Gendered fields

What is the effect of the anthropologist's gender on the process of fieldwork? *Gendered Fields* explores a cluster of issues to do with gender and fieldwork from within the framework of recent feminist and postmodernist debates.

International in its scope and in the background of its contributors, the book bridges the gap between practical experience and theoretical investigation by taking a gender perspective and showing how it actually takes shape in inter-personal or group dynamics in the field. The contributors cross disciplinary boundaries and draw on the work of philosophers, literary critics, linguists, historians and postmodernist thinkers to build on and advance a dialogue between anthropology, feminism and postmodernism. They highlight the complex posi-tion of the ethnographer in the field, exploring the uncertainties of dealing with male–female relationships at both a personal and cultural level, and showing the extent to which the anthropologist becomes dependent on learning through experience. The contributions reveal how personality, intuition, ingenuity and self-analysis become tools of research as ethnographers sort out meaningful ways of understanding gender in context.

Gendered Fields will appeal to students and teachers in anthropology, social sciences and gender studies. Its insights on gender, knowledge and power – by both women and men – will enable future anthropologists to carry out fieldwork with greater sensitivity and caution and will stimulate experienced ethnographers to rethink their own fieldwork.

Diane Bell is Henry R. Luce Professor of Religion, Economic Development and Social Justice, Holy Cross College, Massachusetts; **Pat Caplan** is Professor of Social Anthropology, Goldsmiths' College, London; and **Wazir Jahan Karim** is Associate Professor, School of Social Sciences, University Sains Malaysia, Minden, Penang.

Gendered fields

Women, men and ethnography

Edited by
Diane Bell, Pat Caplan and
Wazir Jahan Karim

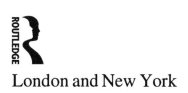

London and New York

First published in 1993
by Routledge
11 New Fetter Lane, London EC4P 4EE

Simultaneously published in the USA and Canada
by Routledge
a division of Routledge, Chapman and Hall Inc.
29 West 35th Street, New York, NY 10001

Typeset in Times by LaserScript Limited, Mitcham, Surrey
Printed and bound in Great Britain by
Biddles Ltd, Guildford and King's Lynn

British Library Cataloguing in Publication Data

A catalogue record for this book is available from the British Library.

Library of Congress Cataloging in Publication Data

Gendered fields: women, men and ethnography / edited by Diane Bell, Pat Caplan, and
Wazir Jahan Karim
  p. cm.
  1. Ethnology – Field work. 2. Sex role. 3. Feminist criticism. I. Bell, Diane,
  1943– . II. Caplan, Patricia. II. Wazir-Jahan Begum Karim.
  GN346.G46 1992
  305.3–dc20   92-18807
                                                     CIP

ISBN 0–415–06251–9
     0–415–06252–7 (pbk)

This volume is dedicated to
LEELA DUBE
who was one of the first anthropologists to consider seriously the relationship between gender and ethnography.

Contents

Contributors

Allen Abramson currently teaches in the Department of Anthropology, University College London. He is finishing a book on hierarchy, sexuality and mythical categories of tragedy, based on fieldwork in the interior of Eastern Fiji. He has also begun research on categories of epic and ordeal in rites of the modern labour process.

Ifi Amadiume, an African resident in London, obtained her Ph.D. in social anthropology at the School of Oriental and African Studies, University of London. She now prefers to consider herself a social historian and works as a freelance lecturer and part-time community education worker. She has given lectures in Nigeria, Canada and the USA and she has also taught West African ethnography at SOAS. Her main publications are *Male Daughters, Female Husbands: Gender and Sex in an African Society* (Zed Books Ltd, London 1987) and *African Matriarchal Foundations: The Igbo Case* (Karnak House, London 1987).

Les Back is a social anthropologist trained at Goldsmiths' College, University of London. He has conducted ethnographic work with young people in two multi-ethnic neighbourhoods in south London. For the past few years he has been a Research Fellow at Birkbeck College, University of London, researching the politics of race and social change in Birmingham. He has recently been appointed to a lectureship in sociology at the University of Birmingham. He has published a number of articles on his research.

Diane Bell is currently the Henry R. Luce Professor of Religion, Economic Development and Social Justice at Holy Cross College, Worcester, Massachusetts. She holds a Ph.D. in anthropology from the Australian National University and is a trained teacher. She has published articles, chapters and reviews in anthologies, edited volumes and journals of anthropology, history, law, women's studies and comparative religion. Her books include *Daughters of the Dreaming* (1983); *Law: The Old and the New* (1980–4) (co-authored); *Religion in Aboriginal Australia* (1984) (co-edited); *Generations: Grandmothers, Mothers and Daughters* (1987); *This is My Story* (1990) (co-edited).

Pat Caplan teaches social anthropology at Goldsmiths' College, University of London. She has carried out research in Tanzania, Nepal and South India. Her publications include *Priests and Cobblers: Social Change in West Nepal* (Chandler 1972), *Choice and Constraint in a Swahili Community* (OUP 1975), *Class and Gender in India* (Tavistock 1985), *The Cultural Construction of Sexuality* (Tavistock 1987); she has also co-edited a number of other volumes and published numerous articles.

Kamala Ganesh is at present Secretary, Commission on Women, International Union of Anthropological and Ethnological Sciences. She is also a member of the Oriental and Occidental Book Selection Committees and the Resource Mobilisation Committee of the Asiatic Society of Bombay. Her publications include *The Fort Dwellers: Caste and Seclusion in a Tamil Community* (Hindustan Publishing Corporation, Delhi 1990), and she is co-editing a volume (along with Nukhet Sirman) on anthropological perspectives on teaching and research concerning women.

Otome Klein Hutheesing was trained as a sociologist at Leiden University in the Netherlands, and then spent five years as a senior expert at the Unesco Research Centre in Delhi, India. Then she taught at Baruch City College in New York for seven years after which she became associate professor at the University Sains Malaysia in Penang. She temporarily opted out of university teaching to do fieldwork among the Lisu people in the Golden Triangle of Thailand. Her publications are mainly in the area of the perception of class and caste, gender in minority groups, the culture of the homeless, ritual change and the appraisal of development projects. She is currently involved in research on mental stress among hill women and principles of hierarchy in the guardian spirit cults of the Lisu, as well as the documentation of ancient Lisu songs.

Wazir Jahan Karim is Associate Professor at the Department of Anthropology and Sociology, School of Social Sciences, University Sains Malaysia in Minden, Penang. She is also Director of the Research Unit on Women's Studies and Human Resources at the University and is author of the books *Ma' Betisek Concepts of Living Things* (Athlone 1981), *Emotions of Culture: A Malay Perspective* (Oxford University Press 1990) and *Women's Contributions to Culture: Malay Women in Adat and Islam* (Berkeley 1990). She has also published several articles on Ma' Betisek religion, Malay women and Islam and is currently researching the anthropology of madness in western and non-western cultures.

Martha Macintyre is Senior Lecturer in the Sociology Department at La Trobe University in Australia. Compiling a bibliography of the Kula inducted her into the ethnography of the Massim area (now better known as Milne Bay Province), Papua New Guinea. A teacher and historian before she turned to anthropology, she was educated at the University of Melbourne, Cambridge University, and the Australian National University. Her fieldwork was carried out on the small island of Tubetube in Papua New Guinea, mainly during 1979–83, and she has published numerous articles based on her research there. She is the author of *The Kula: A Bibliography*, and joint editor (with Margaret Jolly) of *Family and Gender in the Pacific: Domestic Contradictions and the Colonial Impact.*

Lisa Moore is a graduate of the College of Holy Cross, Worcester, Massachussetts, where she majored in philosophy. As a recipient of a Watson Foundation Fellowship, she spent from September 1989 to March 1990 conducting independent research in several refugee camps in Thailand. Her interests include theatre and the impact of development on Third World women, and she intends to carry out postgraduate work in the social sciences.

Oonagh O'Brien carried out fieldwork on ethnic identity, education and language in the Pyrenees in France and is completing a Ph.D. on North Catalonia at University College London. She has taught anthropology at the University of Barcelona and currently teaches anthropology and other related and unrelated subjects at Hammersmith and West London College, London.

Ingrid Rudie is Lecturer at the Department of Social Anthropology, University of Oslo. Her fieldwork experience is in both Norway and Malaysia. She started in anthropology in the sixties, her main preoccupation being with the ecology and economics of household organisation. More recent interests are in the person and the reproduction of culture with special reference to gender and modernisation. She has published numerous articles and co-edited (with T. Bleie and V. Broch-Due) *Gender: Practice and Representations*, Berg Press (in press).

Joke Schrijvers worked for twenty years at the University of Leiden, where she co-founded the Research and Documentation Centre on Women and Autonomy (VENA). She carried out fieldwork in Sri Lanka (1977–8), and supervised research projects in Indonesia, Egypt, Mexico, India and Sudan. One of the outcomes of her research in Sri Lanka was the organisation of a collective women's farm. Her main publications are on Sri Lanka, including *Mothers for Life: Motherhood and Marginalisation in the North Central Province of Sri Lanka* (EBURON, Delft, 1985), and articles on a variety of topics including feminist anthropology and the politics of research. Since 1989 she has been director of the Institute of Development Research Amsterdam (INDRA), University of Amsterdam, where she was appointed as Professor of Development Studies in 1991.

Penny Vera-Sanso is at Goldsmiths' College, University of London doing postgraduate research on the Working Women's Forum, India. She conducted her fieldwork in Madras between July and December 1989 and returned for a further 12 months study during 1990–92. She has been involved in the co-operative housing movement in London since 1978.

Peter Wade was educated at Cambridge University and, after travel in Latin America, he carried out fieldwork in Colombia on ethnic relations in a frontier town for his Ph.D. He subsequently held a Research Fellowship which enabled him to do further fieldwork in Colombia, this time on black migrants to Medellín. He is currently Joint Lecturer in Geography and Latin American Studies, Liverpool University and is finalising a book *Blackness and Race Mixture in Colombia*.

Preface

In the summer of 1988, Leela Dube organised a pre-conference session to the Twelfth IUAES (International Union of Anthropological and Ethnological Sciences) Congress in Zagreb. Its title was 'Anthropological Perspectives on Research and Teaching Concerning Women' and out of the ensuing discussions was born the idea of publishing a book on gender and fieldwork, on which there was felt to be a dearth of material. Golde's pioneering work *Women in the Field* (1970) had appeared almost two decades earlier and a re-examination of its themes seemed timely. Initially, the project was called 'Women in the Field Re-visited' and, on the basis of the ideas which had come up in the discussion, Diane Bell drew up an initial list of questions for contributors to address.

The three editors, all of whom had attended the Zagreb workshop, each agreed to solicit articles so as to achieve as wide a geographical coverage as possible. In the event, despite the many letters of invitation, this did not work out quite as hoped, for, although Africa, Europe and Latin America are all represented in this collection, the greatest number of articles are concerned with Asia.

Ultimately, perhaps like most volumes, the final collection represents the editors' networks. Two of the original workshop participants volunteered papers (Schrijvers and Ganesh). Karim is linked to Rudie and Hutheesing through their work in a common area (South-east Asia), Bell to her contributors through teaching (Moore was her student), and colleagueship (Macintyre) and Caplan similarly through teaching (Back and Sanso are currently her postgraduate supervisees) and colleagueship (Amadiume, Abramson, O'Brien and Wade all trained in other London departments, as indeed did Karim).

Because of the problems of geographical distance – Bell in the United States, Karim in Malaysia and Caplan in London – it was decided that each should take primary responsibility for the articles she had solicited. Bell therefore worked with Moore, Macintyre and Schrijvers, Karim with Rudie and Hutheesing, and Caplan with Abramson, Amadiume, Back, Ganesh, O'Brien, Sanso and Wade.

In the spring of 1990, the three editors met in London for further discussions, and it was decided that it was important to address the question of male ethnographers in the field. At this point, the focus shifted somewhat, the title of the volume was changed, and a number of men were also invited to contribute. In the end, only three did so (although many more declined), and the majority of the articles are by women.

There was a further meeting in Amsterdam in the spring of the following year. At this point, we had fifteen articles which we wanted to publish, and space was inevitably problematic. Most of the authors have had to shorten their original articles, sometimes drastically, and this too has meant that the volume has taken longer than we originally envisaged in coming to press. Bell and Caplan met in Boston in August 1991 for some final sub-editing.

In between meetings, discussions took place by telephone, letter and fax, indeed, it is impossible to think of completing such a task without the aid of modern technology. Even with its help, however, the process has not been easy, and perhaps most difficult of all has been the attempt to write a joint introduction. In the end, Bell wrote the first part, which contextualises the volume in terms of recent debates in both anthropology – particularly the development of feminist scholarship – on the one hand, and reflexivity and postmodernism on the other. Caplan was responsible for the middle section, which discusses the contributions in this volume. Karim wrote the last section, which focuses particularly upon the issue of 'nativising' research: dealing with the ambiguities of the relationship between the researcher and the researched when both are 'natives' and comparing this to the ambiguities raised by committed researchers such as feminist anthropologists.

The editors decided to accept the publishing offer from Routledge in London, and inevitably, therefore, much of the liaison with the publisher and contributors fell to Pat Caplan, the London-based editor. The round of correspondence dealing with illustrations and maps was done by Wazir Karim, while Diane Bell was responsible for the production of the map locating the fieldwork areas described in this book.

Acknowledgements

We have to acknowledge the help of a number of people in completing this work. We have dedicated it to Leela Dube for two reasons. One is that she herself was a pioneer in the examination of some of the issues raised in this volume. Secondly, for the past decade she has been the main driving force behind the Women's Commission of the IUAES, and in that capacity, her organisation of the Zagreb workshop first brought us together.

The conference was jointly funded by Unesco and the International Social Science Commission, and we have to thank Serin Timur and Evelyne Blamont respectively for their practical and organisational assistance, as well as their contributions during the event. The other Zagreb contributors – Lourdes Arizpe and Margaret Velasquez (Mexico), Deborah D'Amico-Samuels, Joan Mencher and Karen Sacks (United States), Neera Desai, Veena Mazumdar, Kamala Ganesh and Vidyut Bhagwat (India), Joke Schrijvers (the Netherlands), Nukhet Sirman (Turkey) and Olga Supek (the former Yugoslavia) – helped generate enough enthusiasm not only to begin this project but to see it through its three-year-long gestation.

The Henry Luce Foundation supported Diane Bell's journeys to London and Amsterdam while the British Academy and the Norwegian Social Science Council supported Wazir Karim's trips to London and Amsterdam respectively. Our various institutions – College of the Holy Cross, Worcester (Bell), Goldsmiths' College, London (Caplan) and KANITA, University Sains Malaysia (Karim) – provided infrastructural support. We are grateful to all these institutions, which have made this joint editorship possible. Sue Greenwood systematised the various manuscripts and floppy disks into a single compatible form. Many others have helped out, and we are mindful of the meals cooked for us, the weekends and holidays forgone, and crises born by our families and friends. They will be almost as happy to see its completion as we are.

Diane Bell, Pat Caplan, Wazir Jahan Karim

August 1991

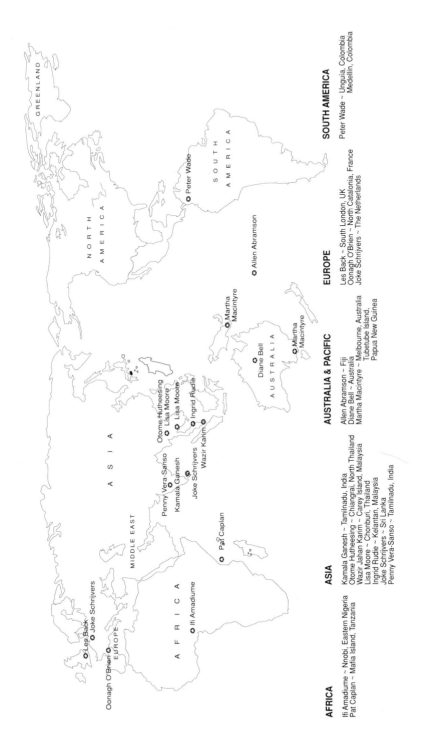

Location of field sites mentioned in this volume

AFRICA

Ifi Amadiume ~ Nnobi, Eastern Nigeria
Pat Caplan ~ Mafia Island, Tanzania

ASIA

Kamala Ganesh ~ Tamilnadu, India
Otome Hutheesing ~ Chiangrai, North Thailand
Wazir Jahan Karim ~ Carey Island, Malaysia
Lisa Moore ~ Chonburi, Thailand
Ingrid Rudie ~ Kelantan, Malaysia
Joke Schrijvers ~ Sri Lanka
Penny Vera-Sanso ~ Tamilnadu, India

AUSTRALIA & PACIFIC

Allen Abramson ~ Fiji
Diane Bell ~ Australia
Martha Macintyre ~ Melbourne, Australia
Tubetube Island,
Papua New Guinea

EUROPE

Les Back ~ South London, UK
Oonagh O'Brien ~ North Catalonia, France
Joke Schrijvers ~ The Netherlands

SOUTH AMERICA

Peter Wade ~ Unguia, Colombia
Medellin, Colombia

Introduction 1

The context

Diane Bell

What does the ethnographer do? he writes.

(Geertz 1973: 19)

While anthropology questioned the status of the participant-observer, it spoke from the position of the dominant and thus for the 'other'. Feminists speak from the position of the 'other'.

(Mascia-Lees *et al.* 1989: 11)

WOMEN, MEN AND ETHNOGRAPHY*

The dilemma confronting the ethnographer who, as participant-observer, is both detached and engaged, an element in the field of study and the instrument of its articulation has generated a considerable body of literature. Some have opted for increased methodological rigour in an attempt to purge fieldwork of its subjective taint (see Radcliffe-Brown 1958; Friedrichs and Lüdtke 1975).[1] Others have stood aloof (Lévi-Strauss 1961), noted the 'bankruptcy of the mere observer position' (Rabinow 1982: 174) and cast the ethnographer as marginal native (Freilich 1970) or professional stranger (Agar 1980). Still others, declaring the demise of ethnographic authority, have urged stylistic experimentation and issued calls for ethical writing (Clifford 1988; Marcus and Fischer 1986; Clifford and Marcus 1986), looked out from behind a multiplicity of masks (Berreman 1962), explored the intertwining of the hierarchies of colonialism and the academy (Asad 1973) and heard the challenge of the indigenous voice (Deloria 1969). Particularly influential has been Clifford Geertz's (1973, 1988) notion of anthropology as an interpretative quest, ethnography as 'thick description' and 'anthropologist as author'. For the most part, however, these authors have been silent on the issue of gender. The gendered nature of our fields has been left to women anthropologists to ponder and feminist scholars to critique, and even then their work has been largely ignored. Neither the burgeoning body of ethnographic literature by women writers nor feminist theorising about the difference gender makes have set the disciplinary agenda.[2]

The issue of gender arises because we (ethnographers) do fieldwork by establishing relationships, and by learning to see, think and be in another culture, and we do this as persons of a particular age, sexual orientation, belief, educational background, ethnic identity and class. In particular, as far as this volume is concerned, we also do it as women and as men. Women have been conspicuous for their consideration of the impact of their presence in the field as an element in their ethnography. Theirs is the gender-inflected voice, which cannot masquerade as universal: they have a standpoint and cannot pretend otherwise (Barry 1989; Bujra 1973; Gordon 1988; Mohanty 1987; Warren 1988). Women have written of their personal biographies, their age, marriages and children as integral to their ethnography (Cassell 1987; Cesara 1982; Wax 1979; Golde 1986; Powdermaker 1966). Female anthropologists working with women in societies where the sexual division of labour prescribes separate spaces for women and men in daily and ritual life have been especially clear regarding the relational nature of their enterprise (see Papanek 1964; Dube 1975; Weiner 1976; Dwyer 1978; Bell 1983; Scheper-Hughes 1983; Ardener 1986). Such reflections on the gendered nature of fieldwork and fieldworkers have made significant contributions towards mapping the terrain on which we might begin to explore experientially based knowledge (Abu-Lughod 1990; Stacey 1988) and cultures as complex, dynamic collages of intersecting interests of gender, race, ethnicity, class and sexuality (Moore 1988). It is in this context that this volume was conceived, first as an attempt to consider the gendered nature of fieldwork and, secondly, the articulation of gender with other aspects of the self of the ethnographer.

Lila Abu-Lughod (1990), reviewing feminists' critiques of scientific objectivity, traces a shift from their early concerns with constraints on objectivity to the more radical analyses of objectivity as an epistemological stance. Furthermore, profound political critiques of the possibility of a gender-neutral anthropology are raised by the deconstruction of 'objectivity' by Catharine MacKinnon (1987), Donna Haraway's (1988) exploration of the privilege of partial perspective, and proposals regarding women's contextualised, relational moral reasoning by Alison Jaggar (1989) and Seyla Benhabib (1987). Feminist theorising has generated philosophical speculation about a feminist successor science (Keller 1985; Harding 1986), and we are to beginning to speak of the possibility of declaring a feminist epistemology (Hartsock 1983; Mascia-Lees *et al.* 1989; Bell, this volume).

Given that anthropology has a long-standing interest in the relations between the sexes (marriage, kinship, rites of passage), it is ironic that its observations still reflect what are for the most part male standpoints presented as the 'norm'. Male ethnographers need fear no challenge to the legitimacy of their knowledge as case material from one locale is generalised for entire regions, while women's ethnographies remain particularised.[3] For example, the ethnography of male anthropologists such as Lloyd Warner (1937) working in Arnhemland is frequently cited as the 'Australian case' of gender relations in Aboriginal society, while Phyllis Kaberry's (1939) ethnography is usually known as a study of women in the Kimberleys. While women have explored their gendered fields, men have remained free to write of the generic 'he'. It took the postmodern proclamation of a 'crisis of representation' to put the critique of objectivity and the scrutiny of ethnographic authority onto the disciplinary agenda. Those anthropologists who have taken the postmodern turn into textual analyses and plurivocality are forthright in their attention to 'native' as 'other', but tracing a genealogy entirely through males – such as Bob Scholte (1972), Dell Hymes (1969), Talad Asad (1973), Paul Rabinow (1977), Jay Ruby (1982), James Clifford and George Marcus (1986) and George Marcus and M. Fischer (1986) – are silent on the matter of woman as 'other'.[4] Their problematising of the ethnographic endeavour bears a striking similarity to the feminist debates mentioned above, but they appear ignorant of or uninterested in this scholarship (see Mascia-Lees *et al.* 1989; Caplan 1988; Strathern 1987; also Back, and Macintyre, this volume).

Why has mainstream anthropology been so recalcitrant in acknowledging that gender makes a difference to ethnography? Why have the practitioners clung so tenaciously to a gender-neutral neo-positivist paradigm or jumped on the post-modern bandwagon? Why has it been so difficult for feminists to be heard? The tendency to associate engagement with the feminine, and the feminine with the emotional, has locked women out of mainstream anthropology and removed them from accounts in the postmodern schema. Regardless of its rigour and innovative nature, such work will be deemed 'women's', treated as a special case, and placed within the genre of 'confessional literature', or simply labelled 'self-indulgent'. It has been men's excursions into these domains that have informed disciplinary accounts of reflexivity. Meanwhile, feminists' questions have been appropriated, and their experimental moments erased (see Mies 1983; Clifford and Marcus 1986: 19–20; Gordon 1988; Viswaswaran 1988). The self-awareness of the situatedness of the knower, so carefully analysed by feminists (see Hawkesworth 1989; Mascia-Lees *et al.* 1989), often translates in practice into marginality to the academy, the discipline and the curriculum (see Stanley 1990; Lutz 1990).

However, if those with an interest in critiquing and challenging the asymmetry of our gendered fields are not to subscribe to an essentialist conspiracy theory, we need to delve deeper. What is to be done to transform gender-inflected questions into disciplinary concerns? We might look to the so-called awkward relationship between anthropology and feminism, and ask whether that should be char-acterised as one of mocking incompatibility (Strathern 1987), a source of in-vigorating tension (Caplan 1988), or an expression of institutional power to set the academic agenda (Jennaway 1990; Lutz 1990; Stanley 1990). We might seek ways in which women and their contributions can be re-inscribed as central to the discipline by considering a two-pronged approach. First, we need to reclaim the voices of those whose insights and experiments are absent from mainstream genealogies, and, secondly, we need an analysis of the practices and presump-tions that have erased, trivialised and marginalised their voices. Pioneering women anthropologists left clear traces for contemporary scholars: feminist scholars have given us the analytical tools.

A GENDERED GENEALOGY

There is a long and honourable tradition of ethnographic writing in which the voice of the ethnographer pondering her situation, the impact of her presence on the people with whom she is working, and the problematic nature of being both observer and participant is audible. In short, there is a reflexive tradition in which the voices of women are critical. It is summed up well by Margaret Mead's comment that as an ethnographer, one must first 'know thyself' (1976: 905–7). Listen, for example, to Hortense Powdermaker in *Stranger and Friend* (1966) as she takes the reader into four different fields (Lesu, Mississippi, Hollywood, Zambia), and shifts from detached to engaged, even suggesting that the nature of our projects reflects the needs and personalities of the ethnographer quite as much as the problems that the field might pose. This is not to suggest that all women anthropologists saw things in the same way, but that there were the makings of a debate embedded in the ethnographies of the first generations of trained women anthropologists.[5] Attention to the structural and epistemological implications of the insider/outsider positioning of the woman ethnographer constitutes a central feature of the later literature.

Women have sought to contextualise their work both autobiographically, as with Margaret Mead's *Letters from the Field* (1977) and *Blackberry Winter* (1972), and biographically, as with the inclusion of correspondence between herself and her friend and colleague, in *An Anthropologist at Work: The Writings of Ruth Benedict* (Mead 1959). One notable facet of the biographical materials within which we may seek further readings of the ethnographic voice is that, for the most part, women's letters, diaries, biographies and autobiographies reveal high levels of integration of personal and professional selves (see Cesara 1982). By way of contrast, Malinowski's *Diary in the Strict Sense of the Term* (1967) raises a host of questions about the gap between his professional pronouncements and private preoccupations.

Women anthropologists' own biographies are as revealing of academia as they are of themselves. For example, Benedict's work draws on her unerring sense of the power of juxtaposing the familiar with the exotic in cultural critique. Her work contains lyric poetry, Swiftian discoursing on the 'Uses of cannibalism' (Mead 1959: 44–8) and, as Modell (1984) has noted, attention to the aesthetic dimension of human life. None the less, her extraordinary stylistic range has received scant attention from the postmodernists. Geertz (1988: 105–6) suggests that her 'mordant' themes and 'conflation' with Margaret Mead may explain the lack of appreciation of her contribution to the discipline, but perhaps more convincing is Margaret Caffrey's (1989) depiction of Benedict as a woman working in a hostile academic environment at Columbia University where, despite her prodigious output, she was not promoted to full professor until 1948, the year she died[6].

Women have indeed experimented with the ethnographic style, but their achievements in this regard are, with a few notable exceptions, undervalued and under-reported. *Nisa* (1981) by Marjorie Shostak is often cited as a dialogical text

(Marcus and Fischer 1986: 58–9; Clifford 1988: 42) but many other innovative texts are ignored (see Schrijvers 1988, this volume; Marshall 1976). Writing of the American South in the 1930s, in a style that captures the rhythms of local speech, the black American anthropologist Zora Neale Hurston provides a fine ethnography of black kinship systems and social experience in *Their Eyes Were Watching God* (1937). In her next book, *Tell My Horse* (1938), she writes of her fieldwork on folk rituals and sex roles in Jamaica and Haiti. However, scholarly anthropologists resisted Hurston's 'personal' writing style and 'engaged' field-work (including participation in voodoo cults), claiming that she lacked 'objectivity' (see Mikell 1988). Although her work addressed gender issues and was reflexively inclined and experimental, Hurston has no place in the post-modernist genealogy. It is scholars of the Harlem Renaissance who have brought her work to academic attention (see Viswaswaran 1988: 40).[7] A not dissimilar fate befell later experimental writers: Elenore Smith Bowen's *Return to Laughter* (1954) may be the classic ethnographic novel, but its fate is to be routinely cited and rarely explored as a text dealing with field ethics, social change or cultural relativism.[8]

There are also a number of novels by women who are not trained as anthro-pologists but whose work is ethnographic in its capturing of daily rhythms and generational shifts. Kate Simon in *Bronx Primitive* (1982) writes about growing up Jewish in New York City. Works such as *Love Medicine* (1984), the saga of two native American families by Louise Erdrich (who is of German-American and Chippewa descent), and the portraits of the Chinese-American experience by first-generation daughters Maxine Hong Kingston in *The Woman Warrior* (1975) and Amy Tan in *The Kitchen God's Wife* (1991) are also journeys of self-discovery. The ethnographic mode is also favoured by several women writers of science fiction, such as Marge Piercy in *Woman on the Edge of Time* (1976), Margaret Atwood in *The Handmaid's Tale* (1985) and Ursula Le Guin in *The Left Hand of Darkness* (1969). Their writing is less perhaps science fiction than 'future history', in which gender relations are explored through ethnographic narratives, as for example in Le Guin's portrayal of an androgynous society observed by the outsider as ethnological hero.[9]

Another set of intriguing contributions to the ethnographic literature comes from the wives (often untrained) of anthropologists. An early example is Mary Smith's *Baba of Karo* (1954), the recording of the life of a Hausa woman of northern Nigeria.[10] In *Guests of the Sheik* (1969), Elizabeth Warnock Fernea, as a young bride, journeys into a tiny rural village in southern Iraq and provides an outstanding and accessible account of the dilemmas of cross-cultural communi-cation. As she struggles with the pragmatics of daily life – whether to wear the all-encompassing black *abayah*, doing the shopping, cooking rice, visiting the harem, and dealing with men – the complexities of the separation between the sexes is revealed.[11] Without this richly textured account, the 'ideals' of marriage available to the male anthropologist could be taken as actual practice. Similarly, Margery Wolf in *The House of Lim* (1968) offers a portrait of the life of women in Taiwan that provides insights into family life not available to the male anthropologist working with elites.[12] Artist Julia Myerson in *'Tambo* (1990) writes evocatively of village life in the Andes, and contrasts the field problems she faced with those confronting her anthropologist husband, Gary Urton.

Anthropological endogamy has also generated some remarkable texts.[13] Daisey Dwyer (1978) and her husband Kevin Dwyer (1982) have written separate accounts of their fieldwork in Morocco, although hers deals directly with gender and is more personal than his. Catherine Berndt, who has produced ethnographies of Australian Aboriginal cultures based on her own work with women and joint research with her husband Ronald (Berndt 1950; Berndt and Berndt 1983), likens her model of Aboriginal women's roles – 'independence within a framework of interdependence' – to their own 'together-but-separate' fieldwork pattern (see Kaldor 1988).[14] The Berndts were able to test ideological and mythic representations of gender roles against practice, as did Yolanda and Robert Murphy in *Women of the Forest* (1974), an exploration of the 'battle of the sexes' in an Indian tribe of Amazonian Brazil. Barbara Gallatin Anderson, in *First Fieldwork* (1990), looks back to the fifties when she accompanied her husband Thor to his field site, a Danish maritime village. Pregnancy had prevented her from pursuing planned independent work in Africa and following her 'first fieldwork', she refocused her research interests in a way that complemented those of her husband. Carobeth Laird's *Encounter with an Angry God* (1975), set in the 1920s, is a graphic exposition of her anthropologist husband's exercise of male power in both professional and personal domains.[15] Again, despite the centrality of this text to any discussion of the ethics of the ethnographic endeavour, it is rarely cited.

Peggy Golde (1986: 3) contended that women's interest in feelings made them better anthropologists, but it has taken the feminist critique of the gendered nature of binary oppositions to move beyond what could be construed as a crudely essentialist position (see de Lauretis 1989). Of particular interest to the ethnographic project, with its focus on the conditions of production of knowledge and the mode of representing that experience, is the work of Alison Jaggar (1989) and Seyla Benhabib (1987) on relationality and women's particularised moral and ethical stances. Jaggar (1989: 92) argues that women's distinctive social experience, including that of gender domination, makes them sensitive to the domination of others; that is, their experience generates a standpoint. Similarly, Benhabib's (1987) thesis is that the requirement of impartiality – namely, treating individuals as interchangeable, and writing of an abstracted, generalised 'other' – runs counter to women's experience. Or, as Jaggar (1989: 97) states, 'impartiality may undermine our personal integrity'. In terms of the ethnographic project, Benhabib (1987: 78) goes one step further: 'The contextuality, narrativity and specificity of woman's moral judgement is not a sign of weakness or deficiency, but a manifestation of a vision of moral maturity that views the self as being immersed in networks of relations with others'.[16] Within this schema, women's experimental texts, with their preference for autobiography, biography and dialogue, are a manifestation of their search for a mode of presentation that represents their experience as affective and their knowledge as grounded in specific relations. Forced always to acknowledge their partial perspective, yet knowing the specific truths of their ethnography, women are thus reflexively predisposed. Ethnographic accounts of 'other' as detached and disembodied thus constitute a violation of women's distinctively embedded 'self'.[17]

Jean Briggs in *Never in Anger* (1970) permits a rare view of the impact of emotions on ethnographies (see also Karim, this volume). However, there have been other women ethnographers who have found the genre as constructed by the academy too restrictive, and have experimented with other forms that permitted their emotions to be vented and allowed them to explore the complexities of writing as women with an interest in gender. Hilda Kuper's short stories about the Swazi, her novel *Bite of Hunger* (1965) and play *A Witch in my Heart* (1970), explore themes of tension and conflict through fictional characters (see Moran 1988). Drawing on her fieldwork and hoping to dispel some popular mis-conceptions, Gladys Reichard (1939) created a fictional Navajo family in her novel, *Dezba, Woman of the Desert* (see Leacock 1988). In *White Moth* (1920) Ruth Underhill turned to the novel to explore gender relations in the business work environment (see Griffen 1988). *Too Many Bones* (1943), the first murder mystery of Ruth Wallis, had a physical anthropologist as heroine (see Case 1988). Rejected by the academy, Zora Neale Hurston turned to writing novels, folklore and drama (see Mikell 1988). As Aisha Khan argues in her introduction to *Women Anthropologists: A Biographical Dictionary* (Gacs *et al.* 1988: xvii): 'A comparison of the fictional and ethnographic writing of these anthropologists is another point of departure in the explorations of the articulation between aesthetic and scientific perspectives, between "subjective" and "objective" depictions of reality.'

To begin to explain the omissions, erasures and marginalisation from the canon of the foregoing literature, it is helpful to compare the 'other' of postmodern anthropological discourse and the 'other' of feminist discourse. Only if each is given a history, a context, a polity can we begin to unravel their respective impacts on the discipline. From the 1970s onwards as white western males have had to reflect on their otherness in the face of challenges from minorities, women and ex-colonials, the neo-positivist paradigm has come under threat and the western male has been decentred as authority. In a sense the discipline has been forced to become reflexive. Yet this has not necessarily included an awareness of gender (see Nash and Wintrob 1972; Stocking 1983). A prime example is *A Crack in the Mirror* (Ruby 1982), a text that has become a touchstone in critical theory. In their overview, Barbara Myerhoff and Jay Ruby (1982: 1–35) explore reflexivity as a cultural phenomenon, as anthropological praxis, and, unlike many other advocates of experimentation, provide their own confessional texts; in this way, they succeed in writing reflexively of reflexivity. But although they note in passing the questions raised by early women anthropologists such as Benedict and Mead, they appear indifferent as to why the discipline set these insights aside for so many decades. They write as if the upsurge in feminist critique is a spontaneous, ahistorical factor, whereas their discussion of postmodern *Angst* is exquisitely historicised. Again we see the appropriation of a women's tradition, for awareness of self as an instrument of observation – that is, reflexivity – once named and analysed, is given a male genealogy and becomes central to the critiques of culture by the postmodernists.

The apparent isomorphism of these two fundamental critiques – feminist and postmodernist – of the ethnographic endeavour is at best illusory, at worst misleading. The 'other' of postmodern writing is distanced from self by geography, and by cultural, racial and ethnic identity. It would appear that feminist critiques are more unsettling. They reveal that the 'other' of the feminist – namely, the beneficiaries of patriarchy – are the very authors of the 'new ethnography' who, under the guise of democratising ethnography through plurivocality, avoid scrutiny of their own power. By reducing ethnographic encounters to texts, the postmodernists have mystified the power of the ethnographer, and their experimentations mask the location, and hence the ability of the author to structure and choose text and voice (see Birth 1990: 550). Yet the consequences of tracing a genealogy through women's reflections and experiments would be to position postmodernism not as a withering critique of the 1980s, but rather as a somewhat peevish, peripheral, self-interested and, in particular, male construction (see Geertz[18] 1988; Gordon 1988; Mascia-Lees *et al.* 1989). On the other hand, a disciplinary account of critical perspectives that was sensitive to gender would compare the trajectories of the recent postmodern concern with the 'politics of representation', on the one hand, with the feminist perseverance with the 'politics of knowledge' on the other. It would also note the enduring nature of gender-blind accounts.[19] In order to generate the terrain for productive dialogue regarding the ethnographic project, and for this to be truly reflective, gender must be incorporated into the analysis. In the next section, some attempts to do that are considered.

ETHNOGRAPHIES OF ETHNOGRAPHERS

Peggy Golde's *Women in the Field* (1986), first published in 1970, remains a base line for those wishing to reflect on issues of gender in the field. It is, as Pierrette Hondagneu-Sotelo (1988: 612) says, the 'grandmother' book of the genre. Although, according to Golde (1986: vii), her book was not 'conceived in a feminist furor', it is evident from her other publications that the treatment of women in the academy has long been an item of concern to her. Contending that the sex of the fieldworker was the simplest of variables to hold constant, Golde asked that her original twelve women contributors interweave in their narratives 'three separate but related kinds of materials and reference points: (1) the personal and the subjective, (2) ethnographic, and (3) theoretical and methodological' (ibid.: 4). From these she identified five central themes: protection, initial suspicion, conformity, reciprocity and culture shock. While subsequent works in this genre also include men, they none the less lean heavily on Golde's insights (see Whitehead and Conaway 1986: 4, 289–301), although unfortunately the sensitivity and the prophetic nature of Golde's analysis of her themes have not always been fully acknowledged.

Arguing that her introduction to the 1970 edition had stood the test of time, Golde decided not to rewrite it for the 1986 edition but simply added a preface, an updated bibliography showing the growth in the area, and two new articles. The last prompted her (Golde 1986: viii) to comment that the 'participant-observer is ageing at a different rate from those being observed', and her comments on the changing conditions of fieldwork are instructive. For the most part the original contributors write of their first field trips as young fieldworkers, whereas Diane Freedman (1986) and Rena Lederman (1986) extend the insights of Mead in the 1970 edition of *Women in the Field* by addressing issues that arise when one returns to the field (see also Caplan, Rudie, O'Brien, this volume). For her new preface, Golde also notes that it is now more likely that women anthropologists will be accompanied by a non-anthropologist husband. One wonders whether eventually there will be another ethnographic sub-genre consisting of the reflections of the 'field-husband', although it is doubtful that his profile will be in accord with Mead's (1986: 326–7) sketch of anthropological endogamy and the 'complete intellectual obliteration, selfless typing, proof-reading and making of bibliographies' of the working wife (but see also Sanso, this volume).

Between Peggy Golde's book and the next collections on gender and fieldwork (Whitehead and Conaway 1986; Cassell 1987), there is a striking gap in the literature. Of course this is the period in which feminist anthropologists began publishing (Rosaldo and Lamphere 1974; Reiter 1975; Caplan and Bujra 1978; MacCormack and Strathern 1980) and the conceptual framings of gendered writing were explicated. Distinctions between an anthropology of women and feminist anthropology were drawn. Feminists first worked with and then deconstructed the private/public dichotomy, disputed whether sexual asymmetry was a universal or historical transformation and moved from simplistic formulations of sex inequalities to complex readings of the intertwinings of gender, race and class (see Leacock 1981; Poewe 1980; Rosaldo 1980). In this period numerous articles appeared in journals, and a good deal of fieldwork related to gender was carried out by women.

Some ethnographers also experimented with voice and reflected further on the gendering of their fields and their relationships with their 'informants' (see White *et al.* 1985). Here, the work of Leela Dube (1975) is of particular interest because of its candour, its comparative nature, and because it prefigures many of the themes addressed in this volume. Working in India, in three different field situations, Dube had to negotiate her caste, marital and religious identities (compare Ganesh, this volume). She writes of reactions and responses of the peoples among whom she worked to her and to her femininity, of how they tried to fit her into their own social and cultural worlds, and of the demands of conformity they made (ibid.: 174). When she undertook work towards her doctorate in Central India between 1947 and 1950, Dube was still a young woman finding her feet. Under the protection of her father-in-law and aware of the failures of previous lone female researchers, she discovered the ease of sharing with other women, and became aware of the gendered aspect of learning and the limits of work with male informants (ibid.: 161). Next in North India, as a research assistant to her anthropologist husband, Dube explores both the complementarity of her role, and the constraints imposed by her sex, age and caste on her research (ibid.: 166). She distinguishes between the expectations of a woman who is an 'insider' from one who is an 'alien', stating that in her view the former is a more difficult status to negotiate. In her third field, working with Muslims in South India, Dube was a stranger to them but they were 'known' to her through research (ibid.: 169).

Tony Larry Whitehead and Mary Ellen Conaway in *Self, Sex, and Gender in Cross-Cultural Fieldwork* (1986: 1) address the 'systemic relationship between the experience of doing cross-cultural fieldwork and the fieldworker's sense of gendered self'. Having reviewed the literature on the role of sex and gender in the field, the editors point out that we need to hear from male fieldworkers on these propositions which hitherto have focused exclusively on women. Whitehead and Conaway (1986: 4) set out to test the following:

1 Female fieldworkers receive greater pressure to conform to local gender ascriptions than do male fieldworkers (Golde 1970: 5–6).
2 Female fieldworkers receive greater pressure to have sexual relations than do male fieldworkers (Golde 1970: 1–18).
3 Female fieldworkers are allowed greater freedom in crossing local gender boundaries than are male fieldworkers (Bovin 1966: 24; Golde 1970: 67–9; Papanek 1964: 160–2; Cesara 1982: 15).
4 Females are more sensitive than males to the field situation and therefore more likely to understand the systemic relationship between the fieldwork process and the fieldworker's sense of self (Golde 1970; Rohrlich-Leavitt, Sykes and Weatherford 1973; Cesara 1982).
5 Sharing the field site with a spouse, children or a colleague can be prohibitive to the fieldwork process and to the type of introspection necessary for growth of self and objectivity, particularly for women (Powdermaker 1966: 14; Cesara 1982).

Although the contributors were not asked to address these views directly, Whitehead and Price consider it possible to interpret the articles in this frame. They find views 1 and 2 to be contradictory and the evidence to support a range of interpretations; 3 not to be sustainable; 4 and 5 to be problematic. In conclusion, they argue for a broader view than 'male versus female' (ibid.: 301).

Whitehead and Conaway asked their contributors to reflect on three aspects of the ethnographic endeavour – the presentation of self, data collection, and overall research orientation – and the result is sixteen portraits of ethnographers getting into the field, doing fieldwork, adjusting, agonising, growing, learning, failing and being transformed. The book is a contribution to the reflexive tradition, and the contributors evince an awareness of the importance of gender for women and men, and pay attention to the 'contradictions' between experience and objectivity in anthropology (ibid.: 2). However, their conclusions remain restricted to the case material: there is no sustained or explicit attempt to engage with feminist or postmodern critiques of the ethnographic endeavour, and the preoccupation is with a 'self' that reflects the American training of the contributors.

Joan Cassell's edited *Children in the Field* (1987) appeared a year after Whitehead and Conaway. The book has examples of children conceived in the field and dying in the field and of children who both facilitate and constrain field communication (see Schrijvers, this volume). The focus on children provides for the reflexive ethnographer a person other than the self about whom to speak of the fears and the all-too-real risks faced in the field. However, Cassell's book reinforces the proposition that children are largely a woman's responsibility. For having children, whether as single parents, co-parents, or in blended families, seems particularly to emphasise the vulnerability of the woman fieldworker. Furthermore, although three pieces are co-authored by couples, the contributors are predominantly women; only one man reflects on the theme of children in the field, and that is with respect to his own childhood.

It is only very recently that some anthropologists, including the contributors to this volume, are writing about fieldwork with an awareness of both feminist and postmodernist debates. Particularly problematic and painful has been the voice in which we speak when addressing the articulation of gender, race and class. Lila Abu-Lughod (1990: 26), borrowing the term from Kirin Narayan, calls herself a 'halfie' (to gloss her location between cultures) and Frances Mascia-Lees, Patricia Sharpe and Colleen Ballerino Cohen (1991: 403) also emphasise the many bases on which they speak. Similarly Trinh T. Minh-ha in *Women, Native, Other* (1989) extends the bases of a critical dialogue that embraces a postmodern critique but is not blind to gender. The diversity of positions adopted by those reflecting on ethnographic experience points to possibilities for future dialogue, albeit one that is characterised by tensions, contradictions and dilemmas. *Gendered Fields*, a text firmly located within the context of the shifting frames of anthropological and feminist discourse, is a contribution to this dialogue.

ACKNOWLEDGEMENTS

* I gratefully acknowledge the assistance of Genevieve Bell, Pat Caplan, Christine Greenway, Susan Rodgers and Karen Turner in locating sources and reading drafts of this section of the introduction.

NOTES

1 See also Herskovits 1948; Lindzey 1961; Radin 1966; Williams 1967; Beuchler 1969; Naroll and Cohen 1973 as examples of attention to method; see Van Maanen (1988: 45 ff.) on the category of ethnographic writing which he terms 'realist tales' and the 'Doctrine of immaculate perception' (1988:73).
2 Although there are many sub-fields of anthropology, it is still possible to speak of the discipline and to establish the priorities of its practitioners by reference to key journals, reviews, appointments (tenure and promotions) and grant allocation. Despite the challenges from various schools of critical theory, including feminism, the dominant paradigm remains neo-positivist/scientist (see Rabinow 1982; Jennaway 1990; Birth 1990).

3 Male dominance as an enduring, unrelenting reality has been generalised across Aboriginal cultures with vastly different social organisation, ceremonial structures and histories, while the works of a number of women anthropologists (Kaberry 1939; Goodale 1971; Bell 1983) are cited as particular cases of the specific groups with whom they worked. See Rohrlich-Leavitt *et al.* (1973) and Gregory (1984).

4 See Gordon (1988) for a feminist critique of the work of Clifford and Marcus (1986). Arguing that 'feminism had not contributed much to the theoretical analysis of ethnographies as texts', Clifford and Marcus prefer to deal with women in footnotes (1986: 19–20, n9–10) and by reference to male perspectives (1986: 17). Clifford (1988) begins with a poem about 'Elsie' but does not pursue gendered ethnography (pp. 1–2, 4, 7). Marcus and Fischer (1986: 135) cite Carol Gilligan (1982) but appear unaware of feminist debates about gender differences.

5 Mead (1932: 133) wrote that a 'woman from another culture can enter a primitive society and, as soon as she can speak a few words, can find a hundred points of interest to discuss with native women', whereas Powdermaker (1966: 114, 156) suggests that as a woman she had limited access to certain data. Some ethnographies are only now coming to light, for example see Medicine (1988) on Deloria (1988).

6 Khan (1988: xvii) lists a number of American women anthropologists who have been unemployed or underemployed throughout their careers: Ruth Bunzel, Ella Deloria, Erna Gunther, Isabel Kelly, Ruthe Landes, Eleanor Leacock, Zelia Nuttall, Hortense Powder-maker, Gitel Steed, Gene Weltfish. See also the experience of Caplan, this volume.

7 See also Pratt (1986), who suggests that the accusations of plagiarism levelled at Florinda Donner (1982) masked academic discomfort with the personalised narrative style of her ethnography of the Yanamamo in *Shabono*, i.e. the dispute was not about ethnographic accuracy *per se*.

8 Elenore Smith Bowen was the pseudonym adopted by Laura Bohannon, who draws on work undertaken with her anthropologist husband, Paul Bohannon.

9 Le Guin, daughter of anthropologists Alfred and Theodora Kroeber, began publishing at about the same time as her mother, who, freed of domestic duties, turned her attention to her own career. *Ishi in Two Worlds* (1961), a biography of the 'last wild Indian in North America' and *The Inland Whale* (1959), her retelling of Californian Indian folktales with particular attention to women as heroines, locate Theodora Kroeber on the genealogy of women's experimental writing (see Buzaljko 1988).

10 Anthropologist husband M.G. Smith.

11 Anthropologist husband Robert Fernea.

12 In her preface, Margery Wolf notes that she lived in the village because her husband, Arthur Wolf, was an anthropologist, a qualification she declares she lacks. The 'Foreword', by Maurice Freedman needs to assure the reader that the 'story is not a whit less anthropological for being marvelously told'.

13 See, for example, the work of George and Louise Spindler (1971), Alfred and Theodora Kroeber (1961), also Khan (1988: xvi).

14 He was the Chair of Anthropology at the University of Western Australia 1963–81, whereas she worked part-time to allow flexibility and to avoid being burdened with administration. This is represented as a joint decision (see Kaldor 1988).

15 The biography of her anthropologist husband, John Peabody Harrington, is filled out in the 'Foreword' by Harry Lawton, who speaks of him as a brilliant, cruel, data-hungry researcher who left no personal papers. Of the author we learn she later married George Laird, her Native American lover, and her manuscript dealing with the lives of his people, the Chemehuevi, written some fifty years after her marriage to Harrington, was only 'discovered' in 1972 (see also Gacs 1988).

16 Birth (1990) argues that ethics requires an accountability that he notes is lacking in the postmodern exposition of the new ethnography. Yet it is clearly present in feminist writing. Jaggar (1989) and Benhabib (1987) move beyond Gilligan's (1982) dichotomies in their contextualisations of women's distinctive ethical stance.

17 This high level of attachment and ethical accountability may also, in part, explain the large number of women anthropologists who engage in work concerning public policy and other applied research (see Khan 1988: xvii).

18 To Clifford Geertz, Clifford and Marcus (1986) constitute 'an interesting collection of the good and the very bad, the knowledgeable and the pretentious, the truly original and the merely dazed'; Marcus and Fischer (1986) 'a somewhat breathless review'; and Clifford (1988), Fabian (1983), Ruby (1982), Asad (1973) and Hymes (1969) are 'other straws in the same wind' (1988: 131, n. 2).

19 Geertz's (1988) *Works and Lives*, a helpful re-examination of the ethnographic project, does not engage directly with the gender question, although he does allow that Ruth Benedict has not 'always been sufficiently appreciated' (1988: 105). John van Maanen's *Tales of the Field* (1988), another useful and most readable overview of the ethnographic project, builds on the postmodernists but defines women's writings out of his classification when he states that he will ignore literature which is experimental, political and personal (ibid.: 6).

REFERENCES

Abu-Lughod, Lila (1990) 'Can there be a feminist ethnography?', *Women and Performance: A Journal of Feminist Theory* 5(1): 7–27.

Agar, Michael H. (1980) *The Professional Stranger: An Informal Introduction to Ethnography*, New York: Academic Press.

—— (1986) *Speaking of Ethnography*, Beverly Hills, CA: Sage.

Anderson, Barbara Gallatin (1990) *First Fieldwork: The Misadventures of an Anthropologist*, Prospect Heights, Illinois: Waveland Press.

Ardener, Shirley (1986) 'Gender orientations in fieldwork', in *Ethnographic Research*, Roy Ellen (ed.), London: Academic Press, pp. 118–27.

Asad, Talad (ed.) (1973) *Anthropology and the Colonial Encounter*, London: Ithaca Press.

Atwood, Margaret (1985) *The Handmaid's Tale*, Toronto: McClelland & Stewart.

Barry, Kathleen (1989) 'Biography and the search for women's subjectivity', *Women's Studies International Forum* 12(6): 561–77.

Bell, Diane (1983) *Daughters of the Dreaming*, Melbourne, Sydney: McPhee Gribble/Allen Unwin.

Benedict, Ruth (1934) *Patterns of Culture*, Boston: Houghton Mifflin Co.

Benhabib, Seyla (1987) 'The generalized and the concrete other: the Kohlberg-Gilligan controversy and feminist theory', in *Feminism as Critique*, S. Benhabib and D. Cornell (eds), Minneapolis: University of Minnesota Press, pp. 77–95.

Berndt, Catherine H. (1950) 'Women's changing ceremonies in Northern Australia', *L'Homme* 1: 1–88.

Berndt, Catherine H. and Berndt, Ronald M. (1983) *The Aboriginal Australians: The First Pioneers*, Melbourne: Pitman.

Berreman, Gerald D. (1962) *Behind Many Masks: Ethnography and Impression Management in a Himalayan Village*, Ithaca, NY: Society for Applied Anthropology.

Beuchler, Hans C. (1969) 'The social position of an ethnographer in the field', in *Stress and Response in Fieldwork*, Henry and Satish Saberwal (eds), New York: Holt, Rinehart & Winston, pp. 7–17.

Birth, Kevin (1990) 'Review article: reading and writing ethnographies.' *American Ethnologist* 17(3): 549–57.

Bovin, Mette (1966) 'The significance of the sex of the fieldworker for the insights into the male and female worlds', *Ethnos* 31 (supplement): 24–7.

Bowen, Elenore Smith (1954) *Return to Laughter*, New York: Harper & Brothers.

Briggs, Jean (1970) *Never in Anger: Portrait of an Eskimo Family*, Cambridge, MA: Harvard University Press.

Bujra, Janet (1973) 'Woman and fieldwork', in *Women Cross Culturally: Change and Challenge*, Ruby Rohrlich-Leavitt (ed.), The Hague: Mouton, pp. 551–7.

Buzaljko, Grace Wilson (1988) 'Theodora Kracaw Kroeber', in *Women Anthropologists: A Biographical Dictionary*, Ute Gacs, Aisha Khan, Jerrie McIntyre and Ruth Weinberg (eds), New York: Greenwood Press, pp. 187–93.

Caffrey, Margaret (1989) *Ruth Benedict: Stranger in This Land*, Austin: University of Texas Press.

Caplan, Pat (1988) 'Engendering knowledge: the politics of ethnography', *Anthropology Today* 14, 5: 8–12; 6: 14–17.

Caplan, Patricia and Bujra, Janet (eds) (1978) *Women United, Women Divided*, London: Tavistock.

Case, Patricia (1988) 'Ruth Sawtell Wallis', in *Women Anthropologists: A Biographical Dictionary*, Ute Gacs, Aisha Khan, Jerrie McIntyre and Ruth Weinberg (eds), New York: Greenwood Press, pp. 361–6.

Cassell, Joan (1987) *Children in the Field: Anthropological Experiences*, Philadelphia, PA: Temple University Press.

Cesara, Manda (1982) *Reflections of a Woman Anthropologist: No Hiding Place*, New York: Academic Press.

Clifford, James (1988) *The Predicament of Culture: Twentieth-century Ethnography, Literature, and Art*, Cambridge, MA: Harvard University Press.

Clifford, James and Marcus, George E. (1986) *Writing Culture: The Poetics and Politics of Ethnography*, Berkeley: University of California Press.

de Lauretis, Teresa (1989) 'The essence of the triangle or, taking the risk of essentialism seriously: feminist theory in Italy, the US, and Britain', *Differences* 1(2): 1–37.

Deloria, Ella Cara (1988) *Waterlily*, Lincoln, NB: University of Nebraska Press.

Deloria, Vine (1969) *Custer Died for your Sins: An Indian Manifesto*, London: Macmillan.

Donner, Florinda (1982) *Shabono: A Visit to a Remote and Magical World in the Heart of the South American Jungle*, New York: Delacorte Press.

Dube, Leela (1975) 'Women's worlds – three encounters', in *Encounter and Experience: Personal Accounts of Fieldwork*, André Béteille and T.N. Madan (eds), Delhi: Vikas, pp. 157–77.

Dwyer, Daisey Hilse (1978) *Images and Self Images: Male and Female in Morocco*, New York: Columbia, University Press.

Dwyer, Kevin (1982) *Moroccan Dialogues: Anthropology in Question*, Baltimore, MD: Johns Hopkins University Press.

Ellen, Roy (ed.) (1984) *Ethnographic Research: A Guide to General Conduct*, London: Academic Press.

Erdrich, Louise (1984) *Love Medicine*, New York: Bantam Books.

Fabian, Johannes (1983) *Time and the Other: How Anthropology Makes its Object*, New York: Columbia University Press.

Fernea, Elizabeth Warnock (1969) *Guests of the Sheik: An Ethnography of an Iraqi Village*, New York: Doubleday.

Freedman, Diane (1986) 'Wife, widow, woman: roles of an anthropologist in a Transylvanian village', in *Women in the Field*, Peggy Golde (ed.), Berkeley: University of California Press, pp. 333–58.

Freilich, Morris (ed.) (1970) *Marginal Natives: Anthropologists at Work*, New York: Harper & Row.

Friedrichs, Jürgen and Lüdtke, Harmut (1975) *Participant Observation: Theory and Practice*, Westmead, Hants: Saxon House.

Gacs, Ute (1988) 'Carobeth Tucker Laird', in *Women Anthropologists: A Biographical Dictionary*, Ute Gacs, Aisha Khan, Jerrie McIntyre and Ruth Weinberg (eds), New York: Greenwood Press, pp. 202–7.

Gacs, Ute, Khan, Aisha, McIntyre, Jerrie and Weinberg, Ruth (1988) *Women Anthropologists: A Biographical Dictionary*, New York: Greenwood Press.

Geertz, Clifford (1973) *The Interpretation of Cultures*, New York: Basic Books.

—— (1988) *Works and Lives: The Anthropologist as Author*, Stanford, CA: Stanford University Press.

Gilligan, Carol (1982) *In a Different Voice*, Cambridge, MA: Harvard University Press.

Goffman, Erving (1959) *The Presentation of Self in Everyday Life*, New York: Doubleday & Co.

Golde, Peggy (ed.) (1970) *Women in the Field: Anthropological Experiences*, Chicago: Aldine Publishing Co. (2nd edn, Berkeley: Universitiy of California Press).

Goodale, Jane C. (1971) *Tiwi Wives: A Study of Women of Melville Island, Northern Australia*, Seattle, WA: University of Washington Press.

Gordon, Deborah (1988) 'Writing culture, writing feminism: the poetics and politics of experimental ethnography', *Inscriptions* 3/4: 7–24.

Gregory, James (1984) The myth of the male ethnographer and the woman's world', *American Anthropologist* 86(2): 316–27.

Griffen, Joyce (1988) 'Ruth Murray Underhill', in *Women Anthropologists: A Biographical Dictionary*, Ute Gacs, Aisha Khan, Jerrie McIntyre and Ruth Weinberg (eds), New York: Greenwood Press, pp. 355–60.

Hammond, Phillip E. (ed.) (1964) *Sociologists at Work: Essays on the Craft of Social Research*, New York: Basic Books.

Haraway, Donna (1988) 'Situated knowledges: the science question in feminism and the privilege of partial perspective', *Feminist Studies* 14(3): 575–99.

Harding, Sandra (1986) *The Science Question in Feminism*, Ithaca, NY: Cornell University Press.

Hartsock, Nancy M. (1983) 'The feminist standpoint: developing the ground for a specifically feminist historical materialism', in *Discovering Reality: Feminist Perspectives on Epistemology, Metaphysics, Methodology, and Philosophy of Science*, Sandra Harding and Merrill B. Hintikka (eds), Dordrecht: D. Reidel.

Hawkesworth, Mary E. (1989) 'Knowers, knowing and known: feminist theory and claims of truth', *Signs* 14(31): 533–57.

Herskovits, Melville (1948) *Man and his Works: The Science of Cultural Anthropology*, New York: Knopf.

Hondagneu-Sotelo, Pierrette (1988) 'Review article: gender and fieldwork', *Women's Studies International Forum* 11(6): 611–18.

Hurston, Zora Neale (1937) *Their Eyes Were Watching God*, Philadelphia: J.B. Lippincott (reprinted, Urbana, IL: University of Illinois Press, 1978).

—— (1938) *Tell My Horse*, Philadelphia: J.B. Lippincott (reprinted, Berkeley, CA: Turtle Island Foundation, 1982).

Hymes, Dell (ed.) (1969) *Reinventing Anthropology*, New York: Random House.

Jaggar, Alison (1989) 'Feminist ethics: some issues for the nineties', *Journal of Social Philosophy* XX(1 & 2): 91–105.

Jennaway, Megan (1990) 'Paradigms, postmodern epistemologies and paradox: the place of feminism in anthropology', *Anthropological Forum* 6(2): 167–89.

Kaberry, Phyllis M. (1939) *Aboriginal Woman, Sacred and Profane*, London: Routledge.

Kaldor, Susan (1988) 'Catherine Helen Webb Berndt', in *Women Anthropologists: A Biographical Dictionary*, Ute Gacs, Aisha Khan, Jerrie McIntyre and Ruth Weinberg (eds), New York: Greenwood Press, pp. 8–16.

Keller, Evelyn Fox (1985) *Reflections on Gender and Science*, New Haven, CT: Yale University Press.

Khan, Aisha (1988) 'Introduction', in *Women Anthropologists: A Biographical Dictionary*, Ute Gacs, Aisha Khan, Jerrie McIntyre and Ruth Weinberg (eds), New York: Greenwood Press, pp. xiii–xvii.

Kingston, Maxine Hong (1975) *The Warrior Woman: Memoirs of a Girlhood among Ghosts*, London: Picador.

Kroeber, Theodora (1959) *The Inland Whale*, Bloomington, IN: Indiana University Press.

—— (1961) *Ishi in Two Worlds: A Biography of the Last Wild Indian in North America*, Berkeley, CA: University of California Press.

Kroeber, Theodora and Kroeber, A.L. (1961) 'Shropshire revisited', *Kroeber Anthropological Society Papers*, no. 25, pp. 1–17.

Kuper, Hilda B. (1965) *Bite of Hunger: A Novel of Africa*, New York: Harcourt, Brace.

—— (1970) *A Witch in My Heart*, Play with anthropological introduction, London: Oxford University Press.

Laird, Carobeth (1975) *Encounter with an Angry God: Recollections of My Life with John Peabody Harrington*, Banning, CA: Malki Museum Press, Morongo Reservation.

Leacock, Eleanor (1981) *Myths of Male Dominance*, New York: Monthly Review Press.

—— (1988) 'Gladys Amanda Reichard', in *Women Anthropologists: A Biographical Dictionary*, Ute Gacs, Aisha Khan, Jerrie McIntyre and Ruth Weinberg (eds), New York: Greenwood Press, pp. 297–309.

Lederman, Rena (1986) 'The return of the redwoman: field work in Highland New Guinea', in *Women in the Field*, Peggy Golde (ed.), Berkeley, CA: University of California Press, pp. 359–88.

Le Guin, Ursula (1969) *The Left Hand of Darkness*, New York: Ace Books.

Lévi-Strauss, Claude (1961) *Triste Tropiques: An Anthropological Study of Primitive Societies in Brazil*, New York: Atheneum.

Lindzey, Gardner (1961) *Projective Techniques and Cross Cultural Research*, New York: University of Minnesota Press.

Lutz, Catherine (1990) 'The erasure of women's writing in socio-cultural anthropology', *American Ethnologist* 17(4): 661–27.

MacCormack, Carol and Strathern, Marilyn (eds) (1980) *Nature, Culture and Gender*, Cambridge: Cambridge University Press.

MacKinnon, Catharine A. (1987) *Feminism Unmodified: Discourses on Life and Law*, Cambridge, MA: Harvard University Press.

Malinowski, Bronislaw (1967) *A Diary in the Strict Sense of the Term*, New York: Harcourt Brace.

Marcus, George and Fischer, M. (1986) *Anthropology as Cultural Critique: An Experimental Moment in the Social Sciences*, Chicago: University of Chicago Press.

Marshall, Lorna (1976) *The Kung of Nyae Nyae*, Cambridge, MA: Harvard University Press.

Mascia-Lees, Frances E., Sharpe, Patricia and Cohen, Colleen Ballerino (1989) 'The postmodern turn in anthropology: cautions from a feminist perspective', *Signs: Journal of Women in Culture and Society* 15(1): 7–33.

—— (1991) 'Reply to Kirby', *Signs: Journal of Women in Culture and Society* 16(2): 401–8.

Mead, Margaret (1932) *The Changing Culture of an Indian Tribe*, New York: Columbia University Press.

—— (1959) *An Anthropologist at Work: The Writings of Ruth Benedict*, Boston: Houghton Mifflin Co.

—— (1972) *Blackberry Winter: My Earlier Years*, New York: Morrow.

—— (1976) 'Towards a human science', *Science* 191: 903–9.

—— (1977) *Letters from the Field 1925–1975*, New York: Harper & Row.

—— (1986) 'Field work in the Pacific Islands, 1925–1967', in *Women in the Field*, Peggy Golde (ed.), Berkeley: University of California Press, pp. 291–331.

Medicine, Beatrice (1988) 'Ella Cara DeLoria', in *Women Anthropologists: A Biographical Dictionary*, Ute Gacs, Aisha Khan, Jerrie McIntyre and Ruth Weinberg (eds), New York: Greenwood Press, pp. 45–50.

Mies, Maria (1983) 'Towards a methodology of feminist research', in *Theories of Women's Studies*, G. Bowles and R. Klein (eds), London: Routledge & Kegan Paul, pp. 117–139.

Mikell, Gwendolyn (1988) 'Zora Neale Hurston', in *Women Anthropologists: A Biographical Dictionary*, Ute Gacs, Aisha Khan, Jerrie McIntyre and Ruth Weinberg (eds), New York: Greenwood Press, pp. 160–6.

Modell, Judith Schachter (1984) *Ruth Benedict: Patterns of a Life*, Philadephia, PA: University of Pennsylvania Press.

Mohanty, Chandra Talpade (1987) 'Feminist encounters: locating the politics of experience', *Copyright* Fall: 30–44.

Moore, Henrietta, L. (1988) *Feminism and Anthropology*, Cambridge: Polity Press.

Moran, Katy (1988) 'Hilda Beemer Kuper', in *Women Anthropologists: A Biographical Dictionary*, Ute Gacs, Aisha Khan, Jerrie McIntyre and Ruth Weinberg (eds), New York: Greenwood Press, pp. 194–201.

Murphy, Yolanda and Murphy, Robert F. (1974) *Women of the Forest*, New York: Columbia University Press.

Myerhoff, Barbara and Ruby, Jay (1982) 'Introduction', in *A Crack in the Mirror: Reflexive Perspectives in Anthropology*, Jay Ruby (ed.), Philadelphia, PA: University of Pennsylvania Press, pp. 1–35.

Myerson, Julia (1990) *'Tambo*, Austin: University of Texas Press.

Naroll, Raoul and Cohen, Ronald (eds) (1973) *A Handbook of Method in Cultural Anthropology*, New York: Columbia University Press.

Nash, Dennison and Wintrob, Ronald (1972) 'The emergence of self-consciousness in ethnography', *Current Anthropology* 13(5): 527–42.

Papanek, Hannah (1964) 'The woman fieldworker in a purdah society', *Human Organization* 23(2): 160–3.

Piercy, Marge (1976) *Woman on the Edge of Time*, London: Women's Press.

Poewe, Karla (1980) 'Universal male dominance: an ethnological illusion', *Dialectical Anthropology* 5: 111–25.

Powdermaker, Hortense (1966) *Stranger and Friend: The Way of an Anthropologist*, New York: W.W. Norton & Co.

Pratt, Mary Louise (1986) 'Fieldwork in common places', in *Writing Culture: The Poetics and Politics of Ethnography*, Berkeley, CA: University of California Press, pp. 27–50.

Rabinow, Paul (1977) *Reflections on Fieldwork in Morocco*, Berkeley, CA: University of California Press.

—— (1982) 'Masked I go forward: reflections on the modern subject', in *A Crack in the Mirror,* Jay Ruby (ed.), Philadephia, PA: University of Pennsylvania Press, pp. 173–85.

Radcliffe-Brown, A.R. (1958) 'The method of ethnological and social anthropology', in *Method in Social Anthropology,* M.N. Srinivas (ed.), Chicago: University of Chicago Press, pp. 3–38.

Radin, Paul (1966) *The Method and Theory of Ethnology: An Essay in Criticism.* New York: Basic Books.

Reichard, Gladys A. (1939) *Dezba, Woman of the Desert*, New York: J.J. Augustin.

Reiter, Rayna (1975) *Toward an Anthropology of Women*, New York: Monthly Review Press.

Rohrlich-Leavitt, Ruby, Sykes, Barbara and Weatherford, Elizabeth (1973) 'Aboriginal woman: male and female anthropological perspectives', in *Toward an Anthropology of Women*, Rayna Reiter (ed.), New York: Monthly Review Press, pp. 110–26.

Rosaldo, Michelle Z. (1980) 'The use and abuse of anthropology: reflections on feminism and cross cultural understanding', *Signs* 5(3): 389–417.

Rosaldo, Michelle Z. and Lamphere, Louise (eds) (1974) *Woman, Culture and Society*, Stanford, CA: Stanford University Press.

Ruby, Jay (ed.) (1982) *A Crack in the Mirror: Reflexive Perspectives in Anthropology*. Philadelphia, PA: University of Pennsylvania Press.

Scheper-Hughes, Nancy (1983) 'Introduction: the problems of bias in androcentric and feminist anthropology', *Women's Studies* 10(2): 109–16.

Scholte, Bob (1972) 'Toward a reflexive and critical anthropology', in *Reinventing Anthropology*, Dell Hymes (ed.), New York: Random House, pp. 430–57.

Schrijvers, Joke (1988) 'Poor women, partiality and power: problems of dialogical research', Working Paper No. 81, Institute of Cultural and Social Studies, University of Leiden.

Shostak, Marjorie (1981) *Nisa: The Life and Words of a !Kung Woman*, Cambridge, MA: Harvard University Press.

Simon, Kate (1982) *Bronx Primitive: Portraits in a Childhood*, New York: Harper & Row.

Smith, Mary (1954) *Baba of Caro*, New Haven, CT: Yale University Press.

Spindler, Louise and Spindler, George (1971) *Dreamers Without Power: The Menomini Indians*, New York: Holt, Rinehart & Winston.

Stacey, Judith (1988) 'Can there be a feminist ethnography?' *Women's Studies International Forum* 11(1): 21–7.

Stanley, Liz (1990) 'Feminist praxis and the academic mode of production: an editorial introduction', in *Feminist Praxis*, Liz Stanley (ed.), London: Routledge, pp. 3–19.

Stocking, George W. (ed.) (1983) *Observers Observed: Essays on Ethnographic Fieldwork*, Madison, WI: University of Wisconsin Press.

Strathern, Marilyn (1987) 'An awkward relationship: the case of feminism and anthropology', *Signs* 12(2): 276–92.

Tan, Amy (1991) *The Kitchen God's Wife*, New York: Pitman.

Trinh, T. Minh-ha (1989) *Woman, Native, Other*, Bloomington, IL: Indiana University Press.

Underhill, Ruth (1920) *White Moth*.

Van Maanen, John (1988) *Tales of the Field*, Chicago: University of Chicago Press.

Viswaswaran, Kamala (1988) 'Defining feminist ethnography', *Inscriptions* 3/4: 7–44.

Wallis, Ruth Sawtell (1943) *Too Many Bones*, New York: Dodd, Mead & Co.

Warner, W. Lloyd (1937) *A Black Civilization*, New York: Harper.

Warren, Carol A. (1988) *Gender Issues in Fieldwork*, Beverly Hills, CA: Sage.

Wax, Rosalie H. (1979) 'Gender and age in fieldwork education: no good thing is done by any man alone', *Social Problems* 26(5): 509–23.

Weiner, Annette (1976) *Women of Value, Men of Renown: New Perspectives on Trobriand Exchange*, Brisbane: University of Queensland Press.

White, Isobel, Barwick, Diane and Meehan, Betty (eds) (1985) *Fighters and Singers: The Lives of Some Aboriginal Women*, Sydney: Allen & Unwin.

Whitehead, Tony Larry and Conaway, Mary Ellen (eds) (1986) *Self, Sex, and Gender in Cross-Cultural Fieldwork*, Urbana and Chicago: University of Illinois Press, pp. 289–304.

Whitehead, Tony Larry and Price, Laurie (1986) 'Summary: sex and fieldwork', in T. Whitehead and M. Conaway (eds) *Self, Sex, and Gender in Cross-Cultural Fieldwork*, Urbana and Chicago: University of Illinois Press, pp. 289–304.

Williams, Thomas (1967) *Field Methods in the Study of Culture*, New York: Holt, Rinehart & Winston.

Wolf, Margery (1968) *The House of Lim: A Study of a Chinese Farm Family*, New York: Appleton-Century-Crofts.

Introduction 2

The volume

Pat Caplan

The major feminist criticisms of postmodernists have been their marginalising of gender and their side-stepping of the very real issues of politics and power, including the conditions of production of ethnographic knowledge, of which, obviously, gender is a part. But gender is not a thing in itself; it articulates with numerous other aspects of the ethnographer's selfhood – age, sexuality, ethnicity, class. These in turn are in complex dialogical relationships with the subjects of study as is shown by the contributors to this volume and by Wazir Karim in the epilogue.

Who, then, are the authors in this book? Their ages range from the early twenties to sixties at the time of writing, although the majority were in their twenties and unmarried when they first went to the field. The editors were anxious to have a range of 'expertise', from those like Lisa Moore who had just graduated, to those who had spent many years doing fieldwork, publishing and teaching, such as Rudie, Schrijvers and Macintyre.

Most of them are female, for, as already mentioned in the preface, it proved much more difficult to obtain contributions from males, a situation which would seem to suggest either that this is an area which men have yet to take on board, or that many of them find writing autobiographically more difficult than do women.

Furthermore, most of the authors are Europeans (British, Dutch, Norwegian, Irish) or of European descent (Australian, American), with only three non-European contributors (Amadiume, Ganesh and Karim). It is striking that all three non-European anthropologists did their fieldwork in their own countries, whereas only two European anthropologists (Back and Bell) did so. The differences between the native and non-native anthropologist are taken up by Karim in the epilogue. A factor which cross-cuts this difference is training, for, in contrast to Whitehead and Conaway's book all of whose contributors trained and work in the United States, most authors in this volume trained either in Britain or in areas strongly influenced by British anthropology, such as Holland, Norway, India or Australia.

There are, then, both diversities and commonalities between our authors – age, gender, nationality, training – and inevitably this is reflected in the varying styles – narrative, dialogue, autobiography – which they use in their articles.

And what of our intended audience? For whom are we writing? We hope that this volume will be read by other anthropologists and social scientists, including non-feminists. We also hope that it will be read outside the discipline, and even outside of academia, for, like Whitehead and Conaway, we share an interest in 'articulating ethnography for those who are not familiar with it'.

Incorporation into the field

How do anthropologists manage to form relationships when they arrive in the field? A large part of the answer to this question must depend upon who they are, both for themselves and for their subjects. In this volume, as in most cases, the majority of authors were not only young (in their twenties) but also unmarried when they first went to the field. Six were married or divorced (Amadiume, Bell, Ganesh, Hutheesing, Macintyre and Schrijvers), but only two, Schrijvers and Sanso, were with their partners in the field. While five were mothers, only three – Amadiume, Bell and Schrijvers – took their children to the field with them. Being alone or accompanied, being seen as young (the more so if unmarried) or mature, had profound effects on the encounter with the subjects of study, as almost all of the articles in this book make plain.

Another factor is the extent to which close relationships could be constructed where they did not already exist. Few were as fortunate as Amadiume, who went home to do fieldwork, and was surrounded by kin; in fact, the first part of her article is a moving account of her rediscovery of the importance of kinship bonds and the support which they offer. But a number of authors describe how they were incorporated into their societies by kinship, even adoption. Abramson and Karim became respectively the son and daughter of the families with whom they lived, and Caplan too acquired a large number of adoptive relatives. In O'Brien's case, although she was not formally adopted, two older women played a quasi-maternal role towards her. For older women, however, the role of motherhood was thrust upon them in the field – Macintyre, who had left her two children at home in Australia, was given two young girls to mother for the duration of her stay; and Hutheesing, who does not have children of her own, found herself playing a parental role *vis-à-vis* the Lisu. In the case of Wade, his incorporation during both periods of his fieldwork in Colombia came via his status as 'fiancé' (*novio*).

In one case, the anthropologist's own family came to the field. O'Brien describes the visit of her parents, her brother and two of her sisters during her stay in her Catalan village, and emphasises the importance of this, not only in enabling the villagers to see that she too came from a real family, but also in giving her acccess to people with whom she had previously found it difficult to make contact (the male world via her father, the world of young married couples via her married sister). Furthermore, her commitment has been enhanced by her marriage to a Catalan.

Only in the case of Amadiume did the inhabitants of the fieldwork area perceive the ethnographer as immediately one of themselves. This enabled her to act in a way which would be impossible for an outsider, especially in her attempts to raise the consciousness of the Women's Council of Nnobi concerning their rapidly diminishing powers. But in the end she recognises the futility of becoming 'a new kind of missionary' and returns to England to pursue the struggle in other ways.

Back too worked in an area which is both geographically and in terms of class very similar to that of his own childhood and youth. But in his article, he discusses the 'perils of credentialism', noting that his education and status as researcher inevitably set him apart from those being studied, and realises that in their eyes, his dominant role was that of 'youth worker'. At the same time, he feels uncomfortable about turning people like his own family into objects of research.

Much of Bell's article concerns the implications of doing fieldwork in one's own country. She points out that these include the fact that one's 'natives' are also one's fellow citizens and one's audience. This heightens the tendency of the ethnographer's biography, politics and relationships to become part of the field and indeed, for the reverse to happen – for the field to become an inescapable part of one's life.

Several authors point out that the role which they adopted in the field was not necessarily one chosen by themselves, but decided by their subjects. Karim shows how she was made to be a 'real' not just a fictitous daughter to her Ma' Betisé' family and how a commitment was 'forced' out of her. Similarly, Hutheesing working among a Thai aboriginal group, the Lisu, was accorded the role of powerful elder in spite of her own feelings of helplessness and inadequacy.

DIFFERENCE OR SAMENESS?

A major question which arises over and over again in these chapters is the extent to which there are differences and similarities between ethnographer and subjects. Clearly, the majority of ethnographers are separated from their subjects by nationality, race, class, education, and, in the case of some, by age and sex. To what extent can such differences be transcended? Can an ethnographer be incorporated into an alien society, and if so how?

Should ethnographers, then, be stressing difference or sameness – or both? If we consider the history of feminist anthropology, we see a move from its early espousal of notions of sisterhood to a preoccupation with difference. One strand in this is the deconstruction of woman as a sociological category and the fascination, influenced by French feminism, with language, representation and style. Another has been the angry rejection of a western version of feminism on the part of Third World women who seek to define it for themselves, and point out the blindness of early feminism to differences of race (and class). Curiously, this view, which is well expressed by such writers as Amadiume (1987) and Amos and Parmar (1984), resonates strongly with the current views of mainstream, especially postmodernist anthropology, that anthropology is primarily about difference.

Such a view is contested in this volume by Macintyre, who sees feminism as being inevitably preoccupied with the similarities of women's lives. She describes a conversation about childbirth with a Tubetube woman and her halting attempts to find the vocabulary to describe it. The woman replies, 'Oh my sister, it is the same for all women. What you felt, I felt.' As mothers, then, they are sisters under the skin. Yet even their mothering is also different, for the woman goes on to point out that whereas Macintyre has gone through this painful experience only twice, she herself has done so nine times. Furthermore, the episode which Macintyre describes as inducing the most profound emotions in her is the death in childbirth of a close friend of hers, a death which Macintyre sees as unnecessary had proper medical help been at hand. But on Tubetube it is not, in Australia it might well have been, and this is another important difference in the experience of giving birth in the two societies.

Bell, too, seeks to 'reclaim the category of woman', and notes that the senior Aboriginal women with whom she worked found her sufficiently like themselves in biography (especially her divorce, her 'pension' and her stage in the life-cycle) to consider her a suitable candidate for instruction in secret ritual. They themselves worked to incorporate her, even as she did to learn from them.

Wade, like other ethnographers, seeks transcendence: indeed, he readily admits that it was his own attraction towards black music and culture which led him to choose the fieldwork he did in the first place. He is frustrated by difference but, unlike Macintyre and Bell, he seeks to overcome the boundary between self and other through relations with the opposite sex, twice embarking on serious affairs with Colombian women. He recognises that this is a perilous path, and that such a relationship implies equality of emotions at a particular moment in time, yet also profound inequality, not only because of the race and class differences between himself and his black Colombian lovers, but also because he is the one orchestrating the encounter, including deciding the moment of ending.

It is, however, perhaps in instances of transgression of accepted codes that boundaries may dissolve. Abramson's single sexual encounter is a moment of rebellion against the dominant ideology of proper behaviour, but at the same time it is the fulfilment of the expectations of his peers, the moment when he truly becomes one of them. Even so, his interpretation of this event as one where he regains control of his selfhood is perhaps belied by his own account, which makes it clear that it is the woman who instigates the encounter, and that her grandmother condones it. Schrijvers, too, finds that the confession to her Sinhalese informants of her divorce enables her to cross a barrier, to be seen as 'just like us'; namely, fallible. But in other instances, transgressing local codes may not lead to acceptance by subjects, but to greater understanding on the part of the ethnographer, as in Sanso's opening story in this volume.

Sometimes the codes transgressed are less those of the society under study than the anthropologist's own society. Threatening a subject with violence, as Back graphically describes in his chapters, would certainly not be underwritten by an academic ethical committee, although paradoxically, in this case it led to a deeper relationship between anthropologist and subjects. Falling in love with one of the 'natives' (Wade, Karim), even engaging in sexual relations (Abramson, Wade), is certainly not the kind of behaviour enjoined upon postgraduate students in their training seminars back home, yet all three articles show how it enables a kind of transcendence of the self–other dichotomy to take place.

SEX AND SEXUALITY

Not all authors tackle sexuality directly, although there are sometimes hints that preoccupation with clothes, hair and jewellery is part of a concern for an appropriate projection, or even a disguising of sexuality (Caplan, Sanso, Ganesh).

Several authors discuss the question of sexuality in the field more openly, although it is striking that, while all three men consider this topic (and for two – Abramson and Wade – it is a major focus), only one of the women (Karim) is courageous enough to discuss it at any length and no woman acknowledges a sexual experience in the field. This perhaps indicates that for women sexual activity or, even more so, 'confessing' it, still has very different consequences than for men. Furthermore, none of the ethnographers in this collection makes any mention of homosexual attraction or relations in the field, and indeed, the silence in the literature with respect to this topic is even more deafening than that concerning heterosexual relationships.

Wade's chapter is primarily about his relations with two Colombian women, each of which lasted most of the duration of a visit. Abramson, too, discusses a single sexual encounter, and the importance this incident had in his sense of himself in the field. Back describes the problems of being a young, single male and gaining access to young, although not to older women.

Several women who went alone to the field, and who were not married at the time, consider potential sexual relations in the field. Moore discusses her feelings of vulnerability to rape and assault in the lawless atmosphere of the refugee area of Thailand where she worked. Bell describes her anger when it is assumed by a black male activist that she must be sexually available. Hutheesing notes that although she did not consider herself sexually vulnerable, local Thai officials cautioned her to beware of Lisu men.

Women who were married when they went to the field seem to have stressed this aspect of their status as betokening not only normality, but also 'unavailability' (Ganesh, Macintyre), although in the latter's case, her celibacy was greeted 'with mirth'. Karim discusses the pressures on her to take a local husband, who was actually chosen for her, although she preferred someone else, a hunter who gave her a pet deer. Her account of the end of this unconsummated affair – when her field-family killed and cooked the deer and served it up to her for breakfast – has elements of both comedy and tragedy, but Karim records that she was glad to have experienced at least some of the emotions of a Ma' Betisé' woman.

The question of sexuality is a complex one and needs to be considered both separately and in articulation with sex and gender. For all ethnographers, it is an area of vulnerability not merely in the physical sense, but in the sense that in the field we are even less free than elsewhere to construct our own sexuality – it is largely constructed for us and sometimes in spite of us.

EQUALITY, INEQUALITY AND VULNERABILITY

What, then, of the issue of equality between informants and researchers? Many authors are acutely conscious, indeed self-conscious, about this topic. All have been influenced by recent debates on it and are painfully aware of their own privileged position on the grounds of race, class, education or whatever. Yet paradoxically, what comes through in many of the chapters is also the vulnerability of being a researcher. Lisa Moore makes this the main subject of her article, but it is there for others too. Abramson, in spite of his early positioning as a Fijian 'chief', is vulnerable not only to the wrestlings of his own conscience, but also to the opposite pulls of field-parents and the requirements of 'proper behaviour' on the one hand, and the 'fucking about' (both literal and metaphorical) of the young men who are his peers and companions. Ganesh, armed with high caste and class status, and letters of authority, none the less experiences fear when she begins fieldwork behind the high walls of the Kottaipillaimar fort where, outside friends warn her: 'Even if they cut you up and bury you, we won't be able to help you.'

Macintyre's vulnerability lies, as does that of many researchers, in the area of language. She struggles painfully to be able to say what she wants, to ask questions, to understand. O'Brien too, graphically describes how her learning of Catalan not only gives her a role as 'une sérieuse', but opens new doors as she gains increasing command.

But some find that their vulnerability is purely imaginery. Hutheesing records the stereotyped view of Thai officials that the Lisu, like other tribals, are predatory and dangerous, especially to a woman like her. Schrijvers finds that her marital past, guarded as a secret lest it spoil her image, actually ties her to others when it is finally revealed.

The self, the other and changes over time

A theme which emerges from many accounts is the extent to which ethnographers use the field to work through other parts of their lives. Hutheesing addresses this most directly, linking her interest in the Lisu to her early childhood in Sumatra with 'brown-skinned grannies' (ayahs, presumably). She also recognises the extent to which the scars of her own puritanical upbringing are healed by her experience of living with the Lisu. What can also be read between the lines of her account is the anger of an older western woman about her consignment to oblivion and the balm of encountering a society where age means elderhood, respect and power for women as well as men.

For several authors, going to the field, becoming an anthropologist, is a moment of rebellion, an attempt to escape the expectations of one's own society. Bell graphically describes her determination to go beyond the confines of being a working-class single parent. Caplan writes of her desire to escape what she saw as her parents' 'humdrum' existence. For Ganesh and Karim, both products of middle-class, highly educated families, doing fieldwork seems to have been an expression of a search for the exotic and adventure, although paradoxically, both end up feeling that the boundaries, the difference between themselves and their subjects, are relatively unimportant.

Moore, the youngest contributor in the collection, and the only one without formal training, uses her journey to the Thai–Cambodian border as a way of exploring her own selfhood, both as an American, and thus a representative of the dominant power in the region, and as a woman, vulnerable like all other women to rape and attack.

Caplan, in her account of three field-trips to the same area, and the periods in between, sees resonances with the development of her personal life, both domestic and professional. Neither can be disentangled from the other, but through fieldwork it is possible to pose different questions about the relationship of marriage and its sexual division of labour. Schrijvers' chapter in particular utilises the themes of work and motherhood to explore not only Sinhalese gender relations, but her own feelings as a mother and as a professional woman.

Several authors describe their societies over a period of time. Many of those who have only visited their fieldwork area once still take an historical perspective: Amadiume through oral history, Back through archival work on the transformation of working-class communities, Ganesh and O'Brien through both written and oral history.

A major theme which emerges from these, as from many other studies, is the effect of historical transformations on gender relations. Both Karim and Hutheesing record finding the cultures they studied as relatively 'ungendered', but becoming increasingly gendered as these remote tribal peoples are incorporated into nation states and the world economy, often with disastrous results. Amadiume too documents the 'loss of matriarchy' among the Igbo, with the Women's Council losing power and finally being written out of the constitution of the town. Schrijvers notes how Singhala peasant women have never been 'written in' either by anthropologists or development workers, being assumed to be confined to the home when in fact they carry out a large portion of agricultural work. Rudie shows how Malay peasant women, traditionally landowners and farmers, are losing out in terms of ownership of land and control of production.

Some can see such processes happening before their eyes, especially when they have carried out fieldwork over a relatively long time-span. Hutheesing conducted her work over a five-year period and saw profound changes taking place among the Lisu. Karim too has continued to re-visit the Ma' Betisé' and to record changes occurring in their environment, especially the loss of the mangrove forest. Both Caplan and Rudie have been working in the same area for twenty years, and a major focus of both of their chapters is seeing the society each time through new eyes, although Rudie focuses upon historical change, changed local perceptions and changes in anthropology, while Caplan also considers changes in herself and the way in which this affects people's perception of her and thus the fieldwork process. Schrijvers, too, records more than one visit, but her emphasis is on the changes in her own perceptions of motherhood.

For Caplan and Schrijvers, as for many of the authors, the boundaries between field and non-field become increasingly permeable over time. For others, their field lives spill over into their other lives. Karim writes of her becoming a 'helping spirit' in the human battles to retain control over land and forest resources. Hutheesing is caught up in the Lisu struggle for survival and sees her writing as her contribution to that struggle. Bell is involved in court cases for Aboriginal land rights, especially those of women.

THE QUESTION OF FEMINIST ETHNOGRAPHY

Most of the contributors to this volume would define themselves as feminists or engaged by feminist scholarship, and most grapple with the notion of what constitutes feminist anthropology and its practice, ethnography. Indeed, this is the major focus of Bell's chapter, as she vigorously adumbrates her notion of what constitutes a feminist ethnography and how she has sought to practise it at three moments in time. Each of her three projects is set in Australia – a study of women and religion among Aborigines, research and defending Aboriginal land claims in Australian courts, and writing a feminist ethnography of Australia for the bicentenary – and it is perhaps only now that she is living in the United States that she can, with the benefit of geographical distance, contrast and compare them. In each case, she herself is part of the picture, but it is only recently, with the development of standpoint theory, that she can construct an epistemology which validates this.

A number of contributors write about how their views of feminism had to change as a result of fieldwork. Macintyre, for instance, anxious to make Tubetube women aware of the dangers of Depo-Provera, a contraceptive recognised in the west as having undesirable side-effects, is made to understand that in the Tubetube context it may be the contraceptive of choice in both senses.

Hutheesing describes how the feminism with which she entered the field had to accommodate to a relatively ungendered society, but underwent a resurgence in the latter part of her stay as she realised the extent to which the Lisu were losing out, the women more so than the men. Karim too notes that as the Lisu became 'more endangered' so too did they become more 'gendered'.

Both O'Brien and Caplan record that their early lessons in feminism were taken from the people with whom they worked. Yet Caplan also found that the women whom she had defined after her first field-trip as strong and autonomous, were also suffering from greater morbidity and heavier work-loads than men, as well as more pregnancies than they wanted, and less food than they needed.

Rudie's chapter tackles some of these issues head on, in her examination of the term 'autonomy' as used by herself (and others) during the 1970s. She shows how her description of women in Malaysian society as 'autonomous' was a riposte to those who would see segregated women as necessarily inferior. However, it only described one aspect of their lives, and might even misrepresent them, for they are not individually autonomous, as women in the west might wish to be, but are members of kinship groups and families. However, with the incorporation of this peasant society into the world economy, gender roles are changing. At this point, Malay peasant women may develop a concept of autonomy, not only in terms of the 'elicited knowledge' generated by the anthropologist's questions, but also in terms of an awareness of what they are losing.

In her understanding of Malay society in the 1980s, then, Rudie rejects or reinterprets her 1970s characterisation of her first fieldwork. Schrijvers, on the other hand, argues implicitly that the term 'autonomy' still has validity, that the *raison d'être* of her fieldwork was to assist in the creation of a development project which would give women greater autonomy, and thereby improve their lives. Her views would seem to resonate with those of Macintyre, who argues that it is impossible to assert that outsiders cannot comment, as this only gives the choice of silence or complicity. But are 'insiders' or 'natives' better able to comment? This is a question taken up by Wazir Karim in her epilogue to the book.

1   Yes Virginia, there is a feminist ethnography[1]

Reflections from three Australian fields*

Diane Bell

It was only a glance. I was crying and so was she. It was two full years after the official mourning period, but there we were at the women's ceremonial ground, quietly crying for her father. The other women were intoning the songs that recalled the travels of the totemic ancestors and it was of her father's country that they sang. The falling cadence and the words were familiar. What had caught my eye was the finely crafted design being painted across her breast. It was not appropriate to speak, so I had signed: 'Whose?' She responded: 'My father's.' We had visited his sacred places shortly before he died and although he was blind, he had 'seen' the country. Now it was time to revisit the store of ritual associated with him, and this symbolic representation of her relationship was the signal that she was assuming the responsibility for that country. It was her decision when, where, with whom, and how the rituals would be reactivated. Without her skill, creativity and dedication to the religious life, this knowledge would disappear. The first to learn of her decision and to see the designs were the women, all close ritual kin, with whom we sat. Then would come the performance and men would attend. This time it was special because an Aboriginal land claim to her country was in progress and officials of the court would be present. The ceremony for which we were preparing was the women's evidence of ownership and exercise of responsibility for their land. In this moment the interdependence of the separate worlds of men and women in the maintenance of sacred knowledge was stark. But, how was I, as the anthropological consultant to the judge on this case, going to give expert evidence on the local system of land tenure?

There are moments in the field when we move so finely attuned to the logic of the host culture that it feels as if we belong; participant observation becomes almost indistinguishable from living the culture; ethical dilemmas dissolve; and possibilities for tracing the rhymes and rhythms of the society in an ethnographic text seem boundless. The truth of the moment is blinding, it sears into the consciousness, yet when we come to write of our fieldwork, we move back from that profound experience, almost embarrassed to admit we've been taken out of ourselves into another world, been transformed in some subtle, immediate way.

The indelible imprint of these field encounters on our personalities and characters is revealed in anecdotes, diaries, letters, sometimes novels, but, with

Diane Bell and Nampijinpa winnowing the seeds of *acacia coriacea*, Central Australia 1976.

notable exceptions, has not been the stuff of professional discourse. We don't have the language to begin to talk about the emotionally charged moments in which the jigsaw pieces of another culture arrange themselves with clarity, only to defy description, to be beyond scientific discourse. It is the association of objectivity, the hallmark of science, with an absence of connection to one's subject matter, that have drawn the ethnographic lines in the sand. If one passes beyond the line, speaks of self as feeling, interacting, or as an element in a relational field, one becomes 'subjective', and one's work is no longer 'good science'. It bears the stamp of the observing-participating self and hence is biased, interested and partial, all terms that are paired with woman in the gender-inflected dualism (partial/impartial, personal/detached, emotional/ rational) of post-Enlightenment rationalist thought.

Feminists' critiques of the cult of objectivity raise the question: should we deconstruct objectivity, attempt to reclaim the devalued term 'subjectivity', or do both (see Abu-Lughod 1990)? My preference is for the latter because my intuition is that perseverance with the doing and writing of feminist ethnography is central to the articulation of a reflexive tradition I find honest and compelling; it encourages ethnographic experimentation that is politically and ethically re-sponsible; it grounds in praxis the deliberations of the so-called 'awkward relationship' between anthropology and feminism; and it allows one to assume a pro-active stance and to resist reactive engagement with the 'new ethnography' on the subject of its neglect of gender (see Caplan 1988). The epistemological sophistication now being achieved in the work of standpoint theorists (see Harding 1986; Hartsock 1983), if taken seriously, turns the criticism of feminists' lack of 'balance' and detachment upside down (see Haraway 1988; Harding 1990). Not surprisingly, mainstream anthropology has been reluctant to engage, and many feminists have moved onto the defensive, or attempted to weld their critiques to those of the postmodernists (see Jennaway 1990).

Rather than asking whether there can be a feminist ethnography (see Abu-Lughod 1990; Stacey 1988; Reinharz 1992), I begin with the assumption that feminist ethnography is what I have been doing, and that more interesting questions concern its politics, style, ethics and epistemology, as well as the tactics of those advocating a more 'balanced' approach to ethnography. I began from a sort of naïve feminist empiricist stance, where I thought that data would make a difference to the portraits of society generated by men talking to men. It seemed so obvious that if the gender of the fieldworker impacted on one's findings, especially given that in my case it was woman to woman, there were good reasons to reflect on the commonalities as well as differences. I stated my interests and orientation and made explicit the research agenda and methodology. The ethnography I wrote was reflexive and it was data-rich, but that was not enough. I found that I was pigeon-holed: my ethnography was designated as feminine and feminist, and was dismissed as subjective and political. The knowledge was tainted. I critiqued male/male encounters masquerading as universal truths. I knew that neither a gender-blind approach nor 'add women and stir' was a satisfactory solution, but at the time all I could do was anticipate a 'feminist paradigm' (Bell 1983: 241–50).

I now see my reflexive feminist empiricism as a first step without which I could not have begun to write of women's culture, but a decade later I want to refine, critique and problematise that stance by reference to standpoint theory. In a sense this is 'work-in-progress', but let me sketch the epistemological dimensions of my feminist ethnography. First, I begin with the proposition that it is worth talking to women about their lives. Woman's knowledge I take to be grounded in her experience, practice, feeling, thinking and being. By privileging woman as knower, man is ethnographically decentred, and this is a profoundly political act. Secondly, I would endorse Catharine MacKinnon's argument: 'A perspectivity is . . . a strategy of male hegemony' (1989: 121). There is no ungendered reality or perspective, but rather the power to declare one universal and the other partial (ibid.: 120–4). Thirdly, I have sympathy with Nancy Hartsock's (1983) feminist reading of historical materialism wherein gender, class and race oppression generate epistemic privilege. Consequently, standpoint theorists acknowledge the need for 'an open-ended and dynamic approach to methodology' (Waters 1990: 6). Fourthly, following Sandra Harding (1986: 249), I am rejecting crude relativism, endorsing a form of 'objectivism', and stating a preference for working within an evaluative framework that is 'anti-sexist, anti-racist, anti-classist' and that distinguishes between 'coercive values' and 'participatory values', on the grounds that such an approach will 'illuminate rather than distort' (ibid).

The ethnography I write is 'situated, perspectival, contextualised, and partial' (Hekman 1990). In short, it is proud to proclaim the possibilities of feminist ethnography, clear regarding its own politics, but not yet sure how to proceed politically in imprinting its understandings on the gendered field of anthropology (see also Viswaswaran 1988). Feminist ethnography opens a discursive space for the 'subjects' of the ethnography and as such is simultaneously empowering and destabilising. It is therefore perhaps no coincidence that as a fully fledged feminist epistemology has become possible, a number of anthropologists appear to have taken a right-hand turn into the postmodern politics of representation and eschewed an interest in the politics of theories of knowledge (see Caplan 1988; Mascia-Lees *et al.* 1989). I want to claim there are distinctive feminist perspectives, and I want to reclaim the category 'woman' from the deconstructions it has undergone in recent years (see de Lauretis 1989). I want to speak in a 'different voice', not because it is feminine, but because it acknowledges the invigorating tensions generated by engaged, rigorous scholarship, is sensitive to difference but not immobilised by it, and promotes a holistic analysis of the conditions of production of knowledge including the politics of the academy that silence, marginalise and mute feminist critiques (see Stanley 1990).

Here, I am focusing on three 'experimental moments' in my doing and writing of feminist ethnography. The first concerns participant-observation work on Aboriginal women's religious beliefs and practices in Central Australia in 1976–8 (see Bell 1983, in press a); the second is applied work in the Aboriginal legal rights arena from the late 1970s to the late 1980s (see Bell and Ditton 1980/4; Bell 1984/5); the third piece of research, on generational links between Australian women, was undertaken in the late 1980s (see Bell 1987b, in press b). A common feature of this work is that it has all been done 'at home'. This has a certain charm, convenience and political accountability that I have pondered in different ways at different times. When I was living in Australia I felt as if I was always in the field. On a daily basis I was enmeshed in the cut and thrust of issues which bore directly on my research and confronted the grim realities of engaging with questions of social justice in cross-cultural contexts (see Bell 1991). Now that I am living in the United States and have a measure of distance – political, emotional and geographic – Geertz's (1988) distinction between being 'there' and being 'here' has some resonance.

Throughout the 1970s and 1980s I reasoned that, as a citizen, I had more direct access to and a deeper appreciation of the political process than an outsider. I was acutely aware that as an insider one's views were never taken as seriously as the 'expert' from abroad whose ideas and stylistic quirks were more exotic than the home-grown product. But I also knew that critiques heard from overseas experts can be contained: the person eventually leaves, can be dismissed as insensitive to 'local conditions', and accused of hypocrisy abroad. So, to my reflections on the pursuit of feminist ethnography, I am adding citizen/alien to the list of gendered dualisms for this autochthonous anthropologist. The transformation from student/girl-child to researcher/female-citizen is never quite complete. It's not only that one has stayed at home, it's as if one is still a child within the family, it's like trying to do one's graduate research where one was an undergraduate.

GATEKEEPERS TO GENDERED FIELDS:
'CHOICES', CONSTRAINTS AND CONFUSIONS

My co-researcher and I needed a few days in town before we headed 'out bush' to begin our project. I applied for access to a university house maintained for researchers. Yes, I could stay there, but my children, who might disturb the 'scholars', were not welcome. I agreed they would not sleep in the house but would bunk down outside. My sincerity in keeping this outrageous provision was never tested, for when I arrived I discovered that the local manager of the property, as a favour, had allowed an old friend from another university, his wife and their children to stay in the house. I learned of this as I opened the door and found the family in residence. I thought this to be a clear case of mismanagement and discrimination, not to mention one of insult and inconvenience, but I needed somewhere for us all to sleep. We repaired to the local hostel. Eventually the university agreed to pay the difference between the hostel and house. There was no apology. Instead, an inflammatory letter addressing my inability to accept the reality of the fact that as a mother, I could not expect to enjoy all the benefits of being a scholar, was sent to the university. I only found this out when, many years later, a member of the cosy club of gatekeepers, administrators and male scholars broke ranks.

Constraints on women's access to the resources of the scholarly world assume diverse forms. Leaving school in the fifties my 'choices' were teacher, nurse, secretary or factory-hand. I trained as a primary school teacher, married, had two children, and divorced. As a single mother in the early seventies, I found my career options severely restricted (see Bell 1987a). I completed high school at night school, gained entrance to university, completed an honours degree and was accepted into a Ph.D. programme. I was 33; my children were 9 and 7; and my combined income from scholarship and government pension was $8,000 per annum. Contemplating fieldwork abroad as a single mother with these meagre resources seemed foolhardy, and I was already too old to qualify for certain fellowships. Had I wanted an allowance to take a dependent wife to the field, there was a category, but a 'single mother' was an anomaly and there was no allowance for dependent children. When I argued the point with the principal of the major grant-bestowing body, he suggested I leave them with someone. I planned to be away for over a year!

During my undergraduate years, I had little time to attend on-campus meetings of women's liberation groups. My consciousness was nicely raised by the daily business of balancing multiple agendas of full-time student, mother and worker. My appreciation of culture as a male construct was heightened as the virtues of Australian egalitarianism were extolled in undergraduate courses as the centre-piece of a national history that yet had little to say of the 51 per cent of the population who were female. As a graduate student, my work was caught in the world of gatekeepers to the field, grants, supervisors and seminar schedules. I raged against the assumption that someone else was maintaining the home, or that I was a solitary scholar. The scheduling of 4.15 p.m. seminars, when I needed to be in the kitchen, I found to be set in customary cement. When I asked for child-care facilities at conferences, I was told this would encourage people to treat the occasions as holidays! My male supervisors/advisers were encouraging as I prepared for the field, but did not suggest I seek out other women who had been in the field. I was at a large research university which specialised in Aboriginal Studies, but there were no women in my chosen field. Along with several interested lecturers and graduate students, I formed a feminist reading group. I had worked on a similar project as an undergraduate and gained a reputation for being obsessed with sensitising the curriculum to gender issues, and attempting to hasten the glacial pace of global warming for women in the academy.

By reading the few feminist texts then available – Germaine Greer, Betty Friedan, Shulamith Firestone, Juliet Mitchell, Sheila Rowbotham – I learned to name the structures of oppression and to identify the pervasive power of patriarchal relations to render my experience personal and private, and men's political and public. The willingness of several women to bend the rules and provide safe spaces for a student-mother sustained my notions of the possibilities of a sisterhood. On the other hand, the hostility which my efforts to get an education aroused in some women underscored what I already knew: 'woman' was no unitary category. Class, educational background, ethnicity, age, marital status and sexual preference intermesh and overlap in significant ways. In the field, this appreciation of our multiple selves deepened, shaping both my own feminism, and my ethnographic presentations.

In locating a field site, I consulted with other anthropologists and was firmly warned by one senior woman in the discipline not to intrude on her territory, but generously offered a small segment of a region she did not intend revisiting: the territoriality of Aborigines is only surpassed by that of their ethnographers. A sort of geographical comity exists and one crosses those ethnographic lines at one's peril. With a dwindling number of 'traditional peoples' to 'study', and the restricted scale of the academic economy in the Aboriginal field in Australia, a quasi-feudal system of field relations has operated. The ability of a few to control the field and to set the intellectual agenda (see Wise 1985; Peterson 1990) has had a dramatic impact on the number of women in the field and the projects they have undertaken. One senior woman told me I was 'ruining my career': working with women would marginalise me and, to boot, Aborigines were the 'most boring people in the world'. This reality counselling was reinforced by the parting *bon mot* from a seasoned anthropologist, who quipped: 'Going to work with women on religion? You'll be back soon. Not much to write about there.' When I came back with data dripping from my notebooks, I was told that it was 'women's business' and *ipso facto* not about religion.

I chose to negotiate entry to a community where there had been no previous in-depth anthropological work undertaken (see Bell 1983) and it was anything but a band of pristine hunter-gatherers. Rather, it was a bitterly factionalised settlement, a monument to the folly of the era of assimilation. My initial approach was to write to the local community, which meant writing to the Village Council, a colonial artefact, all male, with little authority in matters of traditional law and religious life, but none the less the first gate through which I needed respectfully to pass (see Bell and Ditton 1980/4: 5–8). In my first meeting with the Village Council, I simply said I wanted to learn from women of their lives and ceremonies, and to record their stories. I was not sure on what basis they understood my request, but their reply was clear: you are welcome to undertake research here, but confine yourself to the women and children. Such a condition could have rankled a researcher intent on a gender-neutral 'study of mankind', but I was delighted. My intent all along had been to try to establish what women understood of Aboriginal religion and to do so from their perspective.

Fortunately, the then community adviser had some familiarity with the nature of anthropological research and was favourably disposed to having me there. This has not always been my experience, nor that of other fieldworkers. Local advisers are often extremely wary of outsiders, especially 'know-all academics', even worse meddling women and, the biggest nightmare of all, 'women's libbers'. 'First you'll be talking to people outside the store, then in their camps, then you'll be living with them', the area director of the Department of Aboriginal Affairs once sneered at me, 'Just like a woman'. Later, when he saw me working on some old welfare records, he observed, 'I'm pleased to see you doing some proper work'. These records, I hasten to add, were a rich fiction of the accuracy of welfare officers, but considered a sacred point of reference by their authors. It was where they had authoritatively recorded/conferred personal names, place and date of birth, and where they had noted 'consorts' (wife was not available as a classification, as 'traditional marriages' were not recognised by the state). When I began work in the courts, the same individuals were to be found advising local governments and mining interests hostile to Aboriginal land rights settlements. They would trot out their records and impugn the reliability of a woman whom they knew had participated in the daily lives of the persons who were claimants, and who had been seen complaining about the failure of their office to issue Social Security cheques to qualified persons.

En route to the 'field' in 1976, my children and I attended a three-week intensive language course in Alice Springs where we met local Aboriginal politicians, the professionals employed by the organisations, and a frightening array of rights-for-whites, neo-assimilationists and soft-edged paternalists. What bound them together was that this was a highly masculinist culture. The few Aboriginal women I met in the town who were in positions of power were mission-educated and often had spent many years away from their home communities, and were themselves struggling to find comfortable personal and professional niches. Over the next decade, as I got to know some of these women a little better, I heard of their resentment of the positions of power occupied by men, and their conflicts over how best to address the imbalance of power. To identify as a feminist was risky. The media image of feminism as a fearful conspiracy perpetrated by a few frustrated man-haters was prevalent, and several competent women were fired/eased out of their work place for raising questions of sex inequalities in service delivery and the structure of decision-making of Aboriginal organisations.

During this period, I attended a party at which there were both black and white guests – an unusual happening. There was much drinking, and a great deal of humour of a tone I came later to cherish, but it bit hard. One of the most articulate of the black activists regaled me with his story of fighting in Vietnam, but added that his pride in war service was tarnished when he realised that he'd been 'fighting a honky war'. The language of black power had infiltrated the emerging political elites, but had not yet made it into the bush communities. He asked me to dance, and then enquired into my interest in 'making babies'. The notion that white women who worked with blacks could be propositioned with a much different outcome from the advances made towards the wives of station (ranch) owners and welfare officers was novel and had many manifestations. If one declined, the standard retort was 'racist', or 'white trash'. Another Aboriginal activist asked who the hell I thought I was to come up there and think I could have anything legitimate to say or do. I later learned that this was a pass, and the fact that I didn't swoon indicated that I had no sense of humour and that 'southern city girls just can't take it' (see Aickin 1979). I was on the way to the field but I knew I was still at home: resources were gendered, sexism was visceral, to speak of women as a woman was to speak in a gender-inflected voice.

THE FIRST MOMENT: FINDING MY FEET IN FEMINIST ETHNOGRAPHY

'How do you support yourself?' local women asked as soon as I arrived. I later learned this to be a loaded question: could I be trusted with women's secrets, or was there a man who may have felt he had the right to ask about my daily activities? 'I get a pension from the government and a scholarship from the university in Canberra,' I explained. At that time I was in receipt of a single mother's benefit and 'pensioner' was a known category, and a respected one, for a woman: pensioners had an assured income, meagre though it was. Canberra was understood as the source of all wealth and power, so some reconciliation was necessary. The pensioner image was shattered when, three months later, my first grant payment arrived. The local operators of the telegraph system (nominally confidential) received notification that a Canberra-generated cheque was on the way. It was a quarterly payment, but soon the news spread that I was receiving that amount per week. From there it was an easy jump to imagine that I was a government employee; that is, spy. This news of vast amounts of money at my disposal was of greater interest to local men who lusted after second-hand vehicles, than to the women who were already into a pattern of borrowing money from me on the off-pay week and repaying it the next. They knew the extent of my resources and our ledgers were in the vicinity of $20–30, not the thousands which the men sought. When I left the field, the unpaid loans were men's. Women worked on a quick turn-around and sent me off with presents, so I was the one who was indebted.

The Aboriginal women had a restricted range of role models for white women: teacher, nurse, wife. The only other role model was a woman of quite remarkable derring-do, who, it seemed, could shoot and swear like a man. I failed to meet expectations: I don't shoot. I wanted to enter the world of women as another woman, and that integration on the basis of shared experience was high on the list of priorities of the women with whom I eventually became friends and worked. I was asked about my husband. On explaining I was divorced, there was a knowing chuckle and 'just like us' from the ritual bosses of the women's camps. I found myself among women who in temperament were most congenial. They were outgoing, independent of mind, capable of undertaking wide-ranging tasks, raunchy of humour, tolerant of personal traits, willing and patient in teaching a newcomer.

Their constant seeking for explanations for personal preferences, physical features and psychological disposition brought me within the ambit of their law, and was an excellent instructional strategy. The more points of contact between our worlds that could be established, the better I could learn, for it was only by being part of their world that I would be able to read 'the signs of intent' from the landscape. In reflecting on the incorporation of the anthropologist into the field, I have always written as if there were many happy coincidences that positioned me favourably. But it was also that the women worked hard to incorporate me at a level which best suited what they took to be my interests and character. At another level, what I learned was always contingent upon my location within their world, and, as I was given access to a great deal of ritual knowledge, encouraged to participate and entrusted with various items, I have tended to write of these experiences as positive elements of fieldwork.

I went to the field with two children, aged 7 and 9. Had they become ill, I would have had to terminate the work (see Howell 1990; Cassell 1987). I had few options in constructing a field self: the children were vocal and always there. The women ritual experts with whom I wanted to work were all mothers, and certain knowledge was only available after one has raised children. This was, of course, another of those self-fulfilling prophecies: I had access to certain information because I had children of a certain age, a boy nearing the age of initiation and a girl whose betrothal should have been imminent. The anomalous female, old enough to have children, but strangely unaccompanied, faces problems that I did not (see Golde 1970). The down side was that whatever I did in the field entailed planning for the children, carrying a swag (bedding) for three, provisions for three, always thinking through likely conflicts of needs, and taking actions to minimise or obviate problems.

The reflexivity of the self of that ethnography was that of the seventies in terms of the preoccupations of feminists with sexism and bias, and the anthropological critiques of the cultural imperialism of the discipline. The struggle for me was not only to find a way of researching and writing that allowed women's self-perceptions to be accorded legitimacy, but also to contextualise the ethnographic silence towards gender relations within the broader structure and history of Australian frontier society. Women and men spent much of the day apart, participated in sex-specific rituals, and observed a sharp sexual division of labour in economic activities. That ceremonial activity and knowledge was marked as 'women's business' and 'men's business' was acknowledged by both Aborigines and anthropologists. What was contested was how to conceptualise the separation and the points of integration (see Bell 1983).

My initial accounts of Aboriginal religious practice in Central Australia began within the spaces – residential, ritual and discursive – that women control. My preference is still for an ethnographic presentation, but I am now prepared to be more explicit regarding the benefit of feminist ethnography to an understanding of Aboriginal religion *per se* (see Bell in press a). There is little written on Aboriginal women's ritual life, and what does exist mainly ignores women: it is either blind to the historical transformations of gender relations, non-reflectively endorses as holy writ male expressions of power and social reality, or categorically excludes women's activities from the religious domain (see Bell 1983). By beginning with a detailed account of one region, one where the separation of the sexes is marked, it is possible to demonstrate that much of the generalising about women's religious life has been premature and its sureness of vision has constrained research. A woman-centred ethnography reveals that certain behaviours of women, which appear anomalous if mapped with male as ego, are in fact part of a consistent set of practices. It also renders coherent otherwise inexplicable male behaviours (see Bell 1983: 212–26).

THE SECOND MOMENT: FEMINIST ETHNOGRAPHY GOES TO COURT

He claimed he had acted as of right. His wife and her two younger sisters brought sexual assault/rape charges. Despite the evidence of authoritative women – mothers and aunts with a direct responsibility for the abused women – that the violence was not 'customary law', his behaviour was contexualised as cultural and the women's as personal and mission-influenced. He was supported by male lawyers. The court was held many miles from the support of female kin, it was intimidating, and due to a technicality, the rape charges were not pursued. The message heard in the local community was that there was no one to speak for women. There was no one in the court with any expertise in women's law on the matter of violence, and the men who might have spoken out feared for their own safety. It is those who are party to the dispute and their families who know where justice lies and may properly speak, not the local council or other interposing gatekeepers (see Bell 1991: 402–6).

This, and several other 'customary law' cases in which I have become involved, have brought home to me the need to persevere with feminist ethnography; to explore the evaluative frames of standpoint theories that allow one to move beyond cultural relativism and to privilege woman as knower (see Harding 1990).

One dramatic example of the gendering of knowledge occurred in a land claim. It concerned the submission of evidence that, according to their law, women wished to have restricted to other women (see Bell 1984/5). The judge was male, as were the attorneys on the case. The not-infrequent requests from Aboriginal men that their evidence be taken in camera, or that it be marked for 'male eyes only', caused no problem for the court. Eventually the judge ruled that in the interests of justice the women's restriction should be honoured (himself excepted), and that the parties to the action should find themselves women attorneys. This solution was only partially acceptable, because, knowing the hurdles that had to be confronted, women have preferred to have their knowledge remain secret. This has created further asymmetry, since the records generated in land cases become the bases of future rights in the wider society: male attorneys build case by case law and expertise, while 'women's interests' constitute a 'special case'.

The 1970s, as a period of intense legal-political activity for Aboriginal rights, attracted many of us who wanted to work towards change that would create a fairer and more just society. Special purpose legislation, statutory authorities, Aboriginal legal aid services and land councils gave shape to the demands for self-determination. The tenor of things to come was apparent in the composition of these bodies. Aboriginal men of authority (traditional owners) spoke to white men of authority (lawyers, anthropologists, bureaucrats and clergy). Decision-making bodies which were to represent 'Aboriginal interests' began to establish the procedures and precedents, which quickly became sacrosanct practice. Within the academy there was a split between those who pursued 'fundamental' disinterested research and those who engaged in applied work. Could one be an advocate and a scholar? To muddy the waters further, there was appearing a growing number of poorly qualified consultants, maverick anthropologists and refugees from other colonial regimes whose sycophantic ways ingratiated them with various players in the Aboriginal rights drama. The boundaries of the ethnographic field have become increasingly blurred. The 'field' now extends into the law courts, the bureaucracy and, with the emergence of Fourth World agendas and the growth of indigenous feminisms, beyond the nation state into the international arena.

During the late seventies and early eighties, I undertook a considerable amount of applied work in the legal domain, ran a private practice as a consulting anthropologist, appeared as an expert witness in a number of land claims and in cases involving customary considerations, and worked for various Aboriginal and governmental authorities. The self-determination infrastructure had gener-ated a gendered niche, and finding ways of getting women's evidence into a court which was a male arena required not only ingenuity but also a sustained feminist critique of the theory and practice of law (see Bell 1992; Bell and Ditton 1980/4). In setting up work contracts, there were clients and professional researchers, but the brokering was done by paid advisers, not the persons whose lives were the subject of the court case, the land claim or the impact study on which the anthropologist was researching and reporting. The gatekeepers, who had their own agenda, and were decidedly hostile to admitting feminists' critiques, applied subtle pressure and not-so-subtle censorship. I was commissioned by several journals to write about an ethical dilemma confronting anthropologists in the courts in the late eighties (see Bell 1986). I did so, but found that the lawyers on the case had approached the journals and requested that in 'best interests' of Aborigines, the piece not appear. Although one was already typeset, the editor withdrew the piece.

THE THIRD MOMENT: A FEMINIST ETHNOGRAPHY OF A NATION?

'How would you write a book that will be accessible to and reflect on the lives of all women in Australia?' my publisher asked. I decided on an ethnographic approach and, with the assistance of ten researchers, made a series of 'deep slices' into Australian women's culture. We interviewed a hundred women across Australia and we interviewed one another. We negotiated the transcripts of interviews with the 'subjects', and in the process learned more of how they wished to present themselves. What was remarkable was that the range of ethical, practical and philosophical issues raised in this dialogical research replicated those I had confronted in my work in Aboriginal communities. Cultural sensitivity was required, confidences were to be respected, and there were spaces that women considered their own. In listening to my tapes I am struck by the linguistic shifts in tone and content when men intruded on these domains. A distinctive humour, built on references to shared experiences and yes, having children, was a great facilitator when it came to talking about conception: one woman recounted the moment for each of her eight children. The narratives we recorded were richly textured, candid and intimate. The telling of the stories was informative, cathartic, redemptive and indulgent.

All the dilemmas of being a home-grown anthropologist were compounded when I was commissioned to write the landmark volume on women in Australia to celebrate the 1988 bicentenary (Bell 1987b, in press b). I sought diversity through the assistants themselves, and our 'slices' included women from town and country, recent arrivals and original inhabitants, working class and gentry, young and old. I did not set out to create a 'representative' sample. My suspicion was that such approaches reflect male experience. I was cheered when I realised that each major 'event' of post-federation Australian history was mentioned somewhere in the database we had generated. Also, there was a high correlation of details such as educational background, career choice, marital status and country of birth with statistical profiles of the Australian population.

Was I 'too close' to be able to do anthropology? Many of the women had led very different lives from mine, and it was only once the database was established that I could begin an analysis of the salient symbols of women's culture. There were women's rituals that emerged from the data which, as a member of society I would not have thought about, but as an anthropologist I recognised. The ones concerning menstruation were particularly poignant as woman after woman regaled us with similar folk mythologies, while all the time insisting that this was a private belief. My technique in tracing the contours of women's culture was to track the transmission of objects from one generation to the next, and this made an analysis of social structure and kin systems possible. I could write of the way in which women's transmissions routinely subvert and mock patriarchal rights in property and kin lines. The ethnography entailed a mapping of the mundane, finding structure in the idiosyncratic, searching for ways to read the known, and imprinting these private reflections on the public consciousness of the society in which I was raised.

I had a complex chain of accountability to publishers, the Australian Bicentennial Authority, my research assistants, the photographer, and the women whose lives had generated the database for the book. It was an interdisciplinary experiment in multivocality and dialogical research with all the attendant horrors and revelations. I think the methodology holds promise. Ann Moyal (1989) has already used it in her research on women's use of the telephone in Australia. What continues to sustain and delight me from that project is the correspondence from the women who participated, their families, and the experiments of other women trying to write of their lives.

Those who resisted the notion that a woman-centred ethnography might be a valid ethnography thought my work would be more 'balanced' if I were to work with men also. Received wisdom notwithstanding, I did work with men, in all three fields, but I did so as a woman. In the work on Australian women's culture, I found much of men's knowledge of transmission of objects from one generation of women to the next to be on the fuzzy edge of their consciousness. Frequently they would dismiss their ignorance with a shrug reminiscent of my Aboriginal fieldwork: 'That's women's business.' In my work in Aboriginal communities, I did not ignore men. I was simply not privileging their experiences and assessments of the religious domain. They knew that I had had access to women's ritual worlds and that I respected the knowledge boundaries and would not trespass on male territory. I worked with men on genealogies, on country and dreaming affiliations, on sacred sites locations and mythological associations, on social and local organisation, on dispute settlement and conflict resolution. Senior men sometimes requested that I be present at certain ceremonial exchanges and willingly answered the questions I asked, especially when it had to do with land rights and registration of sacred sites. By that time I knew how to seek information without giving offence. Sometimes my circuitous style would develop into a playfulness, especially with men who stood in the relationship of father or father-in-law, and we could express affection in our exchanges.

GOING TO THE FIELD BY STAYING AT HOME

As my colleagues explain how they have a set of publications which are available locally and ones which are primarily for the consumption of their colleagues, I listen with interest. Such a distinction is a luxury rarely enjoyed for Australians working with Aborigines. The ethics of research and publication are always foremost, and a degree of self-censorship and constraint intrudes. True, anthro-

pologists working in 'remote' villages now face scrutiny, but abroad one may build a fieldworker role that can both mesh with and contrast to local gender expectations. At home all the constraints on women apply and those of the field situation are added.

There is a long tradition of women undertaking fieldwork at home, mainly with exotic minorities, but also with sub-cultures of the dominant society (Dube 1975; Powdermaker 1966). In the late 1980s to early 1990s there has been a resurgence of interest in applying anthropological modes of research and analysis to one's own culture (see Ginsburg 1989). What distinguishes this moment from earlier ones is the sophistication of the discourse regarding the exotic other, the critique of anthropology as complicit in the colonial encounter, and the voices, often angry, of indigenous scholars. What remains constant is the resistance to scrutinising gender (Clifford and Marcus 1986).

In this article I have artificially constructed three moments in order to talk about gendered fields, but in reality they overlap. To ask that relationships between indigenous peoples and the state be scrutinised has become part of our anthropological stock in trade. To ask that we explore the points of articulation between a gendered state and male privilege within the academy, or between a masculinist basis in the framing of rights and the structuring of the institutions of self-determination movements, is a step which the discipline, feminists and political activists are yet to take with any certainty. In Australia it is particularly difficult because the field is so small and the persons with whom one interacts wear many hats. For an autochthonous anthropologist, the 'natives' of the field are one's fellow citizens, one's gatekeepers, and also the audience for one's publications. Publishing a critique of misogynist practice of power-brokers and politicians constitutes a different sort of a threat over 'there' to being 'here'.

Working with a minority population within my own country had many practical advantages which are now difficult to disentangle from my feminist politics. To work at home is less glamorous, and I have been arguing that it is more difficult to be taken seriously, especially if one is a woman. Without being able to assert a distance, the assumptions which attach to being a woman at home are not renegotiated as one enters the field, but simply transported. One's location within the host society is scrutinised in terms of location within one's own society; that is, one's biography, politics and relationships become part of the fabric of the field. For women and more particularly a feminist, the consequences of always being 'there' have drawn me to see the interdependence between feminist critiques of the state, standpoint theories, and feminist ethnography (see Bell 1992). Only in the last few years have those interested in questions of women-centred accounts and gendered knowledge begun to develop a meta-discourse which holds the promise that moments of 'truths' in the field may become legitimate signs on the ethnographic landscape.

ACKNOWLEDGEMENTS

* I thank Pat Caplan for her comments on an earlier draft of this chapter, Genevieve Bell for tracking sources and Kristin Waters for our continuing cross-disciplinary conversation on feminist epistemology.

NOTE

1 'Yes Virginia, there is a Santa Claus' was written by the Editor of the *New York Sun* (21 Sept. 1897) in reply to Virginia O'Hanlon's letter asking, 'Is there a Santa Claus?'

REFERENCES

Abu-Lughod, Lila (1990) 'Can there be a feminist ethnography?' *Women and Performance: A Journal of Feminist Theory* 5(1): 7–27.

Aickin, Mary Rothschild (1979) 'White women volunteers in their freedom summers: their life and work in a movement for social change', *Feminist Studies* 1(3): 466–95.

Bell, Diane (1983) *Daughters of the Dreaming*, Melbourne and Sydney: McPhee Gribble/Allen & Unwin.

—— (1984/5) 'Aboriginal women and land: learning from the Northern Territory experience', *Anthropological Forum* 5 (3): 353–63.

—— (1986) 'In the case of the anthropologists and the lawyers', *Legal Services Bulletin* 11(5): 202–6.

—— (1987a) 'Giving in or giving them hell', in *Different Lives: Reflections on the Women's Movement and Visions of its Future*, J. Scutt (ed.), Ringwood: Penguin, pp. 156–66.

—— (1987b) *Generations: Grandmothers, Mothers and Daughters*, Melbourne: McPhee Gribble/Penguin.

—— (1991) 'Intra-racial rape revisited: on forging a feminist future beyond factions and frightening politics', *Women's Studies International Forum* 14(5): 385–412; 507–13.

—— (1992) 'Considering gender: are human rights for women too? An Australian case study', in *Human Rights in Cross-Cultural Perspectives*, Abdullahi Ahmed An-Na'im (ed.), University of Pennsylvania, pp. 329–62.

—— (in press a) 'Aboriginal women's religion: a shifting law of the land', in *Today's Woman in World Religions*, Arvind Sharma (ed.), SUNY Press.

—— (in press b) 'Doing anthropology at home: a feminist initiative in the bicentennial year', in *On the Other Hand: Studies in Gender and Anthropology*, Kamala Ganesh and Nurket Sirman (eds), New Delhi: Sage Publications.

Bell, Diane and Ditton, Pam (1980/4) 'Law: The Old and the New', Aboriginal History, Canberra.

Caplan, Pat (1988) 'Engendering knowledge: the politics of ethnography', *Anthropology Today* 14(5): 8–12; (6): 14–17.

Cassell, Joan (1987) *Children in the Field: Anthropological Experiences*, Philadephia, PA: Temple University Press.

Clifford, James and Marcus, George E. (1986) *Writing Culture: The Poetics and Politics of Ethnography*, Berkeley, CA: University of California Press.

de Lauretis, Teresa (1989) 'The essence of the triangle or, taking the risk of essentialism seriously: feminist theory in Italy, the US, and Britain', *Differences* 1(2): 1–37.

Dube, Leela (1975) 'Woman's world – three encounters', in *Encounter and Experience: Personal Accounts of Fieldwork*, André Béteille and T.N. Madan (eds), Delhi: Vikas, pp. 157–77.

Geertz, Clifford (1988) *Works and Lives: The Anthropologist as Author*, Stanford, CA: Stanford University Press.

Ginsburg, Faye D. (1989) *Contested Lives: Negotiating Gender in American Culture*, Berkeley, CA: University of California Press.

Golde, Peggy (ed.) (1970) *Women in the Field: Anthropological Experiences*, Chicago: Aldine Publishing Co.

Haraway, Donna (1988) 'Situated knowledges: the science question in feminism and the privilege of partial perspective', *Feminist Studies* 14(3): 575–99.

Harding, Sandra (1986) *The Science Question in Feminism*, Ithaca, NY: Cornell University Press.

—— (1990) 'Starting thought from women's lives: eight resources for maximizing objectivity', *Journal of Social Philosophy* 21(2 and 3): 140–9.

Hartsock, Nancy M. (1983) 'The feminist standpoint: developing the ground for a specifically feminist historical materialism', in *Discovering Reality: Feminist Perspectives on Epistemology, Metaphysics, Methodology, and Philosophy of Science*, Sandra Harding and Merrill B. Hintikka (eds), Dordrecht: D. Reidel, pp. 283–310.

Hawkesworth, Mary E. (1989) 'Knowers, knowing and known: feminist theory and claims of truth', *Signs* 14(31): 533–57.

Hekman, Susan (1990) 'Comments on Hawkesworth's Knowers, knowing, known: feminist theory and claims of truth', *Signs* 15(2): 417–19.

Howell, Nancy (1990) *Surviving Fieldwork: A Report of the Advisory Panel on Health and Safety in Fieldwork*, a special Publication of the American Anthropological Association, no. 26.

Jennaway, Megan (1990) 'Paradigms, postmodern epistemologies and paradox: the place of feminism in anthropology', *Anthropological Forum* 6(2): 167–89.

MacKinnon, Catharine A. (1989) *Toward a Feminist Theory of the State*, Cambridge, MA: Harvard University Press.

Mascia-Lees, Frances E., Sharpe, Patricia and Cohen, Colleen Ballerino (1989) 'The postmodern turn in anthropology: cautions from a feminist perspective', *Signs* 15(1): 7–33.

Moyal, Ann (1989) 'Women and the telephone in Australia: a study prepared for Telecom Australia', Canberra.

Peterson, Nicolas (1990) 'Studying man and man's nature': the history of the institutionalisation of Aboriginal anthropology', *Australian Aboriginal Studies* 2: 3–19.

Powdermaker, Hortense (1966) *Stranger and Friend: The Way of an Anthropologist*, New York: W.W. Norton & Co.

Reinharz, Shulamit (1992) *Feminist Methods in Social Research*, New York: Oxford University Press.

Stacey, Judith (1988) 'Can there be a feminist ethnography?', *Women's Studies International Forum* 11(1): 21–7.

Stanley, Liz (1990) 'Feminist praxis and the academic mode of production: an editorial introduction', in *Feminist Praxis*, Liz Stanley (ed.), London: Routledge, pp. 3–19.

Viswaswaran, Kamala (1988) 'Defining feminist ethnography', *Inscriptions* 3/4: 7–44.

Waters, Kristin (1990) 'Epistemology reclaimed: feminist ethics and systems of knowledge', Paper read at the American Philosophical Association, Eastern Division, Boston, MA (Dec.).

Wise, Tigger (1985) *The Self-made Anthropologist: A Life of A.P. Elkin*, Sydney: Allen & Unwin.

2 Fictive kinship or mistaken identity?

Fieldwork on Tubetube Island, Papua New Guinea

Martha Macintyre

FICTIVE KINSHIP OR MISTAKEN IDENTITY?

Arrival

> Imagine yourself suddenly set down surrounded by all your gear, alone on a tropical beach close to a native village while the launch or dinghy which has brought you sails away out of sight.

(Malinowski 1922: 4)

As one of those who has actually followed in Malinowski's footsteps by choosing to work in the Massim area, and to study the kula, I might be forgiven for harbouring such clichéd fantasies of fieldwork. In the event, and somewhat to my surprise, my fieldwork had quite Malinowskian beginnings. I had not imagined that I would be alone. I had envisaged something a little more bureaucratic, given the red tape surrounding my research visa. The people would be expecting me; perhaps a councillor would accompany me. But there I was alone and aware that I had to present myself and my plans to my startled hosts – who had just mistaken me for a clinic sister on patrol.

It was 1979 and I was 34 years old. My husband and my two young daughters were in Australia. My fair complexion, my inability to speak the language, and my lack of experience of any sort of rural life set me apart from everyone on the island. I was conspicuous and apprehensive as I set my gear down in the small house allotted to me. This tiny house had originally been built as a canteen or trade store, but in the absence of cash, had never been stocked. Unlike other houses on the island of Tubetube, it was set on the ground, which meant that at night large, white, spindly ghost crabs could trundle into my house and scare me out of my wits.

My diary yields nothing about the first day, and my memory is of a jumble of curious faces, conversations mediated by the schoolteacher, and my boxes in disarray as I fell asleep under a mosquito net. I recall the terror of the ghost crabs too – but most of all I remember the exhilaration I felt as I walked around the hamlet the following morning.

Intending to study the colonial experience of a society of traders, I had selected Tubetube as the focus of my fieldwork for historical and anthropological

Martha Macintyre seated at the doorway to her house with people from Dekawaese village, Tubetube. The house was built six months after arrival.
Photo: Mary Moabe

reasons. It had been the site of one of the earliest mission stations in the region; it was the first place in Papua where people cleared their own land and planted copra plantations, and both Seligman (1910) and Malinowski (1922) had described it as the major centre of trading in the southern Massim. I had therefore prepared myself for a community of cash-cropping Christians who probably still participated in the kula. I had not prepared myself for what I found.

The morning was filled with the perfume of frangipani, as two of these trees grew beside my house and were the roosting places for several neighbours' chickens. Along the path that went through the hamlet white agapanthus lilies flowered, and behind these grew brilliant red hibiscus trees, and cannas that were crimson with purplish leaves. I had been steeling myself for encounters with rats, cockroaches and houses made of fibro cement and galvanised iron. As I emerged I saw three children busily sweeping the white sand clear of leaves, the sea, 100 metres from my doorstep, was calm and glittery and the houses, made of sago palm, were all surrounded by trees in flower. I learned later that the flower gardens and the lily-flanked paths were introduced by the missionaries, who also supported government regulations about domestic architecture and so influenced major changes (Macintyre 1989: 164–6). But that morning it seemed as if I had woken on Gaugin's Tahiti.

I walked along the path that seemed to go inland (but in fact turned back towards the beach) and a child began following me. I smiled helplessly, already feeling terrified at the thought of having to speak. She stepped off the path, alarmed, and a swarm of tiny blue butterflies swirled up from a dense patch of wild mint. I pointed to them and raised my eyebrows in query. She said tentatively 'Bebebe'. I repeated the sounds, equally tentatively, and she ran off to tell people of our exchange. I carefully wrote the word in my notebook. I looked at my watch, and wondered if my daughters were dressed and ready to go to school in Fremantle. It was a long time before a day went past and I didn't worry about their punctuality and whether or not they would be collected from school at the right time.

LEARNING TO SPEAK: COMMUNICATING DIFFERENCES

Current theoretical concerns with difference are, in many ways, attempts to preserve conventional boundaries between the ethnographer and her subject. The difference is recognised and expressed in the writing process. But the relationship, and the differences, are not decided unilaterally. In the fieldwork context they are sometimes imposed by others, sometimes apparently uncontrollable and occasionally denied by everyone involved.

From 'the beginning, my experience of fieldwork entailed a search for similarities as the basis for constructing mutuality and understanding. I had to learn the language monolingually, which meant that we began with tangible, shared meanings, by naming items that could be held or touched or pointed at. I used to cry at night as I contemplated my failure ever to speak fluent Tubetube. After three weeks I was desperate. I went for a walk along a beach and worked out a plan. I would give myself three months; if I couldn't communicate reasonably fluently after that, then I would abandon fieldwork. I drew up a daily timetable which required that I spend at least six hours of every day working on the language. I used to tape conversations, ask people to speak into the microphone, transcribe and make drills for myself. I made rules whereby I had to use all the new words in some sort of conversation the following day. My neighbours were enthusiastic participants in the project, and there were several people who would help me make drill tapes. Children used to play 'school' by pointing to things and giving me marks for translation and pronunciation.

Linguistic competence is one of the assumptions of anthropology. Malinowski's ability to speak, accurately transcribe and translate has been attested to by most people who have worked in the Trobriands. I have seen Reo Fortune's fieldnotes and been astonished that he could copy a myth (with no recourse to a tape recorder) that is in perfect Dobuan after a mere two months in the village. Rarely do people acknowledge the frustrations of learning a language, much less the lack of status that is so often linked with an inability to speak. Rendered mute, it is no wonder that anthropologists become convinced of the power of words. It is perhaps too the source of that arrogance as 'cultural translators' that Asad criticises with such vehemence (1986: 141). For the assumption of authority to translate and represent meaning by setting down the words and ideas of one language in another derives from political relations that are fraught with inequalities at all levels. The claim of fluency is perhaps the most blatant reclamation of cultural dominance – even when it is true. But it probably obscures the experience of language learning, where the anthropologist is beholden, ignorant and impotent.

In discussing ethnography, where the relations between the ethnographer as writer and interpreter and the people who constitute her subject are at best ambiguous, the politics of fieldwork as a set of personal relations are rarely examined. This is no doubt because the process often occurs within a context of domination and subjection where the anthropologist is identified with (and sometimes as) the dominator. Certainly in Papua New Guinea, the designation of anthropologists as 'thieves of culture' has some currency among those who have received a tertiary education. But anthropologists do not do their fieldwork in the universities, and villagers are rarely hostile. The focus on the ethnographer then shuts out the problematic status of the fieldworker, who, after all, may never even attain the status of ethnographer. For it is in the village that the tables can be turned.

The first period of fieldwork is classically an apprenticeship to an absent master. Most people embark on it as a rite of passage, and that analogy undoubtedly sustains the dispirited fieldworker through crises where the liminal phase threatens to continue for ever. In most cases (including those of the founding fathers) the longest single stint of fieldwork is undertaken as part of their doctoral research, when they are novices, not 'real' anthropologists. Gaining a reputation as a 'good fieldworker' is no guarantee that one will ever be an anthropologist, much less one who is powerful within the profession, or the discipline. Ethnographers may have authority, fieldworkers do not.

One of the conventional images of the fieldworker is as an outsider endowed with power or status derived from identification with earlier (or current) white colonials. It is on this basis apparently that some women anthropologists assumed or were given the role of an 'honorary male' (whatever that really means). Since political independence, Papua New Guinean politicians have been aggressively anti-Australian in their rhetoric; the educated urban bureaucrats have occasionally translated this into practices that make research difficult. On Tubetube, where the colonial presence had never been more than occasional, and where the only precedents for a visiting white woman were the nurses on patrol and a missionary's wife who was remembered with great affection, my credit was probably high from the start. Equally, the sort of abject deference that is often assumed to be the legacy of a colonial past is absent from Milne Bay Province, and I never experienced it during my fieldwork.

During the initial months my sense of the political relations was dominated by my feelings of impotence. My initial inability to speak the language, my ignorance of basic, everyday skills and my breaches of etiquette meant that I often felt vulnerable and demeaned. I remember the frustration of not being able to frame questions or reply to those that I understood perfectly. There is a stage in learning a language when one's passive knowledge outstrips one's capacity to converse. As I used to record conversations wherever possible, I can still cringe if I play some of these early tapes, for I hear my voice stumbling over simple phrases. There are several where the quaver in my voice betrays my distress at my inarticulate state. In some ways I am now grateful that I could not then understand the comments of people as they observed my struggle to communicate, as both sympathy and correction would have reduced me to abject silence.

One woman, Edi, who was my adoptive sister and closest neighbour, had come to Tubetube as an orphaned adolescent, unable to speak the language. She identified with my plight and spent many hours coaxing me to use the words I knew and explaining new words to me. She spoke no English and was a shy person, so most of my 'lessons' from her were conducted at night when her children were asleep and we could be alone. On many of the tapes I hear her voice saying soothingly, 'Oh my sister, I understand, the tongue gets so heavy, the memory goes'. With Edi, as with many of the women of my age, many conversations were about the differences between our lives, but even those were often premised on an assumed or hoped-for underlying similarity.

In this conversation, which took place after eight months on Tubetube, Edi had been questioning me about the births of my two daughters, about contraception and my ideas concerning the causes of illness in young children. She seized on all similarities and denied the differences. This was often the basis of our discussion. After a while I began to have difficulty in expressing myself because I did not have the vocabulary:

MM: Tell me about birth, teach me the words about it so that I can talk about it.
Edi: Birth, well you know that word! What others? Birth is the same for all women.
MM: What is the word for the beginning of birth, when the woman knows that the baby is coming? (*There is a pause, I recall Edi frowning, baffled.*)
Edi: What do you call it?
MM: We call it 'labour' (*I use the Tubetube word for 'physical work'.*)
Edi: (*Laughing*) Well, we don't call it that but we do it! Yes, that's a very apt word. We just call it 'pain'. Pain. That's the word, great pain.
MM: Is it always great pain? Are there other words for that feeling, like . . . (*Here there is a long pause I recall thinking desperately for a word like 'contraction' in Tubetube. Finally I decided to use terms I'd heard in the context of pottery making*) . . . squeezing or pressing? Can you talk about the abdomen 'squeezing' or 'pressing' the baby so that it comes out?
Edi: No. What you are saying is true, that is how we feel it too, my sister, but we say, 'I am in pain', or, 'The pain has started'. It is just as you say, like squeezing, like that. But we only use those words for the hands, you know, making pots, or sago, or washing clothes. The flesh of the abdomen does not do that. Do you understand? I'm explaining that we don't use those words. But I understand what you say, I understand you. Babies are all born in the same way. What you felt, I felt. But for you, only two, for me, nine times. Oh, my sister!

Thus the similarity between us, our motherhood, became a means of affirming an equality: 'What you felt, I felt'. At the same time, Edi's role as my teacher is combined with her greater status as a mother of nine, to assert her authority over me in this context. But there is one element of the conversation that has been impossible to translate and that is her use of the inclusive form of the first person plural. Whenever she spoke to me as a pupil, she taught me as if this language was going to be the the the one I would speak for the rest of my life, so that 'we' included me. Even in the conversation I have translated, where she is speaking of differences between her culture and mine, she uses the inclusive 'we', thereby emphasising my learning role as one which incorporates. Although I was un-aware of it at the time, except at a subliminal level, women instructed me as if I were being incorporated, whereas men more often use the exclusive 'we', especially as 'we Tubetube people', or 'we Bwanabwana' [small islands] people. It is hard to say, on the basis of the taped conversations I have with women and men if this is a product of the difference in subject matter, gender, or perception of my status as a visitor. Equally, I find it hard in retrospect to know whether my varying uses of inclusive and exclusive references are indicative of my own awareness of differentiation as a means of gaining information, or whether I was simply uncertain of the appropriate term!

There were other occasions when shared experience became the basis for identification. One woman who returned to live on Tubetube some months after my arrival was initially very shy with me. The following excerpt from a letter to an Australian friend captures that recognition of shared experience as women, that became the basis for one of the warmest friendships I had with a Tubetube woman.

> By the time the rain stopped I had been through all my photographs with Kempa asking for more and more 'stories' about them. The others had heard them before but never seem to get sick of them. They all love a photograph of me aged about 21, just before my marriage to P.; it's the waist-length hair that they admire. I'm constantly lectured for getting it cut!
>
> So Kempa and I set off for Kalotau. She was in high spirits and as soon as we were alone said in a low voice, 'Did you get divorced from your husband?'
>
> I told her that I had and that I had then remarried. She looked at me with such joy I thought she'd hug me, but of course she maintained the usual decorum. 'Why did you get divorced?'
>
> 'Well, I'd married as a young woman. I think we grew up and became different, we grew apart. And we had no children, which was hard for both of us.'
>
> You cannot imagine the look of relief on her face, she was delighted and began to tell me about her first marriage, interspersing it with, 'Just like you!' and, 'It was the same with me as with you! Just the same!' She thought, I think, that Europeans didn't divorce, an effect of mission propaganda about civilised behaviour.

The joys of recognition and identification are easy to recall. The problems that arise when there are misconceptions, or when the fieldworker is unable to explain adequately aspects of her enquiry, are less comfortable topics of discussion. It is hardly surprising that many anthropologists resort to self-deprecatory humour when they recount the frustrations of dealing with people who seem to be perversely determined to construct their own view of the ethnographic enterprise, and to ignore all attempts at countering that view. Laura Bohannon's story of Tiv interpretations of Hamlet (Bohannon 1966: 28–33), or Nigel Barley's autobiographical writings (1983) about African fieldwork represent a particular style of comic construction that light-handedly argues about the nature of cultural difference. But such gentle and self-disparaging revelations of fieldwork problems are rare, and easily dismissed as anecdotes. Moreover, the tendency of such writings to burlesque their subjects, as well as themselves, indicates an unease with the self-revelatory genre of writing that exposes the political relations between author and subject.

When people criticise ethnographers for appropriating knowledge and usurping the authority of subjects of research to speak for themselves, they often imply that the material has been acquired furtively, or at least without the informed consent of those it purports to represent. Working in the period when sensitivity to the colonial encounter was at a peak, and having chosen to write about Tubetube history, I tried hard to work in a way that was open, ethical and responsive to Tubetube sensibilities. Of course some problems remain intractable – for the issues that inhere in a particular culture's scholarly tradition are obscure or irrelevant for those whose history is unwritten, or created from within the confines of an alien cultural hegemony. It was sometimes impossible to convey the nature of a particular anthropological debate so that people were able to comprehend the motives behind my queries. But I think that such difficulties can be overestimated. It was usually simply a matter of finding an appropriate time when I could talk to adults at length. I found too that most people understood what I was interested in; occasionally, however, they were baffled by the apparent intensity of this interest. So that rather than being suspicious of my research, they often spoke to me in the tone of condescension that indicated to me that they were humouring me. I even heard a man reprimand someone who adopted this tone with me, saying sharply, 'Don't be disrespectful, she has got to learn all these things, even silly things'.

The apparent irrationality of my enquiry was not a simple incomprehension – often people understood perfectly well that my interest was inspired by some issue that was important to me and to other Europeans, and were prepared to concede that it might be important to them. Thus, when I discovered that several women had had Depo-Provera injections, I asked detailed questions about side-effects, and explained that I was alarmed for their health, and concerned that a drug banned in Australia was being used routinely as a contraceptive in a Third World country. Women who had been reluctant to talk with me about contraception came and talked to me at length, quizzing me about my fears. After our discussions I was able to see that decisions to have these injections were based on experiences and circumstances that are very different from those of white, middle-class Australian women. Faced with the choice between contraceptive pills, inter-uterine devices and sterilisation, some women on Tubetube believed that the risks were minimal compared with the risk of another pregnancy. In a country where women still die in childbirth as a result of minor complications, their views were well founded. The discomforts of fluid retention or headaches, for example, are ludicrous in a population where malaria is endemic and people are accustomed to living with the debilitating effects of chronic illness. Amenorrhoea was considered a benefit. When I tried to translate the English term 'side-effect' into Tubetube, women laughed heartily and made jokes about pregnancies that had been 'unexpected and additional results of some particular activity'. But behind their mirth lies the grim difference between their life expectancy and mine, and their realistic views of the possibilities for dramatic change in their generation, or even for their daughters. The ironies of difference were rarely far from my consciousness when I was living on Tubetube, and they have become more pointed as I have written about the lives of women there (see Macintyre 1986: 248–56).

Over the months of fieldwork I gradually became implicated in the activities of the island community in different ways. The nature of my involvement was sometimes negotiable, but it was rarely my autonomous decision. In trying to fathom the terms of my various interactions, I am aware that I could use a number of analogies, but none of them captures the range of relationships, nor do they expose the contradictions of intense commitment and constant observation. The role of the participant observer is not, however, unique to the anthropological fieldworker. It seems to me that I have always had an internalised capacity to note things with apparent detachment even as I engage in some conversation or activity with passionate involvement; it is something that I have done since childhood. So it is not a quality that emerged in the field. As a fieldworker it developed, so that I can recall gestures, expressions and the way in which people interacted, as if it were all on a film. Participant observation seems an apt description of this engagement, but it does not imply a suspension of commitment to the people with whom one participates.

Like many anthropologists, I was initially taken in as 'fictive kin'. The explanations given to me for this were several. First, as I was going to stay on the island for a long time, I had to live in an appropriate place. I therefore needed to belong to the totemic 'clan' that would enable me to live near to the main hamlet. This was a pragmatic decision. Secondly, as the only person who could translate for me was a young married man, I must become his 'elder sister' in order to avoid scandal. Later, a *post hoc* explanation emerged which drew on a long tradition of incorporating migrants and exiles into the community. My reddish hair, my habit of running my fingers through my hair when nervous, and the way that I hold my head at a slight angle when I listen to people intently, were indicators of my natural connection to Magisubu, the sea eagle clan. This view gained currency as I was 'naturalised', and was proved to everybody's satis-faction when an elderly woman from another island pronounced that the lines on my hand proclaimed me as Magisubu.

An equally pressing reason for incorporating me was the need to minimise the disruption I caused by having no rightful place. People found it difficult to use my first name, as first names are used exclusively by spouses, or in intimate contexts. This left them with the honorific 'sinabada', a form of address for senior women that was used in the colonial context for white women. It is now redolent of subservience and I hated being addressed in this way. In making me a part of the Magisubu clan, Tubetube leaders lessened my anomalous status and gave everyone on the island a way of speaking to me. Set in a large lineage with two older sisters, a mother and three powerful men as my mother's brothers, as well as numerous younger siblings, I could be managed, instructed and guided in ways that did not threaten their dignity or mine. Although I was unaware of it at the time, there was a meeting of people who decided on my fate in these terms within days of my arrival.

The adoption by Magisubu people carried with it numerous obligations, most of which were unknown to me until I was instructed as to their nature. In retrospect, they were advantageous to my research in the sense that I was given a role in various events affecting my adoptive family and so learned within a defined context. Usually, before any occasion where I might be expected to behave in some role appropriate to my (fictive) status, some senior person would explain to me what I should do. So, for example, I was told that I must on no account step over people's belongings nor stand so that I looked down on the head of a senior man or woman, nor sit close to any affines. All of these rules were explained in detail, prefaced by 'As a person of this village . . . ' or, 'Married women must not . . . '. Many of these 'rules' were conveyed to me as normative statements. Often I watched carefully to see if other women of my age or status were behaving in the way that I had been told to do. Over time it became clear that on Tubetube I was expected to conform to patterns of behaviour expected of a married older woman. On neighbouring islands I was treated as an honoured guest, unless I was accompanied by a group of Magisubu people, in which case the hosts would treat me in accordance with my fictive status within that clan. The shifts were clearer to me when I gained some proficiency with the language. Sometimes when I arrived on another island people would refer to me as 'sinabada', but as soon as they heard a Tubetube person call me by some kin term, they would address me with the term appropriate to our new-found relationship.

I often pondered just what the adoptive status meant to people on the island. Sometimes I thought that it was like a game for them. Obviously they liked to show me off to their neighbours, and they sometimes commented on my aptitude or skill in an area they considered unique to their culture. As I involved everybody in my language learning, everybody took credit for my fluency. Like all good teachers, they tended to accentuate my achievements when presenting me to others, reserving critical comments on my failings for when I was alone or in a supportive environment. They would proudly explain to visitors that I could speak the language perfectly within weeks of my arrival, make clay pots as if I had been doing it all my life, and understood all sorts of things about the ways in which their ancestors lived. Fulsome praise and exaggerated claims were not part of everyday interaction, however, and I was never allowed to rest on the laurels they made for public presentation.

Within the hamlet my proficiency at various tasks and my inabilities became ways of caricaturing me. Clearly, women liked to see me do things the way that they did. I could carry baskets of yams on my head, but found that heavy buckets of water made my neck ache. Rather than see me carrying my water with difficulty, my sisters would send an adolescent boy or girl to do it, but I knew that they thought it odd. As most people considered that all Europeans cooked on primus stoves in their own countries, my battles with my primus bewildered them. When it became clear to them that I also failed dismally with a wood fire, and occasionally had problems with my pressure lamp, they dealt with my incompetencies by joking with me, and at my expense.

Two words signalled Tubetube reactions to my behaviour. If I was unable to perform some task or failed to grasp some instruction, people would exclaim, 'O dimdim!' (O, European/white person). I was then a figure of fun, like other visiting whites. If, however, I managed to do something skilfully, or commented in a way that indicated my understanding of an issue, then there would be appreciative smiles and nods, and someone would invariably comment, 'O sanapu!' (O, clever), or 'O Papua!'

Clever or not, my whiteness could not really be denied. But people become accustomed to immigrants and visitors who stay for ages, and so I think I was accepted as an incorporated anomaly. Acceptance and incorporation are difficult to demonstrate, but seem to me to inhere in the ways in which people speak of, and to, a person. After a year some people could express impatience or disapproval at some action of mine that would have gone unquestioned had I been a guest. But when I wrote a preface for my thesis in the Tubetube language I recounted an event that captured all my feelings of belonging. In thanking a small girl who was my adoptive sister's child (and therefore someone whom I called 'my child'), I recounted an exchange which occurred when I returned to the island after an absence of several months. Her baby sister was the only person who did not remember me and so screamed in terror at my white face. The little girl frowned reprovingly and told her firmly, 'Don't be frightened, she's not a white person, she's your mother!' Thus it is perhaps that the fictions of fieldwork become the basis for claims of authenticity in ethnography.

FEMINIST FIELDWORK AND IDENTITY PROBLEMS

When I went to Tubetube I had been involved in feminist studies for some years. In Australia I had been active in the Women's Liberation Movement, and in Britain my commitment to feminism was expressed in the work I did with others in the collective that ran a course called *Women in Society* (Cambridge Women's Studies Group 1981). However, the questions that inspired my doctoral research were historical rather than feminist. I found Malinowski's representation of the Trobriands disingenuous and implausible. Even now the opening sentence of Malinowski's Introduction strikes me as strange. Just as he captures his general subject, he extinguishes it with qualifications drawn from his particular historical perception (one derived from and shared with colonial intruders): 'The coastal populations of the South Sea Islands, with very few exceptions, are, or were before their extinction, expert navigators and traders' (Malinowski 1922: 1).

In a text littered with references to change and to the disappearance of cultural elements or social practices 'with the establishment of white man's influence' (Malinowski 1922: 297), generations of anthropologists have managed only to see the functionalist's static South Sea Island paradise, or have only been able to counter the claim by insisting on persistence (see Weiner 1976). But any reader of Malinowski can find within the text a battle between the artifice of the atemporal whole, and the intrusion of those historical circumstances that constantly threaten, transform and reshape his observed subjects or their world.

I arrived on Tubetube having read accounts of the region by anthropologists, traders, missionaries, patrol officers, explorers and historians who had left their written words, published and unpublished, in places accessible to the diligent scholar. These became the counterpoint for those themes and stories that Tubetube people offered in a variety of contexts. The interweaving was conscious, and the setting down in my words was self-conscious, contrived and composed. I wrote an historical ethnography for my thesis. But with this endeavour there was also the constant interest in women's lives – an interest that fed on my own awareness of differences, and was nurtured by Tubetube women's curiosity about similarities and disparities.

As people defined me quite unambiguously as a married woman with children, temporarily separated from her family, in any social activity it was assumed that I would participate in that role. Indeed, shortly after my arrival two of my new-found sisters insisted that I adopt two daughters to live with me, in order to facilitate this role and maintain my maternal identity. On Tubetube there is a form of temporary adoption called 'esimili gabuna', and on this basis, Mary, aged 14 and Catherine, aged 13, became my daughters and part of my household. I have on occasion tried to write about these two, but words and emotions fail me. Last year as I delivered a seminar on feminist anthropologists, I thought that I might talk about them, but the grief of separation choked my words. It still does, and so in alluding to it I shall simply allow the silence to be read. Sometimes the experiences of the field do not transform themselves into ethnographic prose, and sometimes the language of emotional attachment seems sentimental or inadequate.

In a community where alternating residence between the husband's village and the wife's village is required, and where matrilocality seems to be the most desirable residence, absent husbands are commonplace. So in many respects my household conformed with those of other women. Even the fact that I had a husband and children living elsewhere was simply a matter for sympathy. While most women could accommodate my single-parenthood, they found my celibacy a source of private mirth (Macintyre, n.d.). Feminist concerns of the late 1970s inspired me to seek out the ways in which women there were autonomous, dominated or submissive (Macintyre 1987). But over the months, as I confronted the realities of their world, some of my feminist interests and my political insights altered. My feminism had been grounded in my experiences as a woman in an advanced industrial nation. On Tubetube I shifted my focus. But in setting those words down, I am struck by their banality – a banality matched only by those feminist critics who upbraid anyone who writes as an outsider looking in, thereby giving the choice of silence or impossibility. At the same time, many of my ideas, opinions and political judgements were reinforced, not changed by either my observations or participation in life on Tubetube in 1979 and 1980.

When I went to Papua New Guinea I was well aware of the impact of poverty on its inhabitants. I knew that there were periodic droughts in Milne Bay Province. I knew that maternal and infant death-rates were high. During my time in the field I experienced and observed a drought and the death of a woman in childbirth. Of all my experiences in the field, these have remained in my mind as the most politically disturbing, but they were not transformative.

LIVING THROUGH A DROUGHT

The drought came upon us quickly. For weeks older people had been making gloomy comments about the lack of rain, but there were ripe fruits about and the trees seemed green enough. Yam houses were usually empty by November anyhow, so it didn't seem to me to be a crisis. It was only when three of the senior men came and asked me to give my bag of rice to the school that I realised that stores of food were almost exhausted. My notebooks are filled with descriptions of conversations about the drought and with observations about the ways in which the community responded to the food shortage and with annotations to the taped accounts of past droughts that affected the islands. Each day I recorded the food gathered and divided within each hamlet.

My diary reveals the effects of hunger. I had long daydreams about food. I slept more than I would have usually. I do not record that I felt hungry, and in fact I think that I didn't ever feel starving. It was very hot, and the winds were too strong to think of paddling across to one of the neighbouring islands where we knew that there were coconuts growing. On two occasions I almost fainted after walking in the bush looking for food. Oddly, I did not notice that I had lost more than 30 pounds, until I went into Alotau with three people to ask for government assistance. I weighed myself on the airline scales. I was so startled by my emaciated appearance that I took a photograph of myself in a mirror at the doctor's house. He said that I looked as if I could have tuberculosis.

I also took photos of the cracked earth, the dying plants, the banana trees with dry, frayed leaves, and of every collective effort at food production. Like me, people had little energy, so we sat and talked a lot in those weeks. Then and now, my personal experience of the drought seems to me far less important than my understanding of its effects on Tubetube people. I did not need this experience to learn that an inadequate diet is unpleasant, tiring and debilitating.

Nobody died of starvation, but women grew thin as they gave their food to children. An old man died of kidney failure. A 4-year-old girl almost died of malaria. Malaria was rife and people were ill, listless and wasted. In retrospect I feel angry that the endurance of such privations is barely recognised in studies of village economies, or in proposals for development projects.

At the time I was absorbed in recording the details of how life continued. Some of my observations are transmuted into writing on the economy of the region in a way that recognises the exigencies of minor climatic variation within a specific region. Sometimes I suppose that my lectures are more vivid than they might be if I was drawing only on secondary sources. But the selection of the material that can be incorporated into lectures, articles and other scholarly representations obscures the context in which they were collected, and at a stroke snippets of conversation become quotations or pronouncements. What difference is made by revealing the personalised, speaking subject behind the generalised observation she made in a conversation? Whose generalisations are they anyway? I sit and listen to a tape of a woman and me talking about food taboos in 1979. She begins each statement with an authoritative insistence: 'Here we think . . . ', 'Tubetube people know . . . ', 'You don't know yet, but you will see that we know the correct way . . . '. This voice is disembodied in every way now: removed from Papua New Guinea, coming through my head-phones as I sit at my desk a decade later. The tape is old, the voice sometimes distorted. I think of her neatly combed hair and her dark brown skin, and remember that she once astonished me by wearing a bathing costume to go spear fishing. Whenever I remember her I think of her confident bearing, her vehemence and her energy. I marvel still at the quantity of yams that she could carry on her head, I have a slide of her in a flowered dress, a bush-knife in hand and a basket of seed yams on her head. The etiolated roots of a yam obscure her face slightly. I show this slide when I teach about the sexual division of labour in gardening.

THE DEATH OF A FRIEND

In 1981 this Tubetube woman died in childbirth. She was a trained nurse. Although she lived on a neighbouring island, I saw her often and she became a friend. She had lived in Port Moresby, and her experience of town life, her education and her understanding of my reasons for being on Tubetube enabled her to mediate and to explain my research to others. It was she who told me of misunderstandings, deceptions and puzzlement. Her English was fluent, but after a few months she would insist that we speak in her language. She was sympathetic whenever I was feeling homesick or discouraged and obviously enjoyed our discussions about health, childbirth and the differences in our lives. While I never felt as close to her as I did to my neighbour and sister Edi, I valued her support and friendship and knew that I was greatly in her debt.

Our friendship embodied many of those ambiguities that other anthropologists have written about, but that novelists are usually far better at capturing. She and I discussed and dissected its anomalies as well as the ways in which each seemed to be able to imagine what might be strange or interesting to the other. Within the kinship network I was incorporated into a lineage that had close ties to hers, requiring, however, that our relationship be that of respectful 'cousins' rather than sisters. As she was also related to me as an affine, married into my mother's father's lineage, in certain public contexts we were meant to behave deferentially, with extreme mutual respect, observing strict social and physical distance. Because of our initial friendship, she was able to instruct me in the etiquette of our constructed kinship.

As I became more familiar with Tubetube expectations of my social behaviour, so our use of English declined and interactions became more formal. On the few occasions when we did speak in English it was in private, and it seemed to be assuming an inappropriate intimacy. After one such conversation (March 1980) I wrote:

> D. came around from Tupwana and I asked her lots of questions about diving and fishing and the reasons why people understate the contributions of adolescent girls to the evening meals. She asked me in English to read out all the times girls had caught fish. As we pored over my lists of names and dates and weights, she kept exclaiming and then laughed and said, 'Oh Martha, you are going to shame people, especially all those lazy young boys!' I think we both realised that she had used my name and felt embarrassed – she much more than I could have expected. She became flustered, changed the subject, closed my books and packed them away and kept chattering in Tt. until she managed to back out the door.

My own discomfort was stranger to me than hers. Now, browsing through diaries and letters, I am aware that they testify to a relationship that has no real counterpart in my culture, or in the culture of those most likely to read this piece. To say that I think I learned to behave like a Tubetube woman does to relatives of the class they call 'enaena', says little. Even explaining that gradually I learned how to respond to my adoptive mother's father's second wife's son's wife is hardly informative. I am forced into translating the rules that were given to me: 'Don't sit close to her'; 'Don't eat in front of her'; 'Walk behind her'; 'Don't say her name or the names of any of her senior kin or of the people to whom she is married. Use other ways [that is, tekonyms] of referring to them'. Or I can set down my observations of the behaviour of the other five women who stood in this relationship to D. But any attempt to clarify this relationship and the ways it developed means rendering it programmatic, alien or in some way stranger than it seems to me as an experience. We both became more comfortable as I learned how to behave towards her as a relative.

This was a relationship in which sensitivities to difference loomed large. She was my age, she had two small children, as I did. We were both given to pointing out ironies and drawing wry comparisons between our lives. I could not believe that she bled to death. I felt angry at the injustice inherent in the differences between the provision of health care in rural, insular Papua New Guinea and Australia. It seemed too harsh a way of manifesting the differences in life-expectancy for women in these countries. Then and now I was overwhelmed by the realisation that if we had been able to get her to hospital, she would have survived.

As we mourned her death over the following months, several women remarked to me that they too felt angry. We talked about grief and fear of death in childbirth. D's death became a focus for my concern with difference. My distress at her death confirmed to my sisters that I was no different from them. The distinctions we made and the ways in which we drew closer remain complicated and irreducible.

It seems ludicrous to subsume the sum of all those differences and contradictions in any simple psychic category. The world of Tubetube women was no longer alien to me and I shared many of their responses to it. The nuances and ambiguities of the fictive and fictional relationships we made are not rendered transparent or elucidated by invoking categories of 'otherness'. Current attachment to the label 'other' is expressive only of the theoretical preoccupations of postmodern discourse in the European academy. In the retreat from colonial conceptualisations we abandoned the 'native'; as we discarded evolutionist comparisons we jettisoned 'primitives'. No doubt in the future, as the ethnocentrism or inadequacy of psychoanalytic theories are acknowledged, the term 'other' will then be exposed as partial, discriminatory and exclusive. In the meantime it is to me woefully inadequate as a way of conceptualising the complex relation between the fieldworker and the people with whom she lives, whom she observes, describes and later writes about. It carries with it so many connotations of social distance and is redolent of a particular European feminist tradition, that it seems to me to epitomise the sort of inaccessible, theoreticist writing that so enrages women in the Third World (see Amadiume 1987). 'Other' invariably is restricted in meaning to a culturally defined alternative, where the definition is in the hands of the definer, observer and constructor. Moreover, the vision of the anthropological 'object', or 'other' as a self-representing agent in any text is remarkable mainly for its accord with right-wing liberal views of the essential autonomous subject. It ignores the power relations that it claims to subvert, simply by setting the terms for any dialogue within a literary debate about cultural difference.

In her discussion of feminist anthropology, Henrietta Moore points out the critical problems inherent in questioning the concept of culture as it is expressed in current debates about ethnography as the representation of difference. She notes that querying of the primacy of cultural difference 'throws into question the the primary organising concept of social anthropology: the concept of culture' (Moore 1988: 197).

There is an assumption that differences between people from different countries, or classes, or linguistic groups are elucidated when read as cultural variations. The concept of culture expands, contracts and ultimately includes so much or so little that its conceptual utility is lost. Any difference can be written off as a cultural variation so that crucial disparities are obscured. But access to medical assistance is not a cultural variant, nor is the risk of death in childbirth.

In contemplating the death of a Tubetube woman in 1981, I can conjure in my words some of the differences between us. I can still listen to her voice on cassettes as we talk about health issues on the island, sing hymns with other women, or talk about the dietary taboos and their effects on the health of mothers. I could translate some of these and make them into a dialogic text, for certainly she said things that bear on the enterprise of writing about my fieldwork. But in the end it seems to me that any such use of her words would be more expressive of the inequality that her death has made, than of equity in representation.

Recently I have begun to do research about Salvadorean refugee women in Melbourne. This throws into a different light my experience of fieldwork on Tubetube. For here I work in my own community, and I speak the language that they must learn, as I struggle to learn the language that marks them as immigrants. In this context the questions of power, authority and ethical commitments are present in every interaction. The collection of data cannot be unobtrusive; the class inequalities that prevail are expressed in my clothes, my house, my employment and in all the differences between the material conditions of my existence and those of refugee women. The fictions that can be sustained when one is an alien cannot even be manufactured on home ground.

When my research was conducted in a distant place, in a strange language and within a community where I had no previous links, the political inequalities were less clear. I did not have much money and I did not have many goods that set me apart from my neighbours. While at home I lived in relative luxury, on Tubetube my house did not set me apart from others around me.

I did not attempt to disguise differences between my life in Australia and my life in the field. Rather, it was one of the major ways in which I communicated with people. For my interest in their culture and work was matched by their interest in mine. I had illustrated magazines sent to me and people spent hours quizzing me about the pictures in them. I took photographs of my home and family in Australia, and I tried to describe my life to people who were curious. Conscious of the importance of gift exchange in this culture, I tried to give appropriate return gifts. So, for example, I made knitted bags from brightly coloured yarns and gave them to men and women who had made me baskets or combs. I sewed dresses for the women who taught me how to plant and make clay pots. I taught young girls how to make paper patterns from newspapers and to sew on a manual sewing machine that I gave as a special gift to one of my sisters. It is often very difficult to assess one's success at working within a different system. Miriam Kahn's (1986) description of her farewell feast in the final chapter of her ethnography of Wamiran society evokes all those errors of judgement that can be made by an outsider trying to do the right thing. While I am sure that I too made such mistakes, I was fortunate that there were invariably members of my adoptive family to set me (and my mistakes) right. But my ignorance and capacity for error were such accepted knowledge that no senior person would have allowed me to make drastic blunders. Similarly, my sisters invariably kept me informed if they thought that I was being duped, or failing to recognise my indebtedness. They were committed to the creation of identity so that my identification with them could be assumed. Sometimes they were mistaken, often I made mistakes, but neither of us was committed to maintaining my social distance or otherness.

SEPARATION AND DISTANCE

As I have read through fieldnotes, diaries and letters from the field, I have pondered the extent to which the person writing those words was distinct or separable from the person setting them down. I feel no jarring, no sense of unease or distance from the self who lived on Tubetube. My letters and diaries are filled with my concern for my family in Australia and for people on the island. I move back and forth still.

There is a way of thinking and writing about the category of the person that stresses the partibility of the self. It owes much to various psychological discursive modes. But like ethnography, it is a device for setting down thoughts about aspects of identity and experiences of interaction. In writing about doing fieldwork, or writing ethnography, such conventions of pluralities and separations are most useful. But the self-consciousness that pervades requires a fictional distance from the separate self that is being set down. This fiction is probably no less significant of difference than the artifices of selves and others that currently perplex our discipline.

The experiences of alienation, strangeness and isolation from one's own people are central to our cultural vision of the human capacity for self-knowledge or enlightenment. Anthropologists, perhaps more than others, propel themselves into strange worlds and then attempt to recount their observations while occasionally reflecting on the meaning of that experience. In recognising that this is part of what writing ethnography achieves, we are not really making any new discovery. In seeking to extend the range of voices from different cultures, we need to consider the aim of the exercise. Other people's ethnographies may sometimes be boring. Other people's fieldnotes or transcripts are usually tedious or unintelligible.

The implications of reflexive modes of writing are important for feminist anthropology. But in setting out to expose to critical scrutiny the process and results of field research as an individual activity, we are perhaps more likely to be exclusive and ethnocentric than might otherwise have been the case. In truth, I think that my experiences and the self-awareness I gained during the time I lived on Tubetube are far less interesting than Tubetube people's history and their perceptions of their social universe as they disclosed them to me. The same can be said for Malinowski's work on the Trobriands. His diaries are badly written testimonies of a vain and often arrogant man. His ethnographies, whatever their other fictional qualities, are absorbing and lucidly written. If I were really wanting to find out more about the psyche and soul of an Anglophile Polish emigré who travels and lives in exotic lands, I would much rather read Conrad, whose mastery of the language of representation far exceeds that of Malinowski. For in all the debates about reflexivity and ethnography as fiction, literary skills should be prominent. In teaching about the experience of living in a strange culture, I would suggest that students read Carlo Levi's *Christ Stopped at Eboli* (1982) in order to understand the ways in which an alien observer can become immersed in a different world. The moral dilemmas facing anyone who lives and works in a post-colonial Third World country are dramatically and brilliantly revealed in Nadine Gordimer's novel *A Guest of Honour* (1973). These works of fiction provide evocative and penetrating accounts of living in other worlds and dealing with the moral or personal dilemmas that being an alien observer imposes. While not disputing the view that the best ethnographies are imaginatively inspired compositions, I think that we need to recognise that there are genres of writing in which *mis*representation is reprehensible, and others where it is acceptable as a poetic device. The problem that arises in the context of reflexivity is that the anthropological involution that it inspires entails a necessary relativism which does not permit the possibility of misrepresentations. From a feminist perspective, the political implications of moral relativism are potentially reactionary, as they preclude the definition of either oppression or liberation. For those of us who work in the Third World it seems an abandonment rather than commitment to the women whose lives we shared.

REFERENCES

Amadiume, Ifi (1987) *Male Daughters, Female Husbands*, London: Zed Books Ltd.
Asad, Talal (1986) 'The concept of cultural translation in British Social Anthropology', in James Clifford and George Marcus (eds), *Writing Culture: The Poetics and Politics of Ethnography*, Berkeley: University of California Press, pp. 141–64.
Barley, Nigel (1983) *The Innocent Anthropologist: Notes from a Mud Hut*, London: British Museum Publications (Colonnade Books).
Bohannon, Laura (1966) 'Shakespeare in the bush', *Natural History* 75(7): 28–33.
Cambridge Women's Studies Group (eds) (1981) *Women in Society: Interdisciplinary Essays*, London: Virago.
Clifford, James (1988) *The Predicament of Culture*, Cambridge, MA: Harvard University Press.
Clifford, James and Marcus, George (eds) (1986) *Writing Culture: The Poetics and Politics of Ethnography*, Berkeley: University of California Press.
Donner, Florinda (1984) *Shabono*, London: Triad/Paladin Books.
Evans-Pritchard, Edward (1937) *Witchcraft, Oracles and Magic Among the Azande*, Oxford: Oxford University Press.
Geertz, Clifford (1988) *Works and Lives*, Stanford, CA: Stanford University Press.
Gordimer, Nadine (1973) *A Guest of Honour*, Harmondsworth: Penguin.
Kahn, Miriam (1986) *Always Hungry, Never Greedy: Food and the Expression of Gender in a Melanesian Society*, Cambridge: Cambridge University Press.
Levi, Carlo (1982) *Christ Stopped at Eboli*, Harmondsworth: Penguin.
Macintyre, Martha (1986) 'Female autonomy in a matrilineal society', in N. Grieve and A. Burns (eds), *Australian Women, New Feminist Perspectives*, Melbourne: Oxford University Press, pp. 248–57.
—— (1987) 'Flying witches and leaping warriors: the supernatural origins of power and matrilineal authority, in Tubetube society', in Marilyn Strathern (ed.), *Dealing with Inequality: Analyzing Gender Relations in Melanesia and Beyond*, Cambridge: Cambridge University Press, pp. 207–28.
—— (1989) 'Better homes and gardens', in Margaret Jolly and Martha Macintyre (eds), *Family and Gender in the Pacific*, Cambridge: Cambridge University Press, pp. 156–69.
—— (n.d.) 'Reflections of an anthropologist who mistook her husband for a yam', Paper delivered at ASAO Conference, San Antonio, Texas, 1988.

62 *Gendered fields*

Malinowski, Bronislaw (1922) *Argonauts of the Western Pacific*, London: Routledge & Kegan Paul.

Moore, Henrietta (1988) *Feminism and Anthropology*, Cambridge: Polity Press.

Seligman, Charles (1910) *The Melanesians of British New Guinea*, Cambridge: Cambridge University Press.

Tyler, Stephen (1986) 'Post-modern ethnography: from document of the occult to occult document', in James Clifford and George Marcus (eds), *Writing Culture: The Poetics and Politics of Ethnography*, Berkeley: University of California Press, pp. 122–40.

Weiner, Annette (1976) *Women of Value, Men of Renown*, St Lucia: University of Queensland Press.

3 Between autobiography and method

Being male, seeing myth and the analysis of structures of gender and sexuality in the eastern interior of Fiji

Allen Abramson

INTRODUCTION: THE CONSTRUCTION OF ETHNOGRAPHY AND THE TRANSFORMATION OF THE ETHNOGRAPHER

On types of autobiography in anthropology

Over the years, two kinds of autobiography have turned up in anthropology's archive. The first, from outside of ethnographic texts already composed, speaks to the para-professional theme of 'being an anthropologist'. Undoubtedly, a desire for personal introspection, some impulse towards self-exploration, typifies works in this genre. Objectively, though, the readership of the modernist autobiography was, and still is, a general public keen to romanticise the trade of ethnography. In Susan Sontag's words, this well-informed public wills the anthropologist towards some manner of heroism (Sontag 1970), culturally authorising within the discipline the methodical rulings of a Utopian epistemology (Jarvie 1964).

The eventual surfacing of the subjective has meant the genesis of a second kind of anthropological autobiography, which arises more recently in the wake of the paradigmatic collapse of heroic modernism and the generalisation of a reflexive imperative. Projected into the written work as its self-consciousness and conscience, the anthropologist as author is depicted breathing immanent subjectivity into otherwise lifeless and powerless fragments of cultural alteriority.

I take it, though, that a third kind of autobiography is possible, and that, over the conjuncture for which it might be relevant, its chief task lies in nudging these two autobiographical positions away from the philosophies of pure objectivity and subjectivity that court them. It has to fuse together the substantive insights which they make. Indeed, today these two genres are unstable and a third mode of autobiographical reflection is emergent. The polemical role of this third sort resides in exposing the twin mythologies of, on the one hand, the authorless representation of the objective, and on the other, of the consummate authorship of the subjective. Ideally, these reductions give way to the relatively complex structuring of the intrusive objects which anchor and confine anthropological subjectivity in the field, and which reveal themselves to this subjectivity as a set of understandable signs. Thus this account focuses upon the cultural processing of masculinity at the interface of two imagined worlds, exploring the meaning and exercise of gender at the point where these two worlds meet and impinge. It charts the progress and transformation of one man and an anthropological perspective around Fijian corners and spaces that retain radically different conceptions of being male in the world.

THEORETICAL CRISIS, PARADIGM SHIFT AND THE ABANDONMENT OF METHOD IN THE FIELD

Global crisis of theory

At the end of the seventies, I went to the field with political involvement of sorts in mind. I felt as much a militant as I did an ethnographer. In the Melanesian context, I took it that anthropology had to uncover the exploitative structures that governed the fate of whatever social classes gardened, exchanged and feasted there. I was set to reveal the real, the true identity of the actors hiding behind the masks of Melanesian belief and custom, as it were, to bring both big and little men down to earth.

For this programme in social anthropology, the demystification of ideological forms presented itself as just as much an epistemological imperative as it did a moral choice. Thus, if it was to promote itself as a credible science, let alone as a liberating weapon, anthropological theory and method would have to show (1) how imaginary worlds in Melanesia were produced rationally by strategic powers (consciously or not), and (2) how fictional subjectivities peopling these worlds were less powerful in society than the 'ventriloquist' powers that produced and controlled them. If this distinction could not be made and defended, ethnography and theory could not be called upon to support the rational critique of modern religion and ideology. Thus anthropology as an intervening humanism depends upon it successfully defending a theory of (other peoples') ideology and (its own) objective science. It does this allegorically in the genre of the positivist ethnography: that is, ethnography that establishes the transformation of culture as ideology in specific cases in order to promote the facticity of science over culture generally.

By the end of the seventies, however, the generalised critique of anthropological empiricism had reached a point at which a commitment to contemporary standards and criteria of coherence meant that one could not write an unproblematic Durkheimian or Marxist anthropology of Melanesian forms: or, at least, no theoretical anthropologist could have written one, without a serious rejustification of premises. Collapsing the couplet science/ideology, the elusive foundations for a different sort of anthropological realism had to be laid, one that would build constructively upon the impossibility of ever seeing real structures directly.

It was in these circumstances that, somewhat less than consciously, both the desire to work through Marxist difficulties, and the sense that they might be impossible to work through in the end, influenced the early conduct of my

Visible gender practice: women leaving Serea village to fish in the creek.

fieldwork. In my case, the contradictions of this double-bind surfaced amidst very concrete ethnographic concerns. These related to the hierarchical relationship obtaining between chiefs and commoners in the chiefdom of Serea, a Melanesian place in the semi-remote interior of the island of Big Fiji.

The abandonment of method

For ceremonial contexts I had been measuring the flow of material tribute to the chief of the village-chiefdom of Serea. Here the symbolic implication of hierarchy was realised in the enactment of material flows which thus seemed central to a basic understanding of the society and its history. However, as I saw it at the time (and still do), the volume of 'tribute' circulating through this key relation was much too small to signal the dominance of an exploitative class in production. Influenced by the fracture of paradigm and the dislocations caused by doubt, my perception shifted instead to less palpable aspects of material culture: to symbolic rather than physical tribute.

As a result, I began to perceive myths of the chiefs as constitutive texts with indeterminate political effects rather than as charters with written-in guarantees, and to watch rituals of the chiefs as theatres of material transformations, rather than as class masquerades and metaphors. The economy then seemed to represent itself as the material embodiment of potent signs as well as the source of material livelihood. Thereupon, liberated from always having to look for meaning somewhere else, I began to listen to people in a way I had eschewed hitherto. In effect, I began to listen to them. Thus decentred, fieldwork slipped its tight theoretical moorings. Not knowing any longer where the essence of social life was, and not knowing indeed whether there might be an essence to Fijian social life at all, I surrendered the helm of my ethnographic search to my hosts. I let them and their understandings of me unwittingly steer the flaccid vessel of observation as they would.

Consequently, the balance of information in my notebooks reflects a knowledge of Serean forms which my informants and friends revealed to me rather than of forms that I sought systematically without and despite them. In a sense, in surrendering focus, I quit method (defined in the strictest sense of the term). Doing fieldwork during a 'paradigm shift' (Kuhn 1962), now on indigenous terms, more or less, I postponed the rational pursuit of knowledge. I began to defer to my informants' sense of what was appropriate, and this not because I had become a relativist but because I had been a Marxist, and now was theoretically liminal.

In this respect, it is significant to note that my informants and hosts steered and positioned me according to my gender so that I became singularly objectified and controlled by a Melanesian perception of the surfaces of my sexuality. The pivot upon which the subsequent anthropological project balanced shifted from *my* perception of Fijian class to *Fijian* perception of my gender. Only towards the end of my fieldwork did I rebel against this objectification of my person and gender in a way that I recount towards the end of the chapter.

After about three months in the field only, I became ill and left for the city. I returned to the field after six weeks.

OBJECTIVE GENDER: THE MYTHICAL REALITY OF THE ETHNOGRAPHER IN A CHIEFDOM IN EASTERN FIJI

Installed as chief

First of all, I consider my ethnographic progress, as I passed from the category of 'chief' to 'son'.

The European who comes to visit chiefdoms of the interior of Big Fiji can never expect to roam freely inside the space physically marked out as 'the village' (termed 'na koro' in Fijian). He or she is enclosed by a logic of categories, culturally walled up and objectified inside a village confinement that limits mobility and shapes social vista. In effect, the village, as an impersonal authority, demands the respect and obedience of the European even though (and especially if he is male) at the same time it decisively elevates and incorporates him. (Village authority is such that its various spaces cannot be passed over or through, or turned, even unwittingly, into mere points in a continuing journey.)

As professional ethnographer, I was installed under the sign of the 'vulagi' or sky-spirit and attributed 'mana', the celestial power of the Fijian cosmos. In some senses, therefore, even as I conducted ethnographic work for myself, my 'mana' was also appropriated by my informants to do a work of transformation for them.

Undoubtedly, then, my presence altered the object of study. However, it did so within structures that could accommodate my strangeness, for, like all chiefly figures in Oceania, I had arrived within a ritual cycle of coming and going that was able to stereotype and assimilate it. In public places, at least, the charismatic powers of this strangeness commanded a respect verging on adulation. However, even as my fame as a celebrated stranger ramified, my control over personal movement and physical behaviour weakened. Immobilised, my space *qua* ethnographer became increasingly circumscribed. Culturally speaking, so that it might encompass the 'people of the land', my 'mana' was to be hedged in by specific rules (Hocart 1970). I was, therefore, obliged to exchange European freedom for Melanesian fame. What effect upon my ethnographic project did such massive fame and subjection have?

In fact, I first came to the interior as guest of the Fijian manager of a busy cooperative store that was just outside the boundaries of the large chiefdom of Serea in the province of Naitasiri. The store stood at the end of the road from the capital, Suva, and at the point where villagers from upstream unloaded their goods and disembarked from their boats and rafts. It was a busy junction and a good stopping-off place for both me and them in the semi-remote interior of Big Fiji.

On my first weekend trip (and there were several of these before I took up residence on the other side of the village boundaries) I arrived to discover that a considerable feast had been prepared in my honour. A pig had been killed and earth-baked inside the village boundaries of the chiefdom, taken out of the village and brought over to the store. In fact, as soon as I had stepped off the bus, it was to be shepherded towards a 'kava' bowl, at the 'upper' end of which sat the chief of all-Serea, and where, at the 'lower' end, sat a dozen or so men from inside the village. I was put to the sacred right of this chief and I was introduced as a great, mighty and fecund chief from Great Britain and we began to drink. Those below looked on at me with awe, for they would never rise 'higher' than me in their lifetimes. During the meal, as well as on many occasions afterwards, they would feel obliged to stoop and sit physically 'lower' than me. In effect, the chief and I were kindred spirits in the terrestrial province of a semi-heavenly family of Melanesian aristocrats. We began to call each other 'brothers'.

Thus my arrival seemed to have placed this village at an even higher cosmic junction of forest and sky than that secured by the mythically recounted arrival and presence of the regular chief himself. During this period, moreover, every time anyone from another village in either the Wainimala or Waidina valleys appeared, I was summoned, fieldwork ceased, and I became for the moment the most important and extraordinary chief of them all. A myth is recounted about the ancestors of all chiefs which also served to explain to Sereans my own presence and ritual incorporation within the chiefdom as well as to relate my maleness to the extraordinary maleness of Serean chiefs. A great chief called Tui Waimaro, (or 'Lord of Waimaro'), used to live across the ocean on the high chiefly island of Vanua Levu (or 'Big Land'). One day, as he was peering into the ocean, he saw and was approached by the shark-god Dakuwaqa, or 'Boatback'. The god bade him take some food and sit on his back, which he did; whereupon the shark-god swam across the ocean and upstream towards the interior of Big Fiji. When the food ran out, and when, mistakenly, Tui Waimaro thought he could hear people speaking his native dialect of the Fijian language, he asked Dakuwaqa to let him disembark. The shark-god obliged, putting him ashore some 2 miles down the road from Serea at a place now known as Nasobosobo or 'the disembarkation'. Here, Tui Waimaro was found lost and bedraggled and taken into the neighbouring village of Naluwai as chief or 'turaga'. This was my myth of origin as much as it was the myth of origin of chiefs born in Serea.

Now when my relationship with the ordinary people of Serea and its lines of chiefs was based around my visits to the store and my subsequent return to the city, I was indeed a most powerful chief to whom all of the Serean chiefs deferred. In the store, at the edge of the village but not yet inside, it is easy to see that I occupied the position metaphorically analagous to that of Tui Waimaro himself rather than that subsequently occupied by his sons and their imputed descendants. I had just landed from abroad. I was lost. I spoke a strange language. I had surrendered to the village at its edge – rather than display antagonistic intent – but I had not deigned to enter. In this position, it was revealed that I was regal, aloof and unassailable, attached to a point far too high up in the world to be incorporated into the village itself. Here, too, I was a prisoner of my new-found fame in my veritable 'palace' of a cooperative store. (Really, I was just too shy and timid to spend much time inside the chiefdom.)

With the benefit of hindsight it is impossible to imagine how I could have really done fieldwork within the strictures of this awesome elevation. All I could do was bask in the reflected glory of my imagined autobiography, listen to details of my fantastic story as played back to me by my hosts during the rites put on in my honour. In 'mythical' contexts re-created just outside the village, my story became a sort of catechism to be regularly repeated so that my adulated status could be reaffirmed and so that everyone could feel amazed. It was fortunate, then, that, when I finally came to stay in the interior with every intention of permanently basing myself inside the store, the storekeeper and his wife had gone away and the store temporarily shut. Consequently, I was obliged to cross the boundaries of the village, step into the tracks of the sons of the 'Lord of Waimaro', and begin to make entries in my notebooks under a reformed regime. Immediately, the scene I was trying to depict began to change as novel view-points were made available and new horizons extended to me.

Demotion

I was still considered a Waimaro chief and occasionally asked to sit at the top of the kava ceremony, but only when I was invited: it was no longer my heaven-linked right to preside. Because I was unmarried and much younger than my 'brother', the chief 'official' chief of Serea, I was no longer his lord, and he, without any doubt at all, was certainly mine. Demoted, if not deposed, I was placed in a house that was not his house, which lay, unlike his, parallel to all the non-chiefly houses in the settlement. Within the chiefdom, he thus lived on a different cosmic plane from me. Moreover, because I was unmarried, I was placed in the house of another man in the chiefly clan, and subsequently become known as his 'son'. In public places, I was now imagined to be a junior descendant of the foreign Waikalou people in Serea, rather than a royal emissary sent directly from London and the Palace. I was perceived to have origins in the land as well as manifest linkages with the heavens.

In the context of the kava rites, either as presiding or demoted chief, my fieldwork was conducted in the physical absence of women. Though symbolically encompassed by the rites, women are physically excluded from the ceremonies. The taboo is important because, behind it, lurks the unstated assumption that women's fertility is more important than the symbolics of patriliny suggest. Indeed, as in many Melanesian formations, a muted matriliny weaves its way into the supposedly exogamous constitution of the 'patriclans', subverting their unity, prompting schisms and sorcery. The curse of an elusive fecundity is thus attributed to women's fertility, and consequently Serean women are excluded from the kava rites and their project: which is to elevate and civilise human beings – to a man – without recourse to sex.

The next section of the chapter shows how, in a different context, these terms are inverted, scenarios contradicted and women are attributed power. But the 'programme of truth' (Veyne 1988) carried by the kava ceremony posits an essence to social life, and a male essence at that. Deceived, society is seen as revolving around the kava ceremony rather than about the pivotal point of marriage as well. At the kava ceremony, therefore, men are 'fed' abundant images of a false hegemony. In a sense, they drink wishfully to a state that they forget is ideal rather than fully realised: one that is real enough in the rites but which, in retrospect, appears transient and dubiously powerful.

If Serean men were not also immersed in the context of domesticity, where women lead the processes of transformation, these images would irrevocably mislead. Instead, these images of a false hegemony only temporarily distort. Intersecting with the rise of women's mana in the realm of domesticity, and caught up with the vacillating fate of men overall, the ethnographer's gaze is made to shift, disengage and fall.

Deposed and domesticated

Once set upon the stage of domesticity, it was as if my maleness was stripped of its sacred foreignness and pressed to reveal an autochthonous inner body. Moreover, the revelation of this inner body suggested that I possessed a truly wild disposition which, as far as my unmarried peers were concerned, had to be discharged in deed whenever contexts aroused it. In this domain, the overwhelming logic of my positioning suggested that I had not so much ended a journey as never made one in the first place. In fact, in this realm of domesticity, it is the woman who is said to have made such a journey, a symbolic journey between two lands juxtaposed at the very heart of the wedding ceremony.

In Serea, the structural inversion of the politico-ritual hierarchy is emphasised and reproduced through symbolic aspects of the domestic economy. Thus we men, on the left-hand side of the house, came home to each evening meal having productively expended our labours in the family's plantation. Symbolically, this implied the daily attachment of our bodies to the plantation's sub-soil. By contrast, on the right-hand side of the house, women had come from weeding and harvesting the top-soil of the plantations. They had also been fishing, and these forms of economic involvement in production reproduced women's ritual affinity with the high parts of the world and with the watery horizon just below it. Thus, more often than not, deposed from a high position at the kava drinking ceremony, and lowered even further on the left-hand side of the family's house, I would return home to eat to find that my 'mother' had usurped the high position. I would discover that, in this context, she rather than me, my 'father', and any of my chiefly mates, was the bearer of the powerful mana.

In this dialectical formation, the domestic context reverses the chiefly order of things and 'begins society again'. Indeed, the signified forms and relations of domesticity are founded upon a counter-myth that challenges the account of chiefly origins. This counter-myth says that the shark-god, 'Boatback', brought a female goddess rather than a male god to this region of the interior. She was the Lady, rather than the Lord, of Waimaro. Thus, in the context of domesticity my mana was practically ignored or denied and, as a result, my place and viewpoint was radically changed, so that I was to focus on different things.

LIMITS TO SEEING AND KNOWING FEMALE

Sexual division of labour: engendered separation of knowledges

In the context of domesticity, what the male ethnographer sees is a function of where he is placed, what is presented to him, and what he is prevented from easily seeing. Here, as everywhere else in the chiefdom, space is not just where cultural scenarios unfold. It is where they unfold with definite degrees of visibility and audibility. This is a very important feature of Melanesian social formations that the analysis of ethnography always has to take into account. In this section of the chapter, I examine what the male ethnographer cannot see within domestic space, and why.

Young unmarried men possess a basic but incomplete knowledge of women's roles within domesticity. The same applies to the young male ethnographer, who inevitably has to comply with decisions to place him appropriately within the domestic sphere. Part of this ignorance is due to the separation of men and women in this symbolic space, a separation spatially linked to images and rules of incest and to the premises governing the sexual division of labour. In fact, it is the combination of a system of sexual separation with one of ecological affinities that completes the formation of the genders. Thus, to take the case of maleness, the productive relationship of young boys with the ancestors of the land begins with the gift of a little garden donated by their father. Playful work upon the plot produces little in any economic sense; however, it rapidly cancels the vestigial relationship linking little boys to the heavens transmitted by their mothers. In other words, the symbolic efficacy of an economic relation of production makes real men of partly androgynous males (Strathern 1988). The main function of such relations of production in Melanesia is the transformation of the producers, and not the transformation of the raw material, as it is (or seems to be) in the realm of modern production.

According to the logic of these male-engendering practices, I, too, was encouraged to plant a few shoots in my 'father's' plantation, just as I was often encouraged to marry, throw down roots ('weka') metaphorically, and stop 'fucking about' in the world. I was taken under my 'father's' wing and, consequently, found it impossible to spend as much time with married women in my 'mother's' sphere as I did with men in my 'father's'. I knew the general shape of the domestic sphere and of a woman's role within it. But, along with the other men in the house, I could not acquire detailed knowledge of the woman's role. Thus I never truly approached the other women with whom my 'mother' talked and worked, with whom she travelled to market, and with whom she prepared for ritual occasions. This ignorance formed an intrinsic part of being male and was imparted through me to the content of the ethnographic project.

In practice, as much concerned with the chiefdom's perception of my sexuality as with the progress of my questioning, my 'mother' was party to this effort to keep me in place and keep me male. In her case, this meant drawing two lines: a line inside the domestic sphere between me and the women of the house, and another line on the outer edge of this sphere. This second line she drew to separate my masculinity from that of the 'gang' of young unmarried men. Undoubtedly, I could have 'thuggishly' acquired details of women's fishing, mat-making and market economy. Generally, I could have learnt much more of women's domestic lives by pressing my case more forcefully with the young unmarried men who escorted and chaperoned me and my anthropology about the chiefdom in the course of their daily lives. But to do so would have meant their more or less abandoning me, and this would have struck at the heart of my method, or more accurately, at my patient (anti)method.

Male ethnography and excrement: on seeing male and not knowing female within the domestic context

Indeed, in the subjective context of a certain theoretical collapse, and in the objective context of Serean social structure, I had formed a 'natural' ethnographic alliance with this social category of young unmarried men, and one that I knew, instinctively, it was best not to dissolve. This meant, specifically, not probing against the grain of genderised spaces, not pushing beyond cosmic surfaces taboo to the masculine sensibilities of my methodological allies. A well-known Serean story begins to explain that maintaining male space is not a matter of avoiding becoming and feeling female by pushing beyond tabooed surfaces (as it is with European gender systems). For the young unmarried men of the chiefdom, staying in male spaces was a matter of averting a certain kind of annihilation. I was to be safeguarded from this threat.

The story is about the young boy, Little Vo (basically, 'little shit') who is warned by his male friends not to cross to the other side of the river, otherwise he will be captured by the Devil Woman. Vo declines the advice of his peers and sets out to cross the river and, when he is only half-way across, he is captured in the net of the Devil Woman, who is out fishing. The Devil Woman carries Little Vo to the other side of the river, where he tries to escape by butting her with his head. He fails but, in the process, receives the blunting of his head that is so characteristic of the fish called after him, the Vo. (This fish is a brown-coloured bottom feeder, a scavenger and, thus, an eater of food rotting in the manner of excrement.) The Devil Woman hangs up her net on a tree by the banks of the river and Vo turns into a stream of dripping excrement. He drips onto the bank to become Vo, the fish which is called after excrement and which is regularly caught by women. This is a fish with a very muddy taste.

This fable indicates that for a man to cross over to the women's world and to move anomalously out of place is to court total and utter destruction. This fate is imagined by Fijians as akin to being reduced to excrement. It is important to note that Fijians (in the interior of Big Fiji, at least) do not recognise the potentially fertile properties of human excrement. Excrement is only 'shit'. It is desolate nothingness, matter at a dead end, unrecyclable, untransformable and untransforming substance. In the village, it is deposited in deep latrines. Gardeners would look aghast when I suggested the use of cow dung as manure for their plantations. Thus, to see female and, hence, to be excommunicated socially in the manner that Vo was dissolved biologically was the image that hung like a sword of Damocles over my 'natural' research allies.

It is amusing, I think, to record at this juncture that when I did indeed obtain glimpses of the women's world that was off-limits to my normal gaze, it was when I was ill and confined to the house. My illness was almost always due to the giardia I had contracted early on in my fieldwork. Suffering, I saw beyond the normal limits of seeing male and perceiving things female male. Through the maternal understanding and treatment of a real sickness that seemed to materialise the symbolic threat to maleness, I had, nevertheless, in the process, also become a less passive 'victim' of Serean efforts to determine the focus of my fieldwork by counfounding it with my gender.

BETWEEN DOMESTICATION AND PROMISCUITY: AN ETHNOGRAPHY OF DIVIDED LOYALTIES

A wife's mission in marriage hinges upon her cutting the filaments tying the body of her masculine husband to the collective body of ancestors in the forest. Prior to that, escapades of adolescence will have given this man his masculinity. However, it is the woman's sexual enclosure of her husband that turns this unit of collective masculinity into a distinct and separate body within the chiefdom. The woman's mana achieves this individuation of her husband by exclusively imbuing him with the image of self transported to her and, then, to him by the named goddess of the region, the Lady of Waimaro. This form becomes his publicly recognised self-image. It is her gift to him and, by the nature of the system of kinship and marriage, the essence of her cultural being as a gift (Strathern 1988).

As a result, a married man's role and destiny in domesticity is clearly mapped out for him by his wife, acting under the sign and authority of the Lady of Waimaro. To some extent as well, as an ethnographer-son to such a man and woman, my own body and my ethnographic gaze were subject to the woman's sacred agency. My work was refocused under the goddess's authority as my social identity was individuated by its special concerns. In the house, I sensed myself being individuated at the caring end of an exclusive act of Fijian womanly regulation and control. This contrasted with the aristocratic individuality imparted to me at the top of the kava rites by the collective gaze of the commoners.

However, whereas a husband's body is regulated by his wife as he fully draws her spirit into him, a man's sons are considered to be only marginally enveloped by her power. In gangs that form, break up and re-form every day, sons are pulled in contrary directions. On the one hand, they live under the civilising mana of a mother; on the other hand, they live by what they feel in their bodies to be the savage pull of the powers of the forest. These powers are transmitted through their fathers at birth, and they are the stuff and substance of Serean patriliny.

In this latter respect, right on the edges of married women's power and authority, the unmarried boys are given to roam and fight; to 'skive off' work in their fathers' gardens; to leave the chiefdom to 'fuck about' in the city and, in general, to free themselves from the guardian structures of a married woman's mana. And, in varying degrees, I was party to all of these activities. In effect, it is only at mealtimes, when the physiological requirements of hunger prompt a cultural decision, that the young men of the chiefdom return to the civilising space of the house's regulated interior. Here, in a space wrapped up in the female values of mats and bark-cloth, young men eat as sons in the triple presence of their 'mother', the whale's tooth and the sacred goddess (these three forms representing a sort of household Trinity). After eating, they drink as common men, and leave again to roam the Serean landscape, far less inhibited by the village boundaries than any other group in the chiefdom. I was such a son.

Consequently, the focus of my work was inconclusively pulled towards contrasting zones on the social landscape. Thus because she wanted to maintain my public persona in the visible regions of the chiefdom, I was held in domestic harness by my 'mother', in the spotlight of her mana. As she saw it, it was her mission to try and secure and insure me against the temptations of illicit sex and violence that existed for the ancestors, and to which human women occasionally fell victim. Or, at least, this is how she was brought up to see it. These temptations still emanated from the edge of the forest towards the enclave of a civilising space, that was also the edge of social certainty. In her mind, and in her domain, the progress of my fieldwork and the fate of my body were inextricably linked.

This attitude, for which she was gendered and to which she was structurally predisposed, exerted definite effects on my work. Because of her discourse, I tended, in my notebooks, to describe domesticity in ideal terms.

In other places, and at other times, however, the class of unmarried boys in the chiefdom declared otherwise. They boasted their pre-marital conquests and enjoined me to add to mine, though never loudly or in public. Because they wanted to submerge me in the 'gang', my unmarried peers led me in the direction of the hidden zone where they insisted that fighting and sexual transgression did indeed occur. But the boys did not dare take me right down with them into this zone. In the end, at its margins, and often late at night, I was ultimately left to fend for myself. Normally, I returned wistfully to our house to indulge my imagination and fantasies.

As a result, I formed a split opinion about sexual lives in the chiefdom and I couldn't readily make up my mind as to what was happening normally. Under the strong domestic influence of my 'mother' it was difficult, using normal anthropological methods of investigation, to confirm what the 'gang' boasted and what my 'mother' denied. In the end, I did decide on this point but not by resorting to 'method'.

FLIGHTS OF FANCY, INSIGHTS OF DESIRE: TRANSGRESSION AND THE RETURN OF THE ETHNOGRAPHIC SUBJECT

Deflowered

My mother was afraid that, in pursuing the other boys into forbidden places, my existence would begin to fade. Not that I would be completely lost to the world but that, progressively, my name would become associated with deeds that were collectively thinkable but publicly unspeakable. In Serean thought and practice, this lesser use and diminished circulation of a name is significant, because personal name and self-image is a gift that creates individuality only by being continually renewed and reconstructed. This occurs in the sight and speech of the other, for then self survives as 'name', 'fame' or 'reputation' ('yaca'). In this respect, definable Serean self-image has no introspective reality of its own. When unhailed, unrecalled and unrequired, the phenomenon itself is held to expire. Consequently, by dabbling in a sphere of invisible, unreportable sex, my 'I' would socially expire (Mauss 1985). I might die the social death of a dire Serean unmentionable.

Mostly, I was influenced by what I felt would be my mother's opprobrium towards me were I caught off-limits, and mostly, therefore, I failed to act upon on the amorous opportunities set up for me by the young men. I conformed to the presumptions and expectations of her domesticating discourse, and to the assumption implied by it, that extra-marital sex was available to the boys of Serea only outside the chiefdom. However, towards the end of my first year in the field, after a dance on the outskirts of the village, I drank, danced and found myself answering whispers urged in my ears. I met with my partner on the edge of the village. We walked into the house owned by her mother's brother ('momo'). Her grandmother was present, saw us and thought nothing of my presence. Was she a chosen guard? We moved together to the back of the house and lay down under a mosquito net. But I was frightened and unhappy. She picked up a blanket and urged me to accompany her outside. More confident now, I led her to a 'safe' place in a grove of trees just outside the village. She threw down the blanket. We lay down, caressed each other, spoke a little and 'made love'. I remember that we held each other for a moment (for it was cold), smiled at each other, and then went our own separate ways back home.

Much has been written in social anthropology about the sexuality of other people. And yet, is it possible for the ethnographer to write convincingly about sexual practices without having participated? One would have to argue that probably it isn't. In fact, my single involvement in sex in nearly two years in the field taught me little that I had not already been brought to suspect concerning this hidden realm of social relations. However, it did strengthen a certain suspicion, and this foundation laid the basis for a plausible theory of transgression and betrayal particular to this sociocultural formation.

Thus, within the terms of the dominant culture and the counter-culture alike, invisible sexual practices were negatively valued. For the dominant culture, they were confidently declared a thing of the past, whereas for the counter-culture, they were the nub of the present. The evidence of my participation supported the invisible and muted practice of the latter, and began to make sense of a sexist chieftaincy that physically excluded women from its central ritual as it quietly presumed the women's transgression. Moreover, it was through the hope that particular women might not have transgressed that, just as frequently, the ritual chieftaincy receded to be supplanted by the re-installation of a woman on the sacred right-hand side of the domestic hearth. In the context of making this analytical step anthropologically, my one instance of sexual involvement formed rare and critical evidence.

The return to subjectivity

However, my nocturnal involvement was not intended as an extension of method or a cynical deepening of insight. Indeed, it was not intended at all: though, certainly, it was desired. My 'fling' just happened, but did so in a context in which I was constantly dreaming about sexual pleasures, fantasising that what always happened in my fictions would eventually happen in fact.

I never planned sexual involvement (because it seemed to be in contravention of the unwritten ethnographic code), but through the cultivation of desire, I willed it. In effect, even though I sometimes tell myself that I never initiated an affair that could have had calamitous consequences for both my own safety and that of my partner, I did place myself in the 'right' position, since I had drifted to a site where, if such illicit sexuality was indeed generalised, inevitably I would be caught up by it. Subject to the irrationality of my fantasies rather than the rationality of any listed anthropological technique, I had drifted towards the seductive edge of both the anthropological and the indigenous forbidden. Here, inconclusively objectified, and alternately positioned by 'mother' and 'brothers', I came finally to assert myself against Fijian indeterminacy as the subject of my own actions.

Foucault has written of how western traditions have linked the cultivation of the self with the performance of private sex. Hidden from public surveillance, measurement and regulation, western bodies have been able properly to assert their personal uniqueness only in those rare places that continue to resist the penetrating eye of public power. In western traditions and western arenas, the hiddenness of sex provokes and heightens the sense of an unsurveillable self even as it satisfies the requirements of lust (Foucault 1988).

In fact, to relaunch myself as a subject, I had transgressed with respect to a critical Serean value and an unwritten rule of anthropological code of practice. Yet by proceeding in this way, I had reasserted myself against the psychological stresses of objectification to which my abandonment of 'method' had generally confined me, and in a space opened up by the play of an indigenous ambiguity. It is not surprising, therefore, that, persistently alienated from control over my whole project, and from the ability to construct the sort of human relations that I might have wanted normally, I should dream so much of sex. What is surprising and so ironic is that I should have finally yielded to the sexual retrieval of private self in a field of sexual practices precisely associated by Sereans with the risk (if detected) of a personal 'death'. Right on the edge of the village, I had broken out at a weak link in the chain of cultural objectification to launch the rebirth of myself – and 'objectively', had 'died' in the process. It was only here, under cover of social death, and protected by traditions of Serean secrecy, that I could truly be myself. It was here, too, that by 'being myself' in a place where, as far as the dominant scenarios were concerned, 'I' really did not exist at all, I could confirm what these scenarios denied: namely, that both 'I' and they existed.

CONCLUSION

In the end, this chapter has been about the part played by the anthropologist's gender and sexuality in giving access to significant areas of a Melanesian reality. Unidentified in the first instance, these were areas that subsequently became key foci of the research. This occurred as base and superstructure in the Marxist prototype, for the research flew apart, paralysing a conscious search for expected connections of significance. Subsequently, my fieldwork proceeded as indigenous Fijian subjects pulled me towards the symbolic interiors of particular cultural practices. Only then did I begin to ask questions in little pockets of found freedom.

Underlying and preceding the autobiographical aspect of this account is the structural analysis which shows just how objective aspects of my own sex and gender could have come to play the anthropological role of access and limitation which they did. In fact, it has been argued here that the structural analysis (Abramson 1987) is logically prior to both the autobiography which relates this project in cognition to my life-story, and to an assessment of any methods that might have been applicable. Indeed, in this account of pathways of appropriation, the analysis identifies and signposts the spots from which I was able to participate and observe productively, only because I was mythically subsumed and drawn inwards. In this way, participant observation is theoretically expanded here as a concept of both methodological and autobiographical significance.

Secondly, the analysis shows that it was only by being ill, being categorically out of place and, thus, being on the verge of absolute symbolic destruction, that I seemed painfully to metamorphose as the classically free agent of anthropological participation and observation. Again, it was only transgressing sexually, at a point where structures of objectification indecisively left me 'on the edge' of Fijian oblivion, that I came to assume the role of an active subject in the process of my own ethnographic discoveries. It was not by intent, therefore, but by a fruitful conjunction of accident and a weakness in my objectification that I arrived at the traditional starting point for 'applying methods'. And it was precisely there and then that I could not truly apply them.

REFERENCES

Abramson, A.L. (1987) 'Beyond the Samoan controversy in anthropology: a history of sexuality in the eastern interior of Fiji', in P. Caplan (ed.), *The Cultural Construction of Sexuality*, London: Tavistock.

Clifford, J. (1986) 'On ethnographic self-fashioning: Conrad and Malinowski' in *The Predicament of Culture: Twentieth-Century Ethnography, Literature and Art*, Cambridge, MA: Harvard University Press, pp. 92–117.

Foucault, M. (1988) *The History of Sexuality*, vol. 3, London: Penguin.

Geertz, C. (1988) *Works and Lives: The Anthropologist as Author*, Stanford, CA: Polity Press.

Hocart, A.M. (1970 [1936]) *Kings and Councillors: An Essay in the Comparative Anatomy of Human Society*, R. Needham (ed.), Chicago: University of Chicago Press.

Jarvie, I.C. (1964) *The Revolution in Anthropology*, London: Routledge & Kegan Paul.

Kuhn, T. (1962) *The Structure of Scientific Revolutions*, Chicago: University of Chicago.

Malinowski, B. (1967) *A Diary in the Strict Sense of the Term*, New York: Harcourt, Brace & World.

Mauss, M. (1985 [1938]) 'A category of the human mind: the notion of person; the notion of self', in M. Carrithers, S. Collins and S. Lukes (eds), *The Category of the Person: Anthropology, Philosophy, History*, Cambridge: Cambridge University Press.

Sahlins, M.D. (1981) *Mythical Realities and Historical Metaphors*, Ann Arbor, MI: University of Michigan Press.

Sontag, S. (1970) 'The Anthropologist as Hero', in E.N. Hayes and T. Hayes (eds), *Claude Lévi-Strauss: The Anthropologist as Hero*, Cambridge, MA: MIT Press.

Strathern, M. (1988) *The Gender of the Gift: Problems with Women, Problems with Society in Melanesia*, Berkeley, CA: University of California Press.

Veyne, P. (1988) *Did the Greeks Believe in their Myths? An Essay on the Constitutive Imagination*, Chicago: University of Chicago.

4 With *moyang melur* in Carey Island

More endangered, more engendered

Wazir Jahan Karim

LAST NIGHT AND THE FOLLOWING MORNING

The night before I left the village[1] to prepare to return to London, my field-father sat in his usual corner of the kitchen floor. I made him his favourite milky coffee with the grains floating on top. He said to me,

> When you came here two years ago without any warning, many people from this village said you were a government spy. They said you had come to gather information about the land to resettle us elsewhere. Some said you were a head hunter and had came here to collect a few heads to fortify a new bridge on the mainland. Yet others said you were merely assuming a human form and would transform in the middle of the night into a tigress and eat us all. You were, they said, probably not yet 'cursed' (*tulah*) and could assume animal or human forms.[2]

It had taken him two years to tell me this. I shook my head with disbelief. 'Did you believe them? Why did they say this? Why did they mistrust me, a woman?' I said, regretting the remark instantly. He looked thoughtfully at the nipah palm (*nipah fruticans*) cigarette he had just rolled.

> What difference does it make whether you are a woman or a man? It's the intention and the motive that matters. Formerly animals tried to overrun us by assuming human forms; these 'humans' were not sincere. But I took you in. I knew you did not have these powers. I knew you were properly human. I made you my daughter. I sent Jaman, your sister, to see you, to fetch you home.

I remembered the day, Wednesday, 14 August 1973. I was trying to sleep in the afternoon, two days after arriving. Jaman turned up with two other girls, Enak and Tasak, and some children. They avoided my smiles and stared intently at the floor. Soon they exclaimed at the ticks on the mat and began squeezing them down with the nail of their thumbs. After this strange behaviour, they all left together. I had stared after them, willing them to return. I refocused my thoughts on the present conversation. 'I hope I have been a good daughter to you', I said 'I wouldn't have wanted any other family. Only you as my father and Mijah as my mother.' He didn't reply. After a while he said, 'Your eyes are sleepy, go and

Preparing for a Ma' Betisé' dance (*jo'oh*)

sleep. I want to finish my coffee and cigarette.' I went in and curled next to Milah, my sister, and after some time heard him entering the next room.

I left Carey Island the next day, 26 August 1975. Although I had left the village several times before this, my absence had been brief and unnoticed by others. It was usually to obtain supplies, to visit my family in Kuala Lumpur or to participate in activities in another village on the mainland – weddings, funerals, seeing a sick relative or a harvest ritual (*jo-oh*). Going to London, however, seemed a more permanent departure to the villagers. I realised amidst the tears and messages of advice to beware the white man in England that they were bidding farewell to a real daughter. I was no longer 'fictitious' in their eyes. My mother, Mijah, cried out aloud as she threw roasted rice on me in preparation for my journey to the unknown. 'O Ancestors, take care of your grandchild, don't let her get sick, let her heart remain clear, so she'll remember us.' My father wiped away his tears and handed me a walking stick which he had made from *mo'* (nibong palm). On its curved end was a carved tiger resting on its haunches. My father said, 'The *mangat* (spirit) of the *moyang melur* (the tiger spirit, 'melur'), our most mighty spirit, will protect you and give you strength. No one will ever do evil against you in England. When men look at you, they will look away again because *moyang melur* will be there.' I stared into the dark, haunted eyes of the tiger and was convinced. My familiarity with Ma' Betisé' spirits, potions and spells had fortified me with enough magical knowledge to see my thesis through. *Moyang melur* was an added assurance that I would finish my thesis without any distraction. None the less the thought of substituting my life at Carey Island for thesis-writing left me with an empty feeling.

My confused thoughts about *moyang melur* with me in London guiding my thesis-writing while shaking off the attractions of men was disrupted by my many little sisters around me. More used to the modern ways of the world, they cried out, 'Write to us, elder sister, write to us. We will wait for your letters!' I had grown very fond of them and promised them many letters from London. I had told myself earlier that I would joke my way out of the village and lighten the burden of my departure. I disliked farewells and the tensions they produced within me. Besides, I was coming back. I knew that they had become part of my life. Feelings about one's field-family could not be conveniently structured according to fieldwork and post-fieldwork phases. They edged into the life of an anthropologist like a never-ending story, every practical activity outside the field being a reminder of an event inside it. Boundaries could not be properly established for convenience or self-advantage. However, jokes did not come easily that day. The group which had come to see me off became emotional and affected me similarly. The person I could not bear to leave was my field-father, whom I had grown to love deeply. I knew that I would pine for him quietly in the Ma' Betisé' way, and he would for me. The emotion was *magnu*, to long for a loved one who is long absent, till the 'heart eats up the soul' and the body becomes vulnerable to *tenong* or spirit-attacks.

In London, I received many letters from my sister Jaman who kept me abreast of village politics and gossip. I responded to them happily. I sensed that my fieldwork days were over and that I now had to behave as 'family', assuring them that I was fine and well, that I was missing them a lot and was waiting to see them again. Life at the London School of Economics was as fine as it could possibly be, although I wondered if all my failed romantic attachments were *moyang melur*'s doing, so concerned was he with my thesis-writing and my speedy return home.

As my thesis took shape, I realised that I did not really want to leave London. I loved the independence and solitude it brought me. There was no 'family' for me to worry about and concern myself with, no emotions I could not cope with, and no personal or academic problems I could not solve. The contrast with Carey Island was both frightening and reassuring. I worried that I had switched off family concerns for a *tulah* state of egocentrism and pragmatism, placing myself above the people who had helped me realise my professional ambitions. Was I just responding to new needs and priorities? As I worked on my chapters in my yellow room at Lillian Penson Hall, I sensed that anthropological fieldwork did not really change the kind of person one was. Anthropologists develop a particular kind of anthropology in fieldwork because of both academic convention and practical necessity. Afterwards, what they do with their experiences depends to a large extent on their sense of personal involvement with particular issues concerning the people they have studied, and guidelines to dealing with this involvement do not necessarily enter anthropology textbooks or seminars. Most of this depends on the kind of sensitivity one develops to these issues and problems, and 'letting go' or 'self-restraint' becomes more of a personal reaction than an academic one. Hence the individual, despite belonging to a particular culture, learns to develop a pattern of decision-making based on immediate personal experiences (see Karl and Hamalian 1973).

THE RESEARCHER'S 'CENTRALITY' AND THE PEOPLE'S 'PERIPHERY'

Recalling my field-father's statement that self-motivation and sincerity had nothing to do with gender, I could, in the twilight zone of thesis-writing in the heart of London, recapture my own personal history in anthropology. While I was an undergraduate, Geoffrey Benjamin in the University of Singapore had introduced me to anthropology, and I was fascinated. Why did I choose a discipline which was practically unknown at the time to most people in Malaysia? Why did I venture into a field which horrified my immediate family? It was unconventional for a Malaysian graduate in social sciences to want to live with a group of Orang Asli (aborigines) in the mangrove mudflats of Malaysia or elsewhere. However, it seemed to suit my interests to combine my post-graduate work with fantasy. I knew that living with the Ma' Betisé' in Carey Island would be a completely new experience and I was always looking for new experiences. Fieldwork was an excuse for adventure, on top of which I could get credits for it. My own mother shook her head when I stated my intentions, as if the act could shake me out of her mind and sight. My sisters eventually joked about it. 'She has always been the gypsy in the family,' they concluded. 'Why should she not go? As long as she is properly deloused and dewormed when she comes home, there should be no harm in it!'

The reality of doctoral fieldwork only came later when I experienced a sense of loss and loneliness during the first few months of my fieldwork. I did not realise then that I was being tested for my motives and sincerity. Feeling that I should have been greeted properly, I was shaken by the blank indifference and disdain of the Ma' Betisé'. I knew I was sincere, so why were they unfriendly? It took me several days to realise that my own 'centrality' as a middle-class Malaysian was their 'periphery'. I was completely peripheral to their notion of a proper person. No one without personal or political motive would be wanting to live in the most deplorable conditions merely to experience another culture. I was 'strange', 'anomalous' and, obviously, 'dangerous'. I had no previous experience of 'Aslian' fieldwork and did not realise that Orang Aslis did not have a concept of hospitality like the Malays, to whom I was accustomed. Life went on as usual and a person who wanted to stay on could do so (if he or she wanted to) but no welcoming ceremony was to be provided. Acceptance came through the process of experiential learning and this was a one-way exercise of assessment and observation on the part of the Orang Asli.

Inevitably, I became traumatised by my Malaysian centrality, for it could not fortify me against the loneliness and isolation I felt in the first few months of research. On another level, I realised that my own centrality had made these people peripheral over years of history and I continued fieldwork with an uneasy feeling of guilt. I now had the task of reintroducing their periphery professionally to an outside world of western scholarship which had forced me to regard the Ma' Betisé' initially as a field to be observed, rather than an observant people capable of their own reflexivity. I felt that, though I was personally sincere in wanting to discover their culture, I was also politically culpable for I was part of this intellectual field which western anthropologists had created for themselves. I tried to overcome these feelings by diffusing the 'political culture' of anthropology onto a personal concern with belonging. I reserved my emotional energy and sense of caring for the Ma' Betisé' so that they would like me for myself and dissociate me from the central world which created these political boundaries. Indeed, many months later they did begin to like me to the extent that (as I realised later) I was accepted as a real daughter.

Yet in London I was relieved that I could sit back and think of my fieldwork as a distinct, separate experience, and worried that these people would be real again when I returned. I had not yet, I suppose, come to think of myself as a committed anthropologist. I cared more than anyone else about what might happen to them but I was reluctant to be committed at this stage. I wanted to shake off personal commitments, do a good thesis and contribute academically to this western science. I should say that I only resolved this dilemma some years later, when their persistence and determination to make me belong, to be a real daughter to the family I lived with, forced this commitment out of me and, along with it, a whole lot of other emotions of concern and welfare. I eventually learned to divide my interests between many different levels of relationships to the Ma' Betisé' both as an endangered minority and as individual men, women and children I had come to care for.

Emotions and commitments were not supposed to play a role in anthropology and anthropological research, one was told in the secure comfort of the thesis-writing seminars at the London School of Economics. Yet the most significant revelations in anthropology have been derived from the emotional experiences of doing fieldwork, from the frustration of alienation to the triumph of acceptance, from the guilt of receiving to the comfort of giving. The anthropologist, once accepted, becomes more personal and spontaneous in communication and dialogue, and this is where information-gathering is at its best, when people become as important as the stories they tell.

DEVELOPING FAMILY RELATIONSHIPS AND ALTERNATIVES TO MARRIAGE

My single female status positioned me in the role of a daughter to Mijah, my field-mother. Initially a short-term arrangement, everyone found this to be acceptable, and I finally began to relax and enjoy the fieldwork experience. Eventually, the enjoyment became mutual. People dropped in by day and night ostensibly to visit my family but secretly to amuse themselves by hearing me converse in Betisé' and by listening to my comments on their stories which they seemed to find funny. Information-gathering increasingly became dialogical and spontaneously reflexive. The Ma' Betisé' knew of my interest in their language and culture and were curious to know how I reacted to their stories of monkey feasts, spouse exchange or humans being reborn into flying lemurs. They also felt that I had to earn my information the proper way, which was the Ma' Betisé way of narrating stories with food and drink in the still of the night till the early hours of the morning.

Among others, the village *jugra* (petty-chief), my field-father's elder widowed brother, visited me at night, and I made him cups of Nescafé. He was entertaining, and told good stories of people, plants and animals, of their migratory history and early ancestors, the pioneers of Carey Island.[3] I made him Nescafé regularly for many nights. One night, I decided not to make any more Nescafé. I felt as if he were taking advantage of my role as a daughter. Besides, I wanted to test my role again as an anthropologist. I wanted to seek equality and improve upon my reduced role as 'daughter' and 'sister', which making Nescafé merely reinforced. That night the *jugra* demanded his coffee impatiently, then shrewdly said, 'If you want to hear good stories, I need my *candu* (opium), I need coffee!' I made him a cup, and he laughed in delight and unrolled his leaf cigarette to stuff in the tobacco. 'No stories tonight. I notice your eyes are sleepy. You can go and sleep and I can have my coffee.' He had won this time. He had noticed my professional weakness and reduced me to an inferior again. I resented it, and vowed that the next time he would be telling me stories without even realising it.

I had no choice but to be a daughter to elders, but I felt I could still manipulate the position to my advantage. Everyone eventually opened out to me, women and men a little older than me called me 'little sister' (*adi'*), those younger called me 'elder sister' (*ka'oo'*). Older men and women called me child (*kenon*) and I called them 'father' (*we'*) and 'mother' (*gade'* or *gende'*), depending on my kinship relationship with them within the cognatic group (*opoh*). Through kinship I transcended inter-personal relationships of enmity or distance and eventually had few problems in communication. People would warn me of this kinsman or that kinsman but were more concerned that I conducted my kinship relations well. I did this, combining my role as 'daughter' and 'sister' with the best 'Nescafé maker' in the village and the best 'cook'. A 'daughter' and 'sister' was obliged to do many things like any 'son' or 'brother', and if it meant making Nescafé and driving them in a car to hospital when they usually took a bus, this was what I was supposed to do and it was easier on the whole to comply than to argue.

Eventually, I felt that I could do fieldwork more effectively by assuming my place in a network of family and kinship roles while sharing my material culture with them all. Hence I was only different from other women by my access to outside knowledge and the technology that came with it. They never ceased to be impressed by this. They continued to regard me as a Ma' Betisé' who was more successful than others with the ways of the modern world. They also took full advantage of this. They rewarded me with kindness and affection, and their 'culture' gradually evolved before me, or so I imagined, without much prompting or formal investigation through informants.

For me, my gender and marital status were indeed difficult areas to deal with. Of an age when a woman is already supposed to be married and yet feeling unable to throw in the common line of untruth perpetrated by numerous single women researchers who declare a 'husband' or 'fiancé' back home with photographs of boyfriends as supportive evidence, I was put in the impossible situation of being asked to choose a spouse for the period of fieldwork or even beyond, if the arrangement worked out. People constantly scolded and grumbled: 'It is wrong,' said Mijah. 'I have a daughter who should be married who is not. Your younger sister Jaman, only 16, will soon be married.' It was not so much the worry that I was helpless against 'predatory males' (Giovannini 1986: 110), but that at 24, as a 'daughter' to Mijah, I was and should be ready for marriage. (Davis [1986: 243], researching in Newfoundland, found the same problem – there was no pre-existing social role to place single women in such situations.) For the Ma' Betisé', an 'unmarried daughter' was the best role they could find, but even so, it was quite clearly 'transitory'.

They finally chose a person for me. He did not match up to my expectations, few as they were at this stage. I found myself drawn to men who excelled in hunting, for they seemed to exude a kind of natural male sexuality with every item of game they brought home. Other Ma' Betisé' women said that good husbands were also good hunters, for they brought home lots of food. I was impressed by this. The person they had matched me up with did not hunt but worked in the neighbouring oil-palm estate. As my fieldwork progressed, I began to find him irritating, not to mention boring in the extreme. He was constantly beside me at *jo-oh* ritual dances (see Karim 1981a). The women watched me but did not tease me about this. They were anxious that I should be matched up with him quickly and took his interest in me rather seriously.

There was someone else I thought of constantly, under the haze of the sun and in the evenings after the wicker lamps were lit. He was tall, with a rugged face burned by the sun, but he was married. He was a 'cousin' of mine, through my field-father's first-born deceased brother. He brought me emerald pigeons, mangrove crabs, prawns and cat-fish, and stayed back late at night to relate his hunting trips to me. Once he brought me a spotted deer and I fed it fondly with shoots and cassava till it was served to me one morning in a dish cooked with turmeric and tamarind. It was a bleak morning and I was numbed by the shock of the incident. I mourned my deer and, for once, felt betrayed by my family. I sickened at the sight of my father who had killed it. I even thought that they had done this to shock me out of my interest in the hunter. Were they telling me that my emotions were misplaced? I realised the answer some days later. It was *tulah*, the need to treat hunted animals as 'food resources'. I had confused my boundaries between humans and animals. My father told me casually one day after the spotted-deer incident, 'Your emotions are misplaced on animals, it should be on your food.'

Nothing materialised from my relationship with the hunter. He came by more frequently, and I could sense the growing bond between us. I had thought, in some moments of madness, that I should do what any Ma' Betisé' woman did – that is, openly disclose my feelings for him, but cowardice and fear of disapproval by other men and women led me to avoid him eventually. I was miserable having to make this decision but the situation was developing a complexity I could not fathom. I was also afraid that I could not cope with the consequences of my actions and would eventually be accused of having double standards like a Malay schoolteacher before me, who fell in love with a young Ma' Betisé' girl already engaged to be married to her cousin. People had narrated with disgust the story of this Malay Muslim who wanted to marry the Ma' Betisé' girl but did not want to eat monkey-meat with them. He was, they said, a hypocrite (*bahait*, 'bad-mannered', bad) preferring his religion to theirs, yet wanting one of their women. If this went on, they said angrily, the Ma' Betisé' would be drained of their culture and women, the two being synonymous, since the future of the Ma' Betisé' rested on their ability to keep their women to reproduce the next generation.[4]

The constant reminder of village elders that I should seek out 'the chosen one', Ané', was evidence of their disapproval. Finally, responding to a pointed query from the *jugra* of the village about him, I said that I would make a bad wife, since I could not properly hunt crabs or weave mats. He replied that Ané' could not read or write, so we were both equally stupid! I realised I was in Ma' Betisé' country where notions of superiority in terms of formal education did not really count; however, a marriage never materialised and Ané' finally left the village. I did not see him again until July 1990.[5] The tensions thus created eventually subsided but I was not matched up with anyone else again. There was another hunter with dare-devil eyes whom I liked but not in the same way as the first one. Besides, he was *bahait* (a rogue), they said affectionately. He could not be trusted. Last year, he slept with someone's wife and the couple had to pay a fine. Last week, he sold his uncle's crabs for him and did not return all the money. I never went through a form of marriage with any Ma' Betisé', but, looking back, was glad that at least I went through some of the emotional experiences of a Ma' Betisé' woman and experienced the kinds of relationships some of them would have had in this way. The 'bonding' seems more honest and more complete, and I left feeling less unsure of my conflicting role as anthropologist and Ma' Betisé'.

However, the equality of defining emotions in men and women and the equality of dealing with them was something of a new experience for me. It was the ultimate in gender equality; emotion and emotive action were explained through experiential knowledge rather than sexuality and gender. The Ma'

Betisé' were not an 'engendered' field but I had brought many gendered notions of relationships with me into the field and as a result incurred a lot of problems for myself. Then again, by bonding myself to them through family and kinship, I should have married one of them but I could not fulfil their expectations of me. By choosing to remain unmarried, I drew attention to my own gender and sexuality. If I had married I would have been regarded casually like any other young man or woman, left alone to get on with my daily life. Furthermore, I participated in an interpersonal relationship which would have caused problems all round and subsequently withdrew in a way which drew attention to my 'weaker' female character. It was obvious that at this phase in my life, I could not adequately cope with the power that came with sexual equality.

THE RECURRING CYCLE OF CONFLICT BETWEEN HUMANS AND PLANTS AND ANIMALS

As months went by, the conflicting emotions of 'being female' became less important and I settled down to thinking about things which the Ma' Betisé' talked about – hunting animals, gathering forest products, maintaining food supplies, combating illness and injuries, death, rebirth and new sources of land for the future generation. I found the *tulah* and *kemali'* dualism in human behaviour so complex that it became my major preoccupation in fieldwork. The pragmatic *tulah* view that plants and animals were cursed to be food for humans was offset by mystical retribution of a horrifying kind (*kemali'*) – that humans could be fatally cursed by human and animal spirits when they hunted and gathered in the mangrove forests (Karim 1981a, 1981b). Humanising and dehumanising relationships with the natural world were part of a circular argument for survival.

The first *kemali'* incident I heard of was from my grandfather, now deceased, from Teluk Benut, a Ma' Betisé' village on the mainland. He said a Chinese man had just died after chopping down a *jelutong* (*Ervatama corymbosa*) tree at his village. 'The tree is a *moyang*, an ancestor. How could he chop it down?' he grumbled. 'Yet wood-carvers always chop wood for wood-carving.' I asked, 'Was it just the *jelutong* tree which was *kemali'*?' He shook his head. I soon learned that it was not.

Lingam, a neighbour, hurt his left eye while chopping off a portion of the niréh (*Carapa moluccensis*) tree. The niréh tree was not *kemali'* in the sense that it was positively classified as an ancestral tree. It became *kemali'* the moment Lingam chopped it to carve his *tupin'* (masks) and injured his eye. Lingam eventually became blind in one eye, and several *sawai* (seances) were held to appease the angry spirit-soul (*mangat*) of the tree and to arrange for ritual compensation. The helping spirits of the shaman cried in sadness and frustration at his selfishness. 'Our grandchild does not care for us or he would have given us food. Give us food now, we are hungry. Should we help him? He did not help us.' Threats, apologies, tears and offerings rolled on for five nights. Lingam never regained the sight in his left eye but he was able to carve. Significantly, he only did one carving at a time and not as many as before. He had learned his lesson. His recent death was explained in a similar way, that he had once again angered the spirits with his behaviour. No seance could help him again.

All trees potentially had this vital *kemali'* force, to *tenong* or 'attack' humans who harmed them, in the course of hunting and gathering. The *kemali'* and *tenong* force in animals was equally potent, and could injure or kill depending on the extent of their grievance against the culprit. This grievance was demonstrated later, after the completion of hunting, the preparation of the meat or the meal. An illness in the family, a bodily injury, a natural calamity and the plant and animal world transforms itself into a life-threatening force, necessitating a hold on all forms of economic activity linked to the forests and mudflats (Karim 1981a). Shamanistic seances reinforce the *kemali'* position of the accused and the need for substitution (*tukar ganti*; literally, 'to replace') through trays of spirit-food (*anca', sembuang*) or spirit-huts (*balai*). Once forgiveness is certain, the accused resumes his activity of food-gathering and the plant and animal world becomes *tulah*, a base for human destruction and control. And so the season begins and food is once more bountiful. The accused is now the hunter preying on plants and animals which are now conceived as 'cursed' living things of nature.

Dualistic structures like *tulah* and *kemali'* impose encumbrances on economic activity, like a built-in system of checks and balances of human activity upon the ecology – a kind of psychic environmental impact assessment programme. To the Ma' Betisé', the liberal philosophy that human values must be purposive, progressing singly along a path till the ultimate was achieved in mastery and perfection, was something only to be achieved in the after-life, through the regeneration of the souls of the dead. It occurred to me that they were possibly correct about this, for ultimate success and perfection on earth among the living could only be achieved at the expense of others before us.

I had earlier implied that the *tulah-kemali'* morality provided the Ma' Betisé' with a pragmatic solution to the activity of human production and procreation, which in day-to-day life could only be achieved at the expense of plants and animals (Karim 1986). If this has to be done, argue the Ma' Betisé', let it be done slowly, in cycles, so that these living forms can also regenerate themselves and enjoy their own moments of power. Without any possibility of natural regeneration, plants and animals will rebel against their increasing powerlessness and will make an effort to survive at the expense of humans.

Since humans have caused this to happen, human destructiveness can only be checked if humans are destroyed. Hence human regeneration can only be achieved along with rather than at the expense of plant and animal life. The ecologists confirm the ecological catastrophe of ozone depletion through scientific rather than cosmological language, but the Ma' Betisé' earlier warning of supernatural malevolence, and early man's strategy to contain it along a cyclical path of destruction and regeneration is equally ecological except that the world view is communicated through the language of culture rather than science.

Moyang melur, half-human, half-tiger, is an integral expression of this interdependency between nature and culture. The greatest ancestral spirit of all, he was never completely cursed to be a human or an animal. He represented both living forms, coexisting in tense cooperation. Ma' Betisé' anthropology does not contain the same success story of 'completion' of human conquests, or feats of colonialism or imperialism. Rather, it talks about the incompletion of activity as a necessity, for only by staggering human activity, ambitions and goals in the long term can other living forms survive. Indeed, it questions the morality of forms of conquest of one human over another, and of humans over the environment.

In Carey Island, the interdependence of humans, plants and animals is morally threatened with the depletion of the mangrove rain forests and the food resources within. Daily activities of hunting and gathering food become a burden on the young and old, men and women. Poor health and nutrition result in illness and viral epidemics and suggest the increasing threats of revenge from plants and animals which are being destroyed in the forest. The *tulah-kemali'* morality becomes more visibly threatening, as *kemali'* conditions come into sharper focus. *Tulah* conditions have to be re-created, but land shortage and forest depletion make this a difficult task, suggesting out-migration and nomadism as an alternative. The mythical theme of nomadism narrated to me by elders a decade and a half ago seems now to be a reality. Indeed, nomadism was probably always an integral ideology of survival, dramatised retrospectively through colourful accounts of battles and defeats by marauding Malays. This pervasive nomadism further reflects the nature–culture dialectic, visibly symbolized in *moyang melur*'s mystical character as half-human and half-tiger. The Ma' Betisé' in the village of Sialang, where I conducted my research, are now attempting to move out gradually to other mangrove areas where the balance and interdependency between people and the environment can be achieved at minimal cost to human lives.

GENDER IN THE LONG TERM

It seems strange that in the end I should learn the philosophy of tolerance and survival from animism rather than formal religious or scientific knowledge. It was also revealing that on this level of conscientisation, the philosophy for human tolerance and survival was similar for men and women, devoid of the kind of patriarchal thinking which permeates the great religions of the world, in Christianity, Islam, Judaism, Hinduism and Buddhism. Ma' Betisé' animism was the most reflexive of philosophies, demanding a constant dialogue amongst participants of culture on the morality of acts directed towards plants and animals.

In the long term, the anthropologist learns to link ideas of morality in gender with social change and ecology. An endangered community becomes gendered again when women and children incur higher morbidity and mortality rates as health standards decline. For cultures which are dependent on the mangroves and rain forests for survival, it seems that each new phase of development triggers off other problems of gender: the loss of women to outsiders (government technical assistants, rubber-tappers and farmers), higher morbidity rates among women and children from viral and epidemic diseases and infections and the pressure upon younger families to migrate into ethnically mixed areas which eventually cause them to lose their common identity. Since women are symbolically conceived as the transmitters of history and culture, the loss of women implies a history and a present with no future. Hence, fear over loss of women reinforces in a genderless society a concern for women as a precious resource.

Comparing this long-term concern for replenishing history and culture through women with my own earlier experience of the Ma' Betisé' as 'gender-less', I conclude that gender-consciousness within a people's cognitive universe shifts in accordance with critical phases of survival. The immediate concerns of balance between economy and ecology reduce gender-consciousness while long term concerns enhance it. The Ma' Betisé' have developed a sense of self-containment within an endangered environment, but the continuous endangering of life in the long term suggests new meanings of survival.

THE REFLEXIVE 'NATIVE' AND HISTORY

Gadamer (1985 [1960]) has claimed that reliable knowledge can be obtained without a systematic method which may limit the knowledge obtained. Geertz's interpretive approach, on the other hand, suggests the use of a semiotic method-ology in gaining access to the conceptual world of subjects (1973: 24). Both views, however, support the idea of permeating the cognitive universe of subjects through imagination and experiential learning. I found that this could only be achieved after the anthropologist ceases to think of the subjects as a 'field' and discards them as tools of research.

The anthropologist who seeks subjects through imagination and experiential learning may or may not realise that he or she is also the 'other' which is being subject to observation and analysis by the local community. Singly or collect-ively, he or she will reflect upon this new experience and be caught up in a situation of dealing with two kinds of reflexivity, the 'self' as both 'object' and 'subject' and the other as 'observed' and 'observer'.

To what extent, then, can the anthropologist ensure that the cognitive universe he or she is trying to understand is not one tainted with misconceptions whereby the community begins to view itself as a 'cultural field' and behaves accordingly, thinking that this is what is expected of it by the anthropologist? How often have anthropologists made local populations aware of the existence of 'culture', and how often have the latter attempted to revive their own material and cognitive universe as a consequence of this encounter? The view that reflexivity facilitates good anthropological research must be concerned with the notion of the 'double-bind', that two or more processes of experiential learning are occurring simul-taneously and separately so that the reservoir of 'local knowledge' comprises in part a native discourse, imaginary or concrete, of the anthropological experience and method.[6] Wagner (1981) suggests that culture is both creative and inventive, and states that the study of 'cargo-cults' in Australia, for example, should be conceived as a study of native responses to western culture. In my opinion, this should include the western anthropologist as part of the cargo, since the often-assumed harmony of interest and needs between the anthropologist and the local population can be more accurately translated as a 'political' relationship and one capable of producing tension in the face of social realities.

More recently, Rebel, advocating the return of the political-economy approach in anthropology, suggests that a central theme of 'double-binding' relates to culturally hegemonised social experiences which are a product of material aspects of social formation.[7] He argues that political economists 'can cleave much closer to the hermeneutical projects envisaged by the likes of Hegel, Marx, Dilthey, Weber, Freud and even Nietzsche than the current phenomenological approaches with all their ill-concealed pre-Kantian metaphysical baggage, could ever manage' (1989: 130). The experiences of 'natives' are hegemonised because they are based on historical encounters of unequal or non-reciprocal relationships. Hence, like the Ilongot (see Rosaldo 1980: 74–5) who is forced to take in a guest, one with whom relationships have deteriorated to the extent that such hospitality may pave the way for a game of head-hunting during the night (whose head it is, is not clear), the Ma' Betisé' conception of the anthropologist was deception itself. The guest was some kind of government spy, head-hunter or menacing animal spirit assuming an innocent female human form. This was historically conceived in the context of a struggle for autonomy and self-existence against a prevailing dominant culture. Yet with time, their emotions changed, from disdain and indifference to trust and confidence. They were careful to differentiate 'tested' personal experiences with earlier historical experiences tested by previous generations. Images of anthropology and the anthropologist as 'political' and 'historical' became subsumed by a futuristic vision of life, as the anthropologist became a 'helping spirit' in the human battle with plant and animal spirits to retain control over land and forest resources. Metaphorically, this transformed hegemonised social experience into a supernatural conflict of the future between good and bad humans and, on another level, between humans and other living things.

Although a realistic understanding of minority cultures would inevitably require an analysis from political economy, the anthropologist must also continue to understand hermeneutical readings of the endangered mind, for in it lie the clues of difference. In this chapter an attempt has been made to move away from an earlier direct concern for gender in the reflexive mode, towards one which incorporates gender and the gender of fieldwork as part of a wider system of social relations linked to transformations of ecology.

NOTES

1 The Ma' Betisé' are a group of Malayan aborigines (Orang Asli) living in the mangrove coastal rain-forest areas of Selangor in peninsular Malaysia. Numbering approximately 3,500, they are acutely aware of their minority status through fears of encroachment by outsiders, particularly the dominant Malays and the Chinese on the mainland. My research with the Ma' Betisé' was conducted between 1972 and 1975, and I have subsequently returned for numerous trips to maintain social ties and to conduct more detailed research on the changing ecology and developments on the island.

2 A detailed discussion of this ancestral curse is explained in Karim (1981a). The myths which contain this curse are provided in Appendices 16, 18, 19, 20, 21, 22 and 24.

3 Carey Island, known to the Ma' Betisé' as Telu' Gunjeng, has known Ma' Betisé' settlements for more than 100 years. They trace their migration from Batu Pahat in the southern state of Johore through a certain *Batin* (chief) Limpa, who opened up land on the island before the end of the last century. Each settlement seems to have a life-span of between fifteen and twenty years, and movements out of settled areas are explained in terms of population intrusions, over-flooding due to changes in the position of rivers or the weakening of political leadership by elders, leading to alcoholism and social strife.

4 They further argued that Malay women did not want them, they found them backward and dirty so they had to keep their women to themselves. Their argument was perfectly valid, I thought, and I braved myself to eat monkey-meat, not wanting to be stigmatised like the Malay schoolteacher.

5 My last trip to Carey Island, in July 1990, led me to trace my ailing field-father at a Ma' Betisé' settlement off Pulau Lumut at Port Kelang, also in the State of Selangor. The settlement was developed about fourteen years ago by Ané' ('the chosen one') and some friends when he left Carey Island, and resembles the early Ma' Betisé' settlement, built on stilts along mangrove mud-flats, a natural camouflage against the growing industrial estate outside it. I met Ané', his Malay wife, and their baby of eleven months. His elder child had died in a fire at the settlement a few years back. My field-father, who had been staying there for a few weeks after recovering from a minor stroke, said that there had been many deaths at the village – Ané's 4-year-old child and two other babies had died in the night after a day of fever.

6 The phenomenon of 'double-binding' is extensively discussed in his theory of schizophrenia by Bateson in *Steps to an Ecology of Mind* (1972: 201–78). The 'double-bind' in the context of anthropological fieldwork implies that reflexivity at both ends leads to distortion of messages (misconception of the meaning of the anthroplogist's presence, motives, styles of interaction and misconception of the meaning of the natives' hospitality, co-operation, accommodation, and so on) and the mutual acting-out of behaviour in accordance with these two reflexive modes. It also implies asymmetry in the sense that the native is at a disadvantage since his/her reflexive content will not be known.

7 Rebel's commentary on the 'double-bind' is presented in the first of his two-part article in the *American Ethnologist*, 16(1) and 16(2).

REFERENCES

Bateson, G. (1972) *Steps toward an Ecology of Mind*, New York: Ballantine Books.

Davis, D. (1986) 'Changing self-image: studying menopausal women in a Newfoundland fishing village', in T.L. Whitehead and M.E. Conaway (eds), *Self, Sex and Gender in Cross-Cultural Fieldwork*, Urbana and Chicago: University of Illinois Press.

Fukuyama, F. (1989) 'The end of history', *The National Interest* (Summer 1989/90).

—— (1990) 'The end of history' debate, *Dialogue* 89 (March): 8–13.

Gadamer, H.G. (1985) *Truth and Method*, New York: The Crossroad Publishing Co., first published 1960.

Geertz, C. (1973) 'Thick description: towards an interpretive theory of culture', in C. Geertz (ed.), *The Interpretation of Culture*, New York: Basic Books.

—— (1983) 'Blurred genres: the refiguration of social thought', in C. Geertz (ed.), *Local Knowledge: Further Essays in Interpretive Anthropology*, New York: Basic Books.

Giovannini, M. (1986) 'Female anthropology and male informant gender conflict in a Sicilian town', in T.L. Whitehead and M.E. Conaway (eds), *Self, Sex and Gender in Cross-Cultural Fieldwork*, Urbana and Chicago: University of Illinois Press.

Karim, W. (1981a) *Ma' Betisek Concepts of Living Things*, London: Athlone Press.

—— (1981b) 'Ma' Betisek concepts of humans, plants and animals', *Bijdragen Tot de Taal*, Land-en, Volkenkunde, 35–60.

—— (1986) 'Ma' Betisek economics and ecology', Paper submitted at the Sixth Hunters' and Gatherers' Conference, London School of Economics (Sept.).

Karl, F.R. and Hamalian, L. (eds) (1973) *The Existential Imagination*, London: Picador.

Rebel, H. (1989) 'Cultural hegemony and class experience: a critical reading of recent ethnological-historical approaches (part one)', *American Ethnologist* 16(1) (Feb.): 117–36.

Rosaldo, R. (1980) *Ilongot Headhunting: A Study in Society and History*, Stanford, CA: Stanford University Press.

Wagner, R. (1981) *The Invention of Culture*, Chicago: University of Chicago Press.

5 Facework of a female elder in a Lisu field, Thailand

Otome K. Hutheesing

MAKING THE LISU MY FIELD

The field-trip into the Lisu mountains of Northern Thailand had its beginning in Sumatra where, as a Dutch child, I basked in the warmth of brown-skinned 'grannies'. The intrinsic togetherness which I then shared with them and which so sharply contrasted with the frozen rectitude of Dutch behavioural patterns was to stay with me as a much-cherished memory during my formative years in the Netherlands. It was, however, only after a long, tortuous detour via several teaching jobs as a sociologist in the west and a dissertation on the Dutch class system that I was finally able to connect again with the Orient. Back in Asian universities, my sociological work became more larded with anthropological insights. During those teaching days in India and Malaysia, there were occasional brushes with fieldwork in villages, but the burden of lecturing prevented me from 'doing something real'.

The big break came when, at the age of 52, I decided to opt out of academia for a while and become an independent fieldworker. I was thereby fulfilling a dream of going back to a core of tribal life and acquiring firsthand experience of the social processes that were threatening minority cultures. I wanted to participate to the full in the group life of a people known as the Lisu. It was only by accident that I came to know of them but the fact that they ultimately became my research world could be ascribed to my earlier childhood encounters with the mountain people of Indonesia.

I lived with the Lisu in a village near the Thai–Burmese border for a period of over six years, half of which was continuous and intensive (July 1982 to August 1985) and the other half consisting of interspersed visits (January 1986–90) which I still make to this day, whenever my teaching in Malaysia allows for it. These reunions are undertaken both out of a concern for their suffering as well as an academic curiosity about how their gender relations are becoming more and more polarised. Such visits are also prompted by a vague sense of yearning, of wanting 'to go home'.

It was my original intention not to allow my fieldwork to be bound by a sponsoring agency or development project. I also had no compulsion to write a second doctoral thesis, nor even any inclination to publish a book. My primary interest was to focus on the women of the Thai mountains since they had been sadly neglected in most anthropological writings, and to follow up the kind of research in which I had always been involved on the phenomenon of inequality. Finally, I wanted to use an approach which stressed a two-way learning process between researcher and the researched, and which could ultimately result in enhancing the levels of social awareness of both.

FITTING INTO THE LISU FRAME OF REFERENCE

Given that Lisu culture represented a foreign field to me and that my western ways were equally strange to them, what did this exchange between researcher and researched imply? Was it possible to arrive at any mutual understanding? Initially indoctrinated by the Weberian belief that 'Verstehen' (that is, an understanding at an intersubjective level) could actually be arrived at, I became a follower of ideas concerning the construction of realities (Berger and Luckman 1967: 15), of the self (Goffman 1967: 44, 45) and of gender (Lacan 1982). In the field I attempted to 'see through' my constructions of a meaningful world, as I came to grips with Lisu symbolism. In this laborious and not entirely successful endeavour to 'suspend definitions' of reality, the fixed, intellectual categories such as culture, religion and male dominance, motive and action gradually became dissolved. As a consequence, my fieldwork experience was filled with shifting boundaries in terms of understanding myself and the other. Observing the Lisu, I was confronted by useless academic theories and many contradictory Lisu answers to my queries. There were days when I realised how my intellectual conceptions of womanhood were tainted by both personal life experiences and formal societal representations.

And how did Lisu women respond to a female outsider? In a very matter-of-fact way, they immediately fitted me into their world. They wondered about my spirits, or whether I had ancestor cups on the altar. As a woman I was not considered beautiful, because I was neither young nor fat. When I put on weight during the fieldwork period, much to the delight of the Lisu family who fed me, they commented that I had become beautiful, even though old.

It soon became evident that my role was to a large extent defined not by me but by the Lisu themselves. Both men and women labelled me right from the beginning as an 'elder' (*tsu-mo*, 'people old') – that is, a woman of wisdom, more specifically an elder who has knowledge of medicine, a role which in the old days was held by those Lisu women who were experts in collecting medicinal leaves and communicating with a female medicine spirit (the *nae-tsi-ma*). The powers that were bestowed on me by being cast in this role were at times perplexing: I was once called upon to cure the eyes of a blinded buffalo, and on another occasion asked to pacify a hysterical woman. It appeared that the Lisu had for some time been caught up in a crisis of the cultural depletion of their medicine, and so their traditional ways of healing could no longer adequately check the spread of familiar and unfamiliar disease. The thinning of the forest with all its medicinal wealth and sources of protein was an important factor contributing to

Otome Hutheesing with Lisu females, young and old, on the bamboo bed of her hut.

this problem. The introduction of new epidemic diseases was another. I had arrived at a point in time when they had no choice but to develop a faith in western medicine. Sometimes, however, I would insist that a Lisu elder try out some of the few left-over ancient remedies on me. For example, opium stuffed with a garlic clove proved to be highly effective in ridding me of intestinal problems.

The role of the curing elder who distributed pills and plasters, and who had many other kinds of miraculous expertise (including making wealth or money), was one for which I was not prepared. Despite my protestations of ignorance, my faltering Lisu, my insistence that I was in their midst to learn about their culture (a totally nonsensical enterprise in their eyes), they persisted in pushing me into the role of powerful female elder. Not only was I connected to a beneficial spirit world, but my mastery of the lowland Thai language also imbued me with the power to communicate with the worldly authorities – namely, the district administration, the police and the hospital staff – to obtain necessary papers and documents. Indeed, it was through their cries for help that I was able to understand some of the core problems which were engulfing them. My research interests were thus shaped by the real and very dramatic happenings in their environment: the tragedy of the colonisation of their ecology and the ravaging effects of modern crops on their system of gender relations.

It slowly dawned on me that I was part of a social calamity for which there was no immediate remedy. It required an understanding of both the power processes between the state and minorities, as well as between men and women, and I pursued both these lines of research. I felt it was important to crystallise the findings into a publication, recording not only my fieldwork but also my attempts at conscientisation[1] of the Lisu women and thereby seeking an explanation of the roots of gender inequality in this society (Klein-Hutheesing 1989).

GENDER PERSPECTIVES OF THE 'OTHER' AND THE LISU 'FACE'

Even before going into the field, I had to contend with a series of stereotypes which the dominant Thai lowland population upheld about tribal people. A Thai lowland official wondered whether I was not going to be robbed and/or raped by those 'wild' men of the mountains. This reflected the general attitude of the majority towards the minority groups living on the periphery of their society. Implicit in their stance is the assumption of the tribal male as 'aggressor', which simultaneously incorporates a portrayal of the female counterpart as a loose sex object and prostitute. Equally revealing of male authoritarianism was the query by a European male journalist as to whether 'the Lisu men would ever feel threatened by my study of their women'. This supposition illustrates the tenacity of the male power syndrome, a power which might be undermined by an increased self-consciousness on the part of women, instigated in this case by a female researcher with presumed feminist orientations.

Both opinions concerning the role of the woman as fieldworker demonstrate the stereotypical manner in which men perceive women's research on women, a precarious investigation and a corrupting influence on female innocence. Other casually dropped comments related to the question of women's peripheral status, suggesting that a focus on women *per se* could not elicit important statements about their community life since women were excluded from more vital (male) 'political-religious' arenas of control.

After I had worked for a while in the Lisu village, I recall how astounded I was by such blatantly androcentric beliefs in a universal male supremacy. I had begun to observe the very real power of Lisu women: their boisterous talk during the rice harvest or their drunken moods while cutting vegetables for a wedding meal, the vigorous self-assertion of the Lisu female as she trance-danced, accompanied by the vulgar songs of older women. The peculiarity of the Lisu gender system which involved a different 'seeing eye' with which to interpret signs of the 'superior' and 'inferior' also got me to rethink my own paradigm: that the sexism which existed in the west did not prevail in the same form here, and that Lisu men and women were both 'superior' and 'inferior' depending on the context of the situation and the frame of reference of the observer.[2]

Whatever the case, amidst the muddled memories of my working life with the Lisu, few instances of outright sexual inequality seemed to surface either between Lisu men and me, or between Lisu female and male. In other words, fieldwork did not reinforce my earlier notions that women were at a constant disadvantage. I did not have to play a subordinate role, nor was I denied access to men's so-called secret knowledge.

Perhaps this was to a large degree due to my being middle-aged and thus starting with the great advantage of being an elder, a wise woman whom they (female and male) addressed in respectful 'old people's language' and to whom much 'face' was given. Having a 'face' in this context meant that I was expected to be knowledgeable about when to speak, of what and with whom. I had to become fully aware of the rules of avoidance behaviour, which also included the range of sensitive topics for conversation that would cause shame and loss of face. My face slipped many a time; for instance, when I spoke of pregnancy, which happened to be a tabooed topic in the presence of a brother and sister. Though the Lisu were tolerant of my *faux pas*, they let it be clearly known that it was disturbing to them each time I overstepped the rules. However, my face and reputation were easily saved since an elder is always rebuked in a gentle manner. In the maintenance of a ceremonial order, both men and women were expected to exercise their skills in 'face-keeping' devices so that each was left with a sense of social worth. Becoming a Lisu woman thus meant knowing about 'face'[3] and about giving and receiving honour, but never did this adjustment to womanhood, despite its emphasis on modesty, entail being made to feel a lesser being in comparison with the male.

As a middle-aged foreign woman, I gained an extra prestige dimension to my 'face'. Besides being meted out the usual respect and courtesy, I was also given the privilege of entering the village shrine of the most senior ancestor spirit, an otherwise forbidden domain for women. That I was allowed in this sacred area has to be viewed in the light of my non-polluting, non-threatening sexual status as a post-menopausal person. Being a foreigner, and a 'wealthy' one at that, made me somewhat ambiguous. I possessed more 'silver' (money) than they did, and my financial state was interpreted as having received good karma (*myi* in Lisu) or productive capacity from my spirits. Religious knowledge of rituals and the intentions and peculiarities of spirits otherwise safeguarded by men were freely communicated to me. In this manner I acquired more male expertise than a Lisu woman would. This was not seen as an intrusion into a man's world or as an unsettling event for either male or female. My hovering between female and male status as elder simply signified that I had become an 'honorary man/woman'.[4]

Nor did having a special 'face' to keep up mean that the male had to be held at a distance. Lisu men would come to my hut in search of medicine and money, and on many occasions they sought my advice about what to do with a trouble-some daughter or mother-in-law. In all-male company I was free to speak about licentious girls or female orgasms, provided the company was not incest-provoking. Sexual advances were made with jesting grace, and the erotic over-tures of pinching hands during the New Year dance were carried out in low-key fashion, contrary to the predictions of lowland Thai men. My status as a single person was somewhat odd in their judgement, a situation which they attempted to rectify by trying to marry me off to various types of Lisu men. From time to time I appeared in the village with western male friends who were immediately identified as my husbands. No one seemed to regard my polyandrous wanderings as an offence.

LISU ELDERSHIP AND GENDER

In my pre-fieldwork days in the west, the idea of eldership was never entertained: respect for senior citizens in European countries has been on the wane for quite some time. Even the women of my mother's generation were only seen as playing a minor role in the upholding of tradition as grandmothers. They were for the most part meddlesome matriarchs or 'mothers who know best'. I am aware now of the many conflicts my female friends experienced with their mothers, whom they considered backward; they saw them as silly creatures in their roles of wife and mother, in their awkward attempts to appear young and their frequent escapades in neighbourhood hen-parties.

Being an elder in the European context thus held little honour. What was crucially lacking in comparison with Lisu elderhood was the sense of bonding, not only of young and old, but also between women of the same generation. The strength that emanated from older Lisu women well-versed in customary knowledge was forcefully shown during their negotiations for the setting of bridewealth. I recall the eagle eyes of the female elders at the Lisu New Year festivities as they scrutinised the dancing steps of the young and rectified any misplaced pleat or fold in the garments and headgear of boys and girls. I remember how the gift of divining the pig's liver by a decrepit, cantankerous old lady (who was otherwise impossible to live with) was held in high esteem. Hence Lisu eldership convinced me that I had a very weak notion of female elderhood. As a middle-aged woman I was also accorded the status of grandmother, aunt (older sister of mother) and at times even that of father, all of which implied that I received the honour due to a female of my age, for among the Lisu, similar weightage is given to female or male elders who are knowledgeable about Lisu custom.

What then did being a Lisu female elder involve? The execution of soul-calling rites was one prerogative. This means that she had the power to implore the spirits for the return of the souls of sick human beings and animals. This seemed symbolically similar to the 'soul-calling machine' (medicine kit) I used to recall lost souls to their respective bodies. A female elder was also expected to voice her opinion during the bridewealth deliberations and to be consulted on matters regarding marriage.

I can now place in a clearer light the questions several Lisu addressed to me regarding marriage customs. Some of these were:

Do you think I did right to let my daughter stay for a while in a hut near mine after her marriage? [The Lisu usually follow the rule of patrilocality.]

What do you have to say about the bride-price they just now agreed upon? Is it high enough?

Do you think it is good that my husband wants to become a Christian?

At first I wondered why the Lisu themselves did not have the right answers, but at a later stage I interpreted these queries as traditional ways of consulting the female elder which I apparently had become in their eyes.

Being a *tsu-mo* meant, above all, great deference. Lisu men and women would refrain from teasing or frightening a *tsu-mo*. A *tsu-mo* is also given the licence to act in a liberated fashion; she can participate in obscene dances and games and use foul language without suffering shame, and great tolerance is exhibited in cases when drunken older women fight men. Like older women, they are also given the choicest food, the so-called 'old people's dishes', at the big festivals. They are also offered stools which the young are denied. In short, the elder, whether female or male, is given much honour.

'THEORISING' GENDER THROUGH THE LISU: FIXITY OR FLEXIBILITY?

Much of what has been said above represents an afterthought, where actions or assumptions about gender have been rationalised into a coherent scientific frame of reference. I become more aware of my own self-deception if I trace back how I first approached the field of women's studies, in particular my attitude towards women's issues. Was my ideology on women as the second sex correct? Am I now better informed about women's status in society, and how deeply felt is my sense of injustice towards the exploitation of women?

While I have to sort myself out, I am at least aware that my reading of the scant material on Thai mountain people – curing rituals (Durrenberger 1971), the economy (Dessaint 1972) or the determination of ethnic status (Conrad 1989) – now convinces me that it had mainly been collected by male researchers who had overlooked the contributions of the Lisu female to Lisu society. Thus from the outset of my field study I developed critical questions around the themes of male power – political decision-making, economic control, prestigious work, physical violence and rights to property – mainly as a reaction to this earlier gender-biased ethnographic research.

Hence, I had at first looked at gender as two sharply divided hostile entities of male and female. Armed with the harshness of this dichotomy, I had provoked the Lisu women to tell me the 'truth' about their men. Were they so powerful? How did women see themselves relating to men in equal or unequal terms? In the early stages of my fieldwork, I had a great deal of language learning to do not only in terms of understanding the right concepts of 'power', 'honour' and 'repute', but also in terms of relating them to the convoluted way the Lisu discuss gender through the interplay of seniority, marital status, reproduction and ritual.

While puzzling over their figures of speech – for example, 'the female is an elephant', 'the male is a dog' – I gradually came to grasp their way of looking at gender relations, which centred on the moral evaluations of reputation (*myi-do*) and shame (*sa-taw*). Each of these valuations was guided by the principle of hard work, propriety of speech, knowledge of Lisu custom and the ability to share spiritual and material wealth. Within this moral frame, each contributed their share by exhibiting repute as timid elephants (female) or bold dogs (male). Each of these codes relating to gender behaviour provided the yardstick with which female and male worth could be measured. In the judgements on the value of each

gender no implicit or explicit notion of 'superiority' or 'inferiority' was expressed. Both female and male 'strength' were equally necessary (Klein-
Hutheesing 1989).

LISU METAMORPHOSES

In the early phases of opium production, the Lisu gender system had exhibited
few signs of tension. Both female and male appeared to attain a reputable position
in the economic and moral order of their community life. While men felled trees,
burned swiddens, planted poppies and hunted game, women weeded the paddy
fields, harvested the rice and opium, gathered the vegetables and as a rule kept
the cash from the sale of opium.

However, during the six years of my stay with the Lisu, I witnessed traumatic
changes that occurred in their material way of life due to the prohibition of poppy
cultivation and subsequent introduction of substitute crops. The latter brought
about profound ruptures in the environment, leading to deforestation and with it
the disappearance of the male hunter role. While the male as a trader became
more entangled in modern, alien markets, the female withdrew increasingly into
subsistence activities or opted to become a coolie on a foreign-managed coffee
plantation. With their stress on autonomy, both sexes became deprived of
meaningful localised production processes. A sharpening of gender issues took
place. The women complained about loss of cash while blaming Lisu custom
which did not allow them to 'go outside and far away'. I observed the new
awareness of the female concerning her limited freedom to travel and trade in the
lowlands and overheard their cries of anger and conversations filled with worry.
It was clear that the first kernels of male dominance, exemplified in their control
of cash, had appeared on the Lisu scene. Increased poverty led to their inability
to collect sufficient cash for bridewealth, which in turn had its impact on the idea
of repute for both sexes. Against this backdrop, gender conflict and opposition
between the sexes were emerging. Alienated men resorted to violence, and
disgruntled women ran away from their dishonoured husbands.

My perception of the crisis-filled happenings was no doubt influenced by the
various stages of fieldwork I passed through. As I moved from ethnographic
description to the questioning of cosmologies and kinship rules, I was ultimately
able to arrive at certain interpretations of the mechanisms of change in Lisu
culture. The revolution that took place in their production relations provided a
different dimension in fieldwork, for I discovered some disturbing data centring
on gender and class conflict. Modern trade relations had resulted in economic
control of the Lisu female by her own men and in exploitation of her labour
within the plantation setting governed by the political economy of lowland
forces.

I discerned voices of discontent, which were expressed in heart-breaking
songs, in perpetual mutterings by women on the theme that 'Men had become
weak, uncaring, unthinking; they were not capable of raising bridewealth for
their sons; men's souls had become bad'. I tried to translate women's anguish in

terms of their loss of repute, and their position as a second sex, but I realised at the same time that men had not been promoted to the status of first-sex colonisers, since they had themselves become economically marginalised in the much larger framework of capitalist world market systems. However, male marginalisation indirectly reduced women's status. The loss of their traditional elephant-like metaphorical strength was expressed in female outrage about the jointly earned cash which was spent by the men in lowland trading centres (on pesticides, prostitutes, huge transistor radios). Teenage girls were similarly angered when their wages were consumed by their father's opium or alcohol addiction. Mothers became infuriated when their sons pawned the silver family heirlooms. While translating these tales of women's woe, I tried to fit them into a more general feminist ideology and in doing so, became incensed by the injury done to womanhood, not inflicted by their own men *per se* but by the male-empowered systems emanating from a foreign centre.

My own standpoint had thus moved through various stages: that of a priori western feminist to anthropologist with relativised concepts of male dominance, thence to a genderless person with many faces, and lastly back again to a conscientised woman fired by the experiences of fieldwork, aware of the all-consuming power of paternalism which upsets the fragile gender balances of outlying societies. In sum, I needed the study of a minority group to understand my own western assumptions of oppression and of the superimposition of male over female.

NOTES

1 The draft of the book was read out to one of the Lisu women as part of a conscientisation process of the injuries done to the traditional Lisu gender system. She was my field-younger sister and, though I had become a Lisu elder, it did not prevent her from criticising what I had written. In several ways we were 'sisters in arms', trying to come to grips with the disfigurement of women's 'face' (that is, repute) on account of a set of relationships which had introduced new dimensions of power into an otherwise balanced set of ideas linked to honour with respect to each sex (see Klein-Hutheesing 1989).

2 The egalitarian Lisu gender set-up is identical to the one observed among some tribal societies of India and South-east Asia. In this vein Leela Dube noted how unencumbered was her role as female researcher among the tribal Gonds, a fact which she associated with the relatively unoppressive social structure of that community. See Dube 1975.

3 While commenting on the concept of 'face' I wish to make a distinction between the Goffmanesque use of the concept and the one embedded in the Lisu idea of 'face'; that is, *pi-mya*. Goffman (1967: 42–5) regards face as part of interaction ritual in face-to-face relations and, as such, an important device to keep the flow of communication in line, so that the balancing of the actor's selves can be maintained. *Pi-mya* for a people like the Lisu is not merely a kind of put-on or mask which prevents embarrassment between members of a group, but it also represents a moral value related to honour or repute which measures the commitment to Lisu custom and the status derived from it. The Lisu are familiar with face as a strategy to make participants feel accepted, but in addition to this the artful manipulation of face to avoid shame is basic to the cultural standing of a person. Not doing injury to the face

of others is interpreted as having much face; that is, being big in repute. When I mention female facework I refer to two aspects: that of impression management, but more so to the repute one derives from being 'a good woman' – that is, one who is knowledgeable about shame.

4 Norma Diamond in her study of a Taiwanese village experienced similar instances of oscillation between female and male roles, when she commented that her sex role became neutral after being involved in all-male meetings concerning village rituals or acquiring knowledge about the fishing industry, a man's preserve (Diamond 1970).

REFERENCES

Berger, Peter and Luckman, Thomas (1967) *The Social Construction of Reality*, New York: Doubleday Anchor.

Conrad, Yves (1989) 'Lisu identity in Northern Thailand: a problematique for anthropology', in J. McKinnon and B. Vienne (eds), *Hill Tribes Today*, Bangkok: White Lotus-Orstom, pp. 191–222.

Dessaint, Alain (1972) 'Economic organization of the Lisu of the Thai Highlands', Ph.D. thesis, University of Hawaii.

Diamond, Norma (1970) 'Fieldwork in a complex society: Taiwan', in G.D. Spindler, *Being an Anthropologist*, New York: Holt, Rinehart & Winston, pp. 113–41.

Dube, Leela (1975) 'Woman's worlds: three encounters', in A. Beteille and T.N. Madan (eds), *Encounter and Experience: Personal Accounts of Fieldwork*, Delhi: Vikas Publishing House, pp. 156–77.

Durrenberger, Paul (1971) 'The ethnography of Lisu curing', Ph.D. thesis, University of Illinois at Urbana-Champaign.

Goffman, Erving (1967) *Interaction Ritual: Essays on Face-to-Face Behavior*, New York: Doubleday Anchor.

Klein-Hutheesing, Otome (1989) *Emerging Sexual Inequality among the Lisu of Northern Thailand: The Waning of Dog and Elephant Repute*, Leiden: Brill.

Lacan, J. (1982) *Feminine Sexuality*, J. Mitchell and J. Rose (eds), London: Macmillan.

6   A hall of mirrors

Autonomy translated over time in Malaysia*

Ingrid Rudie

This chapter focuses on how I discovered the importance of economically active women in the peasant economy of post-independence Malaysia, and how this finding has been conceptualised in different ways through the filter of changing analytical paradigms and experiential frameworks – my own, those of my informants, and the ones that we create together out of our conversations about shared reference material. The lapse of time is a long one – from a first field study in 1964/5, to a re-study through three consecutive field trips in 1986, 1987 and 1988.

My discussion turns the problem of cultural translation into a question of mediation between different lived cultures, between different 'voices' within each culture, and between different theoretical vantage points. This process of mediation involves a choice between playing on similarities and playing on differences. Both options carry traps, and seemingly innocent catchwords may evoke wrong notions.

In this case a risky catchword has been 'autonomy'. In my fieldwork in Malaysia I have encountered women who seem highly autonomous in relation to their husbands. If this is described as 'autonomy' to a western audience, it suggests a degree of individuation which gives an incorrect representation of identity structures. My informants' most basic identity is as complementary family persons rather than free-floating, culturally 'complete' and potentially single individuals, which is a notion of autonomy derived from a modern background. Yet, Malaysian society is passing rapidly into modernity, and male and female identity structures are undergoing change.

TIME: SOCIAL AND DISCURSIVE PROCESSES

Together with my informants I compare two situations in the middle sixties and the late eighties. In my orientation back to the field in the eighties there is a multistranded process to keep track of.

First there are the processes in the world. Economic and political structures change; demographic movements change the composition of cities and villages; religious and political rhetoric and mass communication affect value parameters.

Secondly, there are processes in people's perception of their world. Back in the field after a long absence, I observed some such changes. Areas of life which had been taken for granted were brought to attention and described in new ways. Bourdieu (1977) suggests a perspective on such processes: the areas of a culture which are taken for granted and not reflected on are regarded as constituting a 'doxic' field, which is only revealed in contrast to the universe of discourse or opinion (1977: 168). The line of demarcation between doxa and discourse is changeable. This approach is suited to exhibiting the work done by contrasts and challenges in sociocultural processes. In the present case, challenge is brought before the informants and the analyst both by new events in their lifeworld, and by fieldwork itself as an experience of cultural contrast which stirs both sides.

Thirdly, processes in anthropological theory change the researcher's perception of the field in close parallel to the informants' changed perception of their lived reality. Between my visits gender had come on the agenda, there had been considerable development in the study of large-scale societies, and most anthropologists had developed a heightened sophistication in coping with their double identification as cultural and political creatures on one hand, and would-be detached observers on the other.

Fourthly, there were the changes in my own specific analytical interests, which made it impossible to go back to the field with the intention of following up the old questions of 1965. There had to be another problem, a new set of questions. This landed me in a situation where two points separated in time had to be compared, but the focus of the comparison was skewed.

The problem of mediation has now been set in a hall of mirrors. My positions in 1965, in 1987 and in between reflect the field from different angles. Changes in my informants' lived reality make them perceive their own situation differently at the two points in time. My questions in 1965 and 1987 elicit a different series of data, and start my informants on different trails of self-reflection.

Recent increased self-reflection in anthropology has brought into focus a notion of fieldworker and informants as co-producers of information. *In Culture and Truth* (1989) Renato Rosaldo stresses the importance of insights which can emerge from bringing in more of the fieldworker's personal experience such as is activated when working in cultural borderlands – and more and more of our field experience takes part in such borderlands, where 'open borders' appear more salient than 'closed communities'. Kirsten Hastrup's approach is even more focused on the dynamic of understanding built up as a kind of joint project between informant and analyst:

> Rather than seeing fieldwork . . . as a simple dialogue between two parts and two cultures which are at all times separate, we should see it as a manifestation of a preliminary establishment of a third culture. . . . The point is, that only from this 'third position' do we obtain an insight which is [both subjective and objective].
>
> (Hastrup, in Hastrup and Ramløv 1988: 220–1 – my translation)

No mention of the relationship between mainstream anthropology and feminism has been made so far. I have been searching for an epistemological frame which can convey both. The reflexive vantage point suggested here can be developed into such a frame, although the task is difficult because we can only transcend ourselves in the aftermath. I can unveil my past moves, but not my present ones. The encircling of the problem must take the form of specific explorations of an empirical situation as well as the researcher's particular positioning in time/space and in theoretical affiliations. In what follows I shall switch between passages which describe my encounters with the field, and passages in which I step outside and reflect on these encounters.

THE SUBJECTIVE HISTORY OF A RESEARCH PROJECT

In 1965, before the feminist movement had seriously begun its urgent call for 'making women visible', I returned from my first visit to Kelantan in Malaysia with field material in which the women were very visible. They had to become visible because they had important tasks in the economy and local community. They owned, inherited, bought and sold land in their own right, they took part in agricultural production, and they dominated bazaar trade.

At the same time there was a clear segregation between the sexes in public and ceremonial situations. Formal religious rules underlined the leadership of men, and when women moved outside their own homes, they had several taboos to observe. Still it would be misleading to say that women were restricted to the domestic sphere. They had a part to play in the public sphere of the village, they had ritual and networking functions of major importance to the viability of household and community.

In the years following this visit a new awareness of gender instructed me to see this as a local system in which the gender discourse contains some elements of tension. It contains arguments for male hegemony, but also corresponding arguments for a more even juxtaposition of women with men. Before I returned in the late eighties I had formed some loose hypotheses to the effect that some of the social resources which women had, and which seemed to further this juxta-position, might be so dependent on a particular division of work and a particular kind of female solidarity that they might not easily be brought along in the process of modernization with its increased demand for geographical and social mobility. I suggested that arguments for male hegemony might then easily come out victorious as local practice was more firmly integrated into large-scale economic and political systems (Rudie 1983, 1985).

Malaysia is a multi-ethnic society, in which the Islamic Malays, together with indigenous groups, constitute 59 per cent of the population. Islam is the state religion, and in a situation of ethnic competition the Islamic idiom takes on high political symbolic value. The dominant economic philosophy is a mixture of capitalist development ideology with elements of government regulation – a combination which is rooted in the country's historical and ethnopolitical situation. In the early seventies the government launched the so-called New Economic Policy, which is a multi-pronged strategy for bringing the Malays closer to the level of the Chinese in control of capital and participation in modern activities in general. Quota regulations are aimed at securing the Malays' admission to educational institutions, and under this protection women are also well represented. Many women are recruited to new kinds of careers, even though there are no formal rules to secure their particular interests. But in some areas of economic activity women's productive roles are overlooked. In particular development initiatives such as plantation projects and adult education programmes the idea of women's reproductive role tends to dominate, while their traditionally strong position as producers in their own right is played down.

In 1985 the Norwegian Council for Applied Social Research launched a major comparative research programme on women and development, and under its auspices there was room for my new project, which I had been thinking about for a long time. In 1987 I returned to the local community in which I did my work in 1965. My new project was set on trying to understand the adaptations which fan out of the community in the form of 'new' and 'old' career types both inside its physical borders and among people who have moved out.

A PERSONAL HISTORY OF MAKING SENSE

This outline is far removed from the fresh field situation; it is already filtered through insights and biases which have formed through a number of later reflections and discussions. Let me now try to get closer to the first fieldwork and its aftermath.

One of my early observations took this form: in some villages in 1965 a large proportion of households were of the extended family type and integrated through links between mother and daughter or between sisters. Moreover, a high proportion of married couples took up residence near the wife's family. This pattern particularly seemed to prevail where gardening and marketing were important elements in the household economy. I wanted to explain the bonds between female relatives on the basis of influences from economic and ecological factors, conventions of division of work between the sexes, and other ideological factors external to 'kinship proper'. I worked seriously on understanding male and female areas of responsibility, but the theoretical framework of my discussion was one in which I led myself to stress *kin* and *family* rather than *gender*.

My research interests at this time were focused on household organisation and change. Important sources of inspiration had been the Firths' pioneering work in Kelantan, and recent developments in the study of domestic organisation set in motion by the Cambridge symposium on the developmental cycle of domestic groups (Goody 1958). I had myself developed some ideas on how domestic organisation could be studied as a 'showcase' for social change and wanted to follow up this analysis. In a wider sense, my theoretical outfit was derived from a variety of contemporary anthropology breaking loose from functionalism and groping for methods to analyse change. This trend was strong in Norway due to the influence of Barth's studies of entrepreneurship, and his other contributions to 'generative anthropology' (Barth 1963, 1966).

I had no feminist concepts among my analytical tools, but in my personal orientation there were attitudes which must be labelled feminist. These attitudes seeped through in personal encounters with informants. I was pleased when I saw the power of decision-making that adult women had, felt provoked about the seclusion of younger girls, and about what I experienced as attempts to limit my freedom of movement as a 'junior woman'. I was puritanical in my conviction that 'science' and 'personal feelings' should be kept apart, but my spontaneous reactions went into my diaries.

In the anthropological discourse at the time 'society' tended to equal 'political structures', which were a male domain. Households were seen as something embedded in political structures. This determined my anxiety level on the professional side: fearing marginalisation among my colleagues, I was afraid of missing important parts of 'the real thing': namely, what men were up to in male-dominated fora. I could not attend Friday mosque, and was hesitant about entering the coffee shops where local women had no place. I could talk to men, but my obvious place for more informal and recreational purposes was with the women.

My knowledge of women's lives was enhanced by my female identification, but the degree to which the information was put to use was restricted by my research design. But it was there as a surplus of information with which I could meet what was going to happen next in the social sciences. For soon after the end of this field stay, questions about the situation of women started cropping up. In discussions of field experiences I was often asked if women in 'my' field were oppressed, and my eagerness to avoid crude 'yes' or 'no' answers led me to stress the measure of economic autonomy of women *vis-à-vis* husbands, and the nature of women's cooperative projects as a system of its own. The coexistence of economic autonomy and social and ritual segregation became my new catchwords (Rudie 1971, 1983). No longer in the field, I could not confront these questions with systematic observation of fresh interaction. Instead, my still pictures in the form of fieldnotes were selected and reflected against changing analytical paradigms over a prolonged period. I selected the picture of the productive and providing women who took decisions on household economy and family politics, and who talked about their acts in the first person singular as they went along.

The history of making sense is to a large extent a history of paradigms, and in my case three dominant trends have had their impact from before the first fieldwork until completion of the last. These are mainstream anthropology before 1970, the new feminist wave which stood behind feminist anthropology, and a reorientation in the eighties that is preoccupied with the relationship between practice and discourse, a reorientation which is an adaptation to a greater theoretical and methodological pluralism (Ortner 1984).

The development of feminist anthropology has been rapid and turbulent. Henrietta Moore sketches its various stages, from criticism of male bias, through a redefinition of the project as the 'study of gender', to a phase where feminist anthropology tries to 'come to terms with the real differences between women' (1988: 11). Marilyn Strathern has drawn attention to the difficult co-existence between mainstream anthropology and feminism. In *The Gender of the Gift*, she claims that we have to give up seeing feminist anthropology as a super-context encompassing both. 'If the beast exists at all, it is a hybrid' (1988: 36). In her view it is more difficult to be a 'feminist anthropologist' than to be an anthropologist and a feminist who tries to keep the identities separated.

But the two positions of feminist and anthropologist are not inert. They both change, and they change partly in response to the practitioners' experience of living in a changing world. It is at this point that the conventional definition of paradigm breaks down. Marilyn Strathern offers a clue to this problem when she notes a flaw in the notion of paradigms as 'basic conceptual frameworks and orientating assumptions of a body of knowledge' (citing Kuhn 1970). This flaw becomes visible when it turns out that scientists become aware of their paradigm shift only after it has happened (Strathern 1987: 281–2).

This will be so because a paradigm does not consist of pure and uncontaminated scientific theory; there is always a residue in our paradigms that we can never thoroughly unveil, and this residue consists of the undiscussed assumptions, the doxa (Bourdieu 1977), in our culture. Before gender came on the agenda for theoretical scrutiny, a few generations of anthropologists had struggled to free themselves of ethnocentrism. They were successful in many ways, but reproduced some of the doxic assumptions of their own societies about men's activities being the most important.

The feminist movement brought the issue of gender out of the doxa of the researchers' community, but may have reintroduced a new dosage of ethnocentrism at another level. Western notions of nature and culture, notions about power and equality, and female role dilemmas between employment and family life have been such danger spots.

My own preoccupation with autonomy falls among all these dimensions. An initial empirical observation was thrust on me through the nature of my field contact. In the 1970s I led myself to describe the Malay women's situation in terms of extensive economic autonomy in order to bring some nuances into a discussion in which some of my more militant feminist colleagues tried to make me say 'oppression'. But in a sense the choice of the concept of autonomy also betrayed my appreciation of an element which was valuable or acceptable in the Malay women's situation. Even if it is a description which my informants could have accepted – and I think many of them would have done so – it still selects one point among many which could have been equally relevant. The notion of autonomy was selected from the feminist corner in my personal paradigm, but was also utilised to oppose what I saw as too crude an analytical framework in the feminist approach. I do not now refute my earlier analysis, but see more clearly how the concept may convey wrong notions if used without proper contextualisation.

RECONTEXTUALISATION

Recontextualisation took place when I returned once again from frozen pictures to live practice during a second period of fieldwork. The notion of the autonomous and self-supporting woman will now be 'interpreted' against my own point of departure, against those of male and female informants, and against the 'macro-level' messages in religious and political rhetoric.

My attempts at re-establishing rapport with my informants had to be based on our shared experience from which we could start a discussion at once more informed and more equal than the learning process that I had been through in the sixties. Our shared experience takes two forms. On the most straightforward level, I share with many informants a chunk of common historical reference material: we all know what the village was like in the sixties. But there is also a more general manner in which we share experience: my informants and I are all experiencing the effects of a global process which can be called the advance of the world capitalist system. Our respective societies are at different stages in this process, and receive it through different cultural filters. This leaves us with bits of experience which are partly comparable, and partly contrasting. Such effects as the breakdown of the domestic mode of production, and reorientation of male and female careers in a way which demands mobility may suggest comparability. But the comparability on this level is thwarted at another level, that of the imagery in which life projects are described (Rudie forthcoming). An informant and I seem to experience similar dilemmas around the problem of holding down a job and taking care of a family at the same time. But while my image of growing old in a happy way is concerned with being personally active and continuing to explore the world, her most cherished image is that of resting and growing old in her daughter's house. Such mixtures of likeness and contrast may exemplify Renato Rosaldo's notion of the cultural borderlands in which contemporary anthropologists mostly work (Rosaldo 1989).

ON CONVERSING WITH WOMEN ABOUT THEIR WORK

On my return to the field I was confronted with a change in the conceptualisation of work. The vernacular word for work – *kerja* – used to cover a wide range of activities including material production as well as ceremonial undertakings, and the broadest translation is probably 'necessary activities'. When I came back in the eighties and asked women about their work, most of them told me that they had none, meaning that they were not in formal, permanent employment. House-work, gardening, petty trade and ceremonial had seemingly fallen out of the work category, and I had to reintroduce these activities one by one if I wanted to discuss them. Whether people keep a double set of work definitions may vary from person to person, but they are at least able to imagine that by 'work' the fieldworker is likely to think about waged work.

The women's narrowed concept of work[1] was a clue to changes in their circumstances. One of the most important changes which had taken place was an increased dependence on the labour market, and a corresponding reduction in the number of small niches for creating household viability. Males fare better in the labour market than females. The labour market in Kelantan differs somewhat from that of the more industrialised west coast. Development in Kelantan has mostly been focused on education and the creation of infrastructure. There are job opportunities for women with specific educational qualifications – in teaching, the health service and clerical jobs – but few opportunities in unskilled industrial work, which would be the outlet for those who lack more specific educational qualifications or have failed to acquire the traditional skills of trade. In contrast, there has been an increase in male opportunities in transport services and construction work following public enterprise. Male job opportunities are thus more evenly distributed to meet different levels of skill and education. It is this development in particular which has tipped the gender balance in the sense that women's importance as providers has become less prominent, relatively, than it used to be.

Most women of working age in 1987 stressed the desirability of having their own income. Some described how they cast about for ideas on how to get into a niche in small-scale trade, others how they stuck to their jobs despite strain, and even despite a husband who thought that there was really no need to be in employment. When I probed further on the positive aspects of having an income, the answers became more varied. Some did not primarily stress the money aspect, but said that they went to work or engaged in trade because they were unable to sit still. 'To sit still' – *duduk diam* – means staying in the house without engaging in any outside activity, being a housewife. Others stressed the advantage of not having to ask the husband for money. When they had earned the money them-selves, they were free to allocate it. A third category of answers was given by those who said that they had to help the husband cover expenses.

Ways of spending money were exemplified in essentially two directions: as buying things for the house, or as helping other relatives, particularly elderly parents. Taking care of the old and handicapped is a family duty which weighs on both men and women, but weighs most heavily on women for two reasons. First, according to the unquestioned productive identity that women had and partly still have, the help had two components which were inextricably inter-twined: material responsibility and personal care. Secondly, with the breakdown of a productive system in which women had a prominent place, women are now worse off in meeting the material part of the obligation. Women who have no independent income have to rely on their husbands in order to fulfil one of their culture's most value-laden obligations.

Readers who know the Malay ethnography may miss something at this point, as it is a well-documented feature that women administer the family's money, and by extension, are entitled to men's earnings. This was also part of normal expectations in Kelantan in 1965, and again in the eighties – but now with the added comment that it did not always work out that way. Informants said that practice was 'half and half'. Cases in which the husband decided about the money were reported by women, usually without strong overtones of negative evalu-ation. This acceptance of different practice is not a sign of women's subjection, but rather something quite different: a certain separateness in marriage, coupled with equality in the project of running a household. There seems to be an implicit rule that whoever brings in the money has the right of disposal over it, and this position is now passing from women to men.

Janet Carsten (1989) argues that there is a division of functions between men and women in Langkawi, another part of Malaysia. Men bring in money as an impersonal commodity and women socialise it – bring it into the sphere of personal loyalties, so to speak, in a household context. The process of transformation from commodity to gift has taken a different shape in Kelantan, because women have had more of the direct responsibility of bringing in the money; in other words, women themselves have been involved in the whole project of acquiring the commodity and transforming it into a gift. In my analysis of the Kelantan state of affairs women are more 'entrepreneurial' and market-orientated than they are in Carsten's analysis of Langkawi; the economic parallelism between men and women seems to have been stronger, the complementarity weaker.

The tenacity of the traditional Kelantan notion of the woman as a total resource person shows in the following paraphrase of an interview with a young girl in the middle of her education. The essence of her view is this:

> I will continue to work and earn my income when I marry. For I have promised to help my parents, help send them on the pilgrimage. I cannot depend on a husband for that; it would be like taking another person's money.
>
> (Azizah, aged 21)

CONVERSING WITH MEN ABOUT WOMEN'S WORK

When I talked to men about women's work, they tended to express one of the following views. First, women don't work, they take care of children. Secondly, sometimes they work to help the husband. And thirdly, Kelantan women are diligent and independent, they will not be stopped.

Kelantan Malay men seem to nurture a myth about the housewife despite the fact that perhaps a majority of women compete for a niche in workforce or market. The male notion of the non-work of women, or at best their role as auxiliary provider, mirrors a world view which is implicit in dominant areas of the political culture, and also the stress on male primacy which is explicit in modern Islamic rhetoric. This has brought the male duty as supporter more clearly into focus. But it also mirrors other, more tangible aspects of the changed position of men in this post-peasant society: not too many years ago, men frequently stayed at home and took care of farming activities, while women travelled to market and brought in the money in a physical and actual sense. With the advent of the wage market and the opportunities of the New Economic Policy, the roles have somehow been reversed. Now it is men who most easily get jobs and often bring in the largest share of income for reasons which were described above.

Women's resource-hunting activities in the informal trade sector are easily lumped together with household activities, and the household is no longer seen as the sphere where production takes place. The third position that some men take – viewing Kelantan women as industrious and independent – is a more accurate description of what we could call the women's work ethic and the reality of the responsibilities that they have been, and still are, expected to take on.

CONCLUDING DISCUSSION

This has been an exercise in dismantling the informants' discourse as well as my own, and the picture should now be reassembled. I have done my best to destroy an expectation that it is possible to isolate the native reality and describe it objectively. The final argument will move through three different stages in handling the problem of practice and representation, and will start with the fieldworker, proceed to the informant, and finally touch on the problem of translation.

The fieldworker's history has been described as a history of passing through personal paradigms which are used to interpret the field, and are changed through this experience. The experience itself is a revelation of contrasts and likenesses, and it is this experience that triggers the selection of what goes into the fieldnotes in the first place. The informants also note the contrasts and likenesses, and start reflecting on their own practice from the same kind of experience. This brings us back to the question of what informant and fieldworker do together. We share a reference material dating back to the sixties, and we share some other elements of common experience rooted in the fact that macro-processes affect different societies in comparable ways. This suggests that the field dialogue is one in which the distinction between the 'emic' and the 'etic' view is partly dissolved. The history of the concept of autonomy in my own and my informants' understanding may serve as illustration once more. It can be summed up in a more narrative style.

In a relatively unchallenged peasant practice women had a considerable amount of economic autonomy *vis-à-vis* their husbands. They themselves did not use the concept of autonomy, although the anthropologist who came there with a different perspective recorded it as an organisational reality. The anthropologist's labelling of the phenomenon was thus based on an 'external' understanding.

In a new economic situation this autonomy becomes threatened, and the women search for ways of guarding their freedom of decision within the marriage relation. They form an idea of a state which can be called 'autonomy', even if it is still not a category in their vocabulary.

Then they are revisited by the anthropologist, who has developed an interest in gender relations and women's affairs. Some of the women quite enjoy the conversations with her, and the mere effort of putting their own experience into words may lead them to formulate some ideas more explicitly than they would otherwise have done.

As fieldworkers we often act as catalysts, we elicit implicit knowledge, or produce knowledge together with our informants. Those who are familiar with Victor Turner's work on Ndembu symbolism will probably also remember how this case has been used by some colleagues (for example, in Sperber 1975: 18–19) as an example of elicited knowledge which might not have been fully explicit even in the expert informant's mind before he entered into the productive discussion with the anthropologist, and it was certainly not commonly shared knowledge in the society. Nevertheless, such elicited knowledge is in rapport with the symbolic repertoire of the culture.

This manner of selectively teasing out information may appear controversial from a conservative methodological viewpoint. But after all, we tease out something which is there. It is not a complete truth, but it is a theme. If the theme can be recognised by a member of the society, it is 'true enough' even if we may disagree on details of what it means. This is not an attempt to create an excuse for inaccurate information; it is an attempt to assess what anthropologists can realistically do. All this is made more acceptable if we agree on a discursive view of culture – in the sense that cultures are multivocal representations of practice.

My simplified scheme of male and female informants plus the assumptions which seem to lie hidden in the political culture reveal that there is no one native view; there are many ways in society of conceptualising women's economic role. There is a main cleavage between male and female representations, but male and female representations also differ among themselves. The variety in views exhibits differential experience – people are differently positioned in a complex situation of change which affects economy, family and the identity structures of individuals. But some men and some women seem to have reached a common understanding of the emerging primacy of the marriage bond and the nuclear family with the male as main provider. This is backed by areas of the political culture, and becomes particularly visible in some development strategies. A dominant view is perhaps emerging of economic development as something bracketed in formal politics, in which the domestic sphere and other fields of local life are reduced to areas of reproduction. Men often contrast their own formal jobs with women's informal economic activities, and see most women as belonging in a domestic sphere. At the same time, some women who are successful in education and career-hunting go along with men into the formal workforce, so that new lines of differentiation are brought about in the female population.

Most young housewives today enjoy higher living standards in an absolute sense than the hard-working gardeners of twenty years ago, but in a relative sense they may have lost an area of control. In the last analysis the issue is not a narrowly economic one, it is one of identity and social attachment. Kelantan women have been used to a share in the control of the whole process of acquisition and allocation of resources. They have themselves been active in mediating between the commodity sphere and the sphere of personal loyalties, and they have had a say as to whom the sphere of loyalties should include. This social issue is the crux of the matter, money is a means, and the mode of acquisition of the means largely decides the control over the ends.

If I say that the issue of identity is an issue about personal fulfilment, I talk within a western modernist and individualist frame of reference. If I say that it has something to do with attachment and belonging, I take care of the Malay idiom at the same time as I do not exclude the possibility of fulfilment. After all, this is a society moving fast into modernity. The ideal of individual fulfilment and the reality of nuclear family isolation are two sides of modernity. Then there are two points in the present process that may be threatening to the social network, namely, the possible weakening of ties between female relatives, and the weakening of local ceremonial cooperation. And this happens while some women may explicitly value not having to work for an income, and some deliberately opt out of ceremonial cooperation because they find it cumbersome or 'old-fashioned'. In doing so they may lose something which has been an important source of attachment. This is a common feature in cultural processes: the practitioners do not foresee all the consequences of their own choices.

Some final remarks should be given to the question of representing ethnographic insights to different audiences. The most obvious demand is that a text[2] should make sense to an audience, and both my informants and a western public are possible audiences. So my description should be a description which the informants themselves could accept, and it should explain something new to a non-Malay audience.

I have already suggested why in all probability some of my informants will accept my description while others will disagree. When it comes to the non-Malay audience, I have to decide on a strategy of presentation which takes care of the problem of knowing where the preconceived notions of this audience are located. When I was carried away by new interests in gender in the seventies I ran the risk of losing the contextual qualifications necessary to put the notion of 'autonomy' in its proper slot. Being autonomous and self-supporting in western society and in Malay society carry elements of meaning which partly coincide, partly differ.

The areas of coincidence are contained within the marriage relation. In western as well as Malay society we will meet the notions of autonomy *vis-à-vis* a husband, and notions of equal or unequal power of decision-making. As soon as we step outside the economic and moral rules of the marriage dyad, the cultural differences become apparent. The issue of being single is perhaps the most dramatically different. Single life is a perfectly normal state in western society; it is often a willed choice, and having children out of wedlock has lost its moral stigma in many countries. Such is the background against which a western audience may read 'autonomy'.

Even though many of my female informants say that the good thing about having one's own income is a degree of non-subjection to a husband, the 'freedom' is enjoyed within a framework of family structures, and not as a free-flowing, self-sufficient, potentially single individual. On this basis it is perhaps not the most apt description to call the women self-supporting. We should rather apply notions from the family set-up: cooperator and contributor, producer and reproducer. This operation brings out contrastive identity models. The individuated individual is clearly set against the complementary family persons whom I encounter in the field.

All these contextualisations were brought back to me with increased force as I approached the field for the second time. But, to paraphrase Heraclitus, one never steps into the same river twice. One is not even the same person. As I said initially, I am not able to transcend my present position. Others may see through it, but I myself have to wait a few years before I can fully unveil the determinants of my 1990 analysis.

NOTES

* A first version of this chapter was read at a symposium marking the twenty-fifth anniversary of the Faculty of Social Science at the University of Oslo. On that occasion Shirley Ardener was invited as a discussant, and I am much obliged to her for her extremely helpful comments, which appear together with my original version in 'Forskningssymposiet 17–18 november 1988' (Festschrift, limited publication). A more empirically orientated description of the research project built on the same original version is being published in Khabar Seberang.
1 A number of Norwegian social scientists have been preoccupied with the work concept, and noted similar processes of narrowing it down to income-generating activities in schemes of popular categorisation (Wadel 1977; Lind 1984; Melhuus and Borchgrevink 1984).
2 For a precise definition, see Fiske 1982: 71, where text is defined as 'messages with an independent existence. A text stands for something apart from itself and its encoder.' Otherwise, the concept of text is rapidly on its way into the toolkit of most anthropologists, and in some instances becomes an alternative way of approaching the culture concept. See also Clifford and Marcus 1986, *passim*.

REFERENCES

Barth, Fredrik (1963) (ed.) *The Role of the Entrepreneur in Social Change in Northern Norway*, Oslo: Universitetsforlaget.
—— (1966) 'Models of social organization', Occasional Paper No. 23, Royal Anthropological Institute of Great Britain and Ireland.
Bourdieu, Pierre (1977) *Outline of a Theory of Practice*, Cambridge: Cambridge University Press.
Carsten, Janet (1989) 'Cooking money: gender and the symbolic transformation of means of exchange in a Malay fishing community', in J. Parry and M. Bloch (eds), *Money and the Morality of Exchange*, Cambridge: Cambridge University Press.
Clifford, J. and Marcus, G.E. (1986) *Writing Culture: The Poetics and Politics of Ethnography*, Berkeley and Los Angeles: University of California Press.
Dube, Leela, Leacock, Eleanor and Ardener, Shirley (1986) (eds) *Visibility and Power*, Delhi: Oxford University Press.
Firth, Raymond (1966) *Malay Fishermen*, 2nd edn, London: Routledge & Kegan Paul.
Firth, Rosemary (1966) *Housekeeping among Malay Peasants*, 2nd edn, New York: Humanities Press.
Fiske, John (1982) *Introduction to Communication Studies*, London and New York: Methuen & Co Ltd.
Goody, Jack (1958) (ed.) *The Developmental Cycle in Domestic Groups*, Cambridge: Cambridge University Press.
Hastrup, Kirsten (1988) 'Sandhed og synlighed', in Kirsten Hastrup and Kirsten Ramløv (eds), *Feltarbejde. Oplevelse og metode i etnografien*, Denmark: Akademisk Forlag.
Kuhn, T.S. (1970) *The Structure of Scientific Revolutions*, Chicago: University of Chicago Press.
Lind, Anne (1984) 'Mødre og dagmammaer', in Ingrid Rudie (ed.), *Myks tart, hard landing*, Oslo: Universitetsforlaget.
Melhuus, Marit and Borchgrevink, Tordis (1984) 'Husarbeid. Tidsbinding av kvinner', in Ingrid Rudie (ed.), *Myks tart, hard landing*, Oslo: Universitetsforlaget.

Moore, Henrietta (1988) *Feminism and Anthropology*, Cambridge: Polity Press.

Ortner, Sherry B. (1984) 'Theory in anthropology since the sixties', *Comparative Studies in Society and History* 26(1): 126–66.

Rosaldo, Renato (1989) *Culture and Truth: The Remaking of Social Analysis*, Boston: Beacon Press.

Rudie, Ingrid (1971) 'Between market and neighbourhood', Unpublished manuscript, 330 pp.

—— (1983) 'Women in Malaysia; economic autonomy, ritual segregation and some future possibilities', in Bo Utas (ed.), *Women in Islamic Societies*. Scandinavian Institute of Asian Studies.

—— (1985) Research Proposal, unpublished, 10 pp.

—— (forthcoming) *Visible Women in East Coast Malay Society*, Oslo: Scandinavian Universities Press.

Sperber, Dan (1975) *Rethinking Symbolism*, Cambridge: Cambridge University Press.

Strathern, Marilyn (1987) 'An awkward relationship: The case of feminism and anthropology', *Signs* 12(2): 276–92.

—— (1988) *The Gender of the Gift*, Berkeley, CA: University of California Press.

Wadel, Cato (1977) 'Hva er arbeid?' *Tidsskrift for samfunnsforskning* 18: 387–411.

7 Among Khmer and Vietnamese refugee women in Thailand
No safe place*

Lisa Moore

REFUGEE CAMPS: SERVING WOMEN

As I ate lunch one day in the market-place at one of Thailand's largest camps for Khmers seeking asylum, a little boy went from table to table asking for food. An old woman scolded him and smiled at me in embarrassment. Beside us sacks of rice stamped UNBRO (United Nations Border Relief Organisation) were being sold to Thai traders. Far from UN conferences and relief agency brochures, corruption and its consequences stood side by side in broad daylight. With the consent, or at least the indifference of the UN, those who had escaped famine and war in Cambodia found asylum at the price of exploitation. The Coalition Government of Democratic Kampuchea uses the hundreds of thousands of Khmers fleeing danger as a power base for their war against the Phnom Penh government.

How had such a situation developed? Ten years ago when famine and war drove Khmers into Thailand, they were all equally powerless. The first people to come to the camps had been completely unorganised and strangers to one another. Amidst the confusion and din of unanswered needs, the voices of those who could command armies were the loudest and the easiest to identify. Groups were designated from without as representative of various political and military interests, given power and legitimised – in particular by China, the United States and Thailand. The complicated web of alliances trapped thousands in a society temporarily strung between Thailand and Cambodia.

The majority of the people in the camps are women and children; their political agenda is survival and stability. Yet their voices have gone unheard. Ten years after Khmers poured across the border into Thailand, the temporary shelters have become permanently temporary, lending the resistance forces who administer the camps a certain legitimacy. Yet the aid given to the resistance forces supports the war, ensuring that the return of the mass of the people to Cambodia will be impossible.

The people in the camps create a life for themselves through a blend of dependency on foreign aid, self-made opportunities impossible under other circumstances, and waiting: waiting for the war to end, waiting to return home, waiting to begin new lives. An organisation called the Khmer Women's

Association provides much-needed support and opportunities. With funds from UNBRO and the COERR (Catholic Office for Emergency Relief and Refugees) the Khmer Women's Association sponsors primary and literacy education, day care and skills training programmes. At a weaving factory, women are trained to make Khmer scarves and sarongs on hand-operated looms. The women are paid in kind and their products are distributed throughout the camp. Day care for all children below school age is also provided free, and staffed by women being trained and paid in kind. Although these programmes were not self-supporting, and could not be replicated without similar quantities of foreign aid, the women involved were learning valuable skills for their eventual repatriation.

However, when the camps were formed, repatriation was not an immediate option. The Vietnamese-installed Phnom Penh government was so abhorrent to donor nations such as the United States and China that they were willing to fund anyone opposed to the Vietnamese. The donor nations scrambled to find or fabricate an anti-Vietnamese force. In their impatience to actualise foreign policy objectives, donor nations funnelled aid through Khmer resistance forces. Groups such as the Khmer Women's Association with long-term goals of rebuilding and recovering their society were not considered significant and not united. Legitimacy was given to men who could command troops. Had the women, who comprise the majority of adult camp inhabitants, demanded and been given priority for their value of stability, perhaps the situation would have been different. Now the camps and the war are intimately intertwined, the end of one meaning the death of the other. Although the people in the camp are civilians, most have relatives in the army. Therefore, it is almost impossible to separate the goals and needs of each. If in the beginning legitimacy had been demanded by and given to the voices that wanted to live in peace, what would have been the results?

DISCOVERY OF COMMUNITY

Perhaps those voices felt too insignificant in their vulnerability. When I began my research, I tended to dismiss my own vulnerability as a single woman as something that hindered me from accomplishing what I wanted. I wanted to discover how Khmer refugees had survived and what they wished to preserve of their past. It became clear that the camps themselves shape refugees' lives as much as their past and hopes for the future. Fearful of violent crimes, official corruption and nearby war, refugee women struggle to provide stability for themselves and their families. I discovered that refugee women's fears dictate their priorities and guide their choices, just as vulnerability plays a role in shaping my goals and how I can fulfil them. Concerns for personal safety and stability traditionally have little relevance to serious research or long-term geopolitical goals. Yet, if personal threats and individual needs are shared by a community, then it is the community itself which is threatened and in need, and which is shaped by these threats and needs.

The camps are really a crossroads for a number of communities. The

English as a Second Language Class for Save the Children, Phanat Nikom Holding
Camp, Chonburi, Thailand, December 1989.

community that works with refugees is closed and protective of information. The
common language is often convoluted and policies are contradictory. There is
little co-ordination; the system consists of individuals and individual organisations making isolated decisions to help as best as they can. The result is a mess.
However, the only way to obtain access to the camps is somehow to be aligned
with the system. I chose to volunteer for a relief agency because organisations
can obtain passes for volunteers much more easily than can individual
researchers. I felt it was important for me, and for what I wanted to discover, to
establish a relationship that involved both giving and receiving. Furthermore,
volunteering gave me an easily recognisable function and satisfied my need for
an identity beyond that of researcher.

Because relief workers are not allowed in the camp at night, I did not live with
the refugees. Faced with two different realities – that of a refugee camp and a
Thai town – I alternately felt aligned with and alienated from Thai culture. The
prevalence and general acceptance of the sex industry informed all my perceptions of Thailand. The glitzy Bangkok bars offering nude dancing women to
whoever will pay are slightly more glamorous versions of the houses of prostitution that are found throughout Thailand. It is socially acceptable, even
expected, for both single and married men to engage prostitutes. In order to
support this lucrative industry, prospective buyers search poor villages for
families who are willing to sell their daughters for a flat fee. Once bought, a
woman can expect to be displayed behind glass with a number around her neck,

or to serve drinks, while prospective customers compare shapes. Every so often a daring government official will burst in on a particularly brutal establishment and save five or six women from their miserable lives. This allows good citizens to shake their heads in disgust and be thankful that justice is done. Perhaps I did not see the complexity involved. I was not able to compartmentalise the sex industry as involving only a segment of the population. The portrayal of women as pleasure-seeking devices seemed to drown out other messages. I chose to become more engulfed in refugee culture, thereby denying the impact of those messages on me personally.

More than anything, I yearned for a woman friend to talk with, someone with whom I did not have to be ashamed of my fears. Until I was completely alone, I did not realise the extent to which I depended on the close confidence of others, even when acting independently. At first I considered this feeling to be sub-versive, anti-feminist. Yet it was when I did have the support of other women that I was the most grounded and able to work the most steadily. When able to share reflections, I could see more and see further. When alone, I was too busy convincing myself I was strong and capable to examine the images that threatened me.

Together with a friend, I found we could face our adversaries in the open. I no longer averted my eyes from the seductively posed women who stared from posters in almost every Thai establishment. When I could see the respect and assurance in a real, live woman's face, the images became impotent and ridiculous. For a moment, a community of two was able to topple a carefully constructed framework of reality. Of course we never really toppled anything; simply saw a different framing.

Feminism, which I had discovered fairly recently, taught me to recognise women's issues as central and multifaceted, not marginal and unidimensional. In contrast, my liberal background had taught me that success and failure are the complete responsibility of the individual. Part of me still believes my liberal education, and true or not, it does give me courage, but I found its explanations inadequate. In undertaking research for a performance on gender and creation myths in 1989, I read authors such as Merlin Stone (1976) and Betty Friedan (1963). In the process, I began to recognise that our society chooses to highlight aspects of our heritage which define women as secondary. If not seen through, the weight of such a heritage can crush the strongest women. Seeing how refugee women depend on one another for strength, I became increasingly aware of the need for community among women.

CAMPS ON THE THAI–CAMBODIAN BORDER

I had the opportunity to interact with two groups of refugees, each facing different challenging environments. Those in Phanat Nikom Camp are officially recognised as refugees and are waiting to be resettled in third countries. Those in the UNBRO camps along the Thai–Cambodian border do not qualify as refugees. Instead, they are classified as 'displaced persons' and are allowed to stay in Thai territory until the conditions inside Cambodia improve sufficiently for their safe return. The Thai government refuses to allow Khmers on the border to be recognised as refugees because they fear more Cambodians will be lured across the border by the chance to be resettled. Furthermore, the guerrillas opposed to the Phnom Penh government use the camps on the border as a power base, thus providing a buffer between Thailand and the potentially hostile Vietnamese-backed Cambodian government.

Although I was interested in learning more about the processing of refugees for resettlement that occurs in Phanat Camp, I was anxious to be in the thick of Khmer life, not where people were counting the hours until their futures would begin to unfold in a new country. With impatience as my guide I set off for Aranyaprathet, a border town near the UNBRO camps. As I waited for the train, a very old woman started an animated conversation with me. I gathered that she wanted to know where I was going. I slowly repeated each syllable of A-ran-ya-pra-thet until she laughed and corrected my pronunciation. From then on she was my travelling companion during the five-hour ride to the border town. She saved a seat for me and told me the names of the towns we passed. As the old woman prepared her betelnut, I watched the rice fields and clusters of houses pass by. I was aware that I was leaving behind everything that had become familiar to me. Struggling not to sink into melodrama, I read about the fighting in Cambodia in *Time* magazine. How different to read about war when it is so close, I thought. Swallowing my apprehension, I reminded myself of the extensive evacuation plan for voluntary staff in border areas.

I stayed in Aranyaprathet for a tense few days, meeting sporadically with an old French priest from COERR and wandering around the streets of downtown Aranyaprathet. The town seemed to operate on a degree of tension that just barely allowed it to function. Or perhaps it was my own nervous energy that filtered everything I saw. During the evening I saw flashes in the sky. I tried to convince myself it was lightning, but was too afraid to ask and find out it was not. I began to realise how little I knew about the lives of refugees. I had read many books and articles before coming but none of them mentioned if shelling lights up the sky, and if so from what distance it can be seen.

The fact that not far from where I was, people were killing and being killed chilled me to my bones. I had anticipated culture shock and language problems, but this I had not. Sitting in the open-air lounge of my hotel so as not to be alone in my oversized bed in my oversized room, I chatted briefly with an American reporter from Cambridge, Massachusetts, who was dressed in black. When two other reporters entered I was introduced and promptly ignored as they discussed the best vantage points to get shots of shelling and the importance of sharp images in 'selling' television programmes. I slunk away to my room and began to wonder what I was doing here. I was repulsed and sickened by the talk and eagerness of those men. Had their excitement been linked to a desire for the world to know what is going on, they would not have appeared so alien to me. I felt terribly innocent and terribly small. Perhaps those men had created a bravado to protect them from the unease they felt inside. Yet now it seemed they were dead inside and all that was living was their bravado. Ashamed of my fear and vulnerability, I shivered to think the only alternative to the fear was an empty display of callousness. Yet the reporters were somewhat like me, they had chosen to come and see someone else's hell. Had I not come with as little or as much understanding of what those images meant to the people who lived them?

PHANAT NIKOM HOLDING CAMP

Deciding to learn more about the lives of refugees in a more hopeful, less dangerous setting, I opted to move to Phanat Nikom, a town far from the border surrounded by rice fields and water buffalo. The camp, located about half an hour's drive from the town, houses Khmer, Hmong, Lao, Mien and Vietnamese refugees. Having already been recognised as legitimate refugees, they remain in Phanat Nikom Camp waiting to be resettled.

For my first day in the camp, a Khmer refugee named Ming guided me through the housing complexes, offices and markets. I felt as if I was swimming in the thick, hot air – one sharp image became blurred as another came into focus, until I felt as if I had lost my ability to focus at all. I wondered how so many contradictory thoughts and feelings could exist in one person. I felt out of breath, as if the world was opening up before me. I had to blink because it was too much for me to see at once. I wanted to run and chase away the thoughts that whirled in my head, and the inexplicable emotions that gathered in my chest and crept up my throat. As Ming told me the story of his life in Cambodia and of his escape, I needed all my strength to keep from scattering into a thousand pieces. Later I would be able to sort through the images and calmly observe the structure of the camp, but on that day I gulped down everything without discriminating.

REFUGEE WOMEN IN THE CLASSROOM

As part of my commitment as a volunteer, I taught English as a second language to Khmer Krom refugees. Khmer Krom are ethnic Khmers from the southern part of Vietnam, an area that was once part of Cambodia. However, some people who qualify for the classification of Khmer Krom were born in Cambodia and moved to Vietnam. Furthermore, there are some Khmers who never lived in Vietnam but who claimed to be Khmer Krom in order to be eligible for refugee status. I cannot blame people for trying to manipulate a system that is clearly so arbitrary in so many cases. Determinations of people's lives often hinge on distinctions that are difficult to determine. One of my students said, 'In Vietnam they call me Khmer; in Cambodia they call me Vietnamese.' Though said laughingly, in a place where so much depends on labels it was hardly a joke.

I felt slightly unnatural in the position of teacher, which actually became my name as well as position. Although the majority of the students were older than me, they stood up to respond to questions as if I were a nun and they were Catholic grade-school students. Though inwardly I cringed, I tried to accept the role I was given; to do otherwise would seem disrespectful to the process of learning which they held in such high regard.

The female students almost never volunteered to answer a question in class, and when called upon usually only replied in a whisper. After class I would discover that they were much further advanced in their speaking skills than I could determine from class. Outside the school, female students would often link arms with me and, without hesitation, ask questions in English about my life. Their reluctance to speak in class regardless of their ability was very familiar to me. My own classroom experiences in the United States were very similar despite vastly different cultures. I wished we could disregard the familiar barriers and communicate in the classroom without fear. Yet, their anxiety was partially fostered by real, immediate dangers of which I had no experience.

Judging from my own fear of being left behind with MOI (Ministry of the Interior) officers when the last bus left from camp, I guessed the extent of their unease. My friend, similarly concerned about the insecurity of the women in Section C, agreed that together we develop an all-women's class where the students could feel more at ease and possibly be encouraged to speak in class. We thought that if the students felt more comfortable speaking individually they would feel stronger. Our instinct was that, as women, we all shared something basic that would allow for greater communication than was possible in a traditional classroom. Our course-work objectives were to teach English for medical problems and emergencies while encouraging class participation. If we made any progress toward our objectives during the short time we ran the course, I did not notice. It would have been unrealistic to expect one course to achieve all we had hoped. A class could not make the nights free of danger or the days free of worry and anticipation.

Once I asked my students to come up with problems so that the rest of the class could practise using the structure 'If I were you, I would . . . '. One student said, 'I have been rejected by all the delegations [of resettlement countries]. What would you do if you were me?' Some of the students offered suggestions like go back to Vietnam, or re-apply to the delegations for more interviews. The student continued to address the question to me even though I had no answer. Although we all laughed, the question was partly in earnest and the laughter was partly to hide the seriousness of the question. When one student said, 'The US Embassy is more powerful than God', many of the other students agreed.

Later, at a teacher training session, I learned that a refugee may apply several times for resettlement in a third country and may be accepted under one programme after having been rejected by others. However, by then it was too late to answer the question. Furthermore, those words would just have been echoes of a policy that must seem empty after years of waiting. The Thai government and UN officials have continually stated that those who have been waiting in Phanat Nikom Camp will be resettled. Nevertheless, many have been repeatedly rejected by third countries. The threat of possible deportation weighs heavily in the minds of those who have not yet been accepted.

GROUPS WITHIN PHANAT NIKOM CAMP

Thinking that I somehow had an 'in' with the American Embassy, many refugees would ask what was holding up their case; because I am white, they assumed I had some power. And, in a way, I did have power, because when I asked a question I would usually receive a reply. When hundreds of refugees asked the same question, they were brushed aside. Sometimes the difference in status was embarrassingly apparent. One morning I came into camp early to tape some Khmer music. The musicians had been asked to leave their usual rehearsal place. The solution was clear to everyone but me; I would simply ask the librarian if we could use an empty room. I explained that since I had no connection with the organisation running the library, it would be better if a musician asked. After all, I said, the library is for refugees, not me. In fact, the librarian only spoke to me and, without asking who I was, agreed to let us use the space provided that I stay.

However, I was confined in the same system they were and just as powerless within that system. Although I had no 'in' with the American Embassy, as a US citizen the power I have over my own destiny is immense. My freedom to live where I want and pursue work or education where I please must seem stunning to refugees fleeing repressive governments and confined in prison-like camps.

Yet, they did not know the different reality I faced when I left the camp to go home. In the evening my bicycle lock became my defensive weapon as I listened apprehensively for motor cycles, hoping that I would not be the next victim of an attack against white women. The tension between local Thais and the camp periodically erupted as aggression against white female relief workers. There had been reports of women being followed and verbally harassed or threatened by men on motor cycles. A woman with whom I worked had been knocked off her bicycle and beaten by a strange man who jumped out of some bushes near her home. When the injured woman mentioned the incident at a staff meeting, she was told she must be unlucky because she had been attacked once before.

Bad luck does not explain why only white women were threatened. Violence against women happens everywhere, yet the very ordinariness of it is demeaning. All women can be intimidated by the threat of physical violence and the fear of sexual assault, but the pattern of attacks directed against white women suggests a reaction against the power foreigners have in their community. By attacking white women, local men assert their power over women and render the white men impotent by proving they are incapable of protecting the women.

To refugees I represented something greater than a frightened individual. With access to a language and a way of life that would soon be theirs, foreign relief workers like myself acted as a bridge between the two worlds. Realising that I was being watched and studied as much as I was watching and studying, I reflected on how most positively to interact with the refugee community. Because the refugees come from varying backgrounds, the community is not cohesive, being often divided along ethnic lines. Unlike the other ethnic groups who mix freely, people from Vietnam are separated from the rest by tall corrugated-metal walls. The Thai rationale for the different treatment is that the

Vietnamese cause more crime and unrest. There is some truth to the Thai perspective, considering that the camp's prison houses a far higher proportion of Vietnamese than those from other ethnic groups. Yet the conclusion that Vietnamese are more violent is simply racist. More likely, the explanation is a combination of elements: the higher proportion of single men, the evident animosity between Vietnamese refugees and Thai administering authorities, and the greater uncertainty involved in Vietnamese cases.

Whereas people from Cambodia and Laos had been transferred to Phanat Nikom after having been accepted for resettlement by a third country, people from Vietnam are in the process of applying and interviewing for resettlement. Also, most people from Laos and Cambodia crossed into Thailand overland, usually travelling together with families or groups, while those escaping Vietnam usually travelled alone because of the high cost and greater danger of leaving by boat or crossing through Cambodia. Considering that the majority of refugees from Vietnam are young single men without the stability of traditional family or community structures and with uncertain futures, the higher incidence of violence seems predictable.

By day, Section C, the area for people from Vietnam, would be calm. Sometimes in the afternoon I would watch the young men playing soccer, children climbing makeshift jungle-gyms, and people carrying buckets of water from the large metal boxes to their homes. At these times the community seemed at peace, and in some way to be working, but then as I left I would be struck again by the sight of the barbed wire fence that surrounds the camp, keeping the refugees penned in like animals, and, even more disturbing, the tall metal walls of the Vietnamese section where those inside cannot even see beyond the wall that encloses them.

At night all the pent-up anger and frustration came out into the open. There had been several rumours of prostitution and rape involving Thai MOI soldiers who guarded the camp. Often I heard stories from co-workers who were involved in counselling or medical clinics. At a women's discussion group on sexual harassment, a few women told stories of unnamed friends who had been raped. In private conversations women would also tell stories about women they knew who had been raped or involved in prostitution. The relatively small number of women in Section C were in a very vulnerable position, particularly the young single women and the women with children. Rape and violent crimes were common. These events belonged to the night, when voluntary staff go home and only MOI soldiers remained to keep the peace or partake in the crimes. Despite the unmistakable intensity of people in Section C, in the morning, it seemed impossible that such rage could erupt.

One morning, in the restaurant where I drank my morning coffee, I was alone long enough to record the impressions that had by then become background. I was far from inconspicuous, usually being the only white person and one of the few women. Most days one of the men would start a conversation with me about the United States but I never became accustomed to the celebrity status given me due to my ability to speak fluent English. It set me apart as someone with whom it was possible to bridge the socially acceptable distances between men and women.

With the distance momentarily restored, I observed that the restaurant is quite dirty. The tables are covered with bright yellow paint that is partially chipped away and partially obscured by sticky black grime. The floor is littered with old tissues and cigarette buts. There are no lights and only one ceiling fan that works. The rafters that support the roof are draped with cobwebs. Flies buzz around the cases of empty soda bottles. Cigarette smoke fills the air. All the while the syrupy voice of a male Vietnamese singer drowns out all other noises.

Perhaps it is best that the music is so loud; after a while people must run out of things to say to one another. With families back in Vietnam or no families at all, little attempt is made to create a community, much less respect the values of a community. They seem to accept the disarray and carelessness of the restaurant as an affirmation of their current lives. Outside a sense of unease lingers in the air. Unlike the sections for the other ethnic groups where children chase trucks carrying volunteer staff and yell in one breath 'hellohowareyouI'mfinethankyou', and where groups of people linger in the shade, or stroll around with no apparent aim, there are very few children in Section C, and people seem to be either driven from place to place or to pace restlessly. People either sit alone in their houses on window frames or congregate around the open-air basketball court, the only common space. Throughout the day, names are called over the speaker system announcing those wanted for interviews. Though they are constructed of the same materials as the buildings in the other areas of the camp, those in Section C look different. Even the way the sun beats down on the main courtyard seems harsher. There is no shelter and few trees. Part of the difference can be explained by the overcrowding in Section C, yet the severity of the atmosphere seems to reflect the way people move and the lines on their faces.

LOOKING BACK

At times I was proud to be one of a group of women who recognised a common goal and a strength in being together. I wonder if I was making a discovery the other women knew all along, and if I was wrongly applying the value of American individualism to women who knew their strength lies in unity.

Although I come from a very different society and have countless more resources available to me, there was a basic set of priorities and sense of myself as a woman that I shared with the women I met. Now that I am back in the United States, I am trying to make sense of the past year. Perhaps if as women we could see a commonality in personal struggles and react as a community rather than as threatened individuals, the shape of the societies we mould would be different. I am still searching for a balance between individuality and the sense of belonging to a larger community.

Within the community I found among refugee women, I was very unusual in that I made choices to leave my home and lead a life many refugee women could not imagine. Sometimes the difference created barriers, but when we could communicate despite our differences, there was joy in discovering what we shared. The daily conversations and gradual getting to know people and understand their lives filled my days. Though life in the camps is very difficult, the day-to-day reality of developing human connections and growing because of them is as important there as where I grew up. I am not sure how my time in Thailand will affect the rest of my life, but I am not likely to forget the intensity of recognising the link between myself and other women.

ACKNOWLEDGEMENTS

* I gratefully acknowledge the support of the Watson Foundation which funded my fieldwork in Thailand. In writing this article, I have drawn on the CCSDPT (1986) and COERR (1989) annual reports and information from the 1989 Annual Conference on Indochinese Displaced Persons in Thailand sponsored by CCSDPT for background information. I thank Diane Bell, Robert Fisher, Francie Mantak, my family and especially my mother, Eleanor Moore, for critical comments on the drafts, but my greatest debt is to the women with whom I worked.

REFERENCES

CCSDPT (Committee for Coordination of Services to Displaced Persons in Thailand) (1986) *Refugee Services Handbook*.
COERR (Catholic Office for Emergency Relief and Refugees) (1989) *Report No. 14 on Refugee Aid Work and Emergency Activities*.
Friedan, Betty (1963*) The Feminine Mystique*, Ringwood: Penguin.
Stone, Merlin (1976) *When God was a Woman*, New York: Harvest/Harcourt Brace Jovanovich Books.

8 Breaching the wall of difference
Fieldwork and a personal journey to Srivaikuntam, Tamilnadu*

Kamala Ganesh

PREAMBLE: MY FIELDS AND MYSELF

The field: a mud-walled fort

I first heard of the Kottai Pillaimar ('Fort Pillais') through an article in a Tamil magazine. It said that because of personal rivalries and political cleavages within the fort of Srivaikuntam, some of the Pillai families had decided to leave and settle down in adjoining Tirunelveli town. This was a historic event, said the article, since the Kottai Pillaimar lived, as was well known throughout Tamilnadu, in a mud-walled fortress into which no outside male could enter, not even government functionaries nor even the police. The women of this sub-caste could not come out of the fort; they had not done so for centuries. The Kottai Pillaimar were strictly endogamous; so far, they had married only within families living inside the fort, who numbered fewer than 100 individuals. The article sounded as though the sub-caste had been written about quite often, and that everyone should have heard about them.

I was absolutely fascinated. In an instant, the Kottai Pillaimar (henceforth KP) became for me the classic 'other'. I saw the KP women as completely different from what I was: educated, metropolitan, modern and, by implication, mobile and exercising options. Though a Tamil-speaking Brahmin, I had never spent much time in Tamilnadu. Except for brief vacations at my grandparents' home, I was unfamiliar with the rural milieu. My 'convent' education and upbringing in big cities in Northern India had made me a stranger to the intricacies of Tamil life and living, except for a selective and limited version of speech, food and rituals which were part of home life, crammed in between conversation, reading and thinking in English. The KP were Vellalas, a high-ranking caste of non-Brahmin land-holders, about whom I had no information. They lived in Tirunelveli district, at the virtual tip of the peninsula. I had never visited the place, nor had any friends there. I was only vaguely familiar with the empirical situation of caste in Tamilnadu, and I had made no linkage between caste ranking and women's seclusion. A mud fortress with high walls, and the women in strict purdah: it sounded most atypical of Tamilnadu. It was more like medieval Rajputana, the age of battle, chivalry and sati. My curiosity was aroused.

Kamala Ganesh with informants.

Even before I set foot in the fort, I was upset by the shrillness of the reportage on the KP. There was a lot of it, including an article in the *New York Times* (8 November 1971) under the headline 'Women of Hindu sect in India live out their lives behind wall of twenty-acre compound'. The articles generally expressed horror at the lack of electricity, running water and women's liberation, at the ignorance of the women about the outside world, the hold of tradition and the anachronism of it all. The same tone was echoed by curious friends, who expected something different, unique. Endogamy in such a tiny group raised fantastic questions of identical-looking females (why not males?), of deformities and hereditary illnesses. Almost everyone I met in Tirunelveli repeated the story of the little KP girl who had inadvertently strayed out of the fort while playing and was killed on the spot by a male kinsman (a story angrily denied by the KP). I also had to contend with my own feelings, and with queries about what I proposed to do by way of intervention, typified by the friend who used to ask me every time I came home for a break between periods of fieldwork, 'Are you at least taking a crowbar with you this time to break down those walls?'

At the time I started researching the KP, I had done a certain amount of reading in social anthropology in preparation for a degree in sociology. My imagination was fired by the classic heroes of anthropology, who travelled to remote places in order to document the strange and the exotic. The mystique remained intact, even though looking at the ordinary, and at everyday life in one's own culture, was an increasingly accepted part of the discipline.

Myself

When I started researching the KP in the late seventies, I had had some exposure to western feminist writing and was looking critically at the givens of my own life. As a young girl, I had observed the rules of space and time that were part of the family culture of a moderately conservative family with a strong government service and professional orientation. The atmosphere in which I grew up was a combination of cosmopolitan approach to language, reading and friendships, with an upper-caste cum Victorian stress on proper feminine behaviour, the post-social reform Indian's zeal for ritual as identity, with a Brahminical emphasis on learning (typically mathematics and classical language), which, however, gave little space to pursue the social outcomes of learning, in which respect anthropology was a strange, vaguely disquieting creature.

I had married early and had a small child. A girlhood that was relatively open to 'modern' ideas made me chafe at the expectations in traditional social arrangements, but I did not respond to the more radical elements of campus politics. Uppermost in my mind, in terms of feminism, were the need to find space and expression within marriage, and the difficulties in reconciling this with a career, though I had begun to feel that the issues were far more broad and basic.

In this respect, I had little rapport with my immediate environment. It seemed to me that my family, close friends and colleagues had limited ideas about and interest in the complexity of gender issues. Any tentative discussion would be shot down with first-principle arguments 'for' or 'against'. The entire exercise seemed to get converted onto a highly personal and specific level. I also had psychological barriers against being articulate and holding my ground with men and seniors, and was completely silent or defensive about the issues that troubled me the most, and about which I was constantly thinking. My reading, at that time, was not filtered through the personal experience of having to fight in a man's world. A reasonably secure and comfortable life was assured, unless one chose to make a fuss about what were considered to be 'after all, symbolic issues'. I took at face value all that I read, and felt very sorry for myself for having been manipulated into all kinds of oppressive situations.

The 'other field': academia

Fieldwork was not only a central phase in my research, it was a crucial experience personally. But my reference point remained the larger society to which I had to get back in order (literally) to 'defend' my thesis – to my supervisor, referees, peers and to the university structure in general. With friends and kin, there was the added burden of having to defend the credentials of anthropology and academic work itself!

My exposure to social anthropology was in the context of a department with a predominantly sociological orientation, a scenario not uncommon in India. Furthermore, at that particular time, the dominant trend was not in favour of narrow caste and village studies, but there was much emphasis on doing macro-studies, preferably on agrarian structure. I was quite apologetic about studying a 'museum piece'. What could be the significance of a detailed study of a quaint, microscopic community on its way out? Furthermore, to focus on women, and – unpardonable *faux pas* – elite women at that: I was worried that the work would be dismissed as trivial, another of those women writing on the 'woman question', as it was called.

THE RESEARCH

The fort and its history

Thus very much on the defensive, I decided that mine would not be another 'status of women' study. I would cast my net wide, pitch my canvas broad. Why did the KP live in mud forts? I followed up some casual remarks about Poligar eighteenth-century military fortifications by people I met in Srivaikuntam and hunted out a big chunk of correspondence in the state archives to build a context. How could such a tiny community survive endogamously? I collected genealogies. Who married whom was a pretty confusing question. Given the rule of preferential cross-cousin and uncle–niece marriage, most couples were related to each other in more than one way. I scanned the literature on in-breeding so as to build a context.

How could the fort be physically maintained if outsiders could not enter? When I came to know about the families permitted entry (FPE), I made detailed calculations on the number of households, average income, conditions of employment, migration rates and so on and compared them with non-FPE families of the same caste to evaluate how working for the KP had affected their professional status. The KP were wealthy landholders who owned or controlled land in six villages around Srivaikuntam. I probed in detail their relationship with their tenants and agricultural workers. How old was the fort? I roped in the staff of the state Department of Archaeology to make rubbings of the inscriptions in the fort's temple, and to date the bronzes in it. I collected and read palm-leaf manuscripts of KP's land transactions more than two centuries old. I traced out, with some effort, the original palm-leaf manuscript which contained the text of an oral recitation of endowments made to Srivaikuntam's major Siva temple (the list included several KP names). Portions of the text, I discovered, were repeated on the walls of the same temple in inscriptions in the fifteenth century AD. I collected the texts of several popular folk ballads in the region, some of which had references to the KP.

How did the fort escape the attention of the British government? As I discovered, it did not. In the voluminous archival records of the Tinnevelly district collectorate and the Board of Revenue, Madras Presidency, the KP suddenly came to life, vigorously pursuing their life-style, petitioning, negotiating and ultimately establishing their rights to the fort.

Undoubtedly my broad-based interest in the KP gave me interesting insights and rich textural understanding of the local scenario. But the motive was to quantify and legitimise. I was keen on establishing structure and patterns – the grammar – and diffident about handling the more fragile area of relationships and sentiments. The mixed English–Tamil narrative of my fieldnotes with its per-sonalised anecdotes, its immediacies and hesitations, its apprehensions and its grey, had to be made into a well-argued, documented, substantiated and defended thesis. But, all the while, my mind and heart were with the women.

I have written this preamble because, in doing fieldwork among the KP, I did not consciously make a selection of theme, location and community on any grounds of academic relevance or practical considerations of funding, safety, accessibility, convenience or representativeness. The usual question of whether I should work in my own culture or a different one did not arise. In fact, I did not even have any specific plans for working for a PhD. It would seem that I stumbled serendipitously on to the KP!

In this chapter, I am concerned with two processes in the field: first, how my gender affected fieldwork – the hassles, the limits, the advantages, the mechanics; secondly, the way in which my feelings and ideas about the structure and articulation of gender differentiation and its implications for power were tossed about in the field, both in a personal and academic sense. Slowly, the 'otherness' of the KP women became more diffuse. At some point I could no longer clearly see the boundary between 'us' and 'them'. All the while, with my inner life being thus churned up, fieldwork and writing-up were going on in the standard manner. I was trying to find out various things about the KP and their fort, their social organisation, institutions, history and relationships. I was looking into the seclusion of women as one among many features of interest and significance.[1]

A WOMAN IN THE FIELD: CASTE, GENDER AND THE ETHNOGRAPHER

The most significant aspects of being a woman in Srivaikuntam[2] had to do with age, marital status and social status, and how far one was perceived as an outsider.[3] In my case, the image was that of an educated, urban, upper-caste woman.

I cannot now recollect at what point my being a Brahmin was clear to the people with whom I worked. I suspect that my vocabulary must have given them a clue pretty early on.[4] As elsewhere in India, caste in Tamilnadu is a visible feature of social stratification at several levels. In addition, Brahminical culture is particularly distinct and influential here, a factor that has contributed to the emergence of vocal and sometimes radical anti-upper-caste movements, which have led to some of the earliest expressions of regionally and linguistically based separatist politics in the country. The KP themselves were very conscious of their caste status and identity as Vellala Pillaimar. I cannot imagine their not taking steps to find out mine. I have argued elsewhere (Ganesh 1982) that KP ideology (and Vellala ideology in general) can be seen as a combination of Brahminical and *kshatriya* (warrior) models (see also note 1). The KP's dominance and influence in the region, as well as its social compositon and economic profile, are typical of paddy-growing, river-valley regions in Tamilnadu.[5] The salience of social stratification and hierarchised interaction and the dilemma of the researcher about how to locate himself or herself in it is a recurring theme among anthropologists working in India.

I was constantly wondering in the field whether my preoccupation with caste ideology was an individual perception, influenced by my own background, or whether it was dictated by the field situation. I spoke at length to several KP men as well as (FPE) men. When they were explicitly asked about caste (as I did after two or three meetings) I noticed that some men, especially the younger ones, were not very comfortable. The general sentiment was that caste was a thing of the past, it was not relevant any more. But, quite contrarily, the language of caste was understood very well indeed; caste was a constant reference point not just in terms of ethnicity but as hierarchised interaction as well. The discomfort was at the concrete labelling, but the principles were operative at many levels, some not immediately apparent. Responses from the FPE to my questions about meat-eating, about goat sacrifice at the *amman* (village goddess) temple festivals, about the worship of *madans* or local semi-devil divinities, were always couched in highly ambivalent terms. Even though these were part of local culture, the more mobile and status-aspiring FPE were hesitant to admit to such practices. It seemed that, regardless of local practice, the referral values were upper-caste ones, and this had to do with more than my own background.

The KP would often describe their domestic habits, rules of interdining, periods of pollution and ceremonies as 'exactly as among Brahmins', but I could sense some reservations which they were too polite to express directly. The KP took great pride in their role as philanthropists, and Brahmin stinginess was the subject of some mockery.

As an upper-caste woman, there was a well-defined role model with a high positive value available to me. Both the people in the field and I were well aware of it. Conformity would ease the process of establishing myself in the field. The impression management did not involve much effort since I was very familiar with the expectations in several contexts at home. To start with, in matters of dress, it meant being modest and 'traditional', not 'modern' (sari, long sleeves, *bindi* mark on forehead, prominent *tali* – the necklace worn by married women – and so on). It meant a certain reticence on public occasions, and the use of a refined manner of speech. In interaction with men it meant a great deal of circumspection. One would avoid interviewing a man alone for a great length of time, and try to arrange meetings with several men present. One would avoid striking up extended casual conversation on the streets even with close male acquaintances.

Walking alone in the streets was all right, but one had to avoid the image of a frequent lone walker, and in any case, walking had to be done purposefully, showing a keenness to reach one's destination. Walking for the sake of looking around or stretching one's legs, which was my usual style, was not the best thing to do. I notice from my fieldnotes that after some weeks of such traversing, I started asking my research assistant, Bebi, to accompany me. If I had to go out after dusk, I would make it a point to find someone to go with. The question was less of safety than of image.

What I call the normative 'upper-caste woman' (usually referred to as 'from a good family', by which caste is implied) at some point merges into the 'good woman' image. This does not imply that women from low-status groups are normatively expected to behave differently; the 'good woman' is a generalised model, an ideal type. But deviations by upper-caste women would be subject to greater comment and speculation. A lone ('unprotected') upper-caste woman with the appropriate behaviour is more likely to be treated by men with respect. Women from the bottom of the hierarchy would doubly have to prove their 'goodness', and even so might be open to rough treatment. Another component of the image was that of 'protected' researcher. For one, I was married and a mother, which compensated for my relative youth. The other signal that I gave – 'educated, knowledgeable' – was not a function of caste, but the association was pretty strong. Formal education (of which knowledge of English is seen as an important part) is given high status throughout India. As the lady from the university, researching local history, I was treated with some deference by most. Among FPE, even very old men would be very deferential, address me as *'amma'* ('mother': a common mode of address to indicate respect, regardless of age), and not look at me directly. The few KP who were sceptical were polite about it.

Looking back on why I did not perceive my sexuality as a problematic issue, I think the public persona I projected (which was the only one that was culturally available to me) in effect played into the first of two stereotypes that my field subjects had been socialised into: to distinguish only between women who should be protected and those who could be mauled.

My friends and contacts in Tirunelveli had warned me against staying inside the fort: 'even if they cut you up and bury you, we will not be able to enter the fort and intervene'. I was taken aback by the drastic tone, but discovered that this was a common usage locally. The KP themselves did not seem comfortable with the idea of my staying in the fort. Eventually, I stayed as a paying guest in the house of an elderly couple: it was on one of the main streets parallel to the town's famous Vishnu temple, and less than ten minutes' walk from the fort. My host was working in the local steel-rolling mill owned by the brother of a friend of a friend. He also introduced me to the secretary of the local cooperative bank who functioned as my local host. The latter was a popular and respected figure in Srivaikuntam and knew several KP personally. Then, of course, I was 'protected' by the KP themselves since I had approached them to study their history and way of life. I was carrying letters to establish my bona fides from the district collector, the commissioner in charge of temple administration, from my university and sponsors. My husband had 'permitted' me to do research, my mother was looking after my child. Thus, armed with the insignia of protection from authorities, kith and kin, did I enter the field.

RESEARCHING MEN, RESEARCHING WOMEN

Playing such a role had its problems. I see on reading my notes that finding suitable space for interviewing men was an irritant. It was not feasible to call people to my room in my host's house.[6] Though the KP lived inside the fort, each family had built a house on the street just outside the fort. This was called the *cer* ('granary'). Some of the rooms were used to store grain. The *cer* were also used as an office by KP men to conduct transactions with FPE, accountants, tenants and labourers, and also to receive acquaintances and entertain friends. The men were rarely to be found in the fort, they were in their *cer* most of the time. In the first phase of fieldwork, my interviews were mainly with the KP. I would meet men in their homes or *cer*. They were curious but friendly, cooperative, even expansive. I was still a novelty. They looked upon my research with different degrees of seriousness. As a group, their style of interaction was not direct or confrontational; they were unfailingly courteous and helpful, but it was difficult to gauge their reaction to me. It took time and perseverance to impress upon them the validity and relevance of my work, though they knew I was in earnest.

Gradually, I started meeting others, mainly the FPE. Initially, introductions were given by the KP. This immediately made the FPE wary of me; I was identified with their patrons and employers. At different points, rumours were circulated that I had come from the government, (a) to investigate the possibility of unearthing treasures from the fort, (b) to help the KP's agricultural labourers acquire legal tenancies, or (c) to enquire into the prevalence of bonded labour. It was particularly difficult and time-consuming to get to know the KP's labourers who were from untouchable sub-castes. On their part, the KP were piqued and puzzled as to why I wanted to talk to all these people. What could they know that the KP had not told me? My explanation that I needed to understand their connections with other groups and institutions did not entirely convince them. Some of them were very unhappy when I talked to the FPE on the nature and conditions of their relationship with the KP. It was difficult to find a place to meet the FPE. Initially, they were asked to come to the *cer* by the KP, but they were understandably inhibited. I too felt awkward in the predominantly male environment of the *cer*, in the presence of business colleagues, cronies and hangers-on. Most of the FPE were voluble and cooperative when they turned up, but often they simply would not turn up at the fixed hour. I would wait, then go to the person concerned's house, only to find that he had gone out on business or personal work. After a while, I managed to borrow a room at the cooperative bank, where I could invite people for a chat. This worked better.

In all fairness, the pressure on me to conform to a particular image was not entirely external; some of it was self-generated. It would have been possible to have had a different life-style in the field, especially if one was an 'outsider', but I suspect I would have had to feel my way much more carefully. Conformity, in some ways, was an easy solution. The other side of the coin is of course the fact that it would have been impossible for a man to go into the fort, much less meet or talk to the women. Being a woman imposed some limits on free interaction with male informants. But one could, over time, and having kept up the externals of propriety, develop some depth in interaction. I also noticed that being a woman with a 'traditional' profile put people at ease. I was able to sustain the idea that I was doing academic research out of my own interest, that it might or might not have financial benefits for me, and that this did not reflect on my abilities or status.

The tenor and texture of my interaction with the KP women was quite different from that with the men. Initially, the women felt they had nothing interesting to tell me. When I persisted, they opened up, but still found it difficult to sustain more than staccato exchanges full of self-deprecation. But among the older women, beneath the overt reticence, there was a sense of confidence about the 'rightness' of their life-style. Gradually, with some of the women, I slipped into an easy relationship where we would have extended conversations on all kinds of topics. There was absolutely no problem of access. They were always at home and I was welcome to visit them as and when I liked.

The question of reciprocity bothered me.[7] I felt guilty about taking up so much time, but they did not seem to mind the intrusion. I would ask them the most intimate questions, but when they did the same (and there was a barrage of questions), I could not be equally frank and open. This added to my guilt. I tried to give small gifts and photographs that I took of them. But I felt I was really taking, not giving.

The KP women also wondered what I was getting out of the whole exercise. 'Well, at least a Ph.D.', I would joke, but they were not convinced. Why should anyone leave family and city comforts to spend weeks at a stretch wandering around the KP villages? None the less, once they had got the drift of the questions I asked, their responses were quick. They felt I was genuinely interested in what they had to say. I remembered the smallest things they told me and followed up next time. We were soon locked jointly in the enterprise of discovering their history. Reciprocity was not an issue any more.

THE KOTTAI WOMEN AND THEIR CONCERNS

The other side of seclusion was that even within the fort, there were degrees of restrictions. Prepubertal girls could go anywhere up to the gates, between puberty and marriage, girls were totally forbidden to go out of the house, married women could only visit one another's homes. The widow, like the unmarried girl, was completely secluded in her house – in fact, in one room for the first year of widowhood. Seclusion obviously had to do with sexually unharnessed phases of women's lives. It was emphasised more for upper-caste women, and articulated differentially towards different castes. The danger of female sexuality was expressed in the language of caste purity and the threat to it from women's inappropriate (out of caste) sexual unions/marriages (Ganesh 1985a).

The other striking aspect was that, though the whole edifice of KP ideology and their high status in the locality vitally depended on the women's seclusion, there was a very big gap between the 'secular' prospects and practices of the men and women. The men had links with all important local institutions and were aware of and conscious about exercising power. In contrast to private interviews where they could be informal, their public behaviour was highly ritualised and articulated the Vellala model very elaborately. They had successfully tried to convert their traditional elite status into a modern, secular one by getting involved in the panchayat, schools, charitable trusts and boards of local banks. They carved out a political role for themselves. They consciously excercised their *jajman* status *vis-à-vis* the FPE in private and public. The KP males had many friends and contacts outside; they were fairly well travelled. They were urbane, knowledgeable men of the world, skilled in interpersonal interaction.

For the women, on the other hand, status was a matter of hearsay. They did not know how to convert it to everyday power. Their behaviour with their servants and helpers was spontaneous, generous and unskilled. They were totally dependent on and vulnerable to them. Unused to being in heterogeneous groups, their first response to an outsider was to withdraw. Among themselves or with the few outside women who got to know them, they could be abrupt, and somewhat unskilled in conversational abilities and formal 'feminine' behaviour. Their extreme seclusion and the smallness of their social universe had even blunted the edges of power relations between women based on age and kinship. The women spoke with the distinct local accent and vocabulary, in what was known as 'peasant' speech, unlike the men, who could switch to different modes, including formal literary Tamil and even English fluently.

Though formal education for men has been stressed only in the last few decades, all were literate, and quite adept at handling their money, accounts and transactions. KP women rarely had to handle money; most of them had somewhat vague ideas about their wealth. Much of the leisure activities of the women were what may be termed religious: preparatory jobs of cleaning the domestic area of worship, stringing flowers, lighting lamps and so on. But, barring a few older women, they had little knowledge about the significance of their rituals, or their scriptural basis. The public religious role of the KP, as trustees of temples and givers of endowments and charities, was exclusively male. The worlds of the men and women were two separate worlds. The women were helpless in controlling their immediate environment.

And yet why did the KP women not articulate their problem as being due to seclusion? They had been asked this question by scores of curious visitors and journalists, and had obviously discussed it among themselves and taken a collective stand.There were no serious misgivings. They saw the seclusion as a given, as a custom; they saw the burden of the identity of their group as resting on their seclusion. It did involve some deprivation and hardship, but it also conferred status on the community. They saw themselves as bearers of the tradition of classical womanhood celebrated in myth and literature. In any case, they felt their lives were not so different from those of other upper-caste Vellala women who lived outside the fort. They read magazines and listened to battery-operated transistors. The men 'permitted' all their normal demands, and met all their needs. Maybe they could not visit the cinema or temple, but 'So many women living outside have heard and read about America, can everyone actually go there?'.

I was taken aback. Nor were they alone in this perception of the honour of the community being reflected in the exemplary behaviour of women. The KP men, the FPE and everyone else in Srivaikuntam expressed broadly similar sentiments.

There was a mystique surrounding the KP women: a suggestion that the severe seclusion gave them special spiritual powers like the legendary *satis*. Clearly, seclusion was not enforced at an obvious level. What was seen by me as total lack of power was in fact, paradoxically, considered by them as giving sacred power. Seclusion was definitely a function of high status in the traditional hierarchy, and in turn, this carried a whole lot of privileges, but privileges for whom? The women were unable to experience in concrete or specific ways the privileges of their status. They could not/did not know the exercise of power that accrued from rank, a rank that was in fact, crucially dependent on female seclusion. I tried hard to look for compensations: there was some security, protection from the harsh realities of working outside the house for a livelihood. The privileges were really for the males, but the point was that the women saw themselves as included in this packet of privileges. In fact, the general notion was that not only the KP's identity, but the moral order of Srivaikuntam itself rested on women like them.

The women were defensive in tone, but it was also clear that they had several concerns and worries which they did not see as derivable directly from seclusion. The most important area of strong feeling for them was a realisation of their lack of control over the course of intrafamilial relationships. When I was doing fieldwork, there were serious splits among the KP families due to differences which had been simmering for some years. Though there were many reasons, ultimately it boiled down to issues connected to the closed nature of a small, endogamous, propertied group: who left how much to whom, and whose marriage proposal was accepted by whom. The conflicts had escalated with the murder of a prominent KP by some FPE, allegedly instigated by another KP family. Several families completely broke away from the fort and settled down in Tirunelveli town. The women of the families involved were much more bitter and disturbed than the men; they articulated their helplessness over the disruption of cherished relationships by factors which they could not control. The women had invested much time in developing relationships. They were concerned with handling growing boys and their casual attitudes towards their customs and ceremonies, coping with rumours of husbands' infidelity, accepting widowhood, coming to terms with ageing.

The older women had an amazing sense of past events, through putting together minutae and trivia. Ulagammal's younger relatives were mildly embarrassed by her periodic lapses into 'those old, useless stories', but she was unaffected by such attitudes. She saw the fort now with its ruptured relationships, and the fort of her youth; she saw events in their contexts, with depth, roundness, a strong sense of community and of the general order of things. Sivagami, in her seventies, was living outside the fort in Tirunelveli – she had reflected a great deal on her life, on the lives of the other *kottai* women, on the life of the fort itself. She saw its ups and downs, its glory and fall, and tried to fit it into a scheme of *dharma* and the exigencies of time, modernity and the inevitability of change.

Sivagami had tried hard to get the women to learn to read and write. Three decades ago, she had persuaded her husband to fix up for women teachers to come regularly to teach them. She had done this in secret, for fear of displeasing elders. Janaki, who had not stepped out of her house for eight years since her husband's death went to her mother's house, just two houses away, when her sister's husband died. She wanted to share their sorrow. She narrated the incident to me in low tones: how she went stealthily at night, surrounded by FPE women, and came back in a day. In the old days, widows would not wear blouses, they would cover themselves in a white sari. Sivagami's mother was instrumental in reducing this to a period of one year after being widowed. There were so many such stories, changes. In their perceptions, life was not static. Janaki, Sivagami and Ulagammal did not see their lives as empty. They had seen difficult times, they said, they had borne pain and sorrow. But the fort's way of life meant something of value to them; the KP men as givers of charity and the women as keepers of chastity and honour symbolised the rightness of things. The rain fell in season because of people like them.

MYSELF AND THEM

I thought I was different from the KP women, but in their life-style and options, I could see myself as I might have been fifty or 100 years ago. I remembered my father's paternal aunt, widowed at 18, who came back to live with her brother, my grandfather. After his death, she lived on in my father's house, an emaciated figure with a white sari and shaven head, never stepping out of the house. I remembered my mother's mother, who had eight sons, all self-willed spend-thrifts who dominated her emotional landscape. Her health fragile with repeated childbearing, she was neither able to take charge of, nor extricate herself from, complex and exhausting relationships. The difference between the women in the fort and me was a matter of chance, of a small variation in time and place.

As I look back on this phase, during the latter part of the fieldwork, it seems to me that in order to reconstruct the process I went through – of identification with the KP women – I need to query why I thought of them as the 'other' to start with.[8] To me the anthropological enterprise is like two snakes gripping each other's tails: the fieldwork experience itself (unlike its representation in text) is unambiguously two-way; both the fieldworker and the field know this to be true. The more 'exotic' and 'different' the field, the more satisfying the inevitable movement from initially defining oneself in contrast, and then in parallel terms to that other. This was so of my response to the KP in a particularly immediate and compelling way. Why had I thought of them as 'other' when they were less so than the white, male anthropologists with whom I had identified, from whom I was separated by history, geography, culture and experience of gender? Why did I choose to skip the intermediate agent – the Indian social scientist working in her or his own society – and go straight to the genre of Malinowski *et al.*? Entering the fort became the equivalent of crossing the seas to faraway lands: the museum visits of childhood, the lazy afternoons of *National Geographic*, the holidays of hurtling train journeys through a hinterland of colour and sound collapsed together into the space of a mud-walled fort.

Eventually this phase too lost its sharpness. It was too easy a way out to look at the KP women as I might have been 100 years ago. They lived in today's world, and our life trajectories and consciousness of our situations were different. Which was more true – the feeling of unity in the field or the sense of distancing when out of it? I am not sure if either was 'true', but I could not ever go back to where I had started from – the social scientist studying the field objectiely.

Being with the KP women made me feel that, despite education and mobility, I too was hemmed in by factors specific to my caste and gender. Though I felt strongly that seclusion was a limiting institution largely neutralised by the process of modernisation in post-independence India, fieldwork made me sensitive to the whole grid of gender relations in which I was as enmeshed as were the KP women. For me, as for them, the hierarchy of gender operated in minute and pervasive ways, forming a vast, unquestioned, unspoken ocean of assumptions. All the same, I felt I could not directly intervene in their lives. It would have been foolish and unfair of me to give them homilies on gender discrimination, given the complex interlocking of privilege and oppression. Understanding had to come from within. But my presence and participation in their lives had stimulated some of them, as theirs had stimulated me, into reflecting on areas to which I had earlier been closed. We had developed some depth and mutuality in our communication. The interaction came to have value in itself, by itself; there was no before or after.

ACKNOWLEDGEMENTS

* Acknowledgements to Leela Dube and Pat Caplan for helpful comments on an earlier draft.

NOTES

1 A brief outline on the KP (based, unless otherwise specified, on Ganesh 1982): The KP are a subcaste of Vellalas, who are a large, heterogeneous caste of agriculturists spread throughout Tamilnadu. (For accounts of Vellala, see Thurston 1909 and Ganesh (forthcoming). The mud fort in which they live is a prominent landmark in Srivaikuntam which is a pilgrim town and historically, an endowed village (*brahmadeya*) for Brahmins The 'fort', located at the heart of the brahminical institutions of Srivaikuntam, is really only a walled enclosure, about 15 acres in area. The KP's agricultural lands are outside, spread out in six villages around Srivaikuntam. The mud fort of the KP can be seen in the context of Tirunelveli district in the 17th and 18th centuries. The poligars, petty military chieftains of the area, had a prolonged engagement with the East India Company, which was worried about the preponderance of their mud fortifications, with their potential for harbouring insurgents. It launched a massive offensive to destroy their forts and annex their territories. The fort's prohibition on entry of outsiders has some exceptions. The KP had formal relations with specific families of 16 subcastes including priests, artisans and untouchable agricultural labourers who could enter the fort for specific tasks: some of these were ritual or ceremonial tasks, and others 'secular'. The elaborate network of reciprocal ties between the KP and the families permitted entry (FPE) closely resembled what are commonly referred to as

'jajmani' relations in the social science literature on India: traditional non-contractual relations between the dominant landholding caste and artisan, and service castes (Ganesh 1985a). As upper-caste vegetarian Vellalas, the KP rank just next to Brahmins in the traditional hierarchy. Simultaneously, their base as large-scale land-holders in rich and irrigated paddy lands, their control over service and labour castes, their links with ruling dynasties and governments as ministers, treasurers, accountants and revenue collectors, and their status as patrons and philanthropists give them a distinct profile. They combine aspects of the 'purity' and 'dominance' models. Some accounts connect them to the large, middle-ranking subcaste of Nangudi Vellalas. (Dumont 1957 and Ramanathan 1969). The KP villages are part of the Tambraparni river basin with a long history of paddy cultivation and continuous rule by Hindu kingdoms till the British annexed the area. Historically this region is characterised by an extensive temple-building activity and a landholding elite comprising Brahmins-Vellalas temples. Such regions typically contain large multicaste villages with visible hierarchised interaction, and with upper-caste values as reference points. Strict endogamy in a tiny population combined with a high rate of consanguineous marriage often raised, especially among early census administrators, the spectre of declining population. In recent decades, KP have been making matrimonial alliances with other local Vellala subcastes. Through putting together varied sources I have traced the presence of the KP in Srivaikuntam up to the 15th century. In the 1840s, there was a protracted correspondence and discussions between E.B.Thomas, Collector of the district and the Board of Revenue, Madras Presidency over the issue of the KP's fort. Thomas tried his best to break down the walls of the fort – he felt it could harbour rebels and insurgents. The KP petitioned to the Board, appealing against interference. Eventually,the Board upheld the KP's right to their fort and its privileges. In spite of much rhetoric about the 'degraded status' of the women, the Board remained true to its policy of not disturbing the traditional landed elite.

2 I was in Srivaikuntam for a total of ten months, spread over one and a half years, during which I made several trips of about a month each. The breaks were in order to go back to Madras to spend time with my son who was then 3 years old.

3 The chapters in Panini (1991) graphically describe the situation of women who do fieldwork in their own cultures.

4 The Sanskritised Tamil I speak at home is rarely used in public or secular fora.

5 Villages with similar profiles in different river-valley regions in Tamilnadu have been researched by other anthropologists: Gough (1960) and Beteille (1971, 1975) in Thanjavur, and Mencher (1975, 1978) in Chinglepet.

6 Mencher (1975: 124) has an interesting point to make. When she took up a house to stay in Chinglepet, Tamilnadu, the owner agreed that she should be free to invite anyone she wanted to. Later, he complained about her having Harijans (untouchables) in her house. When reminded of his promise, he said that by 'people of all castes' he had not meant Harijans.

7 See Bell (1987) for an experimental approach to resolve this dilemma.

8 For those anthropologists working within the country (and this, for various reasons, is the rule), diversities are many and sharp. Working in a different regional or linguistic group is effectively like working in a different culture. Even when working on one's own linguistic and ethnic group, as Madan (1965) does, or even in the village of one's childhood, as Dhruvarajan (1989) does, 'otherness' comes into play as part of the anthropologist. It may be a long period of having lived away, or a different education, or differing perceptions. For 'them' too, we may be the 'other'. Dube (1975) recounts three phases of her fieldwork in three different parts of India. In the Laccadive islands, southwest of the mainland, the matrilineal Muslims she studied looked on her as the Hindu. Among the tribal Gonds of Madhya Pradesh, she was the upper-caste woman. In the multicaste village in the plains of Uttar Pradesh, she was the Brahmani (Brahmin woman). Native or foreign, the anthropologist becomes a counterpoint, and the 'difference' is the spark that creates the dynamic in the fieldwork encounter.

REFERENCES

Barnes, J.A. (1977) *The Ethics of Inquiry in Social Science*, Delhi: Oxford University Press.

Bell, Diane (1987) *Generations: Grandmothers, Mothers and Daughters*, Victoria, Australia: McPhee Gribble/Penguin Books.

Beteille, André (1971) *Caste, Class and Power: Changing Patterns of Stratification in a Tanjore Village*, Berkeley, CA: University of California Press.

—— (1975) 'The tribulations of fieldwork', in A. Beteille and T.N. Madan (eds), *Encounter and Experience: Personal Accounts of Fieldwork*, Delhi: Vikas Publishing House.

Beteille, André and T.N. Madan (eds), (1975) *Encounter and Experience: Personal Accounts of Fieldwork*, Delhi: Vikas Publishing House.

Dhruvarajan, Vanaja (1989) *Hindu Women and the Power of Ideology*, New Delhi: Vistaar Publications.

Dube, Leela (1975) 'Woman's worlds – three encounters', in A. Beteille and T.N. Madan (eds), *Encounter and Experience: Personal Accounts of Fieldwork*, Delhi: Vikas Publishing House, pp. 157–77.

Dumont, Louis (1957) 'Hierarchy and marriage alliance in South Indian kinship', London: Occasional Papers of the Royal Anthropological Institute.

Ganesh, Kamala (1982) 'The Kottai Pillaimar of Srivaikuntam: a socio-historical study', Ph.D. thesis, University of Bombay; under publication as *Boundary Lines: Caste and Women in a Tamil Community*, Delhi: Hindustan Publication Corporation, Studies in Sociology and Social Anthropology (in press).

—— (1985a) 'Women's seclusion and the structure of caste', Paper presented at the 'Women and the Household' Regional conference for Asia, New Delhi; published in Maithreyi Krishna Raj and Karuna Chanana (eds), *Gender and the Household Domain: Social and Cultural Dimensions*, New Delhi: Sage Publications India (1989), pp. 97–117.

—— (1985b) 'Jajmani relations in Tirunelveli district: a case study of the Kottai Pillaimar, 1839–1979', *Indian Economic and Social History Review* 22(2): 175–200 published in J. Krishnamurty (ed.), *Women in Colonial India: Essays on Survival, Work and the State*, Delhi: Oxford University Press (1989).

—— (Forthcoming) 'Vellala', cultural summary for South Asia section, *Encyclopedia of World Cultures*, Human Relations Area Files, Inc., New Haven, CT.

Golde, P. (ed.) (1970) *Women in the Field: Anthropological Experiences*, Chicago: Aldine Publishing Co.

Gough, Kathleen (1960) 'Caste in a Tanjore village', in E.R. Leach (ed.), *Aspects of Caste in India, Ceylon and Northwest Pakistan*, Cambridge: Cambridge University Press.

Madan, T.N. (1965) *Family and Kinship: A Study of the Pandits of Rural Kashmir*, Bombay: Asia Publishing House.

Mencher, Joan (1975) 'Viewing hierarchy from the bottom up', in A. Beteille and T.N. Madan (eds), *Encounter and Experience: Personal Accounts of Fieldwork*, Delhi: Vikas Publishing House, pp. 114–30.

—— (1978) *Agriculture and Social Structure in Tamilnadu*, New Delhi: Allied Publishers.

Panini, M.N. (ed.) (1991) *From the Female Eye: Accounts of Women Fieldworkers Studying Their Own Society*, Delhi: Hindustan Publishing Corporation.

Ramanathan, P. (1969) 'Irunkovel and the Kottai Velalar: the possible origins of a closed community', *Bulletin of the School of Oriental and African Studies* 32: 323–43.

Thurston, Edgar (1975) *Castes and Tribes of Southern India*, New Delhi: Cosmo Publications; first published 1909.

9 Motherhood experienced and conceptualised
Changing images in Sri Lanka and the Netherlands

Joke Schrijvers

The children are becoming more and more Sinhalese. Maurik now climbs into the palm-tree besides our house within a few seconds and Tijmen often becomes annoyed because our pronunciation of Sinhala still sounds so Dutch. He also feels that I look queer, the least I could do would be to wear my hair in a bun. (He calls it 'a little bump', as he forgot the Dutch word.) When I think about it, I feel that the boys have a better life here than in the Netherlands, life is more calm and – literally as well as figuratively – warmer. Never before did I find mothering so easy as here: it is spread over the whole village. I don't feel 'a bad mother' by having a job, I can go wherever and whenever I want to and I don't have to worry as there is always someone to look after them.

(Diary, 15 February 1978, quoted in Schrijvers 1985: 108)

In 1977/8 I carried out anthropological research on the changing conditions of women in the North Central Province of Sri Lanka. My partner and two children of 7 and 5 years old accompanied me, and after having lived in the village of research for three months I wrote that happy statement. However, it is not my intention to romanticise Sinhalese village life, nor do I plan to glorify anthropological 'mothers in the field'.

In this chapter, drawing on diaries and letters and in interpretations, I reflect on the dialectics of my changing conceptualisations of motherhood in Sri Lanka and the Netherlands over more than a decade. In contrast to an orthodox, positivist view, a dialectical approach considers the creation of knowledge as the non-replicable outcome of a socially and historically specific research process. Knowledge is a construct, it is created

in the interaction between researchers and those whose ways of living they try to understand. In a wider sense knowledge is created in the interaction between researchers and the whole situation in which they find themselves. The dialogue is continued after the fieldwork proper is over.

(Kloos 1988: 228)

The experience of living 'in the field' forms a significant, but not isolated, part of this process. Personal aspects of the field encounter and the history of the private background and experiences of the author are inevitably, but usually implicitly, reflected in her or his written constructions of 'reality', and in the theoretical concepts used. I label this 'the personal in theory'(Schrijvers 1985: 225).

The call for making explicit the relationship between 'ego' and 'alter' is not new. For over twenty years, feminism and feminist science have fundamentally questioned the dichotomy between the personal and the academic, and advocated the deconstruction of subject–object dichotomies (Caplan 1988 a and b; Warren 1988). More recently, a similar trend is noticeable in the postmodernist, reflexive turn in anthropology (Okely and Callaway 1992).

However, what puzzles me is the gap between (feminist) theorising and the actual praxis of experimenting with alternative approaches. In my view, one of the challenges of a dialectical conception of knowledge is to find ways of deconstructing the established dichotomy between 'the personal' and 'the professional' not only epistemologically and methodologically, but also in the practice of academic writing: no easy task. One of the vital questions is how to represent and integrate in the ethnographic account itself the interaction between subject and object, and between the researcher and the wider situation in which the research takes place. This is not merely an academic problem, although recent reflexive publications in anthropology may suggest otherwise (cf. Clifford and Marcus 1986, and criticisms by Scholte 1987; Caplan 1988b). In my view, reflexivity first of all must be an expression of a political stand regarding the relationship between 'ego' and 'alter'. Efforts to turn around the anthropological 'research gaze' (Marcus 1992), and to integrate critical self-reflection into the constructed images of 'the others' can be part and parcel of a fundamental criticism of the established 'politics of anthropology' (Huizer and Mannheim 1979).

CONTRASTS: THE COMBINATION OF 'WORK' AND MOTHERHOOD

When I think back to the combination of motherhood and research in the field, thirteen years ago, I primarily remember my enthusiasm at the discovery that in rural Sri Lanka these two spheres of activity were not seen as a problematic combination. There, my work and motherhood could be combined much better than I was used to in the Netherlands.

Influenced since the early 1970s by the women's movement, at that time my main concern as an anthropologist was to make a contribution through my work to the liberation and empowerment of women – in the Netherlands, in Sri Lanka, everywhere. My efforts to combine a profession with motherhood had made me aware of my lack of power to create and define my own life in Dutch society. I had been living in a suburban, middle-class neighbourhood where the ideal of the full-time, happy mother-cum-housewife was still prevalent. The fact that I was the only (part-time) 'working' mother in the street provoked many negative comments from my neighbours. In the ranks of my professional colleagues I likewise felt on the defensive, which at times made me rather miserable.

My plan to do field research, taking my young children with me, did not meet with general approval. Not only neighbours and relatives but also female

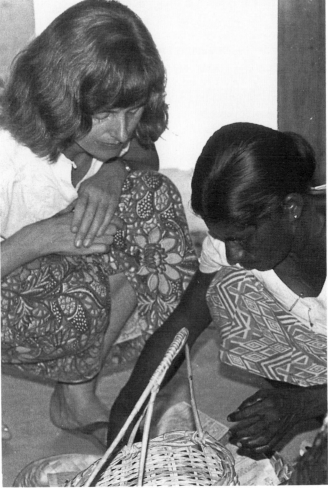

Joke Schrijvers and Ranmenika sorting out her shopping, 1978.

colleagues expressed their doubts. I remember most vividly the warnings of a colleague of my own age, who was also a mother of two sons: 'I doubt whether you will be able to do your work. What if they fall seriously ill? Personally, I would not take the risk.'

No wonder I felt relief after having started work in the capital of Sri Lanka. Most of my Sri Lankan colleagues were combining work and motherhood. I felt that the presence of two little sons influenced my work relations positively. Motherhood as a status and an institution was highly valued, in the urban areas as well as in the peasant interior of the country, as I would soon discover.

In early November 1977 we settled down in Kurunduvila, a *purana* (old, ancient) village in the North Central Province. Academic colleagues in Colombo and officials of different levels and backgrounds in the area itself had given me the impression that Sinhalese village mothers were even more restricted in their movements than Dutch middle-class housewives. According to their view, peasant women in the North Central Province were still backward housewives, busying themselves with cooking and child care.

Yet during our first weeks in the village, when I tried to get acquainted with women and to find out what their activities were, I had the greatest difficulty meeting them at home. It was early November, the height of the main agricultural season (*Maha*). Apart from the very old, the very young and some unmarried girls, the village was empty during the day. Girls, young mothers, middle-aged and older women worked in their *heen* (chenas, swiddens), or they did casual labour, miles away from their homes (Schrijvers 1985: 51). According to my diary I chatted with the women in their kitchens in the early mornings when they prepared food to take to the fields and I went with them on long walks to the swiddens far from the village in the surrounding woods. It was not just acceptable, it was absolutely necessary and therefore self-evident that mothers work outside their homes! They took their infants with them, or left them at home in the care of an older daughter, mother or other relative (in one case a baby was left daily with her aged grandfather, as the grandmother, who was ten years younger, worked as a casual labourer).

The literature available on the region had obscured or distorted the facts about the work and the economic importance of women (cf. Brohier 1975; Ellman *et al.* 1976; Leach 1961; Peries 1967; Samarasinghe 1977; Yalman 1967; Wickremeratne 1977). My own research findings gradually convinced me that, for centuries, women's agricultural labour had been essential for the survival of the population. In Boserup's terms (1970) one could even speak of a 'female crop' (*kurakkan*, finger millet) that had been the main staple food for as long as people could remember. (The significance of this crop was mentioned in the literature, without reference, however, to the gender of the producers.) In short: working outside the home and mothering – the so-called productive and reproductive spheres – were not considered or felt to be opposed to each other; conceptually they were not dichotomised.

Only in retrospect did I realise that this was the first period in my life when I was no exception as a working mother. At the time I did not analyse the emotional and intellectual meaning of this change, I just enjoyed the respect, the freedom of movement, and the sharing of the responsibilities of motherhood.

Besides respect there was of course criticism too. Soon after settling down in the village, I found that as a mother I could have done better: a number of women with whom I soon developed a 'chatting' relationship urged me to continue my childbearing. After one week in the village I wrote to a colleague in Leiden: 'Through *amma*, the woman who cooks for us, we have many visitors the full day round. This morning we were chewing betel together and talked about the daughter I yet have to produce according to them' (letter to a colleague, 13 November 1977). I did not meet their expectations because mothers should have both sons and daughters: sons for general esteem and economic support when old; daughters for help in the household work, and emotional and physical care when old. The idea of having a daughter greatly appealed to me. Later during the research I had recurrent fantasies of having a new baby 'in the field': the idea seemed attractive and uncomplicated.

This fantasy not only sprang from my own adaptation to Sinhalese village life. It was also related to the fact that the children had adapted with amazing ease to our new life.

> The children are fine now, after a difficult start when everybody all the time wanted to touch them, to feel their white skins. After about two weeks they themselves decided to go to the village school, which is just opposite our tiny house. In spite of the lessons in Sinhala, which they still cannot follow, they enjoy going there. . . . Some days we don't see the kids for hours – they are visiting around, playing with their new friends, and 'doing research' as they say. Sometimes they really come home with very useful information.
>
> (Letter to a friend, 14 December 1977)

For the first time in my life as a 'working' mother, I had no fear of neglecting my children, no feelings of guilt in connection with them.

After about five months I became explicitly aware of the significance of this change in my own attitude, when one afternoon a woman whom I did not know very well came to see me urgently. She kept a small shop along the main road and had three small children herself.

> 'I have to warn you', she said, 'about your second son. He came to my shop this afternoon with a ten rupees note and he wanted to give it all to buy cookies! I thought that you would not allow him to spend so much, normally he has enough only to buy one or two sweets. So I thought that he might have stolen the money from your purse.' I thanked her because she was right and I showed my embarrassment. Her reaction was: '*Anee*, isn't he still a baby! We are the mothers, and it is our responsibility to show him the correct behaviour, isn't it?'
>
> (Diary, 10 March 1978)

Her attitude showed that she indeed *shared* responsibility for my son; there was no hint of criticism, only concern. She had given me support – no feelings of guilt for having neglected my child.

A second major change which positively affected the totality of my fieldwork experiences was living with my new partner, Peter, who was an anthropologist.

> Peter and I feel good together although it is not always easy. What I enjoy is the possibility of communicating about all the frictions and controversies. Generally the children have a splendid life here. They have friends, rummage through the village. But Tijmen is still rather tense and Maurik has gruesome dreams at times. They suffer from bad ulcers, one of the effects of the mud mixed with cowdung that is wet and dirty now in the rainy season. It is delightful that I can share the full responsibility of caring and mothering with Peter!
>
> (Letter to a friend, 30 November 1977)

Sharing responsibility obviously facilitated acceptance of the more troublesome aspects of 'mothering in the field'.

Last but not least, in contrast to the situation back home we now enjoyed the luxury of a half-time domestic help. A widow who had to find wage labour in order to feed her family cooked our meals and swept the home and compound, which saved us at least four hours' work a day. Moreover, she kept an eye on the children when she was around in the mornings. The sharing of work with another woman greatly contributed to my good feelings about motherhood 'in the field'.

SOCIO-ECONOMIC DIFFERENCES

Although I was now a working mother among fellow working mothers, there were of course also major differences, both between the mothers in the village and between 'them' and myself. Our domestic help, whom we called *amma* (mother), invariably stressed the sufferings of motherhood. Having brought up her four children in difficult circumstances, and still sharing work, food and income with their families, her experiences as a working mother and grand-mother in Kurunduvila were fundamentally different from those of more well-to-do mothers. Those women worked in their own fields, but did not have to hire themselves out to other farmers in order to feed their children and grandchildren. *Amma's* motherhood was also fundamentally different from mine: I had a good education, came from a rich country, had a well-paid, prestigious job, an equally well-paid and prestigious husband, and we had no difficulties whatsoever in feeding, clothing and educating our children.

We found it highly embarrassing to feel the gap between our socio-economic status and the average village standard. The fact that we had insisted on renting no more than a modest two-roomed house had not reduced our status. With little success we tried to loosen ourselves from the incorporative efforts of the village headman's family. Then, one day, we took a drastic step.

Though worried about our 'loftiness' we were also concerned about our good reputation. We had not told anybody in the village that the children were not Peter's; that both of us had had a divorce; that Peter's two children lived in the Netherlands with their mother; and that in that country, too, lived the *real* father of my children. We knew that in Sinhalese society a divorce was most detri-mental to one's reputation. Revealing these facts of life did not seem the best introduction. But also we did not like to tell lies. We had not yet made up our minds, when we noticed that my sons, whose Sinhalese had become incom-parably better than ours in less than two months, had started to explain the complexities of our family relationships to their friends, and to one or two women whom they addressed as *athamma*, grandmother. '*Ape thaatta*, our father, lives in Holland,' we heard them chatting to a neighbour. As we did not like them to lead a life of deception we decided that it was time to reveal our backgrounds. The quickest way to let the whole village know about our hidden past would be to uncover the facts for our cooking *amma*, emphasising the strict confidence of our confession. So that evening we told her, and when she looked at the photos of our relatives in the Netherlands, especially those of Peter's daughter, she shed tears.

The next day probably everybody in the village had been informed. 'Now we understand', people said, 'why the boys were talking about their father in Holland; we thought they were just talking nonsense, children say many odd things, don't they?' People were most amazed that Peter, who was not the children's own father, behaved like a real father towards them. This greatly increased his moral reputation!

Contrary to what we had been afraid of, our scandalous past did not damage our good reputation. Rather it helped us to be viewed as more or less 'normal' human beings, people who, just like most villagers, had undergone some serious difficulties in their personal lives. Just like the average household, ours too had its own hidden scandal. Immediately after the news had spread through the village women started confiding in me, talking about their own family dramas they had so far kept silent about. We became much closer, and I did not have to rebel any longer against the unwelcome image of the lofty lady maintaining the family status (see Schrijvers 1985: 105).

I was regarded as a very lucky person in having a new partner who behaved well towards me and my children. To be left without a man was about the worst thing that could happen to a woman with children. Not only did it badly affect her reputation (even if all agreed that the man was the one to be blamed), it hit her hard economically. Especially for poor women with infants it was extremely difficult to survive. Here was a marked contrast between 'them and us': divorced mothers in the Netherlands, although both socially and economically badly hit, could at least be sure to survive on social security.

In contrast to casual wage labour, a registered white-collar job such as that of teacher or clerk did not negatively affect a woman's reputation – whether she was a mother or not. For such women, gender restrictions regarding her mobility were highly elastic, and travelling on her own did not negatively affect her reputation. On the contrary, women who did such work were highly esteemed, as I daily experienced myself. Men and women who were lucky enough to find a job in the modern service sector had climbed the ladder, socially and economically.

I saw a marked contrast with the Netherlands of the 1970s. In rural Sri Lanka the combination of motherhood and a regular job in the modern sector was not only accepted, it was so highly esteemed that the gender division of labour was adapted to make room for it. Was this change due to economic rather than cultural differences since, contrary to the past, it was now hardly possible in this area to subsist on agriculture without additional sources of income? The more well-to-do households were those in which at least one adult earned a regular cash income in the modern sector.

EXPERIENCES AND CONCEPTUALISATIONS OF MOTHERHOOD

How did I deal with these contrasting images and experiences? I notice a tendency to romanticise life in Kurunduvila:

> When I came back to the village after a week, I felt accepted and completely
> at home. . . . I often fancy that I could stay here forever, it is like a warm nest.
> But this is a thought without any commitment because I have the choice and
> the money to get out as soon as I feel oppressed. They can't.
>
>   (Letter to a colleague, published in Schrijvers 1985: 106–7)

My economic safety enabled me to stress mainly the positive aspects of being a
mother in 'the field'. When my children fell ill I did not hesitate to jump into my
car and spend money on a private doctor. And, according to my diary and letters
home, they were ill many times: 'The children are fine. The only problem is that
they are frequently ill: festering wounds, a few days' fever, throat infections,
diarrhoea' (letter to a friend, 17 April 1978, published in Schrijvers 1985: 110).
  However, I was happy, and so were the children:

> The children suffer less than us from the heat. They are very well. Maurik became
> eight yesterday. He has grown tall here, walks around with bare gums because of
> losing teeth. He feels more and more at home and I find him much more balanced
> than half a year ago. Tijmen is going native, he throws himself body and soul into
> the new environment, merrily chattering in Sinhala. He teaches us new words and
> writes beautiful Sinhalese letters in his exercise-book at school.
>
>   (Letter to a friend, 10 March 1988)

As indicated before, I was selective not only in my feelings at the time, but also in
my subsequent memory of that period. Before re-reading these letters I mainly
remembered my enjoyment of motherhood during the research. I had completely
forgotten my worries about the frequent illnesses of the boys. This contrasts strongly
with my negative memory of the period before the research: I have never forgotten
the long winters in the Netherlands when I was forced to stay home from work,
immobilised by toddlers who took turns in having colds and infections!
  However, there was another side to Sinhalese village ideologies of motherhood which shocked me.

> Women are viewed, and view themselves, as bodies full of pollution (men-
> struation etc.). They are attractive for devils who crave for blood and dirt. And
> because of this they are afraid to move independently, they feel the need of
> protection and are excluded from culturally important activities such as
> threshing or funerals.
>
>   (Letter to a colleague, 15 February 1978)

Thus the biological capacity of women to become mothers, to create life, was
conceptualised as the natural cause of their weakness and subordination. I
revolted against the women's internalisation of it. I knew that such cultural
legitimations of women as the weaker, subordinate sex were to a certain extent
comparable to the dominant gender ideology prevalent in my own Christian
culture, where ideas regarding female pollution formed the background of the
Roman Catholic rejection of female priesthood. However, during fieldwork I
projected my aversion to such ideas mainly onto 'the other culture'.

In contrast to my own joys, the women with whom I talked about their lives without exception stressed the sufferings of motherhood:

> Now when you are born as a woman you menstruate and what a bother it is. See the trouble when you have to give birth to children. Man's life is better; men can go anywhere and do as they please – no dirt, no filth, no household work, no trouble from children. . . . Women have a lot of trouble. . . . Now look at me. I have three daughters. I am not blessed with a son. Perhaps because I have sinned in a previous life I am deprived of a son in this birth. If I had a grown-up boy, I would not have fallen into such poverty, into such a mess as this.
>
> (Narrated to me by Ranmenika, June 1978; cf. Schrijvers 1983: 185)

Gradually I realised that the hardships and pains were connected with motherhood in a life of poverty.

> Now that a number of women really confide in me and we have got to know each other better, a lot of things come up. They emphasise their own misery, their poverty, the extra burdens connected with a woman's life: pregnancies, deliveries, menstruation, humiliation, caring, cooking, fetching water and firewood, feeding the family somehow or other – together with all the work in the fields their burden of work and life is indeed heavier than that of the men. The longer we live here, the more I get the feeling that there is so much I do not yet understand. But I learn a lot from the life-histories of the women: about their fear of another pregnancy and a new mouth to feed; their anger if their husbands forbid them to practise birth control; the failed abortions.
>
> (Letter to my colleagues, 17 April 1978,
> published in Schrijvers 1985: 110–11)

I wrote: 'They emphasise their own misery', because I was becoming aware of a sharp contrast between verbal and non-verbal expressions of motherhood: the explicit, verbalised agonies were complemented by feelings not expressed in words. Increasingly I also observed the joys, the affection, the esteem, the power of motherhood, and I was deeply touched when I realised that these feelings were not altogether dependent on material conditions. Some of the poorest women were so obviously happy with their babies and infants.

I wrestled with this seemingly paradoxical reality, listening to the rhythm of words repeating the mothers' sufferings, and at one and the same time observing the relaxed joy and profound satisfaction with which they handled their babies and infants. By asking unorthodox questions I gradually elicited the women's criticism of the dominant gender ideology (cf. Omvedt 1979). My previous conceptions of their general powerlessness began to change:

> I am amazed about all the things women now feel free to chat about: their private lives, even about sex, and the management and expenditure of income. It induces marvellous insights; women have considerable power, much more so than I first thought.
>
> (Letter to a colleague, 7 May 1978)

In this period I frequently participated in female 'rituals of rebellion', in which the dominant power relations were turned upside down. This *sellam karanava* – 'playing', as they called it – took place during tea breaks on the fields far from the village (cf. Schrijvers 1985: 219–20). Women who were past the menopause would, for instance, imitate the act of giving birth, not as a passive, silent act of suffering and pain (the cultural norm), but as a joyful, screaming act of rebellion, a victory of life.

In the last months of research I was able to support this view of women's resistance by helping to organise a collective farm. However, it was not until 1978, five years after I left the field, that I was able to recollect entirely this vision of women's power. In my early writings I focused almost exclusively on the powerlessness, the poverty and the marginalisation of these rural women. Only in 1983 did I begin to realise that in my analysis I had to include not solely their sufferings, but also their joys and powers.

I shifted my emphasis from 'manipulated motherhood' to a focus on both the vulnerability and the strength of motherhood, and I called the two sides of the coin 'the paradox of motherhood' (Schrijvers 1983: 188; 1985: 225). What happened after I left the field, and why did I first predominantly stress the aspects of vulnerability?

WRITING MOTHERHOOD

Above, I tried to trace back the connections between my personal experiences and my conceptualisations of motherhood in the field. Can I find a connection, too, between the changes in my written images of motherhood in Sri Lanka, and my experiences after I returned to the Netherlands? How did I experience life during the years when I was writing and constructing my images of those 'other mothers'?

After we left the village in November 1978 I stayed with the children in Colombo for another six weeks. Peter had already left for the Netherlands. Re-reading my diary for this chapter I am amazed to find that in that period I was rather preoccupied with the question of whether or not to have another baby. I had forgotten that this problematic issue was on my mind as early as then.

> Having come home I re-read Peter's letter. He writes about the option to have a baby together. I would love to experience pregnancy and birth together with him. But after that . . . I am afraid, I do not want to sit incarcerated with a child who most probably will have continuous colds, and for whom we'll have to organise a baby-sitter all the time. . . . I want our child and I want my freedom. My condition is that Peter actually takes half a share both of the responsibility and the actual care. . . . I am not at all such a nice mother and I do not have enough patience. I am always quickly irritated if for the sake of the children I have to set aside my own longing for rest and withdrawal.
>
> (Diary, 8 December 1978)

My social network in Colombo did not take a neutral stand on this dilemma. The gentle moral pressure to continue childbearing that I had undergone in the village was taken over by my urban Sinhalese friends:

> D., just before I left: 'When you come back to Sri Lanka you'd better bring a little daughter.' Coincidence? I turn it into a joke, saying that I am not sure I can bring her when I come back in six months, but perhaps the year after. And I ask: 'How can you guarantee that it will be a daughter?'
>
> (Diary, 10 December 1978)

Two weeks after we returned to the Netherlands I stopped writing my diary, thereby reproducing the artificial gap constructed by anthropology between 'us' and 'them'. I started it again in June when I returned to Sri Lanka for six weeks. But that diary does not provide any information on the above question.

What I now remember of my feelings during the five months' interval in my own country is the pressure of combining work (writing my field report) and child care, and the social isolation. In contrast to the period in the field, my memory has retained the many worries about the children's physical and emotional well-being. In the first week after they had gone back to their Dutch school, Maurik fell ill with hepatitis, and two months later Tijmen developed nervous complaints. As a mother I felt pressurised and guilty again! Back in my own country the organisation of mothering was mainly my responsibility, as I was writing at home while Peter was occupied full-time with teaching and administrative work at the university. I felt socially isolated and rather lonely. I especially missed the warm contacts with other women, with my co-mothers in Sri Lanka. My Dutch friends and colleagues were all over-burdened like me.

During that year, 1979, my writing on Sri Lanka had more and more to be squeezed into general management tasks for the VENA research centre,[1] supervision of a new research project in Egypt, and monitoring of the women's farm in Kurunduvila.

At the end of that year, all four of us went back to Sri Lanka for a month of additional fieldwork. Again we settled down in our former house in the village. I cannot unearth my diary of that period – or, did I keep one? I was extremely busy with problems in the organisation of the women's farm. I remember, though, that again the decision of whether or not to have another baby occupied our minds. I even asked advice from a wise friend in Colombo. She straightforwardly voiced her opinion: 'Yes, it will be good for your relationship and for the integration of your family, if Peter and you could have a child together.' In the village our still non-existent daughter was the talk of the day. I vividly remember one night in January, lying awake under the corrugated iron roof of our house. The right decision then seemed so simple. Emotionally, I had made the turn. One year later, when the first joint publication of the research project came out (Postel and Schrijvers 1980), in December 1980 our son Jonatan was born.

My first paper after the birth of our son was entitled 'Manipulated motherhood; a case of agricultural policy in Sri Lanka'. The introduction says:

> In my analysis I emphasise motherhood as one of the key institutions through which the discrimination and manipulation of women is made possible. . . . From rather independent subsistence cultivators these peasant women have been manipulated into a completely marginal position. Still, motherhood holds them responsible for bringing up the next generation.
>
> (Schrijvers 1981: 1–2)

The paper ends on a rather pathetic note, which echoes many of my personal feelings of the time:

> Ironically, the manipulation of women to continue their mothering, even without resources, is about the strongest conservative force. It guarantees the unlimited possibility of further exploitation of the rural poor. One of the best things men can do in support of the international women's movement is to implement new types of mothering fatherhood.
>
> (Schrijvers 1981: 16)

I found it extremely difficult with the new baby to readapt myself to a much more limited scope of life, and to integrate my mothering and intellectual tasks, in spite of the fact that Peter took his fathering responsibility seriously. The situation became worse when gradually we became aware that our baby was rather slow in his development. Finally a test confirmed Down's syndrome. We were told that he was a relatively 'good case'.

One month later, in September 1981, I had to go back to Sri Lanka for the women's farm. There I received an abundance of warmth and comfort, and horoscopes were drawn that gave much hope. And I did need a lot of consolation. Again, the same friend who had earlier advised me on these matters guided me: 'If you can afford to have another child it would be much better, for Jonatan, for the parents and for the whole family.' What exactly did she mean by 'afford to'? The words had both an economic and an emotional connotation. Ten months later, in July 1982, David was born.

Those were heavy years, and I did not publish anything substantial before 1983, when I enjoyed a sabbatical year. I felt energetic again and happy in our big family that had the size and flexibility of a middle-class Third World household (though without the luxury of a full-time servant!). We had been able to organise motherhood and fatherhood in such a way that I could be quite mobile (for instance, I went back to Sri Lanka several times between 1980 and 1986). Moreover, compared to the early 1970s, the ideological climate in the Netherlands regarding 'working' mothers had changed. It was now – at least, in my own social circles – quite normal to combine motherhood with a job.

These changes in my personal life and feelings reflected themselves in my writings of that year. Apparently all of a sudden I no longer supported the cultural rhetoric of suffering. Instead of reproducing the victimisation of 'the others', I started analysing the conditions of women's resistance against physical violence, and the sources of their power and influence. Although perhaps rather belatedly,

I had at last recollected my earlier image of women's power, and realised that a one-sided portrayal of these 'others' as passive victims of (neo)colonialism, patriarchy and capitalism was not correct, nor did it exactly add to their dignity. I began to search my material more systematically, and found more notes in my letters and diary in which I had seen motherhood and sexuality as sources of women's influence and power.

The turn in my focus was influenced also by the changing theoretical approach and tone of 'mainstream' feminist studies. In the 1980s, empowerment rather than the oppression of women became an important concept. Also, in the Netherlands, the dominant feminist climate became somewhat less hostile towards motherhood, and towards mothers and children. Theoretically, too, more room was created for the vast differences between women, in terms of their social and sexual preferences, their culture, class, age and ethnicity. Black feminist critiques had finally entered into the academic rampart of western Europe, and the first confrontations took place.

In that same period I received some critical reactions to the published version of 'Manipulated motherhood' (Schrijvers 1983) from Sri Lankan colleagues. Some considered the linking of motherhood and powerlessness as an utterly Eurocentric bias. In their eyes the Sinhalese mother – in contrast to the western or European mother – had always been a powerful person, and motherhood a source of strength and dignity from the old days to the present time. The dominance and depth of this cultural ideal was affirmed in some publications by Sri Lankan scholars (cf. Jayawardena 1977; Goonatillake 1979). However, Jayawardena (1979: 24) had given an explicit warning: 'Romantic idealisation of women, and a sentimental attitude to motherhood are also notable features of our society today.' Not having an urban, middle-class background, the village women I knew had never romanticised woman or motherhood. Without exception they had indicated as the best periods in their lives the years before they married and had their children. Before they became mothers they had to work less, had fewer worries and more fun, they were plumper, sturdier and healthier. I had, in my earlier analysis, tried to integrate these aspects of the women's own experiences and views of their situation. Now, as a result of the dialectical process I described, I could also integrate the more hidden counterpoints to the sufferings of motherhood, and conceptualise it as a 'paradox of powerlessness and power'. In this light, I find it especially interesting (and amusing) that, in this later emphasis on motherhood as a source of influence and power, I concentrated predominantly on the relations between mothers and sons (cf. Schrijvers 1985: 199–223). There I was, with my four sons!

DISCUSSION

The differences and changes in the experiences and conceptualisations of motherhood that I have tried to trace in the foregoing text were shaped by historical, cultural and ideological factors. These factors were cross-cut by urban–rural and class contrasts as well as by my own personal experiences and those of the other subjects of research. All this happened within the continuum of changing life experiences which formed the setting for anthropological research and writing.

It is, indeed, all very complex, especially if one tries to capture the dialectical process of research and writing in academic discourse. I have often felt a literary text, such as a poem, to be a more convincing and illuminating image of reality than an academic text! But we have also to reflect further on the established epistemologies and paradigms that in my view create fractured and often Eurocentric images. I here refer to the need for a critique of positivist social science with its dichotomisation of subject and object, ego and alter, knower and known, thinker and doer, the academic and the political, the intellectual and the emotional. In contrast to the positivist model, a dialectical and reflexive approach ideally makes room for a plurality of views, for a multivocal discourse: the knowledge produced is seen as an outcome of dialogues, of inter- and intra-subjective communications, and of the confrontations of differing images of reality. Knowledge, in this view, is a temporary construct, determined historically, locally and personally.

The problem remains, however, to what degree researchers can share their *defining power* (Schrijvers 1989) with the other subjects concerned, and with whom, and why, they choose to share this power (cf. Mbilinyi 1989). The politics of research have to be taken into account, especially in the light of the post-modernist relativism that has become *bon ton*, in anthropology as well as in feminist studies.

Is it possible to combine a dialectical, reflexive approach, which makes maximum room for intersubjectivity and multivocal constructions of knowledge, with an explicit political stand regarding the relation between knowledge and change (cf. Scholte 1969, 1987; Schrijvers 1991)? In dealing with the continuous choices springing from the paradox of combining relativity with morality, I have been directed by holding to 'a view from below' (cf. Huizer 1979). In this chapter, I tried to reconstruct the process of my changing conceptualisations by confronting different experiences and images of motherhood, of myself and the other subjects involved. By trying to bridge the conceptualised gap between subject and object, and between the field and 'back home', I attempted to make room for counterpoints to the dominant discourse. I found this approach helpful in problematising and analysing the dynamics of research and writing, and in experimenting with an alternative to the established politics of ethnography.

ACKNOWLEDGEMENTS

I wish to thank Diane Bell, Pat Caplan, Peter Kloos, Kamala Peiris, Marijke Priester, Cora Vreede-de Stuers and Karin Willemse for their comments on an earlier draft.

NOTE

1 The research projects on the changing conditions of women (in Sri Lanka, Egypt and Burkina Faso) were carried out under the responsibility of the Research and Documentation Centre on Women and Development, later Women and Autonomy (VENA).

REFERENCES

Boserup, Ester (1970) *Women's Role in Economic Development*, New York: St Martin's Press.
Brohier, R.L. (1975) *Food and the People*, Colombo: Lake House Investments Ltd.
Caplan, Pat (1988a) 'Engendering knowledge: the politics of ethnography' (Parts I and II), *Anthropology Today* 4(5): 8–12; 4(6): 14–17.
—— (1988b) 'Genderising anthropology; possibilities and necessities for a feminist anthropology', Paper presented at the International Seminar on Anthropological Perspectives on Research and Teaching Concerning Women, Zagreb (July).
Clifford, James and Marcus, George E. (1986) *Writing Culture: The Poetics and Politics of Ethnography*, Berkeley/Los Angeles/London: University of California Press.
Ellman, A.O., Ratnaweera, D. de S., de Silva, K.T. and Wickremasinghe, G. (1976) *Land Settlement in Sri Lanka 1840–1975: A Review of the Major Writings on the Subject*, Agrarian Research and Training Institute, Research Study Series 16, Colombo.
Goonatillake, Hema (1979) 'Women in creative arts and mass media', in *Status of Women in Sri Lanka*, Colombo: University of Colombo, pp. 143–254.
Huizer, Gerrit (1979) 'Anthropology and politics: from naiveté toward liberation?' in G. Huizer and B. Mannheim (eds), *The Politics of Anthropology*, The Hague/Paris: Mouton, pp. 3–41.
Huizer, Gerrit and Mannheim, Bruce (eds) (1979) *The Politics of Anthropology*, The Hague/Paris: Mouton.
Jayawardena, Kumari (1977) 'Some aspects of the status of women in Sri Lanka', Asian and Pacific Centre for Women and Development, Bangkok, selected country papers presented at the ACPWED Expert Group Meeting, Tehran (Dec.), pp. 11–33.
—— (1979) 'The People's Rights: Documents of the Civil Rights Movement of Sri Lanka 1971–1978', Civil Rights Movement of Sri Lanka.
Kloos, Peter (1988) 'No knowledge without a knowing subject', in R.N. Burgess (ed.), *Studies in Qualitative Methodology* I, London: JAI Press, pp. 221–41.
Leach, Edmund R. (1961) *Pul Eliya, a Village in Ceylon: A Study of Land Tenure and Kinship*, Cambridge: Cambridge University Press.
Marcus, Julie (1992) 'Racism, terror and the production of Australian auto/biographies', in J. Okely and H. Callaway (eds), *Anthropology and Autobiography*, London and New York: Routledge.
Mbilinyi, Marjory (1989) '"I'd have been a man"; politics and the labor process in producing personal narratives', in Personal Narratives Group, *Interpreting Women's Lives*, Bloomington, IN: Indiana University Press.
Okely, Judith and Callaway, Helen (eds) (1992) *Anthropology and Autobiography*, London and New York: Routledge.
Omvedt, Gail (1979) 'On the participant study of women's movements: methodological, definitional, and action considerations', in G. Huizer and B. Mannheim (eds), *The Politics of Anthropology*, The Hague/Paris: Mouton, pp. 373–93.
Peries, O.S. (ed.) (1967) 'The development of agriculture in the dry zone', *Proceedings of a Symposium of the Ceylon Association for the Advancement of Science*, Colombo: Swabasha Printers.
Postel, Els and Schrijvers, Joke (eds) (1980) *A Woman's Mind is Longer than a Kitchenspoon*, Research and Documentation Centre on Women and Development, Colombo/Leiden.

Samarasinghe, S.W.R. de A. (1977) *Agriculture in the Peasant Sector of Sri Lanka*, Peradeniya: Ceylon Studies Seminar.

Scholte, Bob (1969) 'Toward a reflexive and critical anthropology', in Dell Hymes (ed.), *Reinventing Anthropology*, New York: Vintage Books, pp. 430–57.

—— (1987) 'The literary turn in contemporary anthropology', *Critique of Anthropology* 7(1): 33–47.

Schrijvers, Joke (1975) 'Vrouw, werkende moeder, antropoloog' (Woman, working mother, anthropologist), *ANTRO* (1974–5) 2: 11–16, Leiden: Institute of Cultural and Social Studies.

—— (1979) 'Een vrouwenboerderij begint met mannenwerk' (A women's farm starts with men's work), *Intermediair* 15(13): 31–9.

—— (1981) 'Manipulated motherhood: a case of agricultural policy in Sri Lanka', Working Paper No.7, Leiden: Institute of Cultural and Social Studies.

—— (1983) 'Manipulated motherhood; the marginalization of peasant women in the North Central Province of Sri Lanka', *Development and Change* 14(2): 185–211.

—— (1985) *Mothers for Life: Motherhood and Marginalization in the North Central Province of Sri Lanka*, Delft: Eburon.

—— (1989) 'Dialectics of a dialogical ideal: studying down, studying sideways and studying up', *Kennis en Methode* 13(4): 344–62; reprinted in L. Nencel and P. Pels (eds) (1991), *Constructing Knowledge: Authority and Critique in Social Science*, London/Newbury Park/NewDelhi: Sage Publications, pp. 162–79.

—— (1991) 'Knowledge and change: a view from below', paper presented at the Third Sri Lanka conference, Amsterdam (April).

Warren, Carol A.B. (1988) *Gender Issues in Field Research*, Qualitative Research Methods Series 9, Newbury Park/Beverly Hills/London/New Delhi: Sage Publications.

Wickremeratne, L.A. (1977) 'Peasant agriculture', in K.M. de Silva (ed.), *Sri Lanka: A Survey*, London: Hurst & Co., pp. 236–55.

Yalman, Nur (1967) *Under the Bo Tree: Studies in Caste, Kinship, and Marriage in the Interior of Ceylon*, Berkeley, CA: University of California Press.

10 Perception, east and west

A Madras encounter

Penny Vera-Sanso

As I sat down amongst a group of women from the slums of Madras, India,[1] my research assistant turned to me, saying, 'They say you slippered an old man last week.' 'No! Where?' I was confused as to what could be the basis for such a serious accusation, for in India the sole of the foot is one of the most polluted parts of the body, and one of the gravest insults is to be slapped with a used shoe. 'At the bus stop.' With these words the scene came flooding back. During the Friday rush hour I had been chatting with a woman at the bus stop. In a half-conscious way I was watching the mass of tired workers fight their way onto an already overpacked bus and in the scramble an obviously poor, middle-aged woman left one of her sandals behind on the road. Knowing that footwear is a luxury for the poor I rushed forward and, grabbing the sandal, slung it low onto the floor of the departing bus. Immediately I knew I had done the wrong thing, for people were staring and my companion quite clearly wished to distance herself from me. I was very relieved when several minutes later my bus took me away from this uncomfortable situation.

By the following week this incident had been embellished in two ways. In the more elaborate story the sandal had hit an old man in the face and, having returned to the stop, all the passengers streamed off the bus in search of the culprit. In the alternative story the bus driver turned the bus back to find the sandal which was, of course, not there. In both stories chaos and confusion were the outcome.

At the time my act seemed to have little significance and was something I had often done with scarves and gloves back home in London. In Madras, however, the act was very significant, for in picking up this poor, illiterate, probably low-caste woman's shoe I, an educated, middle-class foreigner, had behaved as though I was of a much lower social status than this woman.

In this chapter I wish to highlight complexities in the relationship between the researcher and subject which, in the context of India, arise out of divergent cultural discourses on the individual, respectful behaviour and hierarchical structures. In particular, the chapter emphasises the very different readings, misreadings and reinterpretations of behaviour by both the anthropologist and subject.

In choosing my research topic I wanted it to be of value both socially and academically. I had, and still have, severe misgivings about the way in which many development projects are designed and assessed, especially in terms of the emphasis on the economic over the social, and the unfamiliarity of the designers and assessors with the social group concerned. In particular, I had doubts about the social impact of production cooperatives which often replicate manager–worker relations. I wanted to concentrate on employment since it is the most critical issue for poor people and, although I was perhaps better qualified to do research on housing, I knew that after the previous twelve years spent working with housing cooperatives, such a topic would not sustain the level of interest required. I also wanted to do research about women. In sum, I needed to find a 'grass-roots' cooperative which helped to facilitate employment for women in order that I could assess the implications of this type of project for gender relations.

A large credit cooperative operating in South India appeared to fit the bill exceptionally well. Its aim was to strengthen poor working-class women's position both in the family and in the community. In providing credit it sought to help women to improve or start their own business and thus release them from total dependence on the male income. It sought to improve women's status in the community by providing a focal point around which women could organise over such issues as the improvement of squatter settlements, police harassment and violence against women. The organisation's aim was to enable women to 'come out', meaning to rise out of their subordinate role in the family and their more or less strict confinement to the home and to take an active and equal role both in their family and society.

The organisation appeared ideal in terms of my research proposal; none the less, I found the whole idea repugnant. How could I, a representative of the old colonial power, go into the slums of Madras and take up people's time with questions about what must appear to them as too obvious, not to mention personal and often painful questions? I thought they would, quite rightly, give me short shrift. I put the project aside while I struggled with these issues. Talks with both Indian and British academics and activists about the importance of investigating this type of development initiative, and the positive and negative effects of the fieldwork process on the interviewees, gave me some encouragement. Finally, after being invited by the organisation itself to do the research, I began preparation in earnest and tried to put all doubts out of my mind.

By the summer of 1989 I was able to leave England to conduct a five-month study of the organisation, with the object of doing some preparatory work prior to a twelve-month study in the following year. This first visit highlighted the complex and contradictory nature of the fieldwork process. What was striking were the areas of convergence and divergence of researcher's and subjects' interpretation of behaviour. The area of divergence was most apparent in attitudes to expressions of hierarchy, and further complexity was derived from the difference between India and Britain in the degree of politicisation around certain issues, particularly skin colour. There was an apparent convergence of judgements regarding gender relations, but these were derived from quite different understandings reflecting concrete differences in cultural and socio-economic experience.

DIVERGENCE: HIERARCHY AND RACE

India is a hierarchical society in terms of caste, class, sex, age, education and skin colour. In doing fieldwork I was continually confronted with instances of hierarchy; some were Indian in origin and some were a product of the colonial experience. These instances obviously brought forth very different emotions. In 'out of research hours' they ranged from mild irritation at the obsequiousness towards me of hostel and café staff, through suppressed anger at being proudly told by an individual that he belonged to the highest sub-caste of Brahmins, by which he meant that he and his community were innately superior to everybody else, to expressed anger when a high-caste Brahmin tried to prevent me giving up my bus seat to a poor, tired, low-caste woman who was heavily pregnant.

These were, however, minor problems; the real difficulties came in the research context and they led to major dilemmas for me. For the first week of research a schedule of meetings with large numbers of women was planned by the organisation. These initial meetings were relatively formal. The president of the organisation (if she was present), the translators and my husband and myself were all seated on chairs, while the cooperative members and workers were seated on the floor. Frequently we were garlanded. In India garlanding is a complex institution with the obvious intention of honouring the receiver (and to a lesser degree the giver) but it is also associated with the instrumental relations between god and devotee and between political patron and client. For the members this was hospitality on a grand scale, for me this emphasised distance, was diametrically opposed to anthropological methods, and because of my nationality smacked of colonial relations. None the less such expressions of hierarchy and their automatic placing of me within it, although uncomfortable and problematic, were expected.

What was not expected was the direct way in which the women, without realising it, confronted me with the central issue of British racism, skin colour. After asking them numerous questions in these scheduled meetings, I asked the women if they wanted to ask us anything. Questions were directed at me both as an individual and as a representative of British society. So when I was asked, 'What do you think of our skin colour?', what could I say? A question put like that raises complex issues around aesthetics and the political use of phenotypes in Britain. In the light of British racism these issues are extremely delicate and require sensitive explication which could not be satisfactorily achieved in the context of a large introductory meeting.[2] The dilemma was both difficult and painful; I could not bring myself to describe these racist attitudes to skin colour, and yet only to give my personal opinion seemed deceptive as I was being taken to represent British views. I took the least offensive position, which was not a solution to the problem, of turning the question round and describing how white westerners spend a lot of time and money trying to turn their skins brown. I do not know if they believed me – I certainly felt unconvincing. Several times I was confronted with this problem and to my regret never found an adequate solution.

In South India, although the issue of skin colour finds political expression in the anti-Brahmin movement, it does not have the same degree of political significance as it does to the British. For the majority of people, Brahmin or non-Brahmin, a light skin is seen as a sign of beauty and indicates higher social status as it implies freedom from labouring in the sun. Anti-hierarchy movements, such as the anti-caste movement and nationalist movement have had a long history in India but, in Tamilnadu at least, politics at the mass level is largely based on issues of personality and patronage, on the munificent distribution of resources rather than issues of power and exploitation. So, the expressions of hierarchy I encountered were actually more ambiguous in meaning than my personal view of them. They were a complex intermeshing of hospitality, which requires some indication of service, as well as of relative status and power. For this reason my attempts at changing the terms of relations between the interviewees and myself produced some unexpected results, as will be seen below.

SEEKING CONVERGENCE: GENDER PRESENTATION

Prior to going into the field anthropologists must make some decisions as to how they want to present themselves and what implications this will have on their access to information. In India, westerners are considered sexually promiscuous and lacking in family values. 'Western' is a criticism levelled at the more independent Indian woman, who is often seen as trying to evade the sexual restraints that submission to the authority of the men and elders of the household ensures. I certainly did not want to be seen in this negative light. Nor did I want to be taken for an unmarried western woman, partly because of such stereotypes, and partly because being single might have been an inappropriate marital status for work on gender relations. So I was very glad that my husband could accompany me on this initial trip. Thus I avoided the anomalous position of the unmarried woman, and although I did not share the women's experience of being a parent[3], we did at least share the common status of wifehood. In Indian terms therefore I was considered to be in the somewhat ambiguous position of a woman married for several years without children. In terms of personal qualities I wanted to be seen as understanding, sympathetic, sexually unavailable and as much as possible 'one of them', most of which are the common goals of anthropologists.

Modest appearance and posture was a key element in the strategy. The main objective was not to look like a tourist. I decided initially against wearing a sari, partly because I felt self-conscious, and partly because of the heat and difficulty in wearing them. Instead, I had a tailor make up three sets of matching long dirndl skirts and blouses which were loose and kept me well-covered. To my bewilderment I was continually being told I would look much better in a sari but nobody would say why. It was only after a few weeks into the research, when I noticed a young schoolgirl wearing more or less the same clothes, that I realised I had dressed myself as a prepubescent girl!

In other respects my behaviour, although not conforming to 'traditional' Indian notions of 'woman', did conform to the general aims of the organisation – for despite being married I had decided not to have children until after I finished my education. Although in this way I was quite unlike the vast majority of the women I met, my relatively late return to education and the importance I placed on an independent income, plus the support I 'must' be getting from husband and in-laws, coincided with the direction which several members within the organisation were striving for in terms of greater self- determination. However, for the majority, particularly those with whom I had only brief encounters, there must have seemed little in common between us beyond our sex.

The degree to which my experience of gender relations differed from the women's was most clearly bought home to me over the issue of birth control. In a discussion about decisions on fertility one woman asked me, 'You were lucky, your husband didn't want children, but what if he had?' Coming from a society where men have a much reduced role regarding fertility decisions, where polarised views about having children are not uncommon grounds for divorce, and where divorce is increasingly less of a social stigma, I found the implied suggestion that my husband could have forced me into having a child quite shattering and enormously revealing regarding the women's experience of gender relations. For these women desertion, which is more likely than divorce, has serious social and economic consequences, and so women are much less able to resist the particularly strong pressures to have at least one child within the first three years of marriage. Despite the risks of defying their husband's authority, several women had decided to have tubectomies against their husband's wishes or without his knowledge. Every one of these women was in her late thirties and early forties; by this time women had achieved strong positions in their households both by virtue of having had several children and the support lent to them by adult sons, which shifted the balance of domestic power relations.

In order to be seen as 'one of them', I consciously aligned myself with the workers, and hence members rather than the president of the organisation. I ate with them whenever I could, we shared jokes, they teased me about my Tamil: all in all, relations were generally relaxed. Two-thirds of the way through the research I saw the consequences of this behaviour. On the one hand the more educated women told me I was the first visitor in ten years who had 'come down to our level'(!), and who had also become a friend. On the other hand, several people who occupied lower levels of the various hierarchies of caste, education, income and occupational status were confused by my flouting of etiquette, and did not know how to respond. It was only towards the end of the study that I realised that people wanted me to be of obviously higher status, largely because it reflected well on them. As one group of women put it, in terms of the effect on their community status, my interviewing them in their homes was 'even more important than having relatives to visit'. This was also why they were openly disapproving of my lack of gold jewellery and my inexpensive (and childish) cotton outfits.

DIVERGENCE AGAIN: THE HUSBAND'S ROLE

As can be seen from preceeding paragraphs, anthropologists make varying efforts, with varying degrees of success, to reduce negative associations and to conform to cultural norms. During this preliminary study I was accompanied by my husband, who is not an anthropologist, and this provided some unexpected insights into issues around self-presentation in another culture and how this is perceived and understood. As my husband, David, had intended to come to India for a holiday and only expected to stay with me for a short period, I had made little specific effort to prepare him other than to advise him to avoid using his left hand and not to sit next to Indian women, these being the two mistakes a male traveller is most likely to make. Three examples will highlight some of the ways in which he, unwittingly, behaved in a way which contradicted local gender norms and thus exposed divergences in my perception of gender relations and those of the organisation's members.

David was asked by the organisation if he would like to attend the week of introductory meetings they had arranged for me, and he accepted. This caused me some concern as I was afraid that in Indian society, as in European society, it would be unconsciously, if not consciously, assumed that being the woman I was only the assistant researcher. Fortunately this fear was totally unfounded, largely because the organisation is so 'women-centred' but also because of the role David took upon himself. Seeing the degree to which taking written notes slowed the interviewing process, David volunteered to help with this task and eventually took notes for all the interviews he attended. As I have said, at the end of the interviews the women asked us questions about ourselves and Britain. We were always asked if we were married, if we had children, what David's job was and why he was in India. He said he was an engineer and that he was acting as my 'secretary'. This produced very broad grins and a round of applause: they took this to mean that he had left his high-status job to come and help me with my work by taking up the relatively menial position of my secretary. In India, as in most areas of the world, it is the woman who follows the man to wherever his job leads, not the other way round.

In India, the most significant element of the marriage ceremony is the tying of the golden cord of the *tali* around the woman's neck by her husband. Thus the *tali* is the primary symbol of a woman's married status, and there is some connotation of a woman being claimed by the man as his property by the placing of the *tali* on her. As I wore no *tali* I was often asked what my '*tali*' was, and I indicated that the ring on my left hand (hardly an appropriate hand in Indian eyes), was the symbol of marriage in our country. The first time I was asked this I looked on with horror, as David, not knowing anything about the *tali*, pointed to the silver neck chain I had made for him. This certainly did not conform to Indian gender norms, but the women loved it! They found the idea of a man, or at least David, wearing a *tali* exhilarating because it was both amusing and liberating. This incident did much to endear David to the women.

Tamil language and forms of address actually codify the relative status of husband and wife: a husband addresses his wife using language reserved for inferiors, children or intimates; a wife addresses her husband using language for superiors or non-intimates. In addition, a woman should never call her husband by his name, partly because it is thought to bring him closer to death and partly because it implies equality or superiority. Hence a good wife never calls her husband by his name, always uses honorific language when addressing him, and always responds quickly and willingly to what might otherwise be considered rude forms of address. One evening I was chatting on the veranda with a few women, without the assistance of an interpreter, and David, suffering from a severe headache and exhaustion, had fallen into a shallow doze at the table indoors. I misunderstood the women, who were asking me what I called David. I thought they had asked me to call him, so I did, using his name, and he immediately popped his head up and said, 'Yes?' Being slightly dazed, he thought I had been calling him for some time. The women were very amused that David appeared to play the role of the willing wife.

Thus in several ways David's behaviour did not conform to the normal male patterns and sometimes it was a complete inversion. Interpreting reactions to this is rather problematic. The men we met were very concerned that we had no children, even after several years of marriage, and they quite clearly thought David was, at the very least, misguided in not forcing the issue. Understanding the women's response to David is more difficult. His support for my work, his lack of pressure regarding children, and the level of consultation between us corresponded with many of the objectives of the organisation regarding women's productive and reproductive roles and gender relations. But how was the issue of the *tali*, the modes of speech and my giving David instructions seen? Was he being partially identified with the feminine experience, and, consequently, was I partially being identified with the masculine? Or was it taken as just another, though amusing, variation on human behaviour that abounds in India, where other castes, other religions, other tribes and, now, other nationalities have different ways of doing things?

There were three basic responses, but exactly what was thought I could not ascertain. Several of the young unmarried, or newly married women, thought we had the ideal relationship. Women who had been married longer often had to face considerable opposition from their husbands to their engaging in any activity outside the home. Their husbands thought this would undermine their authority and feared the opportunities for sexual trangressions. The fact that David supported me in my work rather than exhibiting such fears was approved of by these women. I also had the impression that sometimes they thought my behaviour bordered on insolence and his tolerance of this was warmly received. Some of the women in their late forties and fifties were openly disapproving that I had not been provided with the gold jewellery which our status as foreign visitors indicated could easily be afforded and of what they saw as my less than respectful attitude to my husband. In addition, I think they were unconvinced about our reasons for not yet having had children. These older women seemed to think that neither David nor myself were getting what we could expect from marriage and that our relationship had foundered on the lack of children, who are seen as the source of affection and understanding between husband and wife.

Interestingly, David's apparent inversion of South Indian gender norms did not, in the final analysis, undermine the women's perception of him as a man. There were three reasons for this. First, a gendered hierarchy was still seen to operate because I was only a student while he was a practising professional. Secondly, and most interestingly, their judgements were based on assumptions about marriage and gender relations which are deeply rooted in Indian culture. Marriage, despite legislation on divorce, is considered indissoluble for women. A woman once married is unlikely to remarry after widowhood, desertion or divorce because of the strong social pressure against remarriage, especially if she has had children. As a woman's social and economic status is heavily determined by her marital status, it is rare, apart from instances of extreme, usually violent, provocation, that a woman would willingly threaten her marriage. Traditionally, gender roles provide for male authority in most matters. In the light of these ideas about marriage and male authority, women in the cooperative assumed that David condoned my wishes to delay parenthood, to continue my education and to return alone to India the following year. They saw him as displaying a generous and tolerant spirit to a rather demanding wife. Thirdly, variations in customs are commonplace in India and hence play a less significant role in the perception of gender than might be the case in a more homogeneous society.

CONCLUSION

This discussion about attitudes towards gender in South India has concentrated on a foreign husband and wife and others' interpretation of that relationship. The husband–wife relationship is the one which most abounds with stereotypes, and hence such an emphasis obscures the interaction between the many roles an individual can hold. As a result, the chapter both hides and reveals the degree to which gender and identity are negotiable. On the one hand, it hides how our individual identities were seen in different contexts, and on the other, it emphasises the dialogic processes of perception.

In this chapter I have attempted to highlight some of the complexities in the researcher–subject relationship in terms of the interpretation of behaviour. Attempts at directing others' perception of and relationship with the researcher come up against often unexpected difficulties. These are the result of three factors. First, library preparation for fieldwork can only ever be partial, both because of the changing nature of the society being studied and the fragmentary nature of the literature. Secondly, the researcher finds ambiguities in the significance of behaviour. Ambiguities arise from the number and range of different roles and identities an individual may hold, and the way these are signified in particular contexts. This ambiguity is augmented by the contradictory nature of ideologies surrounding differing roles and the use of these contradictions to secure the objectives of groups and individuals. Thirdly, the subjects reinterpret the researcher's behaviour in the light of their own underlying assumptions about the kinds of roles an individual holds. This last is most clearly seen with the women's reinterpretation of David's behaviour and our relationship, so that it conformed more easily to their own understanding of gender roles and gender relations.[4]

I have tried to indicate how the interpretation of behaviour is thus related to personal experience and objectives, as well as to social, economic and political factors. This is particularly obvious in the apparent convergence between the women's and my interpretations of gendered relations, which was in fact based on very different assumptions emanating from concrete differences in cultural and socio-economic experience. This disjuncture between what is expected and what occurs provides revealing insights not only into the nature of the society's values but also into the anthropological endeavour itself.

NOTES

1 This research was funded by the University of London Central Research Fund and a University of London Postgraduate Studentship.
2 At an everyday level in South India skin colour is in the main an aesthetic rather than overtly political issue. This is not to say that the political content of skin colour is not recognised but that it arises in specific contexts and is only one of many markers of difference between castes, classes, North and South Indians, developed and under-developed nations and the old colonisers and colonised. In Britain, the issue of skin colour is much more political because of the nature of British racism, which reduces non-Northern European peoples to physiological examples by not recognising their history and culture.
3 By the age of 32 a majority of Indian women are not debating if and when to have children, as I was, but where their 15-year-old son could expect to find work and who their 15-year-old daughter should marry.
4 This corresponds with Regina Oboler and her non-anthropologist husband's experience with the Nandi in Kenya, where their relationship was reinterpreted by the Nandi so as to conform with their own concepts regarding gender relations.

REFERENCES

Oboler, Regina (1986) 'For better or for worse: anthropologists and husbands in the field', in Tony Whitehead and Mary Conaway (eds), *Self, Sex and Gender in Cross-cultural Fieldwork*, Urbana and Chicago: University of Illinois Press.

11 Learning gender

Fieldwork in a Tanzanian coastal village, 1965–85*

Pat Caplan

In September 1965 I was a young postgraduate student setting off for East Africa to begin fieldwork on Mafia Island off the southern coast of Tanzania. It was not my first visit to this area. In 1962, I had spent a summer vacation in East Africa, travelling from Entebbe in Uganda (where a £60 return charter flight from London deposited me) to Dar es Salaam in Tanzania by a circuitous route, taking in northern Uganda, Nairobi, Mombasa and Zanzibar. My ultimate destination was Kilwa Kisiwani, a small island off the southern coast of Tanzania, which, during medieval times had been an important and wealthy town. Because I was doing a degree in African Studies which consisted mainly of anthropology and Swahili at London University, my tutor had arranged with an archaeologist friend of his, who was conducting a 'dig' on Kilwa, that I work there as an assistant, and so improve my Swahili.

I spent several weeks on the island, working in the mornings on the archaeological site, and in the afternoons visiting the small village which is all that now remains of the once large and beautiful town. Here I talked both to women and men, asking questions about marriage, kinship, ethnicity, Islam, rites of passage and politics (Tanzania had just become independent) and taking lots of notes in order to write a report for my tutor when I got back to London. This trip constituted a sort of rehearsal for fieldwork, as well as providing an impetus for what was to follow. I was determined to return to do anthropological research on the East African coast when I had finished my degree.

At the end of that summer, hitching a lift from Kilwa on a small Italian tramp steamer sailing north up the coast, I stood one night on deck with the captain and asked him the name of the long, low island we were passing. 'Mafia.' Thus did I find my fieldwork area.

THE FIRST TRIP, 1965–7: UNGENDERED FIELD, UNGENDERED SELF

I returned to London to graduate, then enrolled for a master's degree which was completed by writing a dissertation about land tenure on the coast of East Africa. When I went back to Tanzania in 1965, I thus had the considerable advantages of relatively fluent Swahili and a broad acquaintance with the literature on the area as well as a number of local friends and acquaintances. With their help, after only

Pat Caplan reaping the harvest rice in Mgeni's field.

a short period of time, I was able to get my permission for fieldwork, buy my household supplies and set off by plane for Mafia Island.

I wanted to work in the north of the island, which had been much less affected by the plantation economy typical of the Zanzibari Arab, German and British colonial periods, and where a nucleated form of settlement predominated. None the less, in the end, the major deciding factor in my location was the availability of a house. Together with Salum, an assistant, cook and general factotum whom I had hired in Kilindoni, the island's capital, I moved into the only house I could find in the north of the island in Kanga village in October 1965. We were to remain there, with two breaks of several weeks for visits to the mainland and a few odd days in Kilindoni, for a year.

Kanga is a village of around 1,000 people, some living in its nucleated centre, others further afield in small clusters of houses scattered among the coconut palms which provide the main source of cash income. The village is surrounded on three sides by bushland, cultivated on a swidden system, and on the remaining western side lies the sea.

Following on from the work I had already done for my master's thesis, my project was to study land tenure and kinship, in order to try, as my supervisor put it, 'to make sense of the coastal system of kinship and descent'. The eclectic and unsatisfactory literature then available suggested that this might be rather different from the unilineal patterns which seemed at that time to predominate in Africa, although it was not at all clear how 'the system' (if indeed there was a common system) worked on the ground. I later learned that bushland is held by cognatic descent groups which trace ancestry through males and females and both women and men have rights to land (Caplan 1976a).

This latter fact did not, unfortunately, enable me to overcome my own prejudices and training, and attribute as much importance to women as they deserved, at least initially. I was convinced that men held the key to the really important matters and that I should therefore ask them most of the questions. In order to do this, I had to convince them that I was worth talking to.

Kanga is part of the Swahili coastal Islamic belt where women and men are segregated on many public occasions, and women even veil themselves sometimes, albeit rather perfunctorily. The first issue which had to be tackled was dress. In an early letter to my parents, I noted that I did not want to wear local dress because I thought I would then be unequivocally categorised as a woman, and I was convinced that this would jeopardise my fieldwork with the men. At the university in Dar I had asked the advice of a British woman anthropology student who was working on the mainland, and she suggested long, full skirts. I did have a couple made in the district capital, and wore them there, and, at first, in the village. Soon, however, I switched – first temporarily, and then permanently – to a pair of *kanga,* one wrapped round my chest and falling to below the knees, and the other draped over my shoulders, which I found much cooler, and which seemed to please the villagers.

I did not dress entirely like village women, however, for I usually wore no jewellery. I rarely wore any back home, and in the hot, humid climate, found necklaces and bangles an irritant. Towards the end of my stay, on one occasion, I must have been wearing some item of jewellery, because a woman friend remarked upon it, adding, 'Yes, today you look nice. But if someone doesn't wear jewellery, one can't really know if they are a man or a woman.' About the same time, one man remarked thoughtfully, 'You know, we never think of you as a woman at all.'

Such remarks enabled me to consider that I had overcome the question of my sex by adopting a 'genderless' role which made interaction with both men and women possible. This was possibly facilitated by the way the villagers saw me – anomalous in my status as unmarried and childless.

Another factor which enabled me to develop comfortable relationships with a number of men was through relations of adoption into kin networks. Fairly early on, an elderly woman neighbour began calling me 'brother's daughter', and her four sons thereafter referred to me as 'cross-cousin' (*binamu*), a relationship which allows for a great deal of familiarity and joking (*utani*). When their fifth half-brother died suddenly, and I attended his funeral, they invited me to go to the grave-side with the men, which I had never done before. Thereafter I did sit with the men, as well as the women, at funerals.

On other public occasions too, when men and women were segregated, such as at weddings and other rituals, I always spent time both 'in the courtyard' (*uwani*), the women's area, and 'on the veranda' (*barazani*), where the men congregated. The only areas where I never asked to go were into the mosque, which was only attended by men, and to the circumcision operation of boys (see below, p. 175).

In short, then, on the level of day-to-day activity, I projected myself as 'genderless', but there were limits to this in terms of some ritual occasions.

In seeking an 'ungendered' role in the village I knew that I was playing on a number of factors which counter-balanced my sex. One was that I was a foreigner and a European, a status which still carried a good deal of weight in this recently independent country. Another was my level of education in a society where, at that time, most of the adult men and virtually all of the adult women were illiterate in Roman script and only four years of schooling were available to village children, mainly the boys. However, what seemed to impress the men most was that I had read the Koran in English and therefore could quote from it in Swahili, whereas most of them could 'read' it by heart in Arabic, but few could understand.

I soon acquired a number of important male informants, the first and most significant, Mohammed, being an old friend of my cook Salum. Another man, Ali, also became my adopted brother and close confidant. A third was Athman, a middle-aged man who was very active in the spirit possession cults, and was also willing to spend hours discussing land tenure and holdings of coconut trees – he boasted that he knew the owner and history of every tree in the village. A fourth important informant was the imam of the Friday mosque, who had a fund of knowledge about Islam and 'mosque politics'. These, and a number of other men, spent many hours talking in my house, particularly in the evenings. Towards the end some of them, especially Mohammed, kept diaries for me (cf. Caplan 1992) and helped me complete censuses.

None the less, I did not ignore women, nor did they allow themselves to be ignored. My letters home during the first few days of fieldwork record a stream of women visitors with babies and children to my house, and soon they requested me to build a courtyard at the back with a side door so that they could enter without being seen by the men gathered on the veranda of the shop next door.

Some women also became good friends. One such was Mohammed's wife, Mwahadia, and another was Fatuma, the wife of Salum the cook, who visited for extended periods with her 6-year-old foster-daughter Subira. And a middle-aged woman called Mwabora took me under her wing after I had driven her daughter in my Land Rover to the hospital in Kilindoni when she was having a difficult first labour. This child, a boy, was 'given' to me as a kind of god-child (*somo*), and I conferred the name of Hassan upon him. A fourth close friend was a young woman of only 17 who, in spite of her resistance, had been taken away from school in Zanzibar to marry. Bimkubwa bitterly regretted what she saw as her lost opportunities and often came to talk to me. She was expecting her second child during my stay, and when it was born just before I left the field, she named her after me – Patlisha.

Even so, I did not have as many female as male informants, nor did I spend as much time with them. Apart from my initially mistaken views of the greater importance of men, and thus lesser significance of women, the latter simply did not have the same amount of time to come to my house and talk as did men. Men often came in the late afternoon, a time when women were busy with food preparation, or else in the evening after their meal. Even when women did come to my house, or I went to theirs, our conversations were rarely uninterrupted by the demands of small children and babies.

But I did gain a good deal of information about women from ritual, a field in which I became increasingly interested. As I have argued elsewhere (Caplan 1982), most ritual in this area consists of an Islamic (*sheria/sunna*) and a customary (*mila*) element. Whereas men control the former, women are the main actors in the latter. Many rituals, such as weddings and funerals, contain elements of both, but that for a girl's first menstrual period is exclusively *mila* and men are not allowed to be present.

I have described this women's puberty ritual (*unyago*) in some detail elsewhere (Caplan 1976b), and here will note that its purpose is to instruct a young woman not only how to cope with her menstrual periods, but also her impending engagement and marriage, sexuality, relations with husband and in-laws and many other matters. What struck me forcibly when observing the one *unyago* which occurred during my stay (that of the younger sister of Hassan's mother) was its open celebration of women's sexuality and the clear message that although husbands had rights over this, none the less it was quite likely that a woman, like a man, might well wish to have sexual relations outside of marriage.

Coming as I did from a religious and somewhat puritanical background, but influenced by the 'swinging sixties', I was impressed by such messages, and felt that women on Mafia were much less 'hung up' about sex than many of my own peers back home. I began to see women on Mafia as more 'liberated' than I had previously done because of their apparent sexual autonomy, although in retrospect I wonder now if, like so many young women of that era, I confused sexual liberation with feminism.

I also wonder whether women's frequent graphic discussions in front of me about their sex lives and their bawdy jokes were a way not only of testing me out, but also of turning into a joke their own feelings of unease about me – after all, in their terms I was a total anomaly, a young woman in her twenties who was still unmarried. In the early days of fieldwork I had even been asked whether I had begun menstruating yet, and I was hard put to explain how it was that my younger sister was already married when I was still single. Furthermore, I spent an inordinate amount of time talking to these women's husbands, often alone at night in my house, another subject on which women sometimes teased me.

Thus in spite of my attempts to be ungendered, even 'asexual', the women particularly often drew attention to my femaleness, perhaps because they felt that this was something which we had in common. There were, however, other reasons why I became conscious of my gender as never before during the eighteen months I spent on Mafia Island. This had less to do with fieldwork and more with the relationship between my personal life and the development of my career. There was a growing realisation that for me, as a woman, difficult choices and compromises had to be made.

In her account of her fieldwork and her 'discovery' of herself as a woman, Karla Poewe maintains that marriages (and presumably long-term relationships) are subject to great strains as a result of fieldwork. In her case, it meant the end of her marriage (Cesara 1984). In my own case, however, a second lengthy separation from my partner had decided both of us that we did not want to repeat the experience again, and that a long-term commitment was desirable. This was not a straightforward decision on my part, and my letters, particularly after my partner visited East Africa for a month and we formalised our decision, are full of doubts and worries about what marriage might involve, including the apparent inevitability of the kind of 'humdrum' existence which I had entered anthropology to escape.

Such concerns were not only personal, they were also professional: I was well aware that marriage for me would mean recategorisation by fellow postgraduates, and above all, by members of staff, who were important patrons in terms of recommendations and potential jobs. I feared that as a married woman I would not be taken seriously. Two female students in my department who had also done fieldwork in Africa just before me had both married immediately afterwards, a step which was viewed as unwise by our supervisor, who argued that it was best to 'finish the thesis first'. For these reasons, then, my relationship with my partner had not been revealed to the rest of the department.

In spite of these concerns, I had always thought that a single woman was as good as a man – indeed, was a kind of 'honorary male' if she played the game according to the rules – and there were a number of important role models in British anthropology at the time – Lucy Mair, Audrey Richards, Phyllis Kaberry – to reinforce that view. As the end of my grant loomed, I was expecting that, like many of the postgrads in my department, I would be offered an assistant lectureship when I finished fieldwork. This turned out not be the case either for me or the other three women students in the department who were due to complete their doctorates at the same time. I was bitterly disappointed

Coincidentally, around this time, my mother wrote complaining of the fact that in her own job, in spite of holding a more responsible post than her male colleagues, she was receiving less pay and no fringe benefits, such as a company car. For the first time, I felt a common bond with her as an adult woman, and wrote to her that 'We women always have to struggle harder – it's still a man's world'.

During this first period of fieldwork, then, I did not really 'see' gender, partly because my training had not prepared me to do so. I regarded wonen on Mafia as very different from myself – primarily wives (in arranged, and often polygynous marriages) and mothers of many children. They were, then, the antithesis of what I wanted to be: an autonomous professional.

SECOND VISIT, 1976: WOMEN IN THE FIELD, WOMAN IN THE FIELD

It was another few years before I was able to return to Mafia to test out my new hypotheses not only by asking the 'right' questions this time, but by asking them particularly of women. In 1976, I was invited by the BBC to go to Mafia with a film-crew to shoot footage for a film series (later entitled *Face Values*) on cross-cultural values: the focus of the Mafia material was the film to be entitled 'Men and Women' (BBC 1977).

Returning to the village after nine years was a wonderful experience – people were thrilled that I had returned and asked many questions about my husband and children (then aged 6 and 4). I realised that in their eyes I had grown up by becoming a wife and a mother. In Britain, however, I had just spent a year job-hunting unsuccessfully, usually being interviewed for posts which went to males, and often being told that I was 'too old' or even on one occasion being asked by a male anthropology professor if I was 'really serious' about wanting a job – it seemed that two babies effectively cancelled out the two books I had published by this time. On Mafia, however, transition into my thirties meant that even young adults greeted me with the respectful form reserved for their elders and betters – *Shikamoo* – 'I hold your feet'. Age there seemed to have its advantages, as a number of anthropologists have noted in their accounts of fieldwork. By this time, too, I had matured considerably, having experienced not only the birth of children, but also the death of a parent and several other close relatives.

Both because I returned as a familiar person and as a social adult, people treated me differently. Indeed, some of them verbalised this quite clearly: 'Before you were just a young girl; now you're grown up and we can talk to you properly.' I was immediately embroiled in the marital problems of my old friends Mohammed and Mwahadia who had just separated, or rather Mwahadia had left Mohammed, claiming that she had had enough of his profligacy (cf. Caplan 1992). I was urged by relatives and friends to try and effect a reconciliation between them; each of the parties came frequently to talk to me, both to complain about the other's past and present behaviour, and, I suspected, to see if they could find out the other's intentions for the future. Mohammed, as he was quick to point out, had the law on his side – Mwahadia had no right to leave him unless he divorced her (which he refused to do). Yet the majority of villagers supported Mwahadia and berated Mohammed for his past failure as a husband. I was impressed by this, as well as by Mwahadia's resolution, to which she adhered, in leaving him.

On this trip, I not only talked a great deal to women, but also became interested in parent–child relations, something I had not thought to investigate before. Although I had realised from the data that I gathered on the first trip that women had important productive roles, this time I was able to see the significance of female links, especially between mothers *and* daughters, which not only enabled women to be mothers and workers, but also facilitated their remarriages after divorce, since children were usually taken to be fostered by their grandmothers.

Although I found the filming itself somewhat problematic and very intrusive (cf. Caplan n.d.), none the less it did teach me several important lessons about the construction of gender on Mafia. After people had, quite legitimately, objected to being filmed unless they were recompensed, I negotiated a small fee for per- mission to film. Men and women always insisted on being paid separately, and men would say that the permission of a wife had to be sought as well as their own if we were filming a household.

A major event which we followed on film was a lengthy circumcision ritual for the sons of two brothers, the elder of whom was my 'brother' Ali. It was agreed that part of the costs of the ritual should be born by the film producer. One evening, however, Ali arrived in my house and said that my *wifi* (his wife, my sister-in-law) was very upset with me because she had not received any fee for the filming. I replied that we *had* paid a fee, but Ali's answer was that we had given it to *him*, not to *her*. In this way, I came to understand more clearly that men and women hold all property separately, which seemed a distinct improvement on the situation in Britain at the time, where marriage entailed not only community of property, but the taxing of a woman's income with that of her husband.

Another lesson emerged from filming the circumcision itself. I realised, of course, that the ritual was about 'making' potential men by other men. Although I had attended numerous circumcision rituals, recorded the songs and riddles and had them explained to me, I had never asked to attend the actual circumcision operation, feeling that in this case, my sex did constitute a bar. Nor did I do so this time, although I negotiated with the chief circumcisor (for a hefty fee) permission for the camera crew, all of whom were male, to film the circumcision. Afterwards I was accosted by a group of village men, and the following dialogue took place:

Villager: Mama Patlisha, we want to know if those men [the crew] have been circumcised?
Me: I really do not know, but I will ask.
Villager: Because if they have not, then it would have been better for you to be there and have taken the pictures than strangers like them.

Here, then, the right to be present at a circumcision is defined less by sex than by gender identity confirmed not only by a circumcision operation but also by knowledge of its surrounding ritual. Thus, in spite of my sex, my presence was considered preferable to that of men who were both strangers and uncircumcised. I began to realise that the relationship between sex and gender, and other factors too, was more complex than I had previously thought.

Other lessons came from some of the material filmed, particularly the interviews. Ali's ex-wife, now divorced from a subsequent marriage, described how she supported and cared for her aged father as well as herself. Hassan's grandmother was also filmed explaining how she fostered a number of her grandchildren, and paid for their keep. When asked if it was better to have girl or boy children, she replied:

Girls are better – definitely. You bring up a girl, and when she's bigger, she'll pound rice for you, she'll go and fetch water, she'll go and look for firewood, and when you die, she'll wash your corpse. But a boy! He doesn't pound, he doesn't fetch water, he doesn't do anything – except that perhaps he'll dig your grave for you! Girls help you in your work, while boys – well, perhaps you can send them on errands to the shop, that's it.

And when they are grown-up, women are better than men; they have more heart (*moyo*), more sympathy (*huruma*) for people. I think that is the way God created them. A man might even snatch food away from his own mother and go and give it to his wife, while she stays there starving. But a woman, a daughter, would never behave like that. She would remember the day when her mother gave birth to her.

I returned to London to make a film, as well as writing a number of articles, which emphasised the separateness of women and men in the same household, the relative autonomy of women and their sources of power. Looking back now, I can see that from my vantage point at that time, women in Mafia did seem to have solved some of the problems with which I was grappling then because of my gender. Women on Mafia worked as well as having children, and no one accused them of neglecting and damaging their children. Women kept their earnings and property separate from their husbands – there was no common property or tax. Women received help with child care, mainly from their female relatives. Children were desired and valued and their company enjoyed. I published a number of articles on these themes (1978, 1982, 1983):

> I am not trying to present a picture of life as ideal for women on Chole [Mafia]; in many ways their lives are more difficult than those of men. Women certainly work harder, in that they share more or less equally in agriculture, but have a greater burden of household and childcare tasks. They also have fewer economic resources than men because they inherit coconut trees at a 1:2 ratio to men, and have fewer opportunities for acquiring them by buying or planting. Nevertheless women are in this society independent individuals, and not appendages of men.
>
> (Caplan 1978: 174)

INTERLUDE 1976–85

For the decade after my return, most of my research and writing was directed to South Asia, rather than East Africa. By this time, I had a full-time teaching job, and although this was a source of much satisfaction, I found it more of a struggle to write while juggling a heavy load of teaching, administration and pastoral work, not to mention responsiblities to a growing family. During this period, I became aware of the pressures of work-load as never before.

I continued to communicate with people in Kanga, and wrote the occasional article, being determined to return as soon as I could get a sabbatical. In the meanwhile, the anthropology of gender itself was changing, with a greater emphasis on gender relations, rather than a simple concentration upon women. Both my personal circumstances, as well as paradigm shifts, affected the collection of data when I went back for a third time.

THIRD VISIT, 1985: GENDER PROBLEMATISED

I returned yet again to Mafia in 1985, with the specific intention of researching food, health and fertility. The first two topics had become growing sub-fields in anthropology, and I had organised and taught a new course on the anthropology of food at the college where I had been working since 1977. I was thus well aware of the food crisis in Africa, its declining production levels and increasing food imports as well as its periodic and much-publicised famines. I was also aware, from acquaintance with the growing literature on development, that women are frequently marginalised in this process.

Once again, there was a warm welcome – my 'brother' Ali rented me a house he had almost finished building next to his old one – and the research began. This time, I decided that my major method would be intensive observation of a limited number of households whose members I knew well. In addition, I would use statistical materials gained from observation at the Mother and Child Health Clinic which had come into being since my last visit, and from records of the district hospital; these would give me information on fertility rates, pregnancy histories, sex differentials in morbidity rates and so on.

Even if I had not wanted to research this topic, it would have been raised by villagers themselves, both men and women, who asked me why I still only had two children, whether I was afraid of 'this work', and warned me that such a small number was not sufficient to care for me in old age. None of this was really a surprise: I had been previously aware that people valued having children, but conversations initiated by the villagers on my own relative paucity in this respect gave me valuable insights into their reasons for this. Even so, I was not prepared for the nature of some of my findings in this regard.

The first is that in attending the Mother and Child Health Clinic, I discovered that a higher proportion of girl than boy babies and toddlers were failing to thrive. Furthermore, women's pregnancy histories suggested that more girls than boys died at an early age. This situation correlated with other factors, including sex preferences. Although women actively wanted daughters as well as sons, men usually said that they preferred the latter. Men also wanted more children than did women. A woman who bears a daughter is thus likely to try and get pregnant again quickly to please her husband, thus endangering the health of the previous child, who is weaned as soon as the mother knows she is pregnant.

The second factor is that men are supposed to provide the cash needs, which include most protein foods, for the household. The exhortations of the midwife to mothers to give milk and eggs to their weanlings could only be complied with if the husband chose to spend his money in that way – and not all men did so.

The third factor is patterns of eating. Strictly speaking, people on Mafia do not practise sequential feeding in the same way as do those in India, for instance (cf. Miller 1981). But at the household level, women and men often eat separately off two different platters, with boys sharing with their fathers, and girls with their mothers. Women told me that they gave their husbands more and better food: 'Otherwise the men get angry.' Obviously, not only does this sometimes mean that women themselves are inadequately fed, but it is also likely to mean that boy children who eat with their fathers are better fed than girls who eat with their mothers; this ties in with the belief held by both sexes that women and girl children are better able to withstand hunger than are males, 'for that is how God made them'.

In short, then, it became clear to me that talking to women was not always sufficient – women, especially young women who had been to school, did know what kinds of food were good for small children, but they did not control the purse strings. Women usually had clear ideas about the number of children they wanted and the mixture of sexes, whereas men wanted unlimited numbers and had a strong preference for boys. It seems possible, then, that there is a correlation between these factors and the skewed morbidity and mortality rates of small children.

Another area in which it became clear to me this time that women are highly disadvantaged is in terms of work-load. Ten years before, I had assumed that women's involvement in productive labour would have positive consequences for their status and autonomy, and to some extent this remains true. Women are entitled to a half share of the crop if they divorce or separate, and if they cultivate a field apart from their husband they can dispose of the harvest as they please. Furthermore, divorced and widowed women can survive on their own without a husband. None the less, I now saw that women also suffer from far too much work and enjoy far less leisure than men. They are not only responsible for fetching wood and water, for pounding grain, cooking food, cleaning the house and caring for children, but they usually work a much longer day in the fields than do men, many of whom go off after the midday meal to the centre of the village to 'do the shopping' and attend meetings for the rest of the afternoon.

Given their heavy work-loads, frequent pregnancies and sometimes lesser food intake, it was thus scarcely surprising that most women suffered from anaemia and had generally higher rates of morbidity than did men, as both the village paramedic and the district hospital staff confirmed. What was I to make of these data? Had I been totally wrong in what I had 'seen' before?

DISCUSSION

There are, it seems to me, a number of factors which determine the kinds of data we collect, and our interpretation of them. One of the most important of these is our positionality – who are we for them? Who are they for us? Such questions have to be considered not only in the light of anthropology's current paradigms, but also in terms of such factors as our gender, age and life experience, as well as our race and nationality. This raises the question of difference and the comparison which is always implicit in our accounts. In conclusion, I consider such topics in the light of this account.

At the time of my first field-trip I was single and childless, and thought, as my supervisor put it, that 'the world was my oyster'. I saw the villagers, and especially the women as 'other'. Women like them, constantly pregnant or lactating, illiterate, and subject to rules of sexual segregation, were what I, determined to prove myself to be as good as a man, was not. I did not wish to identify myself as that kind of a woman either in the field setting or at home. I was determined to have a career, not be just another woman who would disappear into a world of marriage and babies.

None the less, in spite of my resistance, there did come during this period a growing awareness of the implications of being a woman and its concomitant limitations, which led to a period of struggle over the desire to have a 'normal' private life (that is, be married) and to have a career, which meant being taken seriously by the males who would confirm or withhold approval of work, and give recommendations and jobs.

It was only after my return to London that I began to see the Mafian women somewhat differently: as articulate in discussion (when they had time to hold conversations), important in ritual, and sexually autonomous. At this point, I was comparing them with women in my own society of whose position I was becoming, because of the influence of feminism, and because of my own problems, increasingly critical. As I had foreseen, it *was* difficult to maintain a career as well as have children. Reviewing the material on Mafia, it seemed as if women there had in many respects a better deal than women in the west: they controlled their sexuality and property *and* they were productive workers. I came to see them as different from their men, but not necessarily subordinate, and different from women in the west, but not necessarily worse off.

By the time of the second trip, I was married with two children, and struggling to maintain a career as well. By this time too, feminist anthropology was developing fast. It had criticised mainstream anthropology for its male bias and ignoring of women, and numerous studies of women were being carried out to 'fill in the gaps in the data' and to 'redress the balance'. It was with this kind of aim in mind that I had returned to Mafia in 1976. In retrospect, I realise now that frequently, in discussing issues of gender, I talked mainly to women. I made a conscious effort to seek them out, feeling that there were many areas that I must have missed before. Furthermore, because we were filming material for a western audience, the basis of comparison between them and us was particularly explicit. In showing what life was like for women on Mafia, I specifically wanted to show a western audience that things could be different for women, that there was nothing 'natural' or inevitable about the way they were in the west.

By the time of the third trip, feminist anthropology had changed from a focus upon women to one upon gender relations. It was realised that one needed to understand men in order to understand women, and vice versa, and that men are gendered subjects just as much as women are. Accordingly, this time I talked to men not only because they had been important informants from the beginning, but as men *qua* males. This revealed that men and women have different perceptions and interests on certain issues – for example, numbers of children and sex of children – and also that men have more power in this regard, being able to pressurise a wife to get pregnant and to withhold permission for contraception to be used. Thus, regarding fertility and feeding patterns as women's matters is nonsensical – they are matters of gender relations and the distribution of power in them.

By 1985 feminist anthropology had also abandoned a rather simplistic, neo-Engelian assumption that if women did productive work, their status must necessarily be higher than if they did not. Indeed, for women to work productively may mean that they are grossly overburdened. But another reason why I was perhaps able to see this more clearly was my own life circumstances. I had come to realise that the double shift is not necessarily a bed of roses, and that even with a supportive partner and perhaps paid help, it comes with a high price tag. Energies are limited, time is always too little. With this new awareness, as I looked on my third trip at the work-load and fertility rates in Mafia, I could see more clearly than before overburdened women having too many pregnancies, losing too many babies, not eating enough and suffering a high level of morbidity.

This does not negate, necessarily, what I 'saw' before: autonomous and productive women, rejoicing in their own sexuality, able to lighten their burdens by cooperation, to conduct rituals, and to wield political power by a variety of means. The truth, if there is a such a thing, is that women are all these things, and that gender is a much more complex matter than we have supposed. Much depends on how we contextualise the field 'facts' of women's lives and what is our basis for comparison.

Thus far, I have concentrated on how I saw women and men in Mafia. But of equal importance is how they saw me. When I went to the field in 1965, British anthropology emphasised objectivity. Even had it not done so, my position would have been one of relative distanciation determined not only by me and my training, but also by my subjects, for I came as a stranger, and furthermore, one who by virtue of youth and sex constituted something of an anomaly. In some respects, therefore, there were limitations on what information I was allowed to collect. In addition, I was young in terms of life experience, and lacked the understanding which would have enabled me to empathise more with my subjects.

By the time of my return in 1976, I had matured, a factor which was recognised by the villagers, who also ceased to find me such an anomaly. People related to me very differently, and invited me to become much more directly involved in their lives. I was ready for such an invitation, because part of my maturing was an increasing political awareness which included a dissatisfaction with anthropology in terms not only of the feminist critique, but also of its ethnographic methods. Whereas on the first field-trip I had felt compelled to collect a large amount of measurable data, this time I was more content simply to be around and participate in whatever was going on.

By the time of my third field-trip, all of these tendencies had intensified. I made the decision to focus upon a very small number of households both to provide the kind of case-studies I needed for the topics being researched, but also to provide an ethnography of the everyday. In the process, I became even more closely involved with the lives of several villagers, to the extent that the boundaries between self and other were much less clear-cut than before.

Furthermore, in thinking and writing about this material, and in reading around the area of reflexivity, I have become aware that being an ethnographer means studying the self as well as the other. In this way, the self becomes 'othered', an object of study, while at the same time, the other, because of familiarity, and a different approach to fieldwork, becomes part of the self.

ACKNOWLEDGEMENTS

The fieldwork on which this chapter was based was supported by the University of London and the Worshipful Company of Goldsmiths (1965–7), by the BBC (1976) and by the Nuffield Foundation and the Central Research Fund (1985). I am grateful to Diane Bell, Lionel Caplan and Wazir Karim for comments on earlier drafts.

REFERENCES

Caplan, A.P. (1976a) *Choice and Constraint in a Swahili Community*, Oxford: International African Institute/Oxford University Press.
—— (1976b) 'Boys' circumcision and girls' puberty rites among the Swahili of Mafia Island, Tanzania', *Africa* 46, 1.
—— (1978) 'The Swahili of Chole Island, Tanzania', in A. Sutherland (ed.), *Face Values*, London: BBC/RAI.
—— (1982) 'Gender, ideology and modes of production on the East African coast', in J. de Vere Allen (ed.), *From Zinj to Zanzibar*, Wiesbaden: Franz Steiner Verlag.
—— (1983) 'Women's property, Islamic law and cognatic descent', in R. Hirschon (ed.), *Women and Property, Women as Property*, London: Croom Helm.
—— (1992) 'Sex and spirits: a Swahili informant and his diary', in J. Okely and H. Callaway (eds), *Anthropology and Autobiography*, London: Routledge.
—— (n.d.) *Engendering Knowledge: A Swahili Community over Two Decades* (in preparation).
Cesara, M. (1984) *No Hiding Place: Reflections of a Woman Anthropologist*, London: Academic Press.
Leonard, D. (1976) 'Women's Anthropology Workshop' Mimeo, London Women's Anthropology Group, 1973.
Miller, B. (1981) *The Endangered Sex: Neglect of Female Children in Rural North India*, Ithaca, NY: Cornell University Press.

12 The mouth that spoke a falsehood will later speak the truth
Going home to the field in Eastern Nigeria

Ifi Amadiume

When I was approached to contribute to these essays on 'Women in the field revisited', my first impulse was to turn down the invitation with the genuine excuse that I was very busy with other projects. My feeling was: What is the use? Where would I begin to reach a common understanding with 'privileged bourgeois white women' on any of the issues? It was only after an extensive discussion with an African-Caribbean friend whose political views I respect very much that I was persuaded to write something. She felt that it was important that we put our views across, no matter how controversial these were. It was up to the people we criticise to decide whether our views should be published or not. They are still our teachers, supervisors and editors.

I entered into this agreement with full awareness of the oddity of myself and my position in the field of social anthropology. I also knew that I was not going to be sharing the common experiences of most of the contributors, who were strangers to their host communities. Indeed, my situation was the reverse, for I had 'returned home'. Paradoxically for me, the oddity was that as an African social anthropologist I was supposed to explore an African culture through a methodology and theory designed not for Africa, but for Europe.

My fieldwork was part of my doctoral requirement, but my choice of subject and methodology was a reaction to my experience of British racism and my rejection of basic geocultural classifications in social anthropology. Indeed, I went to the field to begin a process of decolonising my own mind and seeking my identity by reconstructing the social history of Nnobi, my father's village. I can therefore say at the outset that I did not go home to learn to understand or to study 'my people' in order to teach the west about them. Thus my chapter will not dwell on the conventional tradition of gathering, ordering and interpreting data *per se*. Rather, I shall deal more with conflicts relating to the issues of the self and other, or in my own case, the multiple selves: as social subject, a member of an extended family, a daughter and a mother, and a woman with independent political views. All of these selves need to be considered, since they determine the ethnographer's methodology.

Representatives of Inyom Nnobi, June 1988.

FIELDWORK: FIRST VISIT

Getting back home

On Sunday, 8 June 1980, after a day of packing and unpacking by my ten-month-old daughter, Kemdi, I found myself at Heathrow airport with an excess luggage charge. However, I was determined to board the Nigerian Airways flight to Lagos that night, no matter what. In a way, my fieldwork had already begun at Heathrow, when I found myself assessing the situation and letting the ground rules guide my action. After nine years of personal involvement in the political struggle against racism in Britain and only eight months after my mother's death, I was still swimming in a turbulent sea that threatened to drown me, if I did not persistently hold my head above water. I boarded the plane after paying a bribe for excess luggage, an experience which reminded me that I was moving into a different arena of political activity – post-independence Nigeria, a fabrication of British imperialism in Africa.

My older brother Ikem met me at the airport and saw me through customs. I was grateful, particularly because I had excessive luggage which included items which I was going to trade or give away as presents during my fieldwork. I had to raise money for the field, since I had not received any funding. (The Social Science Research Council of Great Britain viewed fieldwork as something done by strangers and not by those returning to their own society. Hence I was immediately ineligible.) Furthermore, dealing with the bureaucracy at the

Nigerian High Commission in London for my tuition fees and maintenance was difficult enough, without introducing other problems relating to proposals for research grants.

My next younger sister, Chinelo, a medical doctor who at the time had two children, lived in Lagos. Because of her medical knowledge, Chinelo decided that it would be advisable that I remain in Lagos for some time with Kemdi so that she could observe how the baby acclimatised, while I pursued the problem of extending my federal Nigerian scholarship to cover my postgraduate studies. After a good night's sleep, I felt refreshed, especially since I was relieved of the anxiety of sole responsibility for my baby. She could now play with other children and pass from the attention of one adult to another. For me, that was the greatest difference between my situation in London and in Nigeria. I could feel my muscles relaxing and could actually concentrate on a conversation without being on my feet every minute trying to find out where Kemdi was or what she was doing.

Kemdi was soon 'acclimatised'. And within a few days, she had eaten worms and sand while playing in the garden. That brought back floods of memories of my childhood days. Which African child did not cook or eat sand? The real feeling of being back was finally there. I felt truly at home when I went to the market to have my hair plaited.

In anticipation of the research work ahead, I sent off some of the goods to another sister, Ego, at Enugu, to begin selling them for me. Some friends in Lagos had already given me some spending money and I felt myself to be once again part of a caring network of relationships. It was different from the experience of social isolation in London. My younger sister had taken full charge of my family, partly because I had been living abroad and did not have a place of my own in Nigeria, but also because, she, as second daughter, had had to step into my place after my mother's death and take full charge of our family. I was grateful to her for that.

Unfortunately, within one week of our arrival, Kemdi started having diarrhoea. I blamed the filthy Lagos water and decided that it was best to leave Lagos for Enugu. Travelling to Enugu was a lonely experience. It was also worrying since Kemdi's diarrhoea persisted. I also felt anxious facing the prospect of a sad homecoming without my mother. On arrival, I relived the experience of the totality of death. My sister Ego tried to make up for what was missing, and my mother's people were also determined to support and comfort me, bringing whole basketloads of food. They had become almost aggressively protective of us after her death.

Once Kemdi was on the mend, I could at last fully turn my mind to the necessary preparations for going to Nnobi. My mother's relatives contributed foodstuffs and I bought liquor as a present, especially the schnapps and gin advised by my father. Again I had a lot of luggage, as I had to spend money buying things to equip my father's house, which was usually empty. Two of my mother's sisters arranged for their children, little Ifi and Uchenna, to accompany me to Nnobi, and we all finally set off.

As a result of the genocide against the Igbo in the 1960s, my parents had had to leave Zaria, in Northern Nigeria, where we were all brought up. We settled at Enugu, the township next to our mother's village, and were consequently very near to her people while our father's house in his village remained unoccupied. My mother had been opposed to the idea of my father taking a second wife, who could have lived in the village house, since theirs was a monogamous church marriage, following the pattern of the elite Christian Creole culture which had developed in the local townships. Thus our village house had only been lived in fully for a short period during the Nigeria–Biafra war, which lasted from 1967 to 1970.

Going back there was a kind of pilgrimage. I came into the village with emotions very raw – my heart felt as if it was bleeding. Private moments of reflection brought pain, bitterness and loneliness. I passed my mother's grave, which was in the compound of my father's house in the village. Reflections of a woman's life and choices persisted during my entire stay in the village. I felt that in collecting and analysing information I was also seeking ways of mending my wounds.

The flow of relatives, who had come to greet me and talk about everyday practical family problems and obligations, made it feel that research had to accommodate itself with a normal routine, and that it was this routine which would finally provide the bulk of the data. At Enugu, my mother's relatives had mobilised themselves to assist and support me. At Nnobi, it was those of my father, but in both cases, it was the women who assisted. My female cousins, who were secondary school girls, were sent by my father's most senior sister, Susanna, to come and wash down the house, which was covered in Nnobi red dust. I remembered my amazement as one of these cousins walked in, because I realised that I could easily be looking at myself. With such a strong family resemblance, I experienced a new feeling of *umunne*, the spirit of common motherhood.

The women began to relate to me their feelings about my mother's death. It was then my turn to make the customary visit to the two sisters of my father who were still alive. By the time I got back, I was utterly exhausted, but as I began cooking while the children played, I started to feel that I had at last settled down. I was mistress of my own independent household in my father's village and mother of all these little children, including another couple from the neighbourhood who had moved in without invitation.

DOING FIELDWORK

Kemdi was getting progressively better but was teething again, which gave her a temperature. My father's sisters, brothers and patrilineage wives (who in classificatory terms were also my 'wives') all brought us things and I was reassured that Kemdi was going to be all right now. I was reminded of the Igbo belief that as soon as your feet touch your native soil, all your illnesses will disappear. They condemned Enugu water for being contaminated, just as I had condemned Lagos water. My mother had in her turn condemned London water! They advised me to wash the roof of the house to enable me to collect the clean water from heaven, as it was the rainy season. We did just that and I enjoyed again cool, sparkling, refreshing water for the first time in many years.

On this visit, with all the comings and going, the house was vibrant and lively. My father spent only a few days with us and then returned to Enugu. Once I had taken charge of things, he became like a guest in my house. Later, when he gave me a wooden bowl and developed the habit of asking me for some kolanuts or drinks for his guests, he began to treat me like a 'male daughter'!

The process of making mental notes, following up incidents by asking questions and participating in discussions and arguments, had already begun. For example, my senior aunt, Susanna, had mobilised her *umuokpu* (patrilineage daughters) to come and clean the house for me as a senior *ada* (first daughter). As she gave the instructions, she explained the duties, rules and obligations of *umuokpu*, even before it was announced that I had come home to study our customs, culture and history. The young girls were simply being instructed and socialised in the usual way.

However, once news got around of the reason for my homecoming, the response was overwhelming and I was hard-pressed to meet the numerous offers of help and the many names suggested for interviews. Indeed, the whole town was in competition as to who knew or could explain best *omenana* Nnobi (Nnobi custom).

The impact of western culture, through the churches, the educational, legal and administrative systems and other state agencies, often resulted in conflict between parents and their children and between relatives. Those of us who were brought up in the big towns, against a cosmopolitan background, experienced this more acutely than others who were still in their native villages. My father was always explaining what was right and wrong within Nnobi normative behaviour. Even my mother, who was not from Nnobi, was also constantly reminding us of Nnobi customs, lest she be accused of turning our minds away from the customs of our father's people in favour of her own. Such leanings often conflicted with the teachings in school and church, but we often formed independent views of the attitudes of our maternal and paternal relatives. The constant prescriptions regarding motherhood in Igbo folktales, songs and statements did not give my father's relatives and their customs much chance in our esteem in comparison with our unconditional love for our mother's relatives. I believe this is the case with most Igbo families, if not all African families. We view with some suspicion and unease many of our father's relatives, while we just take for granted and trust our mother's people.

My decision to live in our house with the children was a source of amazement and happiness to the villagers, particularly since they had considered me emotionally weak. My mother's death, funeral and burial had left me overcome with grief and I had not been able to act as an *ada*, taking charge of and supervising events. Chinelo, my younger sister, was the one who behaved like the *ada*. The test for me, therefore, was not just the ability to manage a household in the village. It was also being able to live alone in the house with my mother's grave right inside the compound. This proved a tougher test than I or others expected, and both my father and the villagers admired and respected me for it. The tenderness of people towards me during that period of research work must be understood in this context. We had all suffered the greatest tragedy for any Igbo person, the death of a relatively young mother, who was only 55 years old when she died.

With our presence, especially that of the baby, Kemdi, it was believed that what had been lost had been replaced. Just before her death, my mother had spent a weekend at the Nnobi house, and the villagers told me that she had cleaned it out thoroughly and had visited practically everyone and had paid the dues owed to her *inyom-di* (organisation of patrilineage wives). She had also done the same at Enugu during that same week. Stories about women who have died a sudden and unexpected death seem to follow this pattern. Through accounts of my mother's actions before her death, the roles and duties of a wife and mother were explained to me.

After a few days in Nnobi, I began to have a clearer idea of the various political groupings in the lineage structure and what their roles and duties were. I also visited our old *obi* (ancestral house), where my father's brother, Johnson, now the *okpala* (first son), lives. He was very happy to see us. He gave Kemdi some money and cut down a coconut for her, explaining her place in the kinship system as he did so. Yes, Kemdi was very special person as she was a *nwadiana* (a daughter's child). Johnson then sang me the song of his father's mother, whose reincarnation Nnobi people say I am. Thus I enjoyed multiple deference and respect as an *ada*, as a very educated woman and as a wealthy and powerful ancestress. As these rights were explained to me, I clung to them as a source of confidence.

Consequently, I knew what status I had and what rights I could invoke in different situations with different categories of people. I knew that even the Igwe of Nnobi, the 'traditional ruler', was my *nwadiana*, (a child of a daughter of my patrilineage) and that if I asked him to bow his head he would do so, and if I told him to kneel down he would have no choice but obey. And indeed, I did have the occasion to tell the Igwe off and he took it in good part and looked ashamed. I also had rebuked Eze Agba, the priest of Idemili, who at first had tried to ursurp my authority, until another relative who was present reminded the priest that he too was my *nwadiana*; again, the priest smiled apologetically.

With this awareness of confidence and authority, I felt fearless enough to approach any senior man or patriarch for interviews or ask them to do things for me. One of them, who still holds on to his African religion, was so amazed that he began to shout that I must be an *Ekwe* candidate possessed by the goddess Idemili. However, it must also be said that I did not always get the upper hand in these power struggles.

These practitioners of our African religion also realised the genuineness of my interest in our traditional customs and consequently embraced me into their fold. In spite of their conflict with the Christian elites, they treated me well when they saw that I was 'on their side'. I did not go to church and they were genuinely surprised by this, since it was my relatives who had first brought the church to Nnobi.

Before long, I had established a routine of finishing my morning chores and going out for visits and interviews. The main market days were usually busier, with many visitors and lots of presents for Kemdi from my relatives as *nni afia* or *ife afia* (presents from the market). I had also started attending life-cycle ceremonies and venturing into more distant villages and towns. During one of my visits to Nnewi somehow unthinkingly I decided to put on a pair of jeans, which I had hitherto not worn in the village. The laughter and jeers which greeted me made me swear never to wear trousers again in these areas. The men called me *'Oga na enwero amu'*, 'Master, who does not have a penis'.

From various discussions and interviews, I had collected a lot of information on the traditional economy, various social institutions, including the 'male daughter', 'female husband', the *Ekwe* institution, the traditional religious system and practically all aspects of social life. During this period, I confined myself to finding out about *omenana oge gbo* (ancient customs). I felt that I had to get these quite clear in my head before I could begin to examine the patterns of change in these institutions.

Throughout my stay in the village, my sisters were constantly sending me money and food items, as well as visiting from as far away as Lagos. Other relatives visited too, and those who came later apologised and said that they came as soon as they learned that I was back or as soon as they could take time off from work. Those nearer the house brought food. By then Kemdi had acquired two cocks of her own, and to my delight would pick guava from the tree. She had started walking quite well by ten months.

By the end of a year of research work in the village, I had a fairly clear picture in my mind of traditional Nnobi economic, social, religious and political systems and the structures of relationships between various interest groups and these systems.

A common experience of social researchers is the feeling of being fully saturated with information and not getting anything new. People had become repetitive in their accounts, and I felt I could even detect distorted versions of similiar stories. I felt that it was time for me to return to London and begin the tedious task of reading, translating, transcribing and arranging data, the tricky phase when the subjective self determines the result, and what brought Geertz (1988) to call anthropology 'literature'.

There was, however, one last task for me to do. I organised an essay competition for both the boys' and girls' secondary schools. My intention, apart from encouraging interest in local research into our customs, was to open up a wider discussion on our history and cultural institutions and, more importantly, to have an overall source of data with which to cross-check my own findings and conclusions.

This technique proved an unbelievable success. Nnobi basked in cultural pride for several days. The town was mentioned on the state radio, which reported the names of winners of the essay competition. It advised other towns and villages to follow the example of Nnobi. In Nnobi, elders, both men and women, felt that this sort of thing should be a regular event.

The general discussions which resulted from this event helped both my understanding and analysis of the politics of meaning. By this time, I was quite knowledgeable in Nnobi history and traditional institutions, and listened in amusement to the various interest groups reconstructing patriarchal ideologies. *Odinana* people (followers of African religion) were feeling particularly triumphant, as they witnessed this new interest and pride in the same culture which the Christians had rejected. They took comfort in the Igbo adage *onu kwulu njo ga emesie kwue nma* (the mouth that spoke a falsehood/ill will later speak the truth/good).

SECOND VISIT

Experiencing matriarchy

Back in London, I finished translating the data by the end of April 1981 and had arranged the material into chapters by the end of September 1981. It was not until December that Kemdi and I returned again to Nigeria. As before, I had to trade to cover my fieldwork expenses. This time, however, my research experience was quite different. I was returning to gather specific kinds of information and as I only had about two months to spend in the village, I had to be more organised and specific about my tasks.

By now, Kemdi was 2 years old, and my family persuaded me to leave her in Lagos with my sister Chinelo, so that I could concentrate on my work and also be able to travel more freely. It was a hard decision for me, but I finally agreed to the arrangement. My family reminded me of our customary values, that I should not think twice about where Kemdi was, as long as she was with one of my sisters. This was our very first separation and it proved very difficult for me. I was determined to work hard and return quickly to my daughter.

My major task in this second visit was to conduct long and intensive discussions and interviews concerning the colonial and post-colonial periods, which formed the database for the second and third parts of my thesis. This was also a period of personal transformation for me. As a result of my friendship with my 'male daughter' Nwajiuba and her wife, I was able to accompany *odinana* (elderly women) to *eke Idemili* (Idemili's open space) and witness them do the ritual sweeping of the grounds.

This particular experience was like a window into the African matriarchal past. I saw women enjoying full control of their rituals and could see their love for one another. I felt a kind of raw female sexuality that I had never experienced or read about before, as I watched them dancing for sheer joy and announcing the coming of their annual religious worship of the goddess Idemili. I could see true sisterhood in practice as these women swept the ground in unison. As I was the only woman there still in her thirties I felt I had been specially treated in being allowed to participate in the ritual. Normally, I would have needed another thirty or forty years to be granted this singular experience.

Attacks on matriarchy

It would, however, be fallacious to suppose that matriarchy continued to flourish in Nnobi. Along with my discovery of matriarchy, I had also become increasingly aware of the extent to which things were changing and women were losing power without even realising it. This issue emerged during my discussions which the *Inyom Nnobi* (the Nnobi Women's Council).

I had asked for an interview with the Council's leader, and she had promised to consult with other members. Much to my surprise, I was told one day by one of 'my wives' (that is, my uncle's wife) that the whole Council was to visit me the following morning. On giving me this news, my 'wife' immediately opened her handbag and gave me a contribution of four kolanuts in solidarity and as a symbol of my high status. The whole of Nnobi had in fact also heard the news that *Inyom Nnobi* was going to visit Ifeyinwa (my full name). When I returned home, my wives were already calling one by one to give me kolanuts and pledge their support in case I needed anything to be done.

As for my father, who was staying with me at the time, he found the news of the impending visit simply overwhelming. He told me that it was the highest honour that they could pay me and proceeded to instruct me on what food and drinks to prepare, the presentation of kola and how to conduct myself. As for himself, his immediate decision was that 'sunrise would not meet him in Nnobi'. He was going to disappear to Enugu because, according to him, if *Inyomi Nnobi* met him at home, his pockets would be emptied as they would demand a big feast.

I now present edited extracts from my dialogue with *Inyom Nnobi*, which raises certain questions about the role of the researcher, especially one doing research in her own community, about women researching other women, and the researcher *vis-à-vis* the oppressed.

The meeting with the Women's Council on 18 January 1982

As soon as the women entered the compound gate, they took control of the whole house, asking me for a list of people who lived there. They kept an eye on the street, making sure that no one entered the compound. In fact, a male cousin whom I had asked to take photographs of the visit was stopped and asked to turn back. According to the women, no man was to enter that compound while *Inyom Nnobi* was holding a conference there.

When the women finally settled down, we exchanged greetings and I then offered the customary kolanuts, which I handed to the leader. After their distribution according to membership of the four quarters of the town, the leader prayed:

> Lord, we want no trouble. We women want no trouble. Any compound we visit gets peace and no more trouble. Let the peace of this year be more

abundant than the others. Let the devil not affect anyone else, our children, husbands or in-laws. Women want peace.

To this I replied:

I do not intend to give a long speech. My aim is to understand things concerning women, especially the organisation of *Umuokpu* and *Inyom Nnobi*. This is a result of a kind of anger I felt in England, where I have lived. Women were angry, saying that they did a lot of work or worked harder than men, but when the time came for public acclaim or material reward, men took all the credit. The same thing happened in this country. Those white men who came to write about us wrote down what suited them and wrote about men not the women.

Those of us who have some knowledge about Igbo culture usually feel that there has been a lot of misrepresentation and misinterpretation of social facts, especially on matters concerning women. By not having the facts ourselves, we are usually unable to correct most of these assumptions. This is why I had asked to speak with your leader to find out what I can about women and events in Nnobi. It seems to me that women no longer have a say in the political organisation of Nnobi, unlike the past when women were organised under the leadership of *Ekwe* titled women.

Nnobi welfare organisation seems to be completely monopolised by men. In all the local elections, all the candidates have been men. I have therefore been asking myself whether the *Inyom Nnobi* has fallen. How is the Women's Council involved in the present type of government? Have men as usual cheated them and monopolised everything? Then I corrected myself and decided that I could not act on assumptions and guesswork, that the thing to do is to go to the women and find out what part they play in the present political set-up. So, could you tell me about the organisation of *Inyom Nnobi* as it is today; whether you are still involved in the governing of Nnobi today and what position you hold? If none, that should also be admitted. This is all I wish to say. Have I explained myself clearly? Have I spoken well?

The women: Yes, thank you, and welcome.

The leader: Yes, you have spoken well. What you have just said, you said it to me then and I gave you a reply. I said to you that one person does not take it upon herself to speak on behalf of others without permission. I said that even if I talked to you, I would invite the representatives, *ndi nku*. These women that you see here are the representatives. We still have our organisation and we have our own seat in the government. We work well together, we women in Nnobi; we do not say that this person is a Christian and that one is a Pagan. These representatives hear things before *Inyom Nnobi* is informed. There are thirty-six of us who judge cases – three from each ward. We deal with many matters. We see there is no trouble in the family, especially with regard to women. We see to the policing of women in the market or even in the streets. Wherever women are, we do not want to hear that they are causing trouble. We wish that all women be at peace with fellow women. Anyone who proves stubborn and disobeys our rules is punished. We have a rule of punishment. If the person refuses, we have a way of dealing with the person. The person will not even refuse. In Nnobi, anywhere a market is conducted, anywhere any kind of meeting or gathering takes place, women sweep them and keep them clean.

I then asked the women about their relationship with the Nnobi Welfare Organisation (NWO), which they complained no longer invited them to their meetings but only called them to work, and asked why they tolerated this.

First woman: They now direct our organisation. We now work with the chairman of NWO. They wrote down certain instructions and gave them to us. They have now given us a set of rules of conduct. We have our own chair at meetings.

Ifi: There seems to be a contradiction in your statement, for you said that they now only invite you for work.

Second woman: That is so. The men have monopolised everything.

Spokeswoman: Listen, do not implicate me. I have no strength for these people. We do have a position in the ruling council.

Ifi: What I am saying is that perhaps things have changed. Since things are like this, you can no longer do anything about it.

Third woman: Granted that they have given us no position, we have been waiting in anticipation to see if they will change their minds and give us our due respect by giving us a position befitting us.

Ifi: But since they have not done so, will you just sit and wait? Will you not try and appeal to and ally yourself with men in power who are sympathetic to women? Of course, in the past you could have applied your customary sanction of mass demonstrations and gone to sing *ahihaa*.

Spokeswoman: We have been given a position in the government. Yes, we do have a position. If there is any meeting or anything that they wish us to do, they send for us and we the representatives go and meet them and discuss it. We discuss as men and women, contributing our own opinion. They do not give orders and tell us not to speak. We have a position, for they gave *Inyom Nnobi* a seat. If we have anything to say to them, we do so. If they have anything to say to us, they do so. Yes, we have a seat. We collect levies from women, they collect from men.

Ifi: But what about titles? I see that there are no more titled women in Nnobi. Men, for example, still take the *Ozo* title.

There are the *Ichie* and the *Nze*. But when titled people appear, there are no women among them.

First woman: No, we will not participate in such things. We will not take titles from them, for we are churchgoers. We are Christ's people.

Second woman: The problem is this. The title that women used to take was known as *Ekwe*, but since the advent of the church, that title-taking was stopped. The only kind of title-taking that we participate in today is in the church.

Ifi: Part of the reason for women's loss of power today is because they no longer participate in title-taking in Nnobi. There is no title which women work hard for and aspire to. There is today no title which guarantees women certain powers in Nnobi.

Spokeswoman: No I do not agree with you. We do have a position. Talking about titles, you say that women no longer take titles, but there are women chiefs.

Ifi: You should get together and assess the new political climate and try and find ways of acquiring power as the men are doing. About this question of wealth, title and power, right now Nnobi is trying to draw up a constitution and from the discussions that I've held with those commissioned to do it, it seems to me that men are going to consolidate and legitimise their monopolisation of important political seats in Nnobi through the revival of various titles for men. The only title that they may consider for women would be a modified version of the *Ekwe* title, which you have condemned as paganistic! You are losing out fast in the new politics!

Second woman: Going back to your point on title-taking, these days, the title which we approve of is Mothers Union. Only those who have been wedded in the church may join the union. Even then, they are still screened for good character. You see, our understanding of the *Ekwe* title-taking is different from your understanding of it. In the past, when a woman took the Ekwe title and women crawled under her, they took her as their *chi*, deity. From our own understanding now, we believe that no human being should be worshipped, except God the creator, *Chineke*. This does not mean that we do not respect people, but to worship a person as a God, no! This is what we mean by faith in Christ. The Bible says it is a sin to worship someone like a God.

Ifi: Listen, let me defend myself. You know that the Vice-President of Nigeria is called *Ekwu eme* and you know that this is also a title. It is a title given by people of a town in appreciation of what someone has done for them. *Ekwu eme*, means one who fulfils one's promise. One proposes and carries out one's proposal. I see no reason why Nnobi should not have similar titles to give to women as a reward and encouragement for hard work. Take this leader of yours, for example. You appreciate and praise her dynamism and efforts. Why should she not be rewarded with a title? Say, something like *odozi obodo*, one who keeps the town at peace, or works for the well-being of the town? In which case, one would feel happy and rewarded and therefore continue in the good work. Perhaps, you now understand what I've been driving at. I do not suggest that you worship another human being. Indeed, I'd be the last person to suggest such a thing.

Women: We thank you and agree with you.

Spokeswoman: Now that we have heard the tone of your voice, we will confide in you. We have in fact been meaning to invite the men and ask them to state the cause of their quarrel with us but we have been waiting for things to cool down a bit before arranging a meeting. But now that we have heard you, we will call them and ask them to speak up and say what the quarrel is about and what benefit they derive from quarrelling. We do not like to quarrel. If it were not that you are leaving so soon, I would have said that we would invite you to be present on the day that we will invite them. On that day, we shall write them a letter and ask for the most troublesome ones, for there are some of them who are the worst offenders. We will invite them to the Igwe's palace.

Ifi: Yes, the point is that those who wrote the constitution are people known to us. I have held discussions with them and know the tone of their voice and their opinion and therefore what they are capable of doing. I do not know whether they have actually written down the constitution, but I know from their attitude to women and from other things which they have written in the past, that they cannot be looked upon to safeguard rights for women or be trusted to fight for women. They are mainly concerned with their own interests. Since women know what efforts they have put into the well-being of Nnobi, it is up to women to demand and safeguard their rights. You should always have your decisions and charter at the tip of your fingers and therefore be quite prepared and equipped to confront or negotiate with the men. Your power is no longer guaranteed. You have to negotiate and fight, even scramble for it. Although you have not taken part in the drawing up of the constitution or been consulted about it, before it is passed, I am sure that there will still be a meeting to which you will be invited. Since

	you now know about it, you can then attend that meeting prepared. To be forewarned is to be forearmed. If one does not know a thing in advance . . .
All the women :	Then one is taken unawares.

At the end of the meeting, the women were appreciative and prayed for me. Their spokeswoman was more articulate than a priest. The traditional matriarch in her surfaced when she ended her prayer by saying, 'We own father, husband, in-law, relatives, we the mothers of all. This daughter of ours, guide her.'

ISSUES RAISED

In *Male Daughters*, I stated,

> I feel a strong moral commitment to deal briefly with the practical consider-ations arising from this study: those with whom I worked in Nnobi expected such a commitment from me. The women especially did not consider me a stranger or a visitor or a scientist divorced from local political problems and politics.

(1987a: 194)

From the conversation with *Inyom Nnobi*, it is quite obvious that I had sided with the women. I had divulged information about the constitution which could have led to a crisis. The women had wanted to 'use' me to raise the issue of their non-representation on the ruling council. There had been several moments of crisis during that meeting with the Women's Council. There was the contra-diction between the orientation and aspiration of Christian women and that of the *odinana* women who still followed the indigenous African religion, the goddess worship. My sympathy and support were with the latter. Indeed, my aggressiveness had been provoked by the statements made by a Christian woman among them – their secretary and a wife of a schoolteacher; I saw her as a member of the *petit-bourgeois* class which historically collaborated in the colonialism of Africa. She had condemned the idea of title-taking for women on the grounds that it was non-Christian, as well as maintaining that women were quite happy and at peace and did not really want anything at the moment.

The issues which this meeting raised for me, then, were whether I would fail the women of Nnobi by not taking up their request to speak to the men in the ruling council on their behalf and by not challenging those writing the constitution of Nnobi to make sure that they included women in it. I even thought about staying on to do political work in awareness and consciousness-raising with *Inyom Nnobi* but in the end decided only to make recommendations for the inclusion of women on the ruling council and for their nomination in electoral politics.

None the less, when I returned to Nnobi again between 1985 and 1987 I found, as I had expected, that the published constitution of Nnobi had not allocated any place for the Women's Council on the Central Executive Committee. During this period, I tried again to take up some of the issues raised by members of the

Women's Council during my previous visit. However, my experiences on this occasion induced a sense of helplessness and alienation, which forced me into a new self-criticism, as well as rebellion in my refusal to become an 'honorary male' or a new kind of missionary in this neo-patriarchal scheme devised by British colonialism. I consequently decided to move back again to racist Britain in a kind of self-imposed exile and continue to do research and write, thus continuing the political struggle with the pen.

DISCUSSION

It is quite clear that the themes identified by Golde relating the experiences of women, protection, initial suspicion, conformity, reciprocity and culture shock did not apply to me in the same way as they did to the contributors in her volume. My initial encounter was based on status and gender rather than sex. By slotting into my rightful kinship place in the society, I was already participating in the social relations expected and accepted patterns of reciprocity.

This calls into question the true meaning of the notion of reciprocity used by social anthropologists. Is reciprocity really the ability to repay services with gifts? Is it not the willingness to stay and take on fully the citizenship granted through kinship and contribute meaningfully to that society? In which case, one can say that there is no reciprocity in social anthropology, as long as western researchers continue to treat African communities as research objects.

Most researchers have confirmed that Africans, once they are sure of their intentions, welcome those who want to learn their history and customs very warmly. They integrate the researcher through kinship. But first, as a number of researchers have stated (Golde 1970: 12; Middleton 1970: 6), a person must become a child in order to learn, and must experience what Turnbull (1986) termed 'role mobility', from genderless childhood to youth and adulthood.

To act as a social subject who is capable of error is, I believe, more correct than to accept useless advice about role mobility and calculated role manipulation. This is shown by the way people accept more easily those who experience the basic life-cycles of birth, marriage or death.

It seems to me, therefore, that what is required is the ability to 'let oneself go'. Had anthropologists done so without prejudice, without racism and without calculated self-interest, West Africanists, for example, might have ended up being Africans. But, really as Golde (1970) suggests, to 'let go' poses a 'threat to one's own system of meanings and values, and consequently to one's own identity'. It is this persistent holding on to 'one's own established perception' and all these manipulative strategies that has led to the widespread accusations that social anthropologists are Eurocentric, racist or even spies. If the stranger or anthropologist is not herself or himself a social subject or part of the field of study, what could possibly justify the study of another society?

Since we know that the work of anthropologists has often been used to serve the interest of western imperialism in Africa, it seems to me incorrect to argue like Middleton on the Lugbara, that 'no harm ever came to them from the fact that they told me about these matters' (1970: 13). The point is not only what they told us, but also what we made of it. From a feminist perspective, for instance, I would suggest that Africanist anthropologists have frequently distorted African history by their use of what was said to them, particularly by missing out the basic matriarchal thinking in African philosophy and so distorting our history. In this way, only a patriarchal version of history has been told. Yet there are fundamental matriarchal elements in many African societies (cf. Anta Diop 1989).

For reasons such as these, then, claims that anthropology has brought into proper perspective the position of our culture as one of many and has challenged universalistic and absolutist assumptions and beliefs about the proper condition of man remain a fallacy. The west is still setting the agenda and calling the tune on the 'proper condition of man'. In this, the African continent continues to be a field of academic enquiry while Africans are excluded from the decisions which are being made. African intellectuals are reduced to schizophrenics, alienated from their own societies and cultures. Yet they are not accepted within the hierarchies of power in the western world, in whose culture they have been socialised through the western-dominated educational systems.

What, then, is to be done? Our role as African intellectuals, as I see it, is first to call into question, and indeed, to deconstruct, much of what has passed for scholarship on Africa. If we are not to be collaborators in self-abnegation, we then need to reconstruct our own history. In this process, we must redefine our own roles, as well as our moral and ideological principles, if we are not to forge new oppressions based on patriarchy and class exploitation, as some are now doing.

So what is the status of anthropology in Africa? We cannot ignore the material that has been collected so far, for unfortunately, most work on Africa has been carried out under that rubric. We have to go through the pile to separate the grain from the chaff and give back anthropology to the Africans. I would suggest that part of this sifting process is a change in methodology. We need more multi-disciplinary research on the indigenous systems of each particular society, as well as on the changes and transformations that have taken place (see Amadiume 1987a, for example). Such an approach implies that for us Africans, the major discipline is to be likened to social history rather than social anthropology, with a greater use of oral history and myths, both matriarchal and patriarchal.

Deconstruction and reconstruction remain valid projects for all radical intellectuals, whether of African origin or from the west. In this way, we can fulfil the Igbo proverb and make '*that same mouth which spoke a falsehood to speak the truth*'.

REFERENCES

Amadiume, Ifi (1987a) *Male Daughters, Female Husbands: Gender and Sex in an African Society*, London: Zed Books.

—— (1987b) *African Matriarchal Foundations: the Igbo Case*, London: Karnak House.

Diop, Cheikh Anta (1989) *The Cultural Unity of Black Africa: The Domains of Patriarchy and of Matriachy in Classical Antiquity*, London: Karnak House.

Geertz, Clifford (1988) *Works and Lives: The Anthropologist as Author*, London: Polity Press.

Golde, Peggy (1970) *Women in the Field: Anthropological Experiences*, Chicago: Aldine Publishing Company.

Hodagmeu-Sotelo, Pierrette (1988) 'Gender and fieldwork', *Women's Studies International Forum* 11(6): 611–18.

Middleton, John (1970) *Expectation and Paradox in Anthropological Research*, New York: Holt, Rinehart & Winston.

Pra, Kwel Kwa (1988) 'A plea for an African anthropological renaissance', *CODESRIA Bulletin*, 2.

Turnbull, Colin (1986) 'Sex and gender: the role of subjectivity in field research', in T.L. Whitehead and M.E. Conaway, *Self, Sex and Gender in Cross-cultural Fieldwork*, Urbana and Chicago: University of Illinios Press.

Whitehead, Tony L. and Conaway, Mary E. (eds) (1986) *Self, Sex and Gender in Cross-cultural Fieldwork*, Urbana and Chicago: University of Illinois Press.

13 Sexuality and masculinity in fieldwork among Colombian blacks

Peter Wade

Sex is not a topic that has received a great deal of attention in anthropologist's accounts of their fieldwork. As Warren (1988) points out, few researchers broach the subject of their own sexuality in the field, perhaps because the personal and intimate nature of this matter might undermine the 'objectivity' of an ethnographic interpretation. Of those who do talk about sex, Warren says, men tend to talk about mutual sexual attractions and desires, while women refer more to the sexual advances they have encountered, usually unwanted. Apparently, then, references to sex in reflexive ethnographic accounts are also structured by a logic of gender.

There is more at issue here than simply taboo areas and the undermining of a façade of objectivity. There is also the question of relevance. As Warren observes,

> It is not always clear why sexual encounters should be reported, beyond a modern 'confessional' impulse. It seems to me that where sexual expectations and encounters are part of public discourse, and where the researcher's participation is analytically salient [. . .] then there is good reason to write about it. Where the discussion of sexuality illuminates little more than the researcher's personal odysseys – then I think that it becomes gratuitous.
>
> (1988: 63)

Some may not be too happy with Warren's seemingly easy distinction between analytical salience and personal odyssey, surely a distinction the terms of which have been under review for some time now. The very problem is to know how 'personal' factors influence the analysis, and, of course, what counts as 'personal' in the first place. It is also the case that analytical salience – taken here to refer to something that impinges on the resulting analysis, or ethnographic account – is not the only area of concern. The whole realm of a fieldworker's relations, intimate and otherwise, with his or her informants is an interesting aspect of the anthropological encounter in its own right, whether or not this affects the end analysis (as in most cases it arguably does).

Nevertheless, I take Warren's point that at some indeterminate and theoretically debatable moment a reflexive account of intimate personal relations can move from the apposite to the merely gratuitous. To put it at a more theoretical level, it is of more concern for anthropology, I think, to examine how a person's gender and sexuality structure fieldwork and the resultant textual productions than it is to examine how fieldwork structures an individual's personal sexuality and gender identity. This is not to say that the latter is therefore 'gratuitous', but that it is more relevant to psychoanalysis and theories of the nature of sexuality and gender in western societies than it is to anthropology. That many might not see a clear dividing line between these fields of enquiry reinforces my point about the difficulty of distinguishing between 'analytical salience' (to anthropology) and 'personal odyssey'.

For example, during two periods of fieldwork in Colombia, studying black society and culture, and processes of race mixture and cultural change, I had two quite long-term relationships with local black Colombian women. Now an account of these could be interesting (or boring) from the point of view of a personal psychoanalysis. It could also provide grist to the mill of an argument about the nature of masculine sexuality in the west which posits, say, a tendency to objectify sexuality in a distinct (and often subordinate) other – although I see no reason why such an argument would lack interest for anthropology with its interest in the social construction of the other.

I would contend that these relationships are also 'analytically salient' for the anthropology I did for a number of reasons which form the substance of this chapter, but which I summarise here. First, they partake of the whole fieldwork encounter between the researcher and his or her informants – an encounter which is inevitably highly gendered. This is, I think, an encounter between self and other which is common to the anthropological endeavour (even when the other is barely exotic and quite domestic) and which, in my case, included, although was not limited to, 'boyfriend/girlfriend' relationships. Secondly, sexual relations between men and women of different racial identities have been and still are important aspects of all New World, and especially Latin New World, societies; they are allied to processes of social mobility and cultural change, for example, and they are imbued with ambiguous but powerful meanings both of equality and hierarchy. I and my Colombian girlfriends inevitably had to contend with these meanings whether we liked it or not, and I think both relationships were ultimately open to interpretation by others as having re-established the meanings associated with hierarchy in ways that again reflect upon the anthropological encounter between self and other, which is also often an encounter between west and rest, or between white and black.

Thirdly, the theories which I elaborate about black society and culture and their relation to the non-black world in Colombia include elements which also refer to a tendency by the non-black world to objectify the black world as possessing an exotic physical and sexual otherness. My own relationships in Colombia, while not derived directly from such a cultural construction – and indeed opposed to it in trying to transcend and deconstruct it – clearly are not disconnected from it either.

In sum, then, the interaction between personal gender identity and sexuality and the field setting is a dialectical one (Whitehead and Conaway 1986), and the

In the gold mines, near Unguía, with Elean, a principal informant, and his wife Cristina

distinction between personal odyssey and analytical salience is more a matter of perspective than it is a hard-and-fast division. It is also, I think, partly a matter of ethics. Anthropology inevitably 'uses' informants' lives and statements to produce texts and, whatever claims the new ethnography might make about giving a participatory voice to the informants, this relationship generally remains unequal (Strathern 1987; Stacey 1988). Unequal or not, this activity tends to be justified by reference to humanist values of knowledge, cross-cultural awareness, liberation and, perhaps, the preservation of disappearing traditions; although people have also pointed out the less explicit role of factors of political control in a colonial or neo-colonial encounter, and of individual career-building in the academic world. Clearly, however, when a reflexive account of intimate relationships becomes a sort of personal confessional anecdote, revealing not only one's own sex life, but that of informants, then the ethical implications become even more problematic, since the unequal textual participation of the subjects involved is orchestrated by no more than a desire for self-revelation.

THE ENCOUNTER OF SELF AND OTHER

I did fieldwork in Colombia on two occasions. First, in 1982–3 as part of a Ph.D. I spent fourteen months in a small village called Unguía near the Panamanian border in a frontier colonisation area, investigating ethnic relations between people in the zone who migrated there from ethnically distinct regions of the country. My particular focus was on blacks who came from the Pacific coastal region, a predominantly black area. Secondly, in 1986–7 I spent twelve months in Medellín, the second largest city in Colombia, studying the position of black migrants from the Pacific coast region in what is a non-black city of the Andean interior.[1]

My choice of black society and culture as a subject area was not entirely a chance one. In retrospect, I think that black music and black culture in England had always interested me, representing for me something inaccessible and yet at the same time powerful and attractive. Clearly, in this sense, I was partaking of some common cultural constructions of western society. Furthermore, after graduating, I spent two years travelling in the Americas with a friend, and much of this time we passed along the Caribbean coasts of Central America and Colombia, areas all rooted in the history of Caribbean slave societies. My experience was something more than that of a tourist, and particularly in Guatemala we made friends among the local Garífuna (black Carib) population. Nevertheless, language barriers and the very nature of our stay there (which ultimately remained locked in the tourist mode) kept these friendships superficial. Antagonisms were also established by theft and what we saw as breach of trust.

When I applied to do Ph.D. research, I was in Cartagena, on the Caribbean coast of Colombia, and 'naturally' I outlined a proposal which focused on my local surroundings. Even though at the time, the proposal was only tangentially concerned with race, there is no doubt that underlying this 'natural' choice was the history of an already multiple encounter between myself as a white westerner and the black world in various Caribbean guises. I thus approached fieldwork with a desire to transcend my experience of the black world as other, to get beyond the cultural construction of otherness, the inaccessibility and power of which had created my initial interest. This was a virtually hidden agenda in my research, and yet I think it is common in some form to most anthropological encounters. Alongside, indeed contributing to, a wish to further values of knowledge, awareness and liberation (for example, by exposing the operation of racism in a so-called 'racial democracy', or by deconstructing stereotypes of blacks), there was also a desire to transcend the apparent separation of self and other, to know another world intimately, be accepted by it, and perhaps to know myself in and through it. My own unarticulated strategy in this – which I can articulate with hindsight – was to try to recreate in the field the types of relationship with both men and women that were connected with intimacy and acceptance in my 'at home' experience. It was an attempt to transcend the self–other separation through creating intimate relations with Colombian blacks, relationships that were comparable in form and structure, if not in content, with certain relationships at home.

The way this transpired was, of course, highly gendered. With men, I consciously looked for a figure which is best glossed as 'elder brother', someone with whom there was relaxed affection and confidence, and mutual participation in drinking and partying – activities associated for me with intimate male friendships in England – but who was also a guide and a protector and would vouch for me to others in the world in which he moved. The element of an apprentice in need of guidance was partly conditioned by the fieldwork setting, but it was also a role I had adopted *vis-à-vis* older male friends in English contexts that were relatively 'foreign' to me – for example, in terms of class. During both periods of fieldwork, I formed at least one such relationship with men who were older than myself and who had families.

There was, however, some difference between Unguía and Medellín in this respect. In Medellín, I ended up sharing a house with Carlos and his family, whereas in Unguía I always lived on my own: the small size of the village made it easier to maintain contact with the network of blacks there. My Unguía friend, Elean, was more immersed in black culture than Carlos, who had spent fourteen years in the city, and although still tightly connected into black networks, had adopted some of the cultural mores of the city. In both cases, however, they were central informants and key people in the networks of informants and acquaintances I built up. In both cases, it was important to me that these men were immersed in black networks and culture, not simply to facilitate access to 'objective' information, but so that, through my relationship with them, I could also be drawn into what I saw as the heart of black culture. My friendship with them was for me an important sign of my acceptance by the black world and my intimacy with it.

With women, there is no doubt that I actively sought a young, single, black woman as a potential partner. In both periods of fieldwork, a relation began to form with one particular woman and there was a period of courtship of several months before the relation became a fairly stable arrangement in which we were spoken of by many and spoke of ourselves as *novios* (literally, fiancés, but generally used to mean girlfriend/boyfriend). In the second case, Roberta (a pseudonym) had begun as a paid research assistant who used her family contacts to get me interviews in the city with black families. She continued to help me in this way after our relationship had stabilised, thus impinging markedly on the whole research process. In the first case, Marcela had less impact, as she was often absent from the village and she did not play the role of guide or facilitator in the same way. As with men in the field, however, my motives for forming these relationships – and I doubt they would have formed in this way had I not pushed them in that direction – were not essentially about gaining access to information in a simple sense, but rather about a desire to transcend the separateness that I perceived as distancing me from the constructed otherness of black culture, by participating in a relation classed as most intimate in my own culture, one not just of sex, but of 'love'. Logically, had this attempt at transcendence been a consciously conceived quest, I would have 'found' a woman apparently closest to the image of the other: poor, badly educated and deeply immersed in black culture and identity. In fact, both Marcela and more so Roberta, who had been born and raised in Medellín, were relatively well educated by local standards, were not from the poorest families and were not particularly attached to black culture and identity. This gendered search for transcendence of otherness was mediated by factors of class – I found someone with whom I could relate on my own terms, and who would not be regarded as too far 'beneath me' by local people.

'Transcendence', at this level of gender-specific intimacy, was not a one-sided submersion in black culture, but an encounter mediated by class factors as they appeared in their local guise.

If my own motives were connected, at least in part, to a desire to narrow the gap between self and other, the motives of Marcela and Roberta are harder for me to fathom and more problematic for me to write about on their behalf. They tended to talk to me about this in terms of a unique personal relationship of mutual attraction. There were also, I think, other factors involved. The relationships were rather different in each case, since that with Marcela was open-ended and lasted beyond the fieldwork period, while that with Roberta started with a mutual recognition of its probable termination with my departure. Despite this difference, I think two common elements underlay both relationships. For Marcela and Roberta, a range of possibilities and encounters were opened up which, first, I think they felt reflected rather well on their own status, and secondly, represented a relatively unknown world which they were interested in exploring. In this sense, I represented an otherness to them, just as they did so for me. This was particularly the case for Marcela who, after I left, ended up living in Bogotá in the house of white, upper-class friends of mine, and who later travelled to England. It was less so for Roberta, within whose world we mostly remained: her involvement in my research, however, did bring her into an educational sphere which she aspired to know better.

At first sight, the idea of my transcending the self/other separation through a sexual relationship seems to fit in with Crapanzano's (1986: 52) observation that interpretation has been understood as a 'phallic, a phallic-aggressive' act: there are obvious parallels between knowing mentally and carnally that easily spring to mind. There are two sides to this, however, and Crapanzano adds that interpretation has been seen as a 'fruitful' act in that not only are meanings engendered (Crapanzano's gloss of fruitfulness), but new relationships and of course, in theory, children. Thus there is more at issue than simply 'penetration' of otherness, there is also fertility achieved through union.

This duality is taken further in Evelyn Fox Keller's work on gender and science in which modern science is seen as a masculine-gendered enterprise in which knowledge is allied to control and dominance. At the same time, the understanding of a female-gendered natural world by male-orientated science is akin to the sexual control by men of female human beings. However, again the situation is two-sided. Keller sees both knowledge and sexuality as having both aggression and transcendence as analytically different modes of operation. She contends that knowledge, especially scientific knowledge,

> serves two gods: power and transcendence. It aspires alternately to mastery over and union with nature. Sexuality serves the same two gods, aspiring to domination and ecstatic communion – in short aggression and eros. And it is hardly a new insight to say that power, control and domination are fuelled largely by aggression, while union satisfies a more purely erotic impulse.
>
> (1983: 122)

Western science, she argues, has become dominated by a culturally constructed masculine emphasis on power, control and domination (and presumably this applies as much to sexuality as knowledge), although it still retains elements of an 'erotic' science in which understanding comes through communion with nature.[2]

I see my relationships with Marcela and Roberta as being linked to this impulse of transcendence and union. Keller observes that erotic or 'pre-oedipal' science has 'fundamentally bisexual yearnings' (1983: 123), and this is supported in some ways by the importance of my non-sexual relationships with male informants. Also, of course, most of my relationships with women were non-sexual. But the fact that my relations with men and women had very different possibilities within them indicates that this erotic impulse of union is still highly gendered. At the same time, the fact that the same impulse of union underlay both sets of relationships suggests that such an impulse is not inherently 'phallic-aggressive', nor even simply phallic. Still, Keller's analysis suggests that dominance and union are closely linked if opposite principles, and in the anthropological encounter (which involves people studying people, rather than people studying 'nature') there are usually enduring inequalities between the knower and the known which subvert the impulse to union, even if these do not convert the relationship into a 'phallic-aggressive' one. When the knower is a man and the known a woman there are further possibilities of power difference, and certainly ideologies of male dominance played a part in determining my sexual relationships with Marcela and Roberta in the field, as I discuss in the next section.

MASCULINITY AND SEX

In my own understanding of how my gender identity and sexuality structured my fieldwork, I see my relationships with Marcela and Roberta as being over-determined by two factors which pressured towards the same outcome. Not only did these relationships derive from the relation between self and other discussed above, but also from the relation between my own perception of my masculine identity and the perceptions of masculinity held by my male friends and informants in the field. Colombian culture is characterised by a certain machismo, although this is not monolithic and varies by class and ethnicity, among other things. Among black men, certainly, especially lower-class ones, sexual continence is odd and to be avoided, while having sexual relations with a number of women is a valued and prestigious practice. Women's attitude to this is ambivalent, and while they may accept it if men are discreet, they also protest at men's 'irresponsibility' when these activities impinge too strongly on their own interests (cf. Wade, forthcoming). Also, polygyny is regarded by both men and women as a male prerogative in some areas, and indeed my principal male friend/informant in Unguía had two common-law wives and families. Therefore, if I was seeking out a sexual/romantic attachment with a woman, other men – particularly my key male friends – certainly expected me to do so. Or more accurately, to chase women in general. They expected a young man, especially one with certain 'advantages' – namely, education, some money, whiteness – to put these to good use in the pursuit of women. They stopped short of actually inventing sexual exploits for me in the manner described for the Caribbean by both Angrosino (1986) and Whitehead (1986), doubtless because there was no apparent need.

In addition, if my own concepts of knowledge included the possibility of knowledge through sexual union, there was also a strong sense in which my black male friends (and other men) included, as part of the learning process they saw me as engaged upon, sexual experience with local women. Comments along these lines were made with laughter and rib-nudging, but these jests were part of a series of conceptions that equated masculinity with penetration and learning. Indeed, as Whitten (1974: 125) points out, part of becoming a man for Pacific littoral blacks involves a process of *andar y conocer* (literally, to walk and to know) which includes carnal knowledge. The local male conception of knowing thus also fitted rather well with Crapanzano's characterisation of the understanding of interpretation both as a 'phallic' act, and as a 'fertilising' act, since sexual relations could lead to children and to the creation and consolidation of new kin networks. Interestingly, my male friends, especially in Unguía, tended to refer to Marcela's family in terms of my relation to her: thus her mother was my *suegra* (mother-in-law), her sisters, my *cuadas* (sisters-in-law) and so on. The emphasis in the local male idea of knowing was, however, much more imbued with male dominance than in Keller's concept of knowledge through union.

I thus encountered a series of expectations, voiced quite openly in Unguía although less so in Medellín, about my masculine identity and my sexual activity. Acting 'like a man' in this situation was not as straightforward, in my view, as, for example, Richard Price's experience among Surinam Bush Negroes where he could fulfil expectations by hunting and fishing 'like a real man' (1983: 15).[3] Local concepts of masculinity were close enough to similar concepts already encountered at home, and towards which I already had a conflictive and ambivalent attitude, to present a threat to my own sense of masculinity in the field. In the Colombian context I was in (as in some English contexts), not to 'womanise' could cast doubts on one's manhood. Angrosino (1986: 65) speaks of adopting a 'comfortable gender identity' which is the least threatening to the host society (although he does not specify which categories of people within the host society one is supposed not to threaten), but there is also the question of threat to the fieldworker's sense of gender identity.

A crucial resolution of this threat for me was to enter into a relationship with a local woman. This would not satisfy expectations of sexual promiscuity, and Elean in Unguía still commented that 'a man like you should be screwing a different woman every two weeks in this town'. None the less, it provided a defensible basis for my masculinity which I could then protect by reference to ideas about fidelity and stability – ideas backed, of course, by some of the values about masculinity current both in Colombia and England. As Whitehead (1986: 229) acutely observes for Caribbean notions of masculinity, the coexistence of, and contradictions between, 'respectable' values of stability and loyalty to one woman or domestic sphere, and 'reputational' values of sexual prowess and promiscuity are traits characteristic not only of the Caribbean but also of the United States and Britain. My relationships did not create a completely solid position for my own sense of myself as a man, since the conflict engendered by ideas about masculinity in Colombia was not divorced from similar conflicts in England, but it did give me a relatively secure basis from which to negotiate my masculinity.

This account of the relation between my masculinity and the social representation of masculinity I encountered in the field tends to oversimplify the situation, and delving deeper into this relation throws some light on the dialectical structuring of gender and fieldwork. To begin with, the social representation of masculinity I encountered was not some objectively learned fact, but, somewhat after Wagner's (1975) use of the term, an 'invention of culture'. This does not mean that it was a personal fantasy on my part, but that it emerged out of my progressive understanding of men's behaviour and discourse, a process inevitably predicated on my own culturally patterned masculinity. Secondly, that masculinity was not in itself a coherent subjective stance, but was rather a range of somewhat contradictory, conflictive and changeable positions – for example, with respect to fidelity and promiscuity.[4] Again, Angrosino's idea of adopting 'the most comfortable version of the appropriate gender identity permissible in the host culture' is too bland and straightforward (1986: 65). As his own account shows, there are different elements at play in 'a gender identity'.

Forming a relationship with a local woman was thus partly understandable as a development of certain positions within the range of masculinities I already knew; and this development was influenced by the way I understood local masculinities in relation to my own. That this was a development of, rather than a choice among, a range of masculine positions is indicated, for example, by the fact that I 'courted' Marcela in a way that was to me both familiar and strange. Familiar in that I had seen it before in England (especially as a media representation); strange in that it was a mode of behaviour I had not previously followed myself. I found that I had to 'pursue' her and, indeed, was counselled in this by Elean. Behaviour on her part that I interpreted as showing lack of interest was reinterpreted by him in what could be termed the 'conquest' perspective, which held more or less that, 'if she talks to you at all, she's interested'. The developmental status of the position I adopted, and indeed its continuing conflict with other positions, is also shown by the fact that on two occasions in Unguía and Medellín I formed relations with other women which bordered on the sexual, behaviour which was (and is) not characteristic of my behaviour in England. Thus, I was still engaged in negotiating, with myself and others, different masculine positions which valued, on the one hand, promiscuity and womanising, and on the other, fidelity and stability. Although these stances did not remain totally stable once they had been developed in Unguía, I was later able to re-adopt them with greater ease in Medellín, even though my main male friend there did not himself have such outspoken expectations about my sexual behaviour.

This illustrates some of the complexities of the dialectical relationship between gender and the fieldwork setting. One upshot of this process was my
forming long-term relationships with two women, something that was already
being generated from the self–other encounter discussed above. Both these
particular relations and the interaction of gender and field setting had important
consequences for my location in the field context, my perspective in it and the
data I gathered.

GENDER AND ACCESS TO DATA

In a general sense, being a male affected me as a data collector in both positive
and negative ways. For example, in Unguía I was sometimes seen as a detective
or spy, a role unlikely to be attributed to a woman in Colombia. In Medellín
shanty-towns, however, I was often seen as a local government official, a role as
likely to be filled by a woman as a man. In general, though, as many others have
noted, male researchers can often represent a greater threat in a variety of ways.
On the other hand, as a male it was also easier for me to travel alone or with a
male guide, both in Unguía and in Medellín. In dealings with bureaucracies I was
possibly taken more seriously than a woman, although women might have other
advantages in such contexts. These, I think, are fairly standard considerations.

More interestingly, my particular relations with men and women had certain
specific results. First, my position in both Unguía and Medellín was consolidated
and legitimated by virtue of my relationships with Marcela and Roberta.
Although the matter of sex was not raised in public, and was officially not known
to Marcela's and Roberta's families, it was widely known that we were 'going
steady' in the community of Unguía and among our network of friends and
acquaintances in Medellín. As a result, many people saw me as part of the
community: the relationship implied some commitment to Colombian, especially
black, society. Especially among people of my own generation, there was improved openness and rapport with me, once I was classified as Marcela's or
Roberta's *novio*. In a small community like Unguía, many people were able to
locate me as something other than an oddity, a pryer or a snooper. The fact that I
had been accepted by a local woman (and her family) made me less threatening.
Whereas Angrosino (1986: 74) defused his threatening status by becoming a
'son', I did so by becoming a 'son-in-law', a position which admittedly still had
threatening aspects as far as my 'parents-in-law' were concerned.

In some areas, rapport with female informants was improved. In general
during my fieldwork, I did not find that the 'women's world' was closed off to
me (cf. Gregory 1984). This is not to say that I had the same access to it as a
female researcher, but it was not a realm of activity or experience that was
impenetrable. I found women would talk to me about their lives, experiences and
activities, and often about their relationships as well. More of my informants
were women than men, whether these were long-term rapports or brief interviews
in Medellín shanty-towns. Only occasionally did I find myself alone with a
married woman who was clearly nervous that my presence might give rise to

injurious gossip. My relationships with Marcela and Roberta, when informants were aware of them, helped this situation because the potential threat of my presence could be defused by my known role as *novio*. For example, one of my best informants in Unguía was a female friend of Marcela's with whom I spent many hours. The possibility of amorous relations between us, which could have been inferred by myself, her or anyone else, was always held in abeyance by the roles we adopted of 'boyfriend' and 'girlfriend's friend'.

In Medellín, Roberta acted much more directly as an intermediary in a field context which, by its urban nature and due to the dispersion of many blacks around the city, tended to include one-off interviews with people, usually women, whom she barely knew herself. The fact that she was black and female, as well as often able to resuscitate some vague link of kinship or friendship with the informant, considerably facilitated the interviewing process and defused the potential threat I would have presented as a young white male working alone.

My relationships with Marcela and Roberta and my friendships with male informants in which women and sex were quite often a topic of conversation also gave me access to some information about gender and sexuality. I think I made less of this than I could have done, in the sense that I did not at the time identify it as a particular area of research and did not explore it in a systematic fashion, except insofar as it impinged on what I had defined as my central concerns: hence the relation between racially mixed unions, upward mobility and changes in identity was of interest to me. Instead, this type of information tended to filter through as personal experience – mainly because I had defined these *novio* relationships as a personal realm of activity, rather than subsumed into my main research strategy. Thus, for reasons I discuss in the last section, data on gender and sexuality did not emerge into the ethnographic products of my research.

SELF AND OTHER IN THE 'COLONIAL' CONTEXT

Strathern (1987) notes that feminism can 'mock' anthropology, especially the new ethnography, for its vision of a transcendence of the separation between the researcher's self and the ethnographic other. Feminism's concept of the other embodies fundamental inequalities which it detects also in the anthropological encounter. Similarly, Evelyn Fox Keller's analysis of gender and science posits a dialectic between aggression and eros, power and union. I have characterised my close relations with both men and women as being influenced strongly by a desire to transcend what I perceived as otherness – a perception that was not divorced from wider cultural constructions of blackness in western society. But inevitably this attempt at transcendence could not be independent of concerns of inequality and power differences. I have already looked at how different ideas about masculinity, some of which were predicated on male dominance, played a part in determining my relations with Marcela and Roberta. Now I want to examine how these relationships in some sense reiterated meanings derived from hierarchies of race and class, mediated through gender.

The Colombian racial order is characterised by a continuum leading from black (or Indian) to white. Classifications along this continuum are made by means of a complex interaction of cultural and physical criteria, subject to negotiation and manipulation. People can move up and down the continuum to a certain extent by attempting to have their behaviour and appearance reclassified. One means of doing this is by marrying a person classifiable as 'lighter' or 'darker'. This clearly also has greater implications for the offspring of such a union. Since the continuum is not morally neutral, but is highly hierarchised with white at the top and black (or Indian) at the bottom, moves up or down the ladder are heavily imbued with meanings related to hierarchy. Thus blacks who marry lighter-skinned people may have an overt motive of *blanqueamiento* (whitening), a strategy of cultural and intergenerational physical change in which blackness, cultural and physical, is bleached out. Such a motive may be absent, but may easily be inferred by others. Or, personal motives apart, the end result of change may be interpreted by other blacks as a betrayal of blackness in a general sense. Equally, whiter people who have sexual relationships with blacker people may be assumed to have some specific motive that induced them to cross the social distance which tends to separate people of markedly different racial identities. A white man may be assumed to be 'using' a black woman for easy sex, especially as his whiteness is often associated with wealth which would allow him to cope more easily with the material obligations a sexual relationship is generally assumed to involve. There is also the idea that black women are more *caliente* than white women, again drawing white men to use them for sexual purposes. Clearly, longer-term relationships and marriage tend to defuse these meanings of easy sexual exploitation. These meanings are powerful, but they are not obligatory. They are available as elements with which to interpret and make sense of people's behaviour, as well as to classify and judge them.

Inevitably, my relationships with Marcela and Roberta were open to interpretations of this kind – which does not mean that they were necessarily always understood in this way. Nevertheless, the inequalities of the situation were palpable. Both women came from poor, black, working-class backgrounds, while I was evidently relatively well off, white and of middle-class origin. I was also high up in the crucial hierarchy of education, and both women were intent on gaining educational qualifications.

From one point of view, then, both relationships were open to being glossed as consisting of a white man, with the material and educational attributes typically associated with whiteness, descending into the black world, where he easily formed sexual relations with women who were attracted by those attributes, typically absent from their own world. Ultimately, however, it was the white man, obeying the dictates of his own world, who abandoned the black women, thus rupturing the temporary transcendence of the union between them, and re-establishing the separation and the inequalities of race and class, reinforced by gender hierarchy.

From another point of view – that which Marcela and Roberta tended to express openly to me – both relationships were expressions of mutual attraction and love between unique individuals, rather than the result of motives derived from structures of race, class and gender inequality. This view is also partly my own, since I related to these women as unique individuals, not just as 'black women'. However, as this essay makes clear, it by no means represents the whole story for me. And as I mentioned earlier, I think Marcela's and Roberta's motives were related to their perceptions of me as connected to a different and higher-status world.

The point is that, whatever the personal interpretations involved, the attempt to transcend the separation of self and other, bespeaking the equality of union, could never be entirely divorced from the inequalities which partly constituted that separation. Thus, the relationships with Marcela and Roberta particularly, but also with Elean and Carlos, emerged out of a context of inequality and difference which was breached mutually, but which was also begun and ended fundamentally by my actions in orchestrating the anthropological encounter. Even in the case of Marcela, who visited me in England, and thus broke much of the classic mould of the anthropological encounter defined as 'us' visiting 'them', the basic power differences existed, since she remained financially dependent on me and my family for this trip. The power (or 'necessity') to direct and withdraw from relationships in this way reiterates the inequalities that form their background (cf. Stacey 1988). Marcela felt betrayed by the break-up which I initiated, although she recognised the inequalities it expressed as those of gender: 'men will go out with you all right, but when it comes to marriage – no way.' Roberta did not, I think, feel betrayed, perhaps because she had less, or I had given her less cause to have, illusions about those inequalities and the final reassertion of them. She knew from the start that when I returned to 'my world', the relationship would become purely epistolary.

WRITING UP

Ironically the most obvious impact of my gendered experiences of fieldwork on the textual productions that succeeded them was the virtual absence of any mention of sexual relations. While both Elean and Carlos appear extensively and Roberta also appears since she participated much more in my data-collecting, I make no mention of the nature of my relationship with either her or Marcela. I saw these relationships as somewhat taboo in terms of anthropological writing, having come across no other instances in the literature. Moreover, I felt in an unarticulated way that in the anthropological community 'sex with the natives' was considered improper and even unethical, as simply the gratification of guilty lusts in an exploitative fashion.[5] While one might have relations of close friend-ship, respect and trust with informants, which were also relations of exchange and mutual benefit in material and information terms, and the timing of which was decided by the anthropologist, when these moved into the realm of intimacy defined in term of love and, more specifically, sex, they seemed to go beyond the anthropological pale. This, I think, must be due to a rather distorted vision of the anthropologist as a professional who could abuse his (*sic*) power to gain sexual favours, a practice as unethical as a doctor using a medical façade to facilitate sexual advances. This is, however, a distorted analogy because, while an anthropologist may have power in a certain sense, he or she cannot really force people into sexually vulnerable positions as a direct result of his or her professional remit, like a doctor ordering a patient to get undressed for an 'examination'. I would argue that sexual relations between an anthropologist and his or her informants – while they may, in the local cultural context, be inadvisable or highly problematic – imply the same kinds of ethical or emotional difficulties as any other relationships between these parties. Such problems, while they may be more intense, are not qualitatively different.

In any event, with this unarticulated moral judgement in the background, I operated with an implicit division between the 'personal' and the 'analytically salient' which located my relationships in the purely personal realm. The intrusion of the personal into the analysis would undermine its validity.

In fact, I think that a good deal of what I wrote is relatively independent of the impact of these relationships on my field experience, but the foregoing factors led me to ignore or even suppress the real importance they had. To start with, all the factors I have mentioned regarding access to data obviously influenced the final product. An illustration of this is afforded by the way in which my gendered experience in the field led me into an analysis of the realm of music and *parranda* (partying). These were personal predilections of mine in England, and ones that I sought to re-create with my male friends in the field. In Unguía and especially in Medellín, this led me into male networks of drinking and music. For a short while, I regarded this as 'personal' activity, rather removed from the 'real' business of interviews and suchlike. It soon became clear that music, dancing and celebration were a cultural focus for black society – even in Colombia, where black culture is generally seen as very Hispanicised – and all these elements were involved in the dynamic and fluid relation between the black world and the non-black world. This ultimately entered my analysis in the writing-up stage. Inevitably, a concern with music went beyond male networks, since it involved dancing and this was almost always done with women.[6] Learning to dance in a style considered appropriate by men and women was a slow and sometimes embarrassing process, but it was crucial in being able to form the kind of intimate relations I wanted, especially with women, but also with men, since a man who could not dance properly was not a good companion for a *parranda*. Thus, the gendered experience of forming close relations with the constructed otherness of blackness led directly to the importance of music, dance and *parranda* for me personally; at the same time, it alerted me to its importance in black culture, and this emerged ultimately in the texts I produced.

Another of the ideas that I work with in writing about black culture and its relationship with the non-black world is precisely the constructed otherness of blackness which has been a theme of this chapter, and the attribution to that otherness of a fascinating physicality, musicality and sexuality. Such a construction has a long and racist tradition behind it, tending to be used as a justification for denying blacks equal opportunities or for exploiting certain aspects of their culture. My intention in writing was partly to explore the nature of this construction and its operation in interactions between blacks and non-blacks. I regard my own encounter with blackness not as a perpetuation of this construction – although it is clearly not divorced from it as a generative context – but as a (flawed) attempt to transcend personally the otherness it entailed, and to deconstruct it analytically as a cultural artefact.

Fieldwork as a whole was a 'personal odyssey' for me (as I'm sure it must be for all anthropologists), and certainly my close relationships with Elean and Carlos and with Marcela and Roberta were also personal odysseys within that overall journey. The interest of them for my analysis is the way they influenced how I as an anthropologist structured the encounter with my own concepts of 'close' relationships and my own concepts of masculinity – always in interaction with local concepts of the same – and how this emerges into the written product of the research. In this sense, the personal and the analytical feed into each other.

NOTES

1 Ph.D. fieldwork research was financed with a grant from the Economic and Social Research Council of Great Britain. Post-doctoral fieldwork research was financed with a grant from the Social Science Research Council of the United States, and by a Research Fellowship at Queens' College, Cambridge.

2 There appears to be a tendency here to equate sexuality with union, despite Fox Keller's own explicit recognition that sexuality can involve aggression as much as eros.

3 Price did fieldwork with his wife, Sally, and this may well have altered the expectations local blacks had of him as a man.

4 The view of the subject as a coherent whole, easily identifiable with the individual, traceable to Enlightenment thought, has of course been broken down in recent years partly as a result of post-structuralist theories. Cf. also Pleck (1981), who looks at the contradictory elements in western definitions of masculinity.

5 Whitehead notes that he considered himself to be highly 'ethical' in sexual matters, and that this involved not getting sexually involved with members of the study community (1986: 217).

6 Only in Medellín in certain *salsa* bars without dance floors did I see men sometimes dance on their own.

REFERENCES

Angrosino, Michael (1986) 'Son and lover: the anthropologist as nonthreatening male', in Tony Whitehead and Mary Conaway (eds), *Self, Sex and Gender in Cross-cultural Fieldwork*, Urbana and Chicago: University of Illinois Press.

Crapanzano, Vincent (1986) '"Hermes" dilemma: the masking of subversion in ethnographic description', in James Clifford and George Marcus (eds), *Writing Culture: the Poetics and Politics of Ethnography*, Berkeley, CA: University of California Press.

Gregory, J. (1984) 'The myth of the male ethnographer', *American Anthropologist* 86(2): 316–27.

Keller, Evelyn Fox (1983) 'Feminism and science', in N. Keohane, M. Rosaldo and B. Gelpi (eds), *Feminist Theory: A Critique of Ideology*, Brighton: Harvester Press.

Pleck, Joseph (1981) *The Myth of Masculinity*, Cambridge, MA: MIT Press.

Price, Richard (1983) *First-time: The Historical Vision of an Afro-American People*, Baltimore, MD: Johns Hopkins University Press.

Stacey, Judith (1988) 'Can there be a feminist ethnography?' *Women's Studies International Forum* 11(1): 21–7.

Strathern, Marilyn (1987) 'An awkward relationship: the case of feminism and anthropology', *Signs* 12(2): 276–92.

Wade, Peter (forthcoming) 'Man the hunter: gender and violence in music and drinking contexts in Colombia', in Peter Gow and Penelope Harvey (eds), *Sexuality, Violence and Cultural Differences*, London: Routledge.

Wagner, Roy (1975) *The Invention of Culture*, Englewood Cliffs, NJ: Prentice-Hall.

Warren, Carol (1988) *Gender Issues in Field Research*, Beverly Hills, CA: Sage.

Whitehead, Tony (1986) 'Breakdown, resolution and coherence: the fieldwork experiences of a big, brown, pretty-talking man in a West Indian community', in Tony Whitehead and Mary Conaway (eds), *Self, Sex and Gender in Cross-cultural Fieldwork*, Urbana and Chicago: University of Illinois Press.

Whitehead, Tony and Conaway, Mary (eds) (1986) 'Introduction' to *Self, Sex and Gender in Cross-cultural Fieldwork*, Urbana and Chicago: University of Illinois Press.

Whitten, Norman (1974) *Black Frontiersmen: Afro-Hispanic Culture of Ecuador and Colombia*, New York: John Wiley & Son.

14 Gendered participation

Masculinity and fieldwork in a south London adolescent community*

Les Back

THE MISUSES OF AUTOBIOGRAPHY

> Looking back to my behaviour after my return I see now that my uncertainty as to my role was expressed . . . by an excitement and a garrulousness concerning the Lugbara, whom I discussed avidly with anyone whom I met and was willing to listen to me. They were *'my people', the object of an intense personal experience* which I was willing to interpret to others although not totally willing to share with them.
>
> (John Middleton (1970); my emphasis)

I have a friend and colleague whose favourite humorous story is about male anthropologists. She warns 'never invite them to your house unless you want to hear an essay on their favourite subject – *themselves*!' What she captures in this jibe is the impulse that many of us feel to turn fieldwork into personal folklore. Through this vicarious form of self-projection we possess the other. The syndrome is neatly captured in the quotation from Middleton, above. He lays claim to the Lugbara as 'his' object, this knowledge received as a sovereign personal disclosure. This way of speaking about fieldwork results in a kind of narcissism whereby an escalation of self results from the reception of knowledge about the other. I feel strongly that we need to challenge this way of talking and thinking about the ethnographic experience.

Although we have a lot to *say* about our ethnographic experience, men have *written* comparatively little (Dumont 1978). Women anthropologists, on the other hand, have produced an extensive literature on their experience of fieldwork (Bohannan 1954; Powdermaker 1966; Golde 1970) and the political implications of a division between self and other for feminist scholarship (Roman forthcoming; Stacey 1988; Caplan 1988a, 1988b). In contrast, our autobiographies are recounted in the confines of the bar-room confessional, or in anecdotes for the amusement of students or colleagues. We need to move beyond generating this kind of folklore and story-telling to a more sensitive appreciation of the politics of research. In short, we need to respond positively to feminist anthropology's critique of methodological practice.

In this chapter, I refer to my own ethnographic work in a white working-class adolescent community in south London. Here I use this experience as a way of focusing on the social and political ground where self and other interact, and on the gendered identities which are produced and the negotiations that take place. First of all, I want to explore the question of what it is that men should try to write about fieldwork. In particular how does our gender affect this experience and what issues should we address?

'THE INVISIBLE MAN?' FEMINIST CRITIQUES AND THE REFLEXIVE TURN IN ANTHROPOLOGY

Reading the current literature on reflexivity and autobiography within social science I am reminded of the H.G. Wells classic *The Invisible Man.*[1] In the novel, the main character becomes visible only upon his death. This is exactly what has happened to the academic discourse which has taken male as generic. It is only with the challenge to this discourse by feminist writers that the gendered author has been made visible. It may be that, as in *The Invisible Man*, this new visibility signals the death of an academic discourse which has focused on male informants as if they represented humanity. Perhaps such an analysis is a little premature in its optimism, but the academic narrative is certainly undergoing important transformations.

The emergence of a 'new criticism' (Fardon 1990) signals one of the most important changes. The substance of what can be characterised as the postmodern turn in anthropology refers to a crisis in intellectual authority which is bound up with a wider aesthetic crisis in signification. However, it is vital to place the postmodernist critique in the context of the pre-existence of feminism. In the first major book which appeared – Clifford and Marcus (1986) *Writing Culture* – Clifford found it necessary to explain why feminist scholars had not been in-cluded in the volume. Clifford claimed that feminism had not contributed to the analysis of ethnographies as texts and that feminist theorists were not conversant with the theory he was interested in developing. He commented that, under the pressure of feminism, ethnographic texts have been shown to portray male domains of experience (Clifford 1986: 18). But, as Pat Caplan has incisively shown, this preoccupation with reflection and textual analysis resulted in a 'token bow in the direction of feminist theory: an acknowledgement of its importance, alongside a total failure to grapple with its implications' (Caplan 1988b: 15; also see Mascia-Lees, Sharpe and Cohen 1989).

In this sense the postmodern turn in anthropology has failed to be interested in the analysis of gender issues in research. This literature exhibits a desperate attempt to manage the deconstruction of anthropological authority and out-think the conditions in which anthropology was born; as Edward Said has noted, the postmodernists develop 'ingenious textual strategies as a way of deflecting the crippling attacks on ethnographic authority' (Said 1989: 211). Such an *aesthetic response* is, he argues, easier to narrate than a political one. The postmodernists have developed new ways of writing which are qualitatively different from 'male as generic' anthropology, but ultimately feminist theory is marginalised, if not excluded, while at the same time acknowledged (Marcus and Cushman 1982).

The 'new criticism' may result in a more self-conscious approach to anthropological writing. However, it carries some important dangers. Prior to the postmodernists, autobiography and reflexive writing within anthropology have been associated with 'women's work'. Dumont (1978) noted a number of years ago that women have published material on fieldwork while men were doing the 'real thing'. But in this context how do we comprehend the postmodernist shift? I think that there are some direct parallels between this development and re-alignments of heterosexual masculine identities in the overdeveloped world.

In Rowena Chapman's analysis of shifts in notions of masculinity in contemporary Britain, she shows how men and women are repositioning themselves around a dualistic definition of masculinity and femininity. Here, 'New Men can adopt a position of moral superiority as proto-females: whoever is most powerful appropriates the most attractive value system' (Chapman 1988: 248). The result is that men are moving toward feminine characteristics and thus towards virtue. In the same way, male anthropologists are moving towards experimental modes of representation which were formerly associated with women anthropologists (Smith 1954; Bohannan 1954; Fernea 1965; Shostak 1981). The postmodernists in this way are responding to the death of the 'male as generic' way of narrating culture and are moving towards 'feminised' intellectual positions. 'Feminised' discourse is not the same as feminist social theory, because the former does not carry the political commitment of the latter. In line with Chapman's analysis, the future of anthropological criticism may be 'female', but it still may belong to men.

I am arguing that feminist criticism has resulted in the death of an academic discourse which has viewed male accounts of society as generic. The male ethnographer has been made visible. Postmodern anthropology has responded to this exposure – albeit elliptically – without addressing the relationship between gender and research. The growth of postmodern/reflexive anthropology constitutes a significant diversion for those who are serious about developing a sensitivity to the gender-loaded contexts in which fieldwork takes place. In the following section I want to examine what this means in the context of re-reading male ethnographic writing and reviewing ethnographic practice for men.

MEN'S STUDIES? MALE ANTHROPOLOGISTS AND GENDER IN ETHNOGRAPHIC ACCOUNTS

In assessing the writing of male ethnographers, it is tempting to justify one's 'soundness' by criticising other men. There is a danger here of constructing a hierarchy of 'liberated' versus 'conservative' men which in itself is the expression of a form of masculine competition. I feel that we need to be wary of this trap. As Jonathan Rutherford has commented:

> Putting masculinity into the picture isn't about insisting that all men should be nice, and fit some stereotyped image. Nor is it about creating a male confessional and a fetish of self disclosure. It's about making ourselves 'seen',

about making our . . . masculinities a basis for discussion instead of assuming that men as gendered subjects do not exist.

(1988: 46)

Equally, we need to be careful when speaking as gendered subjects not to seek an opportunistic purchase on sexual politics. For too long within social science, gender has been viewed as synonymous with women's studies, and sexual politics is a subject on which male anthropologists have been curiously silent (see Nencel and Pels 1990: 87). This raises the question of how men make feminist insights part of their agenda without becoming proto-female and so possessing the ground of virtue in a vicarious way. I do not think there are easy answers to this dilemma. But I feel it is vitally important to explore the basis on which we start to develop a sensitivity to our gender, and the way this informs and affects our work as anthropologists.

In David Morgan's (1981) programmatic article, he stresses that gender differences in fieldwork are not simply a source of difficulty for male and female researchers, which lead to exclusion from particular social situations. Rather, these differences constitute a source of knowledge within a specific situation. It is not a matter of trying to 'overcome' the effects which the gender of the researcher has on a particular field situation, but to explore how the participant observer's gender identity becomes intertwined with the process of knowing.

He shows how knowledge and academic discourse have to be placed in the context of academic institutions which are themselves loaded unequally in relation to male and female professionals: 'Men . . . have to work against the grain – their grain – in order to free their work from sexism, to take gender into account. The male researcher needs, as it were, a small voice at his shoulder reminding him at each point that he is a man' (1981: 95). Pat Caplan has also argued that it is necessary to make a case for studying men *qua* men, and not as if we represent humanity (Caplan 1988a; see also Ardener 1985; Atkinson 1982). However, I disagree with her when she characterises the 'male as generic' literature as 'practising an unmarked discipline as *de facto* men's studies' (Caplan 1988a: 14). My point is that many of the ethnographic texts of the classical period are *not* studies of men as gendered subjects. Although men may have been the ones speaking, they were not 'seen' because they are represented as speaking for 'mankind' (Morgan 1981: 93). I want to explore the implications of this by looking at the absence of any appreciation of gender issues within ethnographic accounts of male, working-class, occupational cultures.

There are a number of studies where ethnographic work has been done in industrial contexts (Roy 1953, 1954, 1960). But this kind of writing is not only confined to the social science that was written before the development of feminist social theory and epistemology. For example, Charles Vaught and David Smith (1980),[2] in their study of relationships in a coal mine, conducted fieldwork in a highly gendered working-class culture without mentioning gender as a significant social parameter. They maintained that the workers' games and dramatic performances subverted dominant mores and values in order to emphasise the 'different world' context of the underground mine. The games which they describe are interpreted as powerful mechanisms for the direct bonding of individuals within a group. However, if one looks closely at the content of these rituals it is possible to offer a very different interpretation.

They describe a number of 'games' which the miners played in order to incorporate new members and to punish established miners. The most dramatic of these are penis games. Penis games are varied and included a 'pretty pecker' contest, where a judge awards a prize for the 'prettiest penis'. However, by far the most exaggerated of these games was 'greasing', which takes on the qualities of an operating-room scene, with a 'doctor', 'nurses' and various attendants. The nurses restrain the patient while the doctor 'operates' (applies the grease to the patient's genitals), and the 'anaesthetist' administers the anaesthetic (rock dust). Other games included 'hanging', 'hairing' and 'jacking off' which were variations on the greasing theme.

The authors stress that while 'the sexual themes and dramatic performances . . . may be viewed as brutal, and degrading if abstracted from the situated milieu in which they occur, within the context of the encapsulated enclave, however, they are a powerfully integrating force for the group, a fact which each new individual (including the senior author) must learn to experience' (Vaught and Smith 1980: 180). Gender does not in any defined way enter into their analysis. Rather, they emphasise how these rituals are the product of an environment where 'the worker is faced with a different role-set than he or she performs outside' (p. 181). However, these rituals are not in fact discontinuous with gendered systems of behaviour outside the context of the mine. Such practices may be exaggerated, but they are not qualitatively different from the kinds of abuse that apprentices are subject to within large engineering factories in Britain. Various kinds of ritual abuse are inflicted on finishing apprentices. These included rubbing 'Engineers' blue' – a blue metal dye – into the genitals, covering the apprentice with dust and Swarfega cleansing agent and afterwards hosing them with a high-powered water jet.[3]

This example shows how gender is ignored within the literature on working-class culture. It is a study predominantly about men, but it is not a study of masculinity. The distinction may seem rather laboured, but it is central to my reading of male ethnographic texts. I am arguing that we need to develop an analysis of the cultural construction of masculinity and apply it to the way we conduct fieldwork and write ethnography. The 'male as generic' approach focuses curiously on men but deflects one from a discussion of masculinity.

MASCULINITY AND PARTICIPATION IN SOUTH LONDON

The fieldwork was conducted within two large public housing estates whose residents were mostly working class. The first is a multi-ethnic neighbourhood and the second is predominantly 'white'. The focus of the study was to try and analyse how notions of race and difference were articulated by young people growing up in these areas. In particular, I was concerned with trying to analyse the conditions in which racist ideas flourished and, conversely, where they were interrupted. The research commenced in 1985, and over a period of three years I carried out extended periods of fieldwork in these areas. This included working as a youth worker in each of these neighbourhoods.

I will confine my discussions to the predominantly white working-class area since each of these fieldwork contexts raised different kinds of ethical dilemmas which have to be dealt with separately in order to do them justice. In the situation I am going to describe I, as a white ethnographer, had to make choices about the way I responded to situations where racist constructs were communicated to me.

In Britain, a central issue within the debate on research practice in the sociology of race has been the ability of white researchers to understand and empathise with black experiences of racism (Lawrence 1982). While it is profoundly true that whites cannot fully comprehend the experiential consequences of racism, we do experience the *transmission* of racist ideas and formulas. This is an important distinction in research within multiracial contexts. The question that is raised is what one does in situations where racist ideas are communicated to the researcher. To say nothing in response to them points to the legitimation of these ideas through silence.

Although the young people within the predominantly white neighbourhood almost unanimously said it was 'out of order' to cuss someone's colour, incidents of racist name-calling recurred within the youth club (Back 1991). On these occasions, within and outside the youth club I stated that I felt this behaviour was wrong. This strategy had its problems (Back 1990), but at the time I felt that it was the only way to conduct myself. During a disco which was held in the club a number of racist name-calling incidents took place. One of the incidents involved a black youth worker and a young white woman. The mother of the young woman entered the club. I was at the door when the latter arrived with another woman called Jane, with whom I was friendly. There was some indecision as to whether Jane should come into the youth club. I remember the mother turning and asking Jane, 'Whose side are you on? The bloody social workers!' Again I was made acutely aware of the division between Jane and me. She entered the club supporting her friend who launched into a tirade of racist abuse.

At the end of the evening when the lights came up the young people and the youth workers divided into two camps – black and white. This may not have been conscious, but I felt as if I had to make a choice and I stood with the black group. There were times, particularly early on in the research period, when I did not confront whites who used racist discourses. However, as the fieldwork period proceeded I found that the only way I could be honest to my informants and to myself was to make clear that I felt strongly that some of the things they said were wrong.

My relationship with young black people in this area was not unproblematic simply because I openly stated that expressions of racism were wrong. Indeed, Errol Lawrence (1982), commenting on this issue, notes that the real question is the degree to which racism structures the relationship between researcher and respondent. While young black people in this area shared their experiences with me, it would be foolish to say that our relationships were free from racism. There were times when I was caught on the other side of the colour line, in particular when I associated with, or talked to, people who were renowned racists. As such the trust that black people offered me was always contingent and in need of renewal.

The proximity of racist attitudes and behaviour meant that my position as a fieldworker was not ordered simply around issues of gender. There were similarities between the ethical dilemmas raised by the sexism and racism exhibited by my respondents. In this sense my whiteness was an integral part of the process of construction and presentation of self in this context.

THE CHOICE OF THE RESEARCH AREA AND THE PERILS OF CREDENTIALISM

> Although few radical (male) sociologists would deny the importance of the personal in precipitating social and political awareness, to admit how their own experience has influenced their choice of subject matter (the politics of selection) seems more or less taboo.
>
> (McRobbie 1990: 68)

Angela McRobbie (1990) points out that there has been a silence on the part of radical male academics with regard to how they chose their research subject. While I agree it is necessary to give some account of the 'politics of selection', I think there are some important issues beyond giving honest justifications for the choice of particular research. I think the most important of these revolves around the way this process may lead to an elaborate, and often completely fictitious, form of credentialism.

My choice of doctoral research was closely related to my own experience. I was born in south London in the early 1960s, of white working-class parents. Later my mother and father were moved to a large council estate outside of the inner city areas. This historical context and the transformation of working-class communities which resulted from resettlement is well documented (Young and Wilmott 1957; Cohen 1972), and I experienced such changes personally.

In particular, during the seventies, I became acutely aware of the popularity of far right political parties like the National Front among my peers and the community of which I was a part. The area where I lived had only a small black population, but there were larger numbers of young black people in schools. The tension between the prevalence of racist ideas and my lived experience and relationship with black friends was highly formative. Thus the two experiences from my youth which have remained a guiding influence on my interests and politics are the already mentioned dramatic transformations which occurred in working-class life and the intensity of racist reactions within working-class communities during the seventies.

This combination of experiences informed my decision when it came to choosing a doctoral research project. At the time I felt quite genuinely that I wanted to try and conduct anthropology within areas about which I had close experiential knowledge. As a result, I decided to do fieldwork within the working-class areas that surrounded the college where I had been an undergraduate. This was little over 10 miles from the place I had lived as a child.

To my present embarrassment, I used my working-class origins as a way of gaining credit for this research and thus fictitiously dissolving the division between self and other. As I began to conduct the fieldwork, however, I realised how infinitely durable and complex this dualism remains within the research process. None the less, I heavily identified with my south London informants, especially those who lived in the predominantly white area which I refer to as Riverview. I decided that I wanted to get involved in the institutions and places where young people went outside of school. As a result I started working as a youth worker in the youth club which was situated in the middle of the estate. Later I rented a room from a friend who lived in a tower block on the estate.

Riverview was in many ways socially close to the area in which I had lived as a child. It is a prestigious council development built in 1966. Although located in the inner-city area of London it shared many of the characteristics of the dormitory developments that were built on the outskirts. The rents on this estate were higher than other rented accommodation within the area. Prospective tenants were 'examined' before being allocated a property, a process which was referred to by the housing authorities as 'selective tenancies'. The residents more incisively speak of it as 'vetting'. As a result, a population of relatively affluent white workers was settled here, and it was some five years before a black family was allocated a tenancy.

Within local folklore Riverview is referred to as a white stronghold. As a young black person from a neighbouring area told me:

I just don't go down them areas. It's not safe for someone like me.
Q: What do you mean?
A black man like me don't go to them areas, I don't know what it is I just don't feel safe.

The first time I visited the Riverview Youth Centre I noticed the letters NF which had been sprayed on the wall next to the entrance. The graffiti had faded and were barely visible, and in a sense this was an apt metaphor for the decline of extreme right-wing political support in the area. In the early eighties a gang of young white men, who were purported to be active National Front members, had dominated the youth club. By the mid-eighties this group no longer used the club, and the user population was by no means exclusively the domain of young white men.

In a sense, my childhood experience was quite close to those of these young men and women. But I had a degree and a university education, and I no longer spoke the language of their experience. True, my south London argot at times showed and was often exaggerated for effect, but to the people who lived in Riverview I was just another educated – and, by implication, middle-class – social worker, one of the 'red spectacles and woolly hat brigade'. In this situation the young people were rightly suspicious. The point that I want to make here is that although I had real experiences which informed the research, it was simply farcical to pretend that I had remained what I once was. In a sense I possessed a language and operated intellectual models that were simultaneously my possessions and yet not mine. There were occasions on which I felt this tension.

I remember one night walking home through the estate to the flat where I was living. I recognised the jacket and frame of my brother ahead of me with his face turned away (my family regularly visited during the time I was doing fieldwork). I rushed up behind him. The man turned and faced me; it was not my brother. At the time I felt a profound discomfort. That man could quite easily *have been* my brother. Yet here I was turning people like him into 'objects' of anthropological study and in the process of constructing the 'other', I was also starkly defining my 'self' as alien and separate. The experience left me with serious doubts about the personal consequences of conducting research of this nature, and for me these issues remain unresolved.

In this context, the claiming of working-class credentials seems to me now quite ridiculous, even though this syndrome does seem pervasive among working-class *boys* who have made good. Much of the sociological literature on working-class communities during the sixties seems tinged with elements of personal nostalgia not unconnected with such a syndrome (Hoggart 1958; Jackson 1969; Jackson and Marsden 1966). I think it is important to avoid hiding behind these claims.

In answer to McRobbie's point with which I started this discussion, it is useful to give honest accounts of the development of the intellectual and political consciousness of social scientists. However, the ethnographic process is not one where self and other interact as equals. Judith Stacey explores this point when she discusses the possibility of conducting feminist ethnography (Stacey 1988). She shows in an honest and sophisticated way the limits of empathy and mutuality in feminist scholarship. She ends her discussion by suggesting that there can be a 'partially feminist' account of culture enhanced by the application of feminist perspectives while recognising that 'conflicts of interest and emotion between ethnographer as authentic, related person (i.e., participant), and as exploiting researcher (i.e., observer) are also an inescapable feature of ethnographic method' (Stacey 1988: 3).

In this situation it is essential to look at degrees of mutuality/intersubjectivity, and the complex texture of the social contexts where researchers replete with gender and class identities interact with their subjects. One thing that I disregarded in claiming identification with the working-class south Londoners I was studying was the existence of gender differentiation and inequality within this community.

MALE ETHNOGRAPHER AND FEMALE INFORMANTS

The feminist critique of androcentric social science (Stanley and Wise 1983a, 1983b; Warren 1988; Oakley 1981) challenges the implicit power inequalities found between male researchers and female informants. This has precipitated two kinds of response from male academics. The first relates to the now dated complaint that men find it difficult to get access to women's world of social experience. The second, more modern response is that it is politically 'inappropriate' for men to do such work: that is, 'the far be it from me' syndrome (Caplan 1988b: 14).

For a long time, I adhered to the second of these responses. In doing so I effectively ignored the question of the role of gender in research. I remember a colleague challenging me after I had proclaimed at a seminar that it was inappropriate for me to speak about young women's experience; she asked, 'What's the matter, Les, has feminism made you nervous?' She was, of course, right. I think that many men feel uncomfortable about this issue precisely because we haven't thought through its implications. As a result the politics of research method is reduced to making sure that sexual symmetry between researcher and researched is established. More dangerously, this response assumes that male/male research relations are not affected by gender.

James Gregory (1984) has shown that the 'myth' which states that male ethnographers are unable to work with women has become a self-fulfilling prophecy. Men do not have to confront the effect their gender has on the process of research within the comfortable confines of this myth. During the early part of my own research I applied for a research grant to employ a woman to conduct 'parallel' ethnographic work. To my own benefit I did not receive the award. The question thus seems to be how to avoid slipping into mythic justifications of why men can't study women while at the same time focusing clearly on how gendered power relations may be at work within the research experience. It is not simply that men cannot study women; rather, the issue is the degree to which power relations between men and women mediate the research process.

During the course of participant observation within the youth-club setting my masculinity affected the contexts where I could speak openly to young women. While I could usually speak openly and freely with groups of young women, if the conversation centred on one or two individuals I would be open to accusations from the young men of making sexual advances. On numerous occasions I was accused of 'fancying' or 'chatting up' particular young women. It became clear that such contact placed the young women themselves in a vulnerable position. I subsequently decided to meet young women outside of the gaze of their male peers.

This produced other sets of issues and dilemmas. The issue was not simply that young men stopped me from interacting with young women on a one-to-one basis publicly but gender mediated the fieldwork process even within private settings. The interview context then opened the young women to the kind of exploitation which the feminist critique has levelled at male researchers. Reflecting on these events I think a variety of dynamics occurred. I do not think that all of my interactions with young women were totally limited by the sexism which was so widely prevalent. But neither did these relationships fully escape the effect of gender inequality.

On one occasion during an interview I remember feeling that adolescent relations between young men and women were being replicated within the interview setting. The following extract is taken from that interview. The two young women involved are Michelle and Lorraine (both aged 13, female, white, with English parents):

Les:	Where are your friends from?
Michelle:	All over the place.
Les:	Do they live in this area?
Michelle:	Na! (*Tone of resentment*)
Les:	(*Looks at Lorraine.*) Is colour important in terms of the friendships you have?
Lorraine:	No!
Michelle:	No it doesn't matter.
Les:	How would you describe yourself?
Lorraine:	I don't know what you mean.
Michelle:	He means in terms of colour.
Lorraine:	I don't know.
Les:	Would you see yourself as white?
Lorraine:	Well I suppose that's what you would see me as, but I ain't white! My skin isn't white like that paper. (*Points at a piece of paper on the wall.*) Black people ain't black neither!
Les:	Well, what do you think 'white' means?
Lorraine:	Do you know what it means? (*Looks at Les*) Go on (*looks at Michelle*), you tell him!
Michelle:	I already told him what I think!

In this interview I was trying to ask about the importance of 'race' within the friendship patterns of these two young white women. It is important to realise that I was trying to introduce a divisive concept and that I am male. This resulted in both the young women resisting not only my introduction of these issues but also male authority. These kinds of interactions took place all the time between young men and women in this area. On a number of occasions in the youth club young men would ask about such subjects as friendship, relationships and sexuality. The young women would adopt the same style of resistance that is shown in this extract. Young women were not passive, and they openly engaged with young men if accusations that they didn't like were made. This usually took the form of 'cussing' exchanges (Back 1990).

While this example is similar to the kinds of exchanges that took place between young women and their male peers, it is also significant that I was older and I could be seen as a teacher/social-worker figure. Therefore these young women were not only resisting my maleness but also my adult/professional authority. My point is that this extract is not simply an example of young women being unwilling to talk to me, 'a problem of data collection', but that this ethnographic experience was constituted by the gendered nature of both adolescent relations and a resistance to authority of 'youth professionals'.

I did feel that dialogue took place between us during these interviews, but our age and gender differences were always important factors that need to be taken into account when assessing the material which was produced. As a result, the young women would not always be willing to discuss the 'private' areas of their lives.[4] To some degree the question was how far it was possible to negotiate these differences. But always our interactions outside the interview setting were subject to comments from other young men and accusations of sexual intention. The situation was very different when interviewing older women, but even so gender differences remained important.

My association with older women was not subject to the same kinds of public scrutiny. I often took up a junior status position with regard to these women which was in line with the wider structuring of gender relations within this working-class community. This does not mean that gender was unimportant. It simply means that the character of our relationships was ordered in line with wider social relations which were ordered by gender. For example, it was easier to develop 'key informant' relationships with older women because I was less likely to be accused of making sexual advances towards them.

However, in some settings, particularly where husbands or partners were present, our gender mediated the kinds of interactions that took place. On one occasion I was interviewing Sheila, a woman in her late forties, and her husband returned home from work. Sheila explained who I was and what I was doing there, and he replied, 'Why are you asking her questions? There's nothing I don't know that she can tell you.' The comment was laughed off. Sheila challenged her husband to remember the date that they moved into their flat. He couldn't remember. Sheila replied, 'See, don't take any notice of him.' In this situation I felt that Sheila's husband was invoking our shared maleness as a way of undermining the validity of Sheila's account.

In sum, the age of the women with whom I was working seemed to be closely linked to the *nature* of the impact that my gender had on our relationships, and this had a profound effect on the situations in which we could meet and talk. Additionally, gender roles/identities found within the wider community manifested themselves within my fieldwork relationships.

MALE ETHNOGRAPHER AND MALE INFORMANTS

My relationships with young men in this area were no less affected by our gender and masculinity. The question here was how far one went along with the kinds of masculine social practices that took place between young men themselves.

I have already commented that much of the literature on working-class male culture has been preoccupied with the negotiation of status within peer groups while ignoring the implications these rituals had with regard to gender identity (Whyte 1955; Roy 1960). The young men I have worked with in south London operated these kinds of play, and they were highly significant in terms of gender and the maintenance of masculine identities. I use the term 'duelling play' to describe the kinds of interactions that took place within this context. This is referred to in the peer groups as 'cussing someone out' (which has overtones of an insult) and 'wind-ups' (which is the process of getting another person angry, then ridiculing their anger by exposing its illegitimacy). 'Cussing' is equally apparent within male and female peer groups, while 'wind-ups' are a predominantly masculine preoccupation, signifying both public statements of peer status and ritualised expressions of masculinity (Back 1990).

The practice of 'wind-ups' must be located within working-class occupational culture in general (Roy 1953, 1960; Vaught and Smith 1980; Willis 1977). The cultural/occupational practices found in the world of work are echoed in male adolescent peer groups. This was made clear to me in a conversation I had with Darren, a 17-year-old bricklaying apprentice in the youth club.

DARREN: APPRENTICESHIPS, 'WIND-UPS' AND WORKING

Les: What are you doing now?

Darren: Well me and Rodders we're on the building now ain't we?

Les: Do you like it?

Darren: Yeah, it's all right innit Rodders? (*Looks over at Rodney playing pool; Rodney looks back.*) Bricklaying, innit all right? Yeah we 'ave a great ... it's all right you know what I mean. The blokes we work with ... they are ... na mean ... everyone gets the piss taken out of them but they are all right. It's like when you are new they suss you out ... make you look stupid. There was this one geezer today and they told him to go down to the stores and get a bag of 'glass nails' and he fell for it – you know what I mean. They are always laughing and joking with you but that's the way it is.

Les: Do they do the same to you?

Darren: Me, not really. I remember once they sent me to the stores for a 'rubber hammer'. (*Laughs*) And another time, they wanted me to get inside a piece of scaffold pole to measure its diameter. I mean there ain't no way anybody is going to get inside a scaffold pole is there. (*Laughs*) Another time they tried to get me to go down to the stores to get some holes for a bag of nuts ... all stupid things like that. But if you don't know what kind of things come out of the stores how are you going to know any better?

There are striking similarities between the content of occupational 'wind-ups' and those practised in male adolescent peer groups. Darren says that 'everyone gets the piss taken out of them', implying that these practices define a notion of group, a group that 'plays'. There is a suggestion that this is a rite of passage: 'when you are new they suss you out ... make you look stupid'. But in the process of defining there is also the attribution of status (Cohen 1986: 56–7). Through various 'wind-ups' (glass nail, rubber hammer, scaffold pole, holes for a bag of nuts) the apprentices are made to 'look stupid', conferring on them a non-adult, junior, subordinate status. It is also in the course of these rituals that notions of masculinity are articulated with status. In particular, notions of hardness and play fighting are connected to these rituals.

As a male ethnographer in this situation the issue is how far one participates in these activities and what one does if crass sexist statements are articulated around one? I want to dwell for a moment on the first question.

These play rituals were very familiar to me. I had experienced them during my own youth and thus was quite capable of participating. However, in the youth club there was a complicating issue. I was employed as a youth worker, and there had been a number of debates among the members of staff about the degree to which male youth workers should get involved in 'wind-ups' and 'play fighting'. This issue had been raised when a male youth worker struck a young man in the youth club in this context. I decided not to get involved in this kind of banter wherever possible. Some of the young men, particularly the ones with whom I had poor relationships, realised this. On a number of occasions I was called a 'poof' and a 'fairy' for not taking up challenges.

This situation changed after a 'wind-up' incident that I did get involved in, which involved a young man from the youth club called Paul, who was 15. During the course of a youth-club session he approached me and asked if I was interested in going to a football match with him the following weekend. He said that he had a spare ticket and he thought I might like to go. At first I was surprised at this but after few minutes I agreed. He told me that he had a ticket worth £7 and he would sell it to me for £5 as a favour. So I bought the ticket. Paul walked away and got on with the organising of a game of table tennis with some young women.

After the youth-club session I walked out of the club with a young man called Steve and two young women. It was Friday night, and we were sharing stories about our plans for the weekend. In order to get to my flat I had to walk past the chip shop which was a 'hang-out' for young people after the youth-club session had finished. As I approached the shop Paul was standing with three older youths leaning up against a railing in front of the shop. As we approached, Peter, one of the older boys, greeted me 'All right Les?' I answered. Paul then launched into a tirade, boasting how he had got me to pay for a ticket which he had picked up for free. His parting insult was, 'Agh what a wanker!' At this point I turned to Paul and told him that we were not in the youth club now and I ended this exchange with, 'You wouldn't get away with that with Steve or anybody else and you are not getting away with it with me.' Peter then looked at Paul and said, 'Watch it, he means it! He'll lump [hit] you . . . you know what I mean!' At this point Paul tried to make light of the situation: 'All right, don't get heavy, I was just winding you up!' I turned to the other two young men, and said, 'I'll see you tomorrow, all right', and left to go home.

The next day as I left my flat for the game, Paul, whose mother lived on the floor above, was walking into the lift. Before I had a chance to say hello he said, 'Yeah sorry about last night, you na mean, I was a bit ready. I was out of order and you know?' I told him to forget it and we left.

This incident was a turning point in my relationship with the young men, for I had defined myself within their terms of reference. I had asserted a masculine status and thus positioned myself within the group. As a result I began to build relationships with them that I would not have otherwise had. Before this incident I am sure that they saw me as a yet another 'social worker', but after this exchange I think they started to relate to me primarily as a resident of the estate.

The issue that follows directly from this is how far men should go in participating in masculine social practices. Should there be limits to our involvement and on what grounds should we make personal or political interventions? Feminist writers such as McRobbie (1990) and Roman (forthcoming) have criticised male ethnographers for not being critical of the sexism of their subjects. In particular, Paul Willis's (1977) analysis of young working-class men's oppositional practices in schools has been critiqued in this way. In the final appendix of the book he ends the text by asking one of his informants if he would go back to college. Joey replies: 'I don't know, the only thing I'm interested in is fucking as many women as I can if you really wanna know' (Willis 1977: 199). By saying nothing in reply to this crass statement, is Willis (albeit unintentionally) colluding with the sexism of his male research subjects? I certainly felt that there were times in my relations with young men in Riverview where I was falling into this trap.

The difficulty was the result of a tension between, on the one hand, the sexual politics of the content of what young men said, and on the other, the desire to remain close to them and participate in their social life. To say nothing and scurry away to write about how sexist these young men were is ultimately dishonest and unethical. Yet, at the same time extolling a radical pedagogy to them also felt patronising.

I did get into a number of arguments with the young men about the implications of using 'slag' as a term of insult directed at young women. On one occasion I questioned Tony, a 15-year-old white male, who used this as part of a string of insults which were hurled at a young woman. When I tried to talk this through with Tony by suggesting that he wouldn't use that term if it was one of his mates, he just said, 'That's rubbish, and what do you know, you don't even come from round here.'

On another occasion, I entered into heated discussion after one of the young men had made one of the young women pregnant. At the time this young man was 'going out' with someone else. I remember having a number of arguments with the young men in and outside the youth club over 'who was to blame' and the responsibilities of the young man involved. Again, my attempts to discuss critically some of the things they were saying were met by calling me an 'outsider' – a 'social worker'. There is a direct contradiction between the attempt to record sympathetically other men's experience while at the same time trying to transform elements within that experience.

MAKING OUR 'SELVES' SEEN: ETHNOGRAPHY AND MASCULINITY

As a fieldworker I possessed a gender identity. This notion was not static, but it formed an essential component in the negotiations that took place between myself and the people I was working with. My masculinity was constructed from outside, and although I was involved in this process I was not always in control of it. As a result, the relationships I developed with female/male respondents were ordered by the *gendered form of participation* which I have tried to describe. As male researchers I feel that it is vital to try and get some purchase on this process so that our ethnographies can be read and evaluated in an honest way.

There are signs that this process is already beginning (Johnson 1986; Whitehead 1986). But we still seem more happy to talk about our sex lives in the field (Turnbull 1986), as opposed to addressing the way gender and power are articulated in the process of participant observation (Warren 1988). Sadly, for too many of my male colleagues the issues of 'sex and gender' in cross-cultural fieldwork rarely moves beyond a discussion of 'sex and sex'!

I realise that there is far from a consensus among male anthropologists on these issues. For example, there are colleagues whose starting point does not begin with the assumption that gender inequality is problematic and in need of attention. Richard Scaglion writes of his experience within Abelam society in Papua New Guinea:

> I hesitate to admit that in the field I too was most comfortable with the perception of sex roles. I have little interest in domestic tasks such as cooking and cleaning, performing them only grudgingly in the United States, so I was euphoric to be freed of them in the field. While my own perceptions of females are certainly different from Abelam males' perceptions, I had no moral or ethical problems in assuming an air of sexual superiority consonant with that of the Abelam male. In fact, I am less comfortable with what are to me the re-defined sex roles of men and women in the United States, for here I find myself trying to 'watch' my sexism.
>
> (Scaglion 1986: 155–6)

This account is not ambiguous. It clearly shows that, for some, gender inequality is not on their intellectual, let alone political, agenda. Yet addressing this issue is fundamental if we are meaningfully to contribute to the debate on gender and cross-cultural fieldwork.

It is important for men to find a voice and do this, but we also need to be careful. If feminism has partially shaken up academic discourse, men might find it strategically beneficial to pick up on feminised academic areas which are now associated with ethical and political virtue. We need to develop a fully gendered perspective without appropriating and transforming feminist social theory and epistemology. If there are changes occurring in male academic life, we need to be sure that they are happening for ameliorative reasons, not simply for personal advantage.

Making our 'selves' seen is about making our masculinities the subject of discussion. This does not mean abandoning identities which are viewed unfavourably, nor is it about creating a male confessional and a fetish for self-disclosure. It is simply a matter of stating that we exist as gendered subjects and that this has implications for the fieldwork we carry out. It is only from here that we can engender some insight on the complex and partial nature of our ethnographic endeavours.

ACKNOWLEDGEMENTS

* I would like to thank Ann Phoenix, Barbara Tizard, Julia Brannen, Parminder Kaur Bakshi, Caroline Hardman, Michael Keith and Pat Caplan for their comments on this chapter and their continuing friendship and support.

NOTES

1 I should acknowledge that the appropriateness of this metaphor came to mind after reading the way it is used in Rowena Chapman and Jonathan Rutherford's (1988) book.
2 I would like to thank John Wrench for introducing me to this important ethnographic example.
3 Thanks to Ken Back for sharing his (I imagine painful) experiences.
4 Meyenn (1979) found similar kinds of fieldwork relations in his study of young white women.

REFERENCES

Ardener, S. (1985) 'The social anthropology of women and feminist anthropology', *Anthropology Today* 5.
Atkinson, J. (1982) 'Review essay: anthropology', *Signs* 8(2) (Winter).
Back, L. (1990) 'Racist name calling and developing anti-racist strategies in youth work', Centre for Research in Ethnic Relations, Research Papers Series, University of Warwick.
—— (1991) 'Social context and racist name calling: an ethnographic perspective on racist talk within a South London adolescent community', *European Journal of Inter-cultural Studies* 1(3).
Bohannan, L. (Elinor Smith Bowen) (1954) *Return to Laughter* New York: Harper & Brothers.
Caplan, P. (1988a) 'Engendering knowledge: the politics of ethnography' (part 1), *Anthropology Today* 4(5): 8–12.
—— (1988b) 'Engendering knowledge: the politics of ethnography' (part 2), *Anthropology Today* 4(6): 14–17.
Chapman, R. (1988) 'The great pretender: variations on the new man theme', in R. Chapman and J. Rutherford, *Male Order: Unwrapping Masculinity*, London: Lawrence & Wishart.
Clifford, J. (1986) 'Part truths: introduction' to J. Clifford and G.E. Marcus (eds), *Writing Culture: The Politics and Poetics of Ethnography*, Berkeley, CA: University of California Press.
Clifford, J. and Marcus, G.E. (eds) (1986) *Writing Culture: The Politics and Poetics of Ethnography*, Berkeley, CA: University of California Press.
Cohen, P. (1972) 'Subcultural conflict and working-class community', *Working Papers in Cultural Studies*, Centre for Contemporary Culture, University of Birmingham, pp. 9–21.
—— (1986) *Rethinking the Youth Question*, Post-sixteen Education Centre, University of London Institute of Education.

Dumont, J.P. (1978) *The Headman and I*, Austin, TX: University of Texas Press.

Fardon, R. (1990) *Localizing Strategies: Regional Traditions of Ethnographic Writings*, Edinburgh: Scottish University Press.

Fernea, E. (1965) *Guests of the Sheikh*, New York: Anchor Books.

Golde, P. (1970) *Women in the Field: Anthropological Experiences*, Berkeley, CA: University of California Press.

Gregory, J. (1984) 'The myth of the male ethnographer and the women's world', *American Anthropology* 86: 316–27.

Hoggart, R. (1958) *The Uses of Literacy*, London: Penguin.

Jackson, B. (1969) *The Working-class Community*, London: Penguin.

Jackson, B. and Marsden, D. (1966) *Education and the Working-class*, London: Penguin.

Johnson, N.B. (1986) 'Ethnographic research and rites of incorporation: a sex and gender based comparison', in T.L. Whitehead and M.E. Conaway (eds), *Self, Sex and Gender in Cross-cultural Fieldwork*, Urbana and Chicago: University of Illinois Press, pp. 164–81.

Lawrence, E. (1982) 'In the abundance of water the fool is thirsty: sociology and black pathology', in the Centre for Contemporary Cultural Studies, *The Empire Strikes Back*, London: Hutchinson, pp. 95–142.

Lees, S. (1987) *Losing Out: Sexuality and Adolescent Girls*, London: Hutchinson.

Marcus, G. and Cushman, D. (1982) 'Ethnographies as Text', *Annual Review of Anthropology* 11: 25–69.

Marcus, G. and Fischer, M. (1986) *Anthropology as Cultural Critique: An Experimental Moment in the Human Sciences*, Chicago: University of Chicago Press.

Mascia-Lees, F.E., Sharpe, P. and Ballerino Cohen, C. (1989) 'The postmodern turn in anthropology: cautions from a feminist perspective', *Signs: Journal of Women in Culture and Society* 15(1): 7–33.

McRobbie, A. (1990) 'Settling accounts with subcultures: a feminist critique', in S. Frith and A. Goodwin, *On Record: Rock, Pop and the Written Word*, London: Routledge (first published 1980).

Meyenn, R. (1979) 'Peer networks and school performance', Unpublished Ph.D. thesis, University of Aston in Birmingham.

Middleton, J. (1970) *The Lugbara of Uganda*, New York: Holt, Rinehart & Winston.

Morgan, D. (1981) 'Men, masculinity and the process of sociological enquiry', in H. Roberts (ed.), *Doing Feminist Research*, London: Routledge & Kegan Paul.

Nencel, L. and Pels, P. (1990) 'Critique and reflexivity in anthropology', *Critique of Anthropology* 9(3): 81–9.

Oakley, A. (1981) 'Interviewing women: a contradiction in terms', in H. Roberts (ed.), *Doing Feminist Research*, London: Routledge & Kegan Paul.

Powdermaker, H. (1966) *Stranger and Friend: The Way of an Anthropologist*, New York: W.W. Norton & Co.

Roman, L. (forthcoming) 'Double exposure: the politics of feminist materialist ethnography'.

Roy, D. (1953) 'Work satisfaction and social reward in quota achievement: an analysis of piecework incentive', *American Sociological Review* 18: 507–14.

—— (1954) 'Efficiency and the fix: informal inter-group relations in a piecework machine shop', *American Journal of Sociology* 60 (Nov.): 255–65.

—— (1960) 'Banana time: job satisfaction and informal interaction', *Human Organisation* 18: 156–68.

Rutherford, J. (1988) 'Who's that man?', in R. Chapman and J. Rutherford, *Male Order: Unwrapping Masculinity*, London: Lawrence & Wishart.

Said, E. (1989) 'Representing the colonized: anthropology's interlocutors', *Critical Inquiry* 15(2): 205–25.

Scaglion, R. (1986) 'Sexual segregation and ritual pollution in Abelan society', in T.C. Whitehead and M.E. Conway (eds), *Self, Sex and Gender in Cross-cultural Fieldwork*, Urbana, IL: University of Illinois Press.

Shostak, M. (1981) *Nisa: The Life and Words of a !Kung Woman*, London: Penguin.

Smith, M. (1954) *Baba of Karo*, New Haven, CT: Yale University Press.

Stacey, J. (1988) 'Can there be a feminist ethnography?', *Women's Studies International Forum* 11: 21–7.

Stanley, L. and Wise, S. (1983a) '"Back into the personal" or: our attempts to construct "feminist research"', in G. Bowles and R. Duelli Klein (eds), *Theories of Women's Studies*, London: Routledge & Kegan Paul.

—— (1983b) *Breaking Out: Feminist Consciousness and Feminist Research*, London: Routledge & Kegan Paul.

Turnbull, C.M. (1986) 'Sex and gender: the role of subjectivity in field research', in T.L. Whitehead and M.E. Conaway (eds), *Self, Sex and Gender in Cross-cultural Fieldwork*, Urbana and Chicago: University of Chicago Press, pp. 17–27.

Vaught, C. and Smith, D. (1980) 'Incorporation and mechanical solidarity in an underground coal mine', *Sociology of Work and Occupation* 7(2) (May): 159–87.

Warren, C.B. (1988) *Gender Issues in Field Research*, Beverly Hills, CA: Sage.

Whitehead, T.L. (1986) 'Breakdown resolution and coherence: the fieldwork experience of a big, brown pretty-talking man in a West Indian community', in T.L. Whitehead and M.E. Conway (eds), *Self, Sex and Gender in Cross-cultural Fieldwork*, Urbana and Chicago: University of Chicago Press, pp. 213–39.

Whyte, W.F. (1955) *Street Corner Society: The Social Structure of an Italian Slum*, Chicago and London: University of Chicago Press (2nd edn).

Willis, P. (1977) *Learning to Labour*, London: Saxon House.

Young, M. and Wilmott, P. (1957) *Family and Kinship in East London*, London: Routledge & Kegan Paul.

15 Sisters, parents, neighbours, friends
Reflections on fieldwork in North Catalonia (France)*

Oonagh O'Brien

> The journey is not linear, it is always back and forth, denying the calendar, the wrinkles and lines of the body. The self is not contained in any moment or any place, but it is only in the intersection of moment and place that the self might, for a moment, be seen vanishing through a door, which disappears at once.
>
> (Winterson 1990: 80)

One of the interesting things about reflexive anthropology as it has developed with regard to fieldwork is the close connection with gender. In a review article Hondagneu-Sotelo (1988: 612) attributes this to Golde (1986, first published in 1970), whose early volume selected only women contributers, and refers to the continued interest in the influence of gender with Gurney (1985), Keller (1985), Whitehead and Conaway (1986) and Warren (1988). Caplan also discusses the effect of the changing sense of self over a period of twenty years of doing fieldwork in terms of the nature of the questions asked and data gathered. She writes that this shift in the nature of enquiry was partially shaped by the answers informants gave and the questions they themselves asked (1988: 11). Field-workers who return regularly to the field are bringing with them their own changing perceptions, as in Caplan's case becoming a feminist and subsequently wife and mother. These changes are implicitly attributed to the world of the fieldworker. However, fieldworkers are also changed by the very experience of fieldwork, and this can affect the 'return' to their own world. Thus there is an on-going dynamic in continuous fieldwork, with both researcher and informants affected by the other.

As my fieldwork area was not far from my 'home', revisiting has been possible and frequent, and periods spent in the community which was studied have affected my life in many ways. Within the complexity of reasons that decide the choice of fieldwork location, my decision to study 'at home' was both tinged with making a decision to avoid exoticism and a feeling of 'not quite doing real fieldwork' which pervaded my departure as well as my return. In fact, I was not studying exactly at home, but in France, an area which was familiar to me, as I had spent many summers in Provence with a close friend and her family.[1]

The focus of the research was not Provence, but the northern part of Catalonia which has been in the French state since the Treaty of the Pyrenees in 1659.[2]

Catalonia, in both the French and Spanish states, has a strong sense of identity, and a widely spoken language. In the Spanish state, Catalonia is well known for its vociferous political activity. The Catalans south of the border accuse their cousins in the French state of assimilation and of loss of the language. I chose to focus on the situation in North Catalonia, particularly language use and education.

Fieldwork was carried out in 1981/2 in a small community in France called St Llorenç de Cerdans with a population of 1,600, about 10 km from the French–Spanish border in the Pyrenees. There had been a flourishing textile and soft shoe industry there since the mid-eighteenth century. It was chosen because of the high proportion of those who spoke Catalan as well as French, and the interesting economic situation.

This chapter discusses some of the issues for women in the field, looking first at relationships with women informants and the impact they have had on myself as a researcher and as a feminist. The women in St Llorenç de Cerdans turned out to be unlike women I had spent time with before. They had spent their lives working in factories, and for the most part were strong and outspoken. They have influenced the development of my ideas on feminism, and contributed to an understanding of my own personal politics. Secondly, the article describes visits I received from my family to the fieldwork area. During my first fieldwork period visits were made by my parents, a brother and a sister. Subsequently my other sisters visited, and my partner, who is himself Catalan. Because family is such a crucial defining factor for women, these visits had a definite impact on my role in the community, as well as relationships within the family itself.

STARTING OUT

Housing is of vital importance in fieldwork, and choices about which part of the village to stay in, whether to stay with a family or not, all have to be taken before anything is known about the community. I was told there was a widow who rented rooms in St Llorenç de Cerdans and who was great fun and would be ideal for me to stay with. I sensed that there was a consensus among the people who had taken me under their wing that she would be an appropriate guardian for me. It was almost as if she was appointed as the representative of the community. I visited the widow, who turned out to have the builders in for a six-month stint. Since otherwise the situation was perfect – a small street right in the middle of the village and a nice, friendly woman was to have been my protector – my disappointment was great. However, the large damp house opposite was empty, and available for rent. Comments were passed about the unsuitablity of my living alone, and in such a cold and damp place, but the proximity of the neighbour-protector meant that I felt it was not impossible, and I moved in.

WOMEN'S WORK

One of the first problems encountered in the field was the fact that women and men between the ages of about 20 and 45 had very little time to see me. The day for working women started at about 7.30 a.m. with shopping, and preparation of the main meal of the day, lunch. The factories started work at 9 a.m., announced by sirens which could be heard throughout the village and which also announced the start of the school day. Women who did not work in factories worked in shops, which opened even earlier. The sirens sounded again at 12, when the shops closed and women rushed home to put the lunch out for the whole family. By 2 p.m. the lunch had to be cleared, the kitchen cleaned, and the workers returned to the factories. At 6 p.m. the factories and shops closed and women went home to prepare the lighter evening meal, and put their children to bed. Everyone was in bed by 10 or 11 p.m. There was simply no room in the lives of working people, particularly women, for an anthropologist to hang around, trying to prise information out of them.

Contact was through formal interviewing and at weekends (although I was loath to disturb their peace at such times). As a result, I spent a large proportion of my time with the retired members of the community, many of whom found time hanging heavily on their hands after so many years of work. Those who had no family were particularly happy to spend hours talking and were a mine of information, as well as being wonderful story-tellers and therefore a pleasure to listen to. The telling of stories had a set pattern to it, and as I have returned to the village over the years, the same stories are still told in an almost identical pattern.

People in their sixties during my first visit had been in their teens and early twenties in the 1930s. For many, the formative years of their life were dominated by the Spanish Civil War, taking place 10 km away, and subsequently by refugees fleeing from Hitler. Finally, the occupying Germans had come to the village itself.

During the first half of the century the village had been engaged in industrial conflict as the workers tried to improve their working conditions through trade unions and cooperatives, and the factory boss, 'Amos', had tried to resist this. My research took on a distinctly historical bias as I tried to make sense of these momentous events.

The village is clearly divided along lines of class, related to the industrial structure of the community. The smallest class group, which I have categorised as the industrial bourgeoisie, owns the factories and much of the property in and around the community, while the petty bourgeoisie own small shops or artisan workshops; until recently the largest class group were the workers from the factories and workshops.[3] However, the factories have closed in rapid succession. The year before my first visit in 1981 there were eight factories. At the end of my stay there were four. Two years later there were only two. As I write in 1991 there is only the 'big' textile factory still open with twelve workers. I became aware that I was recording an era that would shortly no longer exist. Many of the villagers were aware of this too and were keen for me to know how things had been. For many years women had been able to earn as much money as men and there was plenty of work in the factories.

The household was frequently looked after by the grandmother (mother of either partner), leaving the women time to work both in the factories and at home in the evenings doing piecework. Women often worked harder at economic production than men to earn the same money, but the whole family recognised the importance of the woman's wage. Domestic work was divided between the 'wife' and the 'grandmother'. Children were looked after by grandmothers when pre-schoolers, or during the holidays. Cooking, cleaning and washing were shared. Men did not participate in domestic work, but contributed through work in the *horts*, small gardens that were owned or rented. Most of the vegetables for the family were grown there, and often chicken and rabbits were kept to supplement the food supply.[4] The whole community was extremely industrious.

LEISURE

When women were not working, their leisure was spent talking to one another in the street and on benches which were placed at various points around the village. Women also went for walks together. The cemetery was visited each day and was an extension of village life where daily housework was done at the family graves, and even at the graves of friends, removing dead flowers, maintaining plants or fresh flowers as well as cleaning ceramic mementoes and the grave itself. The value of a woman was measured as much by her cemetery housekeeping as her house housekeeping. Women usually visited the cemetery in groups and weather permitting, would then actually 'take a turn' as they walked the path that went up above the village and made a circle to come down on the other side. In winter they visited one another and chatted in their kitchens.

When men relaxed from their work they too sat and talked on benches, but they also went to areas that were out of bounds to the woman anthropologist: the café and, at the weekends, hunting. Despite my knowledge that outsiders should be able to break the rules, somehow I was not quite 'exotic' enough to do this. I had my own personal paranoia too about marching into a café with no other women present.[5] Hunting was a complete taboo; I never went and no one ever suggested that I should. No woman in the community ever had anything to do with any aspect of hunting, whether discussing, planning or excecuting it.

TALKING AND WALKING

I spent a great deal of my time on the first visit with older women, particularly my neighbour, whom I shall call Yveline, from whom I had nearly rented a room. She is inextricably linked with my experience of fieldwork, both in enabling me to learn the necessary language skills in order to communicate in Catalan and so participate in the world of women's talk, and in my position as a woman in the community, by being my 'protector'. If we both leaned out of our windows we could almost pass things from house to house. Messages were shouted across the street, and sometimes conversations between three or four windows would take place. A pattern developed where I visited her on most evenings and we talked, watched TV and drank herb tea. She was my teacher in every sense of the word, not just of language, but also explaining many things about the village. Eventually she succeeded in teaching me to dance the *sardana*, the dance of Catalonia. Food and cooking were also learnt from her, and any new contact could be enquired about, and the connections with other families made clear to me.[6] As Oakley comments, much of the research information that passes from woman to woman is of personal and family events, often centring on emotions and attachments (1981: 41). Our talk, though wide-ranging, also covered topics such as marriage and childbirth, and women's position in general. It was much more than 'gathering data', and often consisted of stimulating arguments as I pitched my ideas against her years of experience. Although she was from one of the better-off working families in the community, her life was full of family tragedy and endless work to support a sick husband. After leaving the village, I had a dream that someone close to me had died. Yveline was in the dream, and said to me, 'Now you are a real woman, you know what it's like to suffer.' In the dream I was initiated into her world, the world of adult women, through the acknowledged sharing of often painful experience.

Shortly after my arrival I heard about a group of villagers who went walking in the mountains every Sunday, and was invited to join them. While I worried slightly that this would not be 'proper' fieldwork, I was also aware that it could produce new contacts. These walks changed many things. I met my second woman friend and major informant, whom I shall call Anne, on those walks. But just as important for my work, I gained a completely new picture of the community. Instead of seeing it as a small settlement, isolated in the mountains, with a mysteriously large (if declining) textile and shoe industry, I started to see St Llorenç de Cerdans as the centre of a web of movement between the small villages scattered around the mountains on both sides of the border. As we walked, Anne pointed out farms and told me who had lived in them, where they were now, and what they had done before they lived there. We passed places that used to be fields, and I was told what used to be grown there. Tiny chapels that are or had been the scene of festivals were also visited. One of the overwhelming impressions of these walks was arriving in one of the small villages on 'the other side' (*l'altre costat* was how villagers referred to El Principat) which were always our destination, and seeing half the group disappear, to go and find an aunt or a cousin of their own or a neighbour. I would never have realised the extent of these cross-border links if it had not been for the weekly walks taken in the mountains. As we passed farms or small villages, there were enquiries about relatives and friends, and messages to pass on. This information changed my focus of research as I began to see a pattern of people migrating from small villages to work as agricultural labourers in the farms dotted around St Llorenç de Cerdans, and then a move into the factories. The final stage of this chain appeared to be a move northwards to Toulouse or Paris as a *fonctionnaire*, working for the French state.

Anne taught me about plants and trees, both their names and whether or not they were edible. She was considered the most knowledgeable person on mushrooms in the village, and showed me the best places to find them. She knew every path for miles around, as when she was a child she had had to bring food up to her father who worked as a woodcutter in the chestnut forests surrounding the community. I felt I was learning for the first time in my life; learning real things that seemed enormously important. Like most villagers she had started working in the factory at a young age, and her wages had been important in supporting her family. Unusually, she had never married, and perhaps because of this saw herself as a bit of an outsider in the village. However, she felt strongly that she had never met the right person, and had not wanted to marry for the sake of conforming.

Anne is someone who has had enormous influence over my life. She has a sharp sense of injustice and oppression as well as an eye for corruption and nepotism. An avid reader, she always has her finger on the political events of the day not only in the community but also at an international level. I still find myself referring back to her for comment on current events, whether they are related to fieldwork or not.

In terms of the dynamic between fieldworker and informants these two women changed my perception of a whole range of issues, not just to do with fieldwork and my research, but also about politics, women and my own personal feminism. In other words, not only did they give me simple objective data, but they also changed me as a person, so that the interpretations I gave to the data I was collecting altered. My relationship with them has continued through visits, letter-writing and telephoning.

Being changed in this way affected my 'reintegration' on return home, and subsequent returns to the field were also affected by the periods in-between. What builds up with repeated visits to the field is a dynamic whereby neither the fieldworker nor the informants are static, but both give and take from the other.

FAMILY IN THE FIELD

My position in the field was such that I was independent, and yet still under the protection of my neighbour. However, villagers asked me continually if I was not 'lonely' in the house, and if my family did not mind me leaving them to come all this way. It was difficult to explain that I no longer lived with my family. Part of this was due to their categorisation of me as a young girl. A number of anthropologists have commented on this type of age categorisation (see Turnbull 1986; and Briggs 1986). In my case I was attributed an age of about 18 rather than 24. This was due to my being alone, while at 24 in St Llorenç de Cerdans I would most likely be married with children.[7] Furthermore, I was not sophisticated in dress, as I did not wear high heels, make-up or elegant clothes.

Another aspect of the categorisation of myself in the community was that no one was quite sure what I was there for. My principles told me to be honest about what my work involved, but the overwhelming piece of knowledge about the 'stranger living in the village' was that she was learning Catalan. Most people never got past this fact, and I often gave up trying to explain that I was doing a study of the whole community, including the family life, people's work and politics as well as language use. To say that I was an anthropologist could bring negative results as it was associated with primitive cultures, folklore and head measuring. Such reactions are common and are hard to overcome. As well as the problem of trying to explain *what* I did, I had a hard time trying to convince the women that I did anything at all. They would comment on all the free time I had to sit around gossiping on the street, or to go visiting (cf. Nader 1986: 100). As Eidham says, he was 'a stranger with no specific task'(1969: 42). This free time was unknown for a woman of my age, and only hard-earned by the older women. I found myself pointedly going to look up records, and telling everyone what I was doing so that they knew I was 'working'. To counteract these accusations by telling them that sitting talking and asking questions was my 'work' seemed tantamount to saying that time spent with them was an obligation.

The problem of this work ethic was particularly associated with being a woman. Women in the community were not permitted time to sit around, their work was endless. The language explanation turned out to have certain advantages (although I still protested when it was used), and indeed my language use did improve by leaps and bounds. The women's use of language was rich and the vocabulary colourful. They were proud of my improvements, and rightly congratulated themselves on being good teachers.

ESTABLISHING CREDENTIALS

Largely due to the protection from my neighbour, there were no serious problems with my role as a single woman living alone, but there was a persistent need to justify and account for my position. I could easily be seen as an 'available' woman and had to be extremely careful about who was invited into my house as well as my overall behaviour. This was both because of living alone, and the difficulty I had in people treating my work seriously. One of the commonest models of 'foreigners' in the area was *les hippies*, young people who had abandoned urban life and had retreated to the mountains to live in decaying farmhouses. Villagers were suspicious of them, suspecting them of sexual promiscuity and drug-taking.[8] I was never accused of being one of these, but was aware that I had to be seen as *sérieuse*, the French word indicating honesty, morality and consistency. Something that altered my position in the community, both in terms of my work and my position as a woman alone, were visits paid to me during my fieldwork period.

Every member of my (rather large) family has now visited the village, and each one has affected my work in different, but largely positive, ways. My parents were the first to visit, and this was as it should be for the villagers. The effects of this visit were manifold. My credentials were established. I had respectable parents, who approved of what I was doing. They had not abandoned me, in fact they were concerned enough to visit. Someone was, as Golde (1986:

7) put it, 'protecting' me. My parents were interested in the village, and my mother, who is from a farming family, was particularly good at trying to converse about vegetable plots and animals. They were quickly accepted, as I had hoped. Both my parents have some knowledge of French, and were able to communicate with people in the village. Looking back over my notes, I have written quite a lot about what I called a 'fixing' process that my parents enabled. By introducing them to people in the village, a number of peripheral relationships were formalised. Closer contacts were also strengthened by introductions. I wrote that I found this useful, and was able, during the fortnight, actually to search out contacts whom I wanted to 'fix'. People in the village were very welcoming to them and keen to be introduced, and so the visit was punctuated with a great many invitations for coffee or drinks, as well as meals from some of the more established contacts.

During their stay my brother also came briefly, and was part of the visit. He speaks excellent French, and was able to communicate easily with people. Looking back on this visit, both my parents have remarked on what a vivid experience it was. My mother felt that the village was very much what she had expected, and that the lengthy correspondence between us prior to the visit probably contributed to what was almost a sense of recognition when she arrived, as well as an ability to distinguish and remember people to whom she was introduced. She was much struck with the contrast of old and new in the community: the washing of clothes in a fountain at the end of my street, and a loud-speaker system rigged up to the dustbin lorry that announced the important events and activities of the community. There were many older people wearing black and with a very basic standard of living, as well as young people still returning to participate in village activities even though they worked elsewhere. She found this 'step forward, step back', as she has called it, remarkable.

An unplanned consequence of the visit was my ability to find out about, and on one occasion even enter, male territory, courtesy of my father. He had played international Rugby for Ireland during the years when they were on a winning streak. North Catalonia is Rugby-mad, and some people in the village knew who he was and when he had played France. He became known as *Le Capitan* in one of the bars, and this led to conversations with the Rugby team on their yearly night out, something I could never have participated in without him. Contact with some of the men was easier after this.

My parents' visit also became a topic of conversation for many people to whom I had not actually talked before. I felt much more confident after their visit and rarely had to justify myself again. I think my own lack of confidence and the difference their visit made was closely connected to being a woman researcher, and in particular to the protection that a community can feel is necessary for a single woman living with them. My father was important in gaining more access to a male world. Both my parents talk about the holiday as a very vivid memory and a unique experience. An important part of that was, as my mother put it, the 'dramatic encounter with people' that resulted from entering into relationships that I had built up.

However, I felt it was important that they understood my work and saw me as an adult. Rather than trying to separate the daughter role from that of researcher, I wanted them to see their daughter *as* a researcher. I was certainly proud, both of them and of the life I had built up in the village, and was anxious to bring the two together. Additionally, their stay was one of the rare occasions where I have been on my own with my parents, and this added to the importance of the visit for me.

It is interesting that few anthropologists seem to have written about visits from family other than spouses or children. My family is very close, and it was I who asked my parents to come to stay. My memories of the visit are overwhelmingly positive. These go beyond the areas mentioned above to include not only my relationship with them, but also their acceptance and understanding of my work. They both read a brief field report while there and engaged in quite a lot of discussion about the ideas I had. Much of my interest in the topic I was re-searching (ethnic identity and language use) had been stimulated by the background of my parents who are both from Ireland but live in Scotland. My father found it interesting that I was studying another 'minority' culture with a number of elements in common with Ireland, and has recently told me that he was fascinated by how much knowledge there was about Ireland in the community.

Visits from my sisters had a quite different effect, which still surprises me. In each case we spent time with a group of people of the same age of the sister, and I was able to get to know that particular group better. A married sister visited alone about two months after my parents during my first fieldwork trip and was asked out by the very young married couples I found it hard to see. Because she came during the summer holiday and the beginning of the *festes* that take place every year, the extra time people in the community had for socialising coincided with her visit. Unlike my parents' visit, I did maintain some formal research during her stay, although since much of it at this time involved observing and participating in the *festes*, it was actually quite useful having her there. She remembers the visit as one in which her identity as my sister, and particularly my married sister, was constantly reinforced. However, she also felt that she saw quite a different side of me while there, watching me participate in a culture she was not familiar with. Again there were many invitations for drinks and meals, and with the festivities going on as well it was quite a lively period. This sister had been living overseas prior to her visit, and for both of us it was a special time together. After her departure, as after that of my parents, I was very lonely and depressed. This was reinforced by the fact that my period in the field was coming to an end and the calm routine of the winter and spring would never be regained in quite the same way. After both visits it took a good week or two to settle down again in the community.

MORE FAMILY IN THE FIELD

The year following the first fieldwork trip I worked in Barcelona and visited at weekends and during the holidays. This period almost felt like a continuity of fieldwork. Since then I have visited four times during the summer.

A second sister visited St Llorenç with me while I was living in Barcelona and we went up for a weekend. She then decided to stay on for three days without me, and although her visit was very short she, like my parents and older sister, says she remembers it vividly. She got to know young students more or less of her own age, and felt that the visit was not so much a holiday as going to a place to which she belonged in some way. While she was made to feel welcome, and even looked after, she also felt a sense of responsibility which continued after her visit, as she undertook to look after some of the young villagers who came to Britain, and wanted to tour Scotland at a time when I was not able to go with them.

Later that summer, while still living in Barcelona, my youngest sister was the last member of the family to visit the village with me. I was busy doing a specific piece of research during that visit, and she spent a lot of time with a group of her own age, the offspring of people who had left the village but returned every summer to visit their grandparents. This was a group I had found very difficult to meet, as their return coincided with the period of most intense activity in the community. She has maintained contact with many of this group, and has returned twice, once with me and once without me. She writes to some of the people she met there, and they have also visited her in Scotland. While she felt that knowing this group of young people was not directly to do with me, the reception she got in shops and generally from older people, enquiring whether she was enjoying herself and how her holiday was going, was closely linked to my relationship with them. She was impressed with the level of activity of the young in the maintenance of festivals, and the sense of warmth and friendliness of the community. This sister also felt a sense of responsibility, and a feeling that she must not let me down, which again led to a feeling of not exactly being on holiday. However, when she returned without me but with a friend, she felt it was more of a holiday. This time she stayed in the camp site, which probably reinforced the holiday feeling, but at the same time felt well looked after by people she had met previously. She also visited informants who were my close friends, thus carrying out some of my obligations.

The village has thus become something which the whole family has to some extent shared in, and also has a special fondness for. They have all felt that their visits were a unique experience enabling them to participate in the life of a community, rather than visiting as tourists. All of them speak of the relationship with people as the factor that set the experience apart from a tourist holiday; they were able to participate in relationships I had already established. What struck the family, and myself, was the extent to which people in the village were hospitable and made them welcome. On the whole the community welcomes visitors. They are a diversion to the monotony of everyday life, and a subject to talk about, and hospitality plays an important role in the value system there. People are proud of the village and enjoy talking about it to strangers. Since the factories have closed, tourists (who are few in number) are seen as an important part of the economy. Besides this, there was a genuine sense of friendship that has developed with some informants and myself, or other members of the family.

There have been some moments of tension for me around particular behaviour, and I have come in for some teasing as I instructed family members on their obligations in terms of visiting, being polite and friendly and wearing appropriate clothes! This probably contributed to the sense of responsibility they have mentioned to me. All the family managed to communicate to varying degrees in French and through me translating. Some of the younger villagers could speak some English. With my parents, the role of daughter and researcher was split to some extent, by suspending formal fieldwork during their visit. This was not so much a conscious decision as a practical one, thinking that it would be difficult to combine the two, and also due to the fact that I felt other benefits would emerge from their visit, such as those described above. In fact, the benefits were greater than I had thought and lasted longer. There are still enquiries about their well-being when I return to the village. With my sisters, and more recently, my partner, there was no such split. I made it clear that work came first, and although there have been occasional tensions, they have never been insurmountable, and have been compensated by for the support I felt I had from the visitor.

MARRIAGE: BECOMING AN ADULT

In my case this continuing relationship with the field has changed the perception of me by the community of St Llorenç de Cerdans, particularly since I married someone from Catalonia (albeit from 'the other side' of the border). This did not seem to come as a surprise to anyone in the village. We had met in London and he visited the village with me before we married, and has returned twice since.

Marriage has changed my status in the community, and I am no longer a young girl in need of protection. It has cemented me firmly in Catalonia as far as informants are concerned, and the fact that my partner is Catalan, and so has a connection with them, gives them a permanent claim over me. He has had a greater share of my tensions and obligations about returning to the village than the rest of my family. This has led him also to have a sense of responsibility about the time spent there. Despite that, he is of course more familiar with the culture and the language, and has an appreciation of my worries as he understands and shares the social codes that underpin village life. It is a great source of pleasure to me that he is willing to visit St Llorenç and especially that he enjoys the company of Anne and Yveline, who likewise approve of him and enjoy his company. This is an important factor in my on-going contact there. He is also aware that it was my position in the community that enabled him to get to know people in the personal and very direct way that he has; he has been considered an extension of me, and immediately included in the confidence of friends.

My return led to a willingness to give information that I had not dreamt of. I had somehow thought that each visit would involve starting all over again, but instead, as much data were obtained in a fortnight as previously had been in six months. Golde comments on this in the introduction of the second edition of her book, where she says,

Two new essays have been added, and these provide an accidental bonus in their common demonstration of the value of returning to the field after a lapse of time. . . . This insight enables one to appreciate the impact of the passage of time on the deepening, enriching, and strengthening of trust and on the quality of sharing that is possible only with repeated encounters.

(1986: viii)

However, on return, not only was data collection concentrated and increased, but so were the tensions so common to fieldwork. Short visits are exhausting, as so many people have to be visited on arrival and again on departure. The feeling of being constantly on show, that had been forgotten on return 'home', came back with a vengeance during later visits. Everybody seemed to have a claim on me, and the calm long winter days of sitting around 'gossiping' with neighbours seem to have long gone. Return visits appear to be rather panicky affairs, with a lot of rushing about, and apologies that I do not have time to spend with people. There is a conflict of interests in that the community sees me as someone who returns on holiday, while I see my visits as opportunities for more data. Even when not planning to do any specific work, I cannot turn off the anthropologist in me and am alert all the time for new information. These visits are preceded by vivid dreams. The dreams are always the same: I am in the village, I have been there for a few days already and I meet someone I have not visited, in the street. The horror at this breach of protocol is so great that it wakes me up!

CONCLUSION

In the introduction to the edited volume *Women in the Field*, Golde (1986: 5) categorises five themes that emerge from the articles which relate to being a woman doing research: protection, initial suspicion, conformity, reciprocity and culture shock. While all of these also apply to male researchers, it is the specific ways in which they apply to women, and in which all of them involve stronger pressures on women researchers, that interest Golde. I would suggest that visits made to me in the field aided my position there in all five of these categories. The visit from my parents was the most important in establishing that I was protected. Although many members of the community continued to be unclear about my work, visits from my family more or less removed suspicion about why I, a woman, was there alone. I was seen to come from a large, close family with similar values to those of the village, and later to have a partner who was approved of. This went a long way to my conforming, and in fact gave me more freedom to be 'myself' without worrying about conformity; my credentials had been checked and accepted.

When researching close to 'home' it is easy to dismiss culture shock. In fact with participant observation, it is the method rather than the measured difference from one's own culture that causes dislocation on arrival and on return 'home'. While visits did not eliminate culture shock, there has at least been some continuity between the two sides of my life. The visits mattered for me as they enabled the family to understand what I was there for, and also share in a very important experience in my life. They helped me with specific areas of fieldwork, to deepen some relationships with informants, instigate relationships with certain groups within the community and have been part of the on-going contact with informants.

Perhaps the most interesting aspect of the visits is the emergence of the give and take of fieldwork. At a time when the discipline is more and more concerned with the representation of culture and the choices made by the fieldworker, the dynamic between the culture studied and the researcher is a vital part of understanding the finished product. In this case that dynamic was affected by the roles of my family and partner in my work. I have thus been able to share aspects of my life with the community, just as I have expected them to share aspects of their life with me.

NOTES

* My first research visit to Northern Catalonia was supported by a grant from the Social Science Research Council, and a return visit, two years later, by the University of London Central Research Fund.

1 Doing fieldwork in a familiar culture is a growing phenomenon due to an increasing sense of unease with the exoticisation of culture within anthropology, and a shortage of research funds. Some of the issues arising from this trend are discussed in the volume *Anthropology at Home* (Jackson 1987).
2 Catalonia includes the eastern area of the Spanish state, with Barcelona as its capital. This is known as El Principat. Valencia, the Balearic Islands and Andorra are also part of Catalonia, along with North Catalonia, which lies within the French state boundary.
3 There is also an extremely important socio-economic group of state workers called *fonctionnaires*, who have a wide variety of statuses. This is the group central to my research, but cannot be called a class as such.
4 These domestic animals have replaced the tradition of each household keeping a pig for a year to make sausages and hams for the winter.
5 Not all the cafés were out of bounds to me, but one definitely was, and another at certain times.
6 Her role as my teacher is still something to which we refer only half-jokingly, since both of us are aware how much she has given me.
7 This was not the case with the female intellectual or professional members of the village; however, it was hard to remember in everyday life, as such people worked elsewhere and only returned for holidays.
8 On recent visits it has become apparent that those 'hippies' who have stayed to persevere with farming are also now considered *sérieux* (Fr.) and are credited with the hard work involved in maintaining a farm. This is particularly the case since concern has grown about some of the more capitalist enterprises that have been developed, largely by foreigners, in the surrounding area.

REFERENCES

Briggs, J. (1986) 'Kapluna Daughter', in P. Golde (ed.), *Women in the Field*, Berkeley, CA: University of California Press, pp. 19–46.

Caplan, P. (1988) 'Engendering knowledge, the politics of ethnography', in *Anthropology Today* 4(5, 6).

Eidham, H. (1969) 'When ethnic identity is a social stigma', in F. Barth (ed.), *Ethnic Groups and Boundaries*, London: Allen & Unwin.

Golde, P. (ed.) (1986) *Women in the Field*, Berkeley, CA: University of California Press.

Gurney, J.N. (1985) 'Not one of the guys: the female researcher in a male-dominated setting', in *Qualitative Sociology* 8(1): 42–62.

Hondagneu-Sotelo, P. (1988) 'Gender and fieldwork', in *Women's Studies International Forum* 11(6): 611–18.

Jackson, A. (1987) *Anthropology at Home*, ASA Monograph 25, London: Tavistock Publications.

Keller, E.F. (1985) *Reflections on Gender and Science*, New Haven, CT: Yale University Press.

Nader, L. (1986) 'From anguish to exultation', in P. Golde (ed.), *Women in the Field*, Berkeley, CA: University of California Press, pp. 97–118.

Oakley, A. (1981) 'Interviewing women: a contradiction in terms', in H. Roberts (ed.), *Doing Feminist Research*, London: Routledge & Kegan Paul, pp. 30–61.

O'Brien, O. (1990) 'Perceptions of identity in North Catalonia', in J. Llobera (ed.), *Family, Class and Nation in Catalonia*, London: Critique of Anthropology and Mare Nostrum editions.

O'Brien, O. (1991) 'Good to be French? Conflicts of identity in North Catalonia', in S. Macdonald (ed.), *Inside European Identities: Ethnography in Western Europe*, Oxford: Berg.

Turnbull, C. (1986) 'The role of subjectivity in field research', in T.L. Whitehead, and M.E. Conaway (eds), *Self, Sex and Gender in Cross-cultural Fieldwork*, Urbana and Chicago: University of Illinois Press, pp. 17–27.

Warren, C.A. (1988) *Gender Issues in Field Research*, Beverly Hills, CA: Sage.

Whitehead, T.L. and Conaway, M.E. (eds) (1986) *Self, Sex and Gender in Cross-cultural Fieldwork*, Urbana and Chicago: University of Illinois Press.

Winterson, J. (1990) *Sexing the Cherry*, London: Vintage.

Epilogue
The 'nativised' self and the 'native'

Wazir Jahan Karim

Said (1978) has argued that western intellectual discourses are bounded by their own political culture and that since the Third World, as the hinterland of western colonisation, has never been completely autonomous from the political culture, one can expect this form of intellectual domination to persist for some time. Cohen (1989) has described as a human rights issue how cultural relativism has succeeded in putting Third World communities in a 'primitive' category, while enhancing the advancement of the west in the field of cultural enquiry.

Within the academic culture of anthropology, reflexivity has to a certain extent served as a defence against Said's critique by offering a dialogue on issues of intellectual hegemony *vis-à-vis* the researcher and the researched (Marcus and Fischer 1986; Rosaldo 1989). While Marcus and Fischer criticise Said for not offering solutions (p. 2), Rosaldo at least recognises the fact that, whatever the solutions are, they would still serve to enhance the western point of view about the culture of the 'other'. He opts for a more balanced approach to an under-standing of the politics of anthropology and highlights the diabolical power relations which surface in fieldwork: one is of the supremacy of the anthro-pologist in relation to the world outside the field, and the other of the supremacy of the 'natives' in relation to the world inside. However, he argues that this power relationship cannot be so simply stated, since the anthropologist eventually gains from this new source of knowledge, putting the researcher again in another advantageous position in relation to the researched (p. 195).

An important argument put forward by Rosaldo which highlights the main points of this discussion is that it is no longer possible to separate clearly the researcher and the native into two neat categories. Not only has reflexive anthro-pology highlighted the ambiguous position of native scholars in anthropology, but it has also renewed interest in the importance of 'anthropology at home' for western anthropologists. Hence the 'nativised' self and the 'native' no longer represent clear-cut oppositions of the 'west' versus the Third World. Although anthropology was historically constructed through colonialism by drawing upon the human and environmental resources of the Third World to develop systems of knowledge and advance western social theory, today non-western cultures are seldom studied purely as ethnographic pieces. Even in the early phases of structural-functionalism there was always an overall concern for developing comparative perspectives, in order to understand similarities and differences between the European and the native (with functionalists like Malinowski recognising universalisms more readily, and social structuralists like Radcliffe-Brown the differences). The idea of 'show-casing' natives as classical works of western ethnographers has never really been developed very successfully. It follows that one of the most successful outcomes of anthropology has been to strengthen the western tradition of social criticism.

The acquisition of knowledge of non-western cultures in a reflexive mode can help generate perspectives on humankind which are more balanced and humanitarian and which can overcome generalisations which border on racism. Even when native scholars argue against the neutrality of the 'humankind approach' in anthropology, they are able to do it through the self-critical mode of anthropology; they can either point out the difficulty of native researchers in proving their expertise on 'white' cultures which have been under the monopolistic control of Europeans and Americans (Hsu 1973; Choong 1990), or reflect upon the inadequacy of the anthropological method in catering for detached neutral observers from western academe (Rosaldo 1989). Whatever the criticism, it is possible to say now that anthropology is less concerned with 'show-casing' ethnography and more concerned with the development of the discipline as a form of 'political writing' which can allow more participation from the researched.

Secondly, reflexive anthropology elucidates the controversies of 'scientifying' culture. It has led western and non-western scholars to question the paradigms of objectivity and detachment which strait-jacketed anthropology for decades as an empirical science. The relationship between 'self' and 'other' is now thrown into confusion, and it is no longer clear 'who is who' and 'what is what' in this soul-searching exercise. The fieldwork process 'nativises' the anthropologist on one level and produces 'self-consciousness' on another, but how exactly the anthropologist deals with these two levels involves a lengthy discussion about the kinds of social and political situations which confront them in the field.

It is interesting to pursue this topic further, by comparing the experiences of 'native' researchers (non-western anthropologists, doing 'anthropology at home' within their own community or outside, and western anthropologists researching on their own communities) with other anthropologists doing fieldwork on other cultures. To a considerable extent, the studies of Karim and Ganesh in this volume reflect the same kind of situation. They are both non-western anthropologists doing anthropology on cultures other than their own within their respective countries. Bell, as an Australian researching Australian 'Aborigines', shares a similar position, except that she is a white Australian, a factor which poses problems relating to her ambivalent position. Back and Amadiume are the only two truly 'native' researchers studying their communities of origin. All these anthropologists record varied emotional and social experiences in relating the 'nativised self' to the 'native'. Bell was subject to a double barrage of prejudices from both 'native' Aboriginal men and white Australians, but in the long term, was able to reposition herself against the 'other' – in particular, powerful white administrators of the law – by becoming an informant on 'Aboriginal' culture in the courts of Australia. In a sense, her 'self' became the 'other', not so much through emulating native conduct as by translating its meaning to others in important positions and by reconsolidating this with her earlier feminist convictions (which emerged forcefully in the field). Karim's experiences with the Ma' Betisé' were, however, completely different. Through them she discovered how western anthropology and her own position in the dominant Malaysian society impeded her metamorphosis into the 'other'. While she so strongly wanted to be completely 'nativised', the long-term commitments of affinity and kinship that were attached to this experience made her even more aware of the contradictions in her roles as anthropologist, native and part of the politically dominant majority. As a result, although the Ma' Betisé' wanted to incorporate her fully as time went on, each phase of involvement made her ever more conscious of her distanciation from them. Her discussion ends on a note of pessimism as she becomes aware that the anthropological experience only succeeds in creating a consciousness of inadequacy heightened by the failure of the anthropological method to deal with the problems of endangered minorities. The helplessness of the men and the fear of the women and children seldom diminish with each new and glossy publication emerging from the field of the endangered.

The experience of Ganesh in India strengthens this argument further, for she shows how closely intertwined is the life history of the female researcher with those of the women researched. Her past personal history converges with the present as she acquires the understanding that women's social seclusion in India is reproduced in history. Anthropology merely serves the function of tantalizing the memory in a '*déjà vu*' situation.

Back and Amadiume, the only 'native' anthropologists studying their culture of origin, seem to have done so in order to evoke a nostalgia for childhood and to develop an understanding of the changes in their own lives in relation to the 'community' left behind. In the case of Amadiume, her choice to 'go native' in her father's ancestral village in Nnobi, Nigeria, was also seen to be the best way to renew her ties with her kinsfolk. From her fieldwork accounts, one can seen her concern for the declining power of women, their loss of the Ekwe title, their weak position in the Nnobi Welfare Organisation and the way they argued against these sources of power as paganistic. Doubtless, a non-native anthropologist might be equally concerned with these issues, but the difference between her and the 'other' is that, as an Igbo, she is personally and emotionally caught up with the changes around her, in particular, the declining power of Igbo women through Christianity and bureaucratisation. She confronts the problem with seeming frustration as she attempts to reconscientise the women through participatory dialogue. Failing to achieve this, she realises that her self-consciousness is another expression of her 'nativeness', which the women themselves have begun to lose. Emotionally and politically this sets her apart from the women.

As in the case of Amadiume, Back as a native anthropologist tries to recapture the past in the present, expecting positive changes and yet resigning himself to the knowledge that the past cannot be expected to remain. For all these researchers, the anthropological method reaffirms the limitations of indigenising experiences; the process of 'nativising the self' reinforces further the empty spaces and silence between the researcher and the researched.

In the case of both the native and non-native women researchers in this volume, it is clear that gender consciousness has played an important role in the research process. In some cases, researchers already had feminist sympathies; in others, these emerged later through the experience of fieldwork, and generated a sympathy for the women being studied. Perhaps their concern for and attempt to advance the position of women in other cultures symbolically expressed their awareness of their own ambiguous position as women and as anthropologists marginalised by their gender. For example, Hutheesing, Rudie and Caplan have become more and more immersed in issues of womanhood and power as their fieldwork experience has shifted from years to decades. For them, one of the long-term consequences of doing fieldwork has been to counterpoise choices in European perceptions of gender relations against those recently emerging in cultures of the Third World. At the same time, their growing realisation that fieldwork relationships are dialectical and political has made them aware of the importance of social commitment and responsibility towards the researched. Both of these can be seen as positive developments.

The native researcher, however, remains discontented, for over and above this consideration is the need to re-establish the 'native' in the 'self' and to reproduce the culture in this image of newly found personhood. When things go wrong, disintegrate or buckle under the weight of politics and development, the failure to generate effective changes towards social and gender equality leads to a questioning of the native role as 'anthropologist' and the role of anthropology as a discipline concerned with the lives of minorities.

REFERENCES

Choong, Soon Kim (1990) 'The role of the non-western anthropologist reconsidered: illusion versus reality', *Current Anthropology* 31(2)(April): 197–200.

Cohen, R. (1989) 'Human rights and cultural relativism: the need for a new approach', *American Anthropologist, Commentaries* 91(4)(Dec.): 1014–17.

Hsu, Francis L.I. (1973) 'Prejudice and its intellectual effect in anthropology: an ethnographic report', *American Anthropologist* 75: 1–19.

Jackson, A. (1987) *Anthropology at Home,* New York: Tavistock.

Marcus, G. and Fischer, M.M.J. (1986) *Anthropology as Cultural Critique: An Experimental Moment in the Human Sciences,* Chicago: University of Chicago Press.

Ohnuki-Tierney, E. (1984) 'Native Anthropologist', *American Ethnologist* ll: 584–6.

Rosaldo, R. (1989) *Culture and Truth: The Remaking of Social Analysis,* Boston: Beacon Press.

Said, E. (1978) *Orientalism,* New York: Vintage Books.

Name index

Abramson, Allen 20, 22, 23, 24, 76
Abu-Lughod, Lila 2, 11, 29, 30
Agar, Michael H. 1
Aickin, Mary Rothschild 35
Amadiume, Ifi 19–21, 25, 58, 197, 249–50
Amos 21
Anderson, Barbara Gallatin 6
Anderson, Thor 6
Angrosino, Angrosino (Michael) 206, 207, 208
Ardener, Shirley 2, 115 n.1, 218
Asad, Talad 1, 3, 13 n.18, 46
Atkinson, J. 218
Atwood, Margaret 5

Back, Ken 231 n.3
Back, Les 3, 19, 220, 225, 227, 249–50
Barley, Nigel 50
Barry, Kathleen 2
Barth, Fredrik 106
Bateson, Gregory 91
Bell, Diane: 'Aboriginal women and
    land' 31, 38; 'Aboriginal women's
    religion' 37; 'Considering gender' 38,
    41; *Daughters of the Dreaming* 2, 12,
    n.3, 30, 31, 33, 37; 'Doing
    anthropology at home' 31, 39;
    Generations 31, 39, 141 n.7; 'Giving
    in or giving them hell' 32; 'In the case
    of the anthropologists. .' 39;
    'Intra-racial rape. .' 31, 37; 'Law: the
    old and the new' (with Pam Ditton) 31,
    34; 'Yes Virginia' 19–24, 26, 249–50
Benedict, Ruth 4, 7, 13 n.19
Benhabib, Seyla 2, 6, 12 n.16
Benjamin, Geoffrey 81
Berger, Peter 94
Berndt, Catherine 6
Berndt, Ronald 6
Berreman, Gerald D. 1

Beteille, Andre 141 n.5
Beuchler, Hans C. 11 n.1
Birth, Kevin 8, 11 n.2, 12 n.16
Bohannan, Laura 12 n.8, 50, 215, 217
Bohannan, Paul 12 n.8
Borchgrevink, Tordis 115 n.2
Boserup, Ester 146
Bourdieu, Pierre 104, 108
Bovin, Mette 10
Bowen, Elenore Smith 5, 12, n.8
Briggs, Jean 7, 239
Brohier, R.L. 146
Bujra, Janet 2, 9
Bunzel, Ruth 12 n.5
Buzaljko, Grace Wilson 12 n.9

Caffrey, Margaret 4
Callaway, Helen 144
Cambridge Women's Studies Group 53
Caplan, Pat: 'Boys' circumcision and
    girls' puberty rites..' 172; *Choice and
    Constraint* 170; 'Engendering
    knowledge' 3, 29, 31, 144, 215, 216,
    218, 224, 234; *Engendering
    Knowledge* 174; 'Gender, ideology. .'
    172, 176; 'Genderising anthropology'
    144; 'Learning gender' 9, 12 n.6, 20,
    23, 25–6, 251; 'Sex and spirits' 174;
    'The Swahili of Chole Island' 176;
    'Women's property, Islamic law. .' 176;
    Women United (with Janet Bujra) 9
Carsten, Janet 111
Case, Patricia 7
Cassell, Joan 2, 9, 11, 36
Cesara, Manda 2, 4, 10, 173
Chapman, Rowena 217, 231 n.1
Choong, Soon Kim 249
Clifford, James: 'Part truths' 216; *The
    Predicament of Culture* 1, 5, 12 n.4, 13
    n.18; *Writing Culture* (with George E.

Subject index

academia, the academy: hostility 4; Indian 130–1; opting out 93; relationship with colonialism 1; treatment of women 4, 8, 32–3; western 249
adoption 20, 52–3, 54, 78–81, 170
age: attitudes to 174; authors' 19; categorisation 239–49; eldership 4–5, 98–9; importance to women's ethnography 2; status 132
Andes 6
animism 88
anthropology: at home 41, 248, 249; feminist 107–8, 179, 180; status in Africa 197; theoretical crisis 64–5
Aranyaprathet 121
Australian: Aborigines 6, 26, 28, 31–9, 249–50; Bicentennial 39–40
authority, ethnographic 3
autobiography 19, 63–4, 215–16, 217
autonomy 26–7, 103, 107–8, 112

Bangkok 119
birth control: Depo-Provera 26, 50–1; husbands' role 151, 163, 179; methods 48, 50–1
black society in Colombia 200–13
Brahmins 128, 130, 132, 161–2
Brazil 6
Britain: anthropological training 19; masculinity 217; racism 161, 182, 183, 196, 220–1

Cambodia 117, 121, 122, 125
camps, refugee 117–27
Carey Island 78–90
Cartagena 202
caste 128, 132–4, 136, 161–2
Catalonia, North 20, 234–46
Catholic Office for Emergency Relief and Refugees (COERR) 118, 121

centrality, researcher's 81–2
changes over time 24–6
chiefdom 66–70
childbirth 22, 48–9, 56
children: adoptive 54; death rates 55, 177–8; illness 88; in the field 10, 11, 20, 36, 143–56, 183–9; responsibility for 11; sex preference 175–6, 177
Colombia 20, 22, 199–213
Columbia University 4
colonialism 1, 196, 201–2, 248
contraception see birth control
cooperatives 160
credentials 221–3, 240–2
culture: concept of 58; expectations 89–90; invention of 207; relativism 248; scientifying 249
customary law 37–9

death 55–9, 76, 88, 186–7, 237
Denmark 6
Depo-Provera 26, 50
difference and sameness 21–3, 58
distance and separation 60–1
divorce: Aboriginal women's attitudes 36; authors' 20, 36, 49, 148–9; Indian attitudes 163, 166; Sinhalese attitudes 148–9; Tanzanian attitudes 174, 178; Tubetube attitudes 49; western attitudes 163
domesticity 69–70, 73
domination 6
dress 133, 162, 163, 170, 188
drought 55–6

eating patterns 177
education 106, 171
eldership 98–9
Enugu 184, 185–7
equality 24